LIBRARY OF NEW TESTAMENT STUDIES

685

Formerly Journal for the Study of the New Testament Supplement series

Editor
Chris Keith

Editorial Board
Dale C. Allison, Lynn H. Cohick, R. Alan Culpepper, Craig A. Evans,
Jennifer Eyl, Robert Fowler, Simon J. Gathercole, Juan Hernández Jr., John S.
Kloppenborg, Michael Labahn, Matthew V. Novenson, Love L. Sechrest,
Robert Wall, Catrin H. Williams, Brittany E. Wilson

A Ricoeurian Analysis of Identity Formation in Philippians

Narrative, Testimony, Contestation

Scott Ying-Lam Yip

t&tclark
LONDON • NEW YORK • OXFORD • NEW DELHI • SYDNEY

T&T CLARK
Bloomsbury Publishing Plc
50 Bedford Square, London, WC1B 3DP, UK
1385 Broadway, New York, NY 10018, USA
29 Earlsfort Terrace, Dublin 2, Ireland

BLOOMSBURY, T&T CLARK and the T&T Clark logo are trademarks of
Bloomsbury Publishing Plc

First published in Great Britain 2023
Paperback edition published in 2025

Copyright © Scott Ying-Lam Yip, 2023

Scott Ying-Lam Yip has asserted his right under the Copyright, Designs and
Patents Act, 1988, to be identified as Author of this work.

For legal purposes the Acknowledgements on p. xi constitute an extension of
this copyright page.

All rights reserved. No part of this publication may be reproduced or transmitted
in any form or by any means, electronic or mechanical, including photocopying,
recording, or any information storage or retrieval system, without prior
permission in writing from the publishers.

Bloomsbury Publishing Plc does not have any control over, or responsibility for, any
third-party websites referred to or in this book. All internet addresses given in this
book were correct at the time of going to press. The author and publisher regret any
inconvenience caused if addresses have changed or sites have ceased to exist,
but can accept no responsibility for any such changes.

A catalogue record for this book is available from the British Library.

Library of Congress Cataloging-in-Publication Data

Names: Yip, Scott Ying Lam, author.
Title: A ricoeurian analysis of identity formation in Philippians : narrative, testimony, contestation / by Scott Ying Lam Yip.
Description: London; New York: T&T Clark, 2023. | Series: The library of New Testament studies, 2513-8790 ; 685 | Includes bibliographical references and index. | Summary: "Scott Yip Ying Lam explores the process through which Paul shapes the identity of the Philippian community against other opponents, via Ricoeur's concept of narrative identity"– Provided by publisher.
Identifiers: LCCN 2022050764 (print) | LCCN 2022050765 (ebook) | ISBN 9780567711014 (hb) | ISBN 9780567711052 (pb) | ISBN 9780567711021 (epdf) | ISBN 9780567711045 (epub)
Subjects: LCSH: Bible. Philippians–Commentaries.
Classification: LCC BS2705.2 .Y56 2023 (print) | LCC BS2705.2 (ebook) | DDC 227/.606–dc23/eng/20230324
LC record available at https://lccn.loc.gov/2022050764
LC ebook record available at https://lccn.loc.gov/2022050765

ISBN: HB: 978-0-5677-1101-4
PB: 978-0-5677-1105-2
ePDF: 978-0-5677-1102-1
ePUB: 978-0-5677-1104-5

Series: Library of New Testament Studies, volume 685

ISSN 2513-8790

Typeset by Deanta Global Publishing Services, Chennai, India

To find out more about our authors and books visit www.bloomsbury.com and
sign up for our newsletters.

Contents

List of Figures	x
Acknowledgments	xi
List of Abbreviations	xii
Introduction	1

Part I Past Approaches to Philippians

1	Critical Review of Narrative Analyses of Philippians	9
	1.1 Narrative Approach to the Pauline Letters	9
	1.1.1 History of Research	9
	1.1.2 Discovery of Narrative Substructure (Richard Hays)	10
	1.1.3 Five Levels of Story (James Dunn)	12
	1.2 A Review of General Narrative Analyses of Philippians	14
	1.2.1 N. T. Wright	14
	1.2.2 Michael Gorman	15
	1.2.3 Richard Hays	16
	1.2.4 Richard J. Weymouth and Stephen Fowl	17
	1.2.5 A Brief Evaluation	21
	1.3 A Review of Narrative Studies on Identity Formation in Philippians	22
	1.3.1 James Miller	24
	1.3.2 Sergio Nebreda	25
	1.3.3 Robert Brawley and William Campbell	26
	1.3.4 Ben Meyer and John Barclay	29
	1.3.5 A Brief Evaluation	31
	1.4 Conclusion	33
2	Brief Review of Introductory Issues	35
	2.1 Compositional Unity	35
	2.2 The Role of Suffering	36
	2.3 The Identities of Opponents	37
	2.4 The Imperial Cult and Exemption for the Jews	37
	2.5 Conclusion	40

Part II Theoretical Framework

3 Ricoeur's Narrative Theory: Contestation of Temporalities, Identities, and Testimonies — 43
   3.1 Threefold Mimesis — 44
      3.1.1 Prefiguration (Mimesis1): Diverse Traditions toward Suffering for the Gospel of Christ — 45
      3.1.2 Configuration (Mimesis2): Narrative Dynamics of Paul's Narrative World amid a Contestation of Narratives — 46
      3.1.3 Refiguration (Mimesis3): Transformative Reading amid a Contestation of Horizons — 51
   3.2 Temporality and the Making of Identity — 56
      3.2.1 Assessing the Degree of Coherence across Narratives — 57
      3.2.2 Nesting of Narratives: Articulating the Processes of Paul's Theological Thinking — 57
      3.2.3 "Alluded Stories": Serving Paul's Agenda in Contestation — 61
      3.2.4 The Narrated Event of Christ's Death: A Christocentric Earthly Upper Limit of Time — 63
      3.2.5 Narrative Identity of a Storyteller Acquired from the Narrative Told — 64
      3.2.6 From Narrative Identity to Ethical Identity: Character and Self-Constancy — 64
      3.2.7 Applying the Threefold Mimesis and Temporality Models to the Narrative Dynamics of Philippians — 69
   3.3 The Hermeneutics of Testimony — 70
      3.3.1 Dialectic of External Narration and Internal Conviction — 70
      3.3.2 The Self-Engaged Nature of Testimony — 71
      3.3.3 Contestation of Convictions: Truthfulness of a Testimony — 71
      3.3.4 Applying Truthfulness to Analyze the Religious Identity of the Philippian Community — 77
   3.4 Conclusion — 77

Part III Exegetical Analysis

4 Nature and Background of the Problem: Double Contestation of Narratives (Phil. 1:3–2:4) — 81
   4.1 Persecution from Political Authorities and Theological Debate with Other "Christ-Followers" (1:27-30) — 82
      4.1.1 Controversy on the Understanding of Πολιτεύομαι (27a-e) — 82
      4.1.2 The Contestation of Allegiance between Caesar and Christ (27f-28a) — 92
      4.1.3 A Manual for Battle: Assurance of the Gospel (27g) — 95

	4.1.4 Contestation of the Meaning of the Philippians' Suffering (28bc)	96
	4.1.5 The Contestation of Testimonies between Paul and the Jewish Christian Leaders (29a-d)	100
	4.1.6 The *Same* Suffering of Paul and the Philippian Community (30abc)	103
	4.1.7 Conclusion	105
4.2	Contrasting Receptions of Paul's Testimony among Christ-followers (1:12-18)	106
	4.2.1 Paul's Understanding of His Chains Deviates from the Philippian Community's Expectation	106
	4.2.2 A Contrast of Truthfulness between Paul and the Jewish Christian Leaders	110
	4.2.3 The Contestation of Testimonies between "Christ-followers"	113
	4.2.4 Conclusion	114
4.3	Assurance amid Doubt: Narrative Logic within Allusion to Job (1:19-26)	115
	4.3.1 Similarity and Difference between Job and Paul	115
	4.3.2 Interpretive Issues within Allusion to Job	116
	4.3.3 Nesting the Story of Paul upon the Story of Job	117
	4.3.4 Conclusion	125
4.4	Christ's Eschatological Era Demands Believers' Discernment (1:3-11a)	125
	4.4.1 Remembering the Community's Past Truthful Witnessing	126
	4.4.2 The Foundation of Paul's Conviction: Inauguration of an Eschatological Era by God and Christ	129
	4.4.3 Discernment of God's Act: Suffering for the Gospel as Essential (1:9-11)	135
	4.4.4 Conclusion	136
4.5	A Contrast of Ethical Dispositions among Contesting Testimonies (2:1-4)	136
4.6	Conclusion	139
5	Contestation of the Manifestation of God: The Paradigmatic Narrative of Christ (Phil. 2:5-11, 3:17-21)	140
5.1	"Beginning": *Forma* of Slave in a Contestation of the Manifestation of God (2:6-7b)	142
	5.1.1 Contestation of Allegiances: Christ versus Earthly Rulers	144
	5.1.2 Contestation of God's Knowledge: The Manifestation of God through a Slave	144
5.2	"Middle": Suffering to the Point of Death in a Contestation of the Paradigmatic Obedience (2:7c-8)	147

		5.2.1 Christ's Identification with Humans: The Ultimate Paradigm for Paul	148
		5.2.2 Meaning of ἐταπείνωσεν ἑαυτὸν: A Voluntary Act in Lowering Himself	149
		5.2.3 The Manifestation of God: Christ the Volitional Agent Narrates Death as Limit	151
		5.2.4 Resonance between Christ and Paul: The Contestation of Discernment of God's Righteousness in Suffering	154
	5.3	"Ending": Vindication of Christ and Believers in a Contestation of Hope (2:9-11, 3:17-21)	155
		5.3.1 God's Total Approval of Christ's Earthly Journey of Suffering	156
		5.3.2 Context of Isaiah: Contestation of Testimonies on Cyrus as God's Instrument	157
		5.3.3 Nesting of Stories of Paul and Christ on That of Isaiah: New Phase of Eschatological Lordship	160
		5.3.4 Contrasting Fates Following Contesting Narratives on the Role of the Body (3:17-21)	162
	5.4	Conclusion	166
6	Contestation of Temporalities: The Exemplary Narrative of Paul (Phil. 3:1-21)		169
	6.1	A: Contestation of Authority in Interpreting the Past Story of Israel (3:1-6)	170
		6.1.1 The Identity of Opponents and Their Influence on the Philippian Community	171
		6.1.2 The Marker of Manipulating or Representing God (Κατατομή and Περιτομή)	173
		6.1.3 The Contestation on the Definition of Circumcision: The True Marker of God's Covenantal People	175
	6.2	B: Contestation of Assurance of God's Righteousness (3:7-9)	181
		6.2.1 The Dialectic of Boundaries between "Old Judaism" and "New Christianity"	181
		6.2.2 Updating God's Old Act in Israel with His New Act in Christ	184
	6.3	B': Contestation of the Mature Way of Thinking (3:12-16)	188
		6.3.1 The Finishing of an Unfinished Yet Assured Future (3:12-14)	188
		6.3.2 Paul's Story: "Golden Rule" and "Golden Example" (3:15-16)	192
	6.4	A': Contestation over the Demarcation of Time (3:17-21)	193
		6.4.1 The Redefining of Circumcision: God's Renewed Covenantal Act in Christ Jesus	194
		6.4.2 The Demarcation of Time within the Jewish Christian Leaders' Testimony	195

	6.4.3 The Demarcation of Time within Paul's Testimony	196
	6.4.4 The Contestation of Temporalities between the Testimonies of Paul and the Jewish Christian Leaders	198
6.5	C: Contestation of the Value of Present Experience (3:10-11)	198
	6.5.1 Not Subjugation but the Power of Christ's Resurrection	199
	6.5.2 The Modification of the Temporal Structure of Jewish Apocalyptic Tradition	201
	6.5.3 "Death of Christ" as the Christocentric Earthly Upper Limit of Time	202
6.6	Conclusion	204

7 The Intended Narrative of the Philippians: Voluntary Retelling of Paul's Testimony (Phil. 2:12-16A) — 206
   7.1 With Fear and Trembling amid the Contestation of Allegiance with Political Authorities (2:12-13) — 206
   7.2 Without Grumbling and Dispute amid the Contestation of Testimonies with Other "God-Followers" (2:14-15b) — 209
   7.3 Suffering to the Point of Death amid the Double Contestation of Narratives (2:15c-16a) — 212
      7.3.1 The "Alluded Story" of Daniel — 213
      7.3.2 The Story of the Philippian Community — 216
   7.4 Conclusion — 218

8 The Stages of the Philippian Community's Collective Identity Formation — 220
   8.1 Mimesis1: The Community Is Forced to Live a Life beyond Previous Narrative Configuration — 221
   8.2 Mimesis2: Aligning with the Tradition of Dispute within God's People Regarding Suffering — 224
   8.3 Mimesis3: The Community's Retelling of Paul's Testimony — 226

9 Conclusion — 230

Bibliography — 235
Index — 255
Scripture Index — 262

Figures

1	The five levels of story model from Dunn	12
2	Three concentric spheres of narrative consciousness	54
3	Three hooked moments inside the nesting of narratives	59
4	After the backward-looking of a narrator, the volitional agent looks forward accordingly	60
5	The story of Paul nested upon the "alluded story" of Job	123
6	The temporal structure of the story of Christ	141
7	The story of Paul nested upon the story of Christ—the "Beginning"	147
8	The story of Paul nested upon the story of Christ—the "Middle"	155
9	The story of Paul nested upon the "alluded story" of Isaiah	166
10	The story of Paul nested upon the story of Christ and the "alluded story" of Isaiah—the "Ending"	168
11	The story of Paul nested upon the "alluded story" of Jeremiah	179
12	"Milestone events" as divergent demarcations of time within competing testimonies for God's master plan of salvation	194
13	The demarcation of time within Jewish Christian leaders' testimony	196
14	The demarcation of time within Paul's testimony	197
15	The story of the Philippian community nested upon the "alluded story" of Psalm 2	208
16	The story of the Philippian community nested upon the integrated "alluded story" of Numbers and Deuteronomy	211
17	The story of the Philippian community nested upon the "alluded story" of Daniel	218
18	When each community member is steadily supporting Paul in a financial manner	222
19	When Paul has been imprisoned, and the community has received escalating persecutions	224
20	When emerging concerns have weakened the community's conviction, Paul writes	225
21	When the Philippian community starts to retell Paul's testimony	227
22	Even after the Philippian community has internalized Paul's testimony	227

Acknowledgments

First of all, I have to give thanks to God, for the way He has led me to the completion of this work through the assistance of many. I am immensely grateful to my primary supervisor, David Horrell, who offered penetrating insights on my work. His gentleness, guidance, and wisdom have helped me in ways too numerous to mention. I am also grateful to my secondary supervisor, Louise Lawrence, who provided me with many questions to improve the coherence of my writing. I have to give special thanks to Jacqui Stewart, who volunteered herself in helping me understand the concepts of Paul Ricoeur. I thank Rebekah Welton for her help with copyediting.

I would also like to thank those who have prayed for me and supported me financially. I am grateful to my fellow brothers and sisters at the Hong Kong West Point Baptist Church. I have to thank three dear doctoral colleagues, Hyunte Shin, Hayoung Kim, and Leanna Rierson for their friendship and encouragement throughout my research. I am particularly grateful to my dear friends in Exeter, Louise Hooper, Cherryl Hunt, Richmond Hunt, and Chris Tsang, who have touched my time in Exeter with so much love and care. Lastly, I would like to thank my family, and particularly my beloved wife, Scarlet Yip, for her perseverance, sacrifice, and love during all these years of hard work. It is to them that I dedicate this work.

Abbreviations

AJBT	The American Journal of Biblical Theology
AJCN	Amsterdam International Electronic Journal for Cultural Narratology
Ant	The Antiquities of the Jews
ATR	Anglican Theological Review
BBR	Bulletin for Biblical Research
BDAG	A Greek-English Lexicon of the New Testament and Other Early Christian Literature
BDB	Enhanced Brown-Driver-Briggs Hebrew and English Lexicon
BDF	A Greek Grammar of the New Testament and Other Early Christian Literature
BECA	Baker Encyclopedia of Christian Apologetics
BECNT	Baker Exegetical Commentary on the New Testament
BHM	Bulletin of the History of Medicine
BibInt	Biblical Interpretation
BJRL	Bulletin of the John Rylands Library
BTB	Biblical Theology Bulletin
CBQ	The Catholic Biblical Quarterly
CBR	Currents in Biblical Research
Conspectus	Journal of the South African Theological Seminary
Cremer-Kögel	Cremer H., Kögel J., Biblisch-theologisches Wörterbuch des neutestamentlichen Griechisch
DLNTD	Dictionary of the Later New Testament and Its Developments
DOTP	Dictionary of the Old Testament: Prophets
DOTWPW	Dictionary of the Old Testament: Wisdom, Poetry & Writings
EDNT	Exegetical Dictionary of the New Testament
ESV	The English Standard Version
ExpTim	The Expository Times
HALOT	The Hebrew and Aramaic Lexicon of the Old Testament HCSB The Holman Christian Standard Bible

HIBD	Holman Illustrated Bible Dictionary
HTR	The Harvard Theological Review
HUCA	Hebrew Union College Annual
JAOS	Journal of the American Oriental Society
JBL	Journal of Biblical Literature
JBMW	Journal for Biblical Manhood and Womanhood
JCSP	Journal of Classical and Sacred Philology
JETS	Journal of the Evangelical Theological Society
JQR	The Jewish Quarterly Review
JRE	Journal of Religious Ethics
JSJSup	Supplements to the Journal for the Study of Judaism
JSNT	Journal for the Study of the New Testament
JSNTSup	Journal for the Study of the New Testament Supplement
JSPL	Journal for the Study of Paul and His Letters
JSS	Journal of Semitic Studies
JTI	Journal of Theological Interpretation
JTS	Journal of Theological Studies
KJV	King James Bible
LALS	The Lexham Analytical Lexicon of the Septuagint
LBD	The Lexham Bible Dictionary
LDS	Latter-Day Saints
LEH	A Greek-English Lexicon of the Septuagint, Revised Edition
LNTS	Library of New Testament Studies
LSJ	Liddell-Scott-Jones Greek-English Lexicon, 1996
LTQ	Lexington Theological Quarterly
NAC	The New American Commentary
NASB95	New American Standard Bible, 1995
NCBC	New Century Bible Commentary
NDBT	New Dictionary of Biblical Theology
NET	New English Translation
NETS	New English Translation of the Septuagint
NICNT	The New International Commentary on the New Testament
NIDNTT	New International Dictionary of New Testament Theology
NIGTC	The New International Greek Testament Commentary

NIV	New International Version
NovT	Novum Testamentum
NPNF	Nicene and Post-Nicene Fathers
NRSV	The New Revised Standard Version
NTS	New Testament Studies
NTSupp	Supplements to Novum Testamentum
OGIS	Orientis Graeci Inscriptiones Selectae
PCNT	Paideia: Commentaries on the New Testament
RevExp	Review & Expositor
RTR	The Reformed Theological Review
SBL	Society of Biblical Literature
SJM	Scandinavian Journal of Management
SJOT	Scandinavian Journal of the Old Testament
SJTh	Scottish Journal of Theology
SPCK	The Society for Promoting Christian Knowledge
SuppVT	The Supplements to Vetus Testamentum (Leiden)
TDNT	Theological Dictionary of the New Testament.
THNTC	The Two Horizons New Testament Commentary
TLNT	Theological Lexicon of the New Testament
TNTC	Tyndale New Testament Commentaries
TynBul	Tyndale Bulletin
VT	Vetus Testamentum
WEC	Wycliffe Exegetical Commentary
WSNTDICT	The Complete Word Study Dictionary: New Testament
WTJ	Westminster Theological Journal
ZKG	Zeitschrift für Kirchengeschichte
ZNW	Zeitschrift für die Neutestamentliche Wissenschaft
ZThK	Zeitschrift für Theologie und Kirche

Introduction

In his work *The Faith of Jesus Christ: The Narrative Substructure of Galatians 3:1–4:11*, published in 1983, Richard Hays shows that the theological thinking of Paul is guided by a narrative substructure "underneath" Galatians.[1] The theology-generating core of Paul's thinking is the "sacred story" of Jesus Christ upon which Paul reflects and which he recapitulates within the discourse of his writing.[2] Since then, scholars have further differentiated the fabric of the substructure into various layers and explored narrative components within Paul's mode of thinking.[3] One particular substructure model to be used in this book is the five levels of story model proposed by James Dunn, who argues that Paul's theologizing consists in his own participation in the interplay between all five levels of story.[4] However, despite scholarship's recognition of the significance of narrative analyses in Pauline studies, a systematic study incorporating the interaction between the stories of Paul and the Philippian community (levels four and five), and the interplay between these upper levels of story and the lower levels of God, Israel, and Christ (levels one to three), is yet to be done. Also lacking has been any attention to the ways in which competing narratives, or competing versions of what it means to live rightly in light of God's saving action in Christ, may be evident in Paul's epistolary discourse. The neglect of this interplay has severely limited the contribution of narrative theories in analyzing Philippians.

First, while previous scholarship has utilized narrative theories in understanding Philippians, attempts have been hampered by not giving enough attention to the contingent situation of Paul and the Philippian community (levels four and five). Paul's concerns in Galatians and Romans are often read into the exigency of Philippians. For example, while N. T. Wright has undoubtedly offered insightful perspectives on the application of a *storied* worldview in understanding Paul, his analysis of Philippians relies too much on his overarching framework of redefining covenant status and treats

---

[1] Richard B. Hays, *The Faith of Jesus Christ: The Narrative Substructure of Galatians 3:1–4:11* (Cambridge: Wm. B. Eerdmans, 2002), 226.
[2] Ibid., 27–9.
[3] Ben Witherington III, *Paul's Narrative Thought World: The Tapestry of Tragedy and Triumph* (Louisville: Westminster John Knox Press, 1994), 6n.7; N. T. Wright, *The New Testament and the People of God* (London: SPCK, 1992), 123; James D. G. Dunn, "Paul's Theology," in *The Face of New Testament Studies: A Survey of Recent Research*, ed. Scot McKnight and Grant R. Osborne (Grand Rapids: Baker, 2004), 328; Bruce W. Longenecker, *Narrative Dynamics in Paul. A Critical Assessment* (Louisville: Westminster John Knox Press, 2002), v–vi.
[4] These five levels include: (1) the story of God and creation; (2) the story of Israel; (3) the story of Jesus; (4) the story of Paul; (5) the story of Paul's churches. Further details will be covered below. For references, see Dunn, "Paul's Theology," 328; James D. G. Dunn, *The Theology of Paul the Apostle* (Edinburgh: T&T Clark, 1998), 18.

the story of Paul in Philippians 3 just as an "abbreviated form of Galatians."[5] As a result, Wright fails to address the contingent exigency of Philippians.[6]

Second, the narrative interplay between stories on levels four and five and stories on levels one to three has not been fully taken into account. While scholars have become more aware of the storied nature of Paul's discourse in Philippians, the majority of their attention has been given only to either the "Christ-Hymn" (Phil. 2:6-11) or Paul's "autobiography." For example, while Richard J. Weymouth, in his PhD thesis *The Christ-Story of Philippians 2:5-11*, recognizes the phenomenon of intersecting stories of Paul, the community, Christ, and others,[7] he limits his analysis to Phil. 2:5-11 and totally neglects the significance of Paul's story with respect to the meaning of the story of Christ.[8] Consequently, Paul's specific concern in Philippians is completely disregarded with respect to the meaning of the "Christ-Hymn."

Third, scholars have had an incomplete understanding of the construals of time within their previous employing of narrative theories.[9] Subsequently, previous analyses of the narrative aspect of the identity formation of the Philippian community, guided and divided by the disparate approaches of William Campbell and John Barclay, have been done based on partial understanding of temporal dynamics and narrative logic.[10] The temporal experiences involved within the identity-making processes of Paul himself and the Philippian community are not fully addressed. A hermeneutical approach that could accommodate perspectives from both camps is needed to produce a more complete picture of the Philippian community's identity formation.

Moreover, while narrative has been identified as the fundamental manner of reasoning through which competing convictions among people should be analyzed, scholars have not given enough attention to the dynamic of competing narratives between Paul and his opponents in understanding Philippians.[11] The epistemology of Paul's narrative thinking and his source of conviction within the context of competing narratives have not been taken into account.

---

[5] N. T. Wright, *Justification: God's Plan and Paul's Vision* (London: SPCK, 2009), 122.
[6] Cf. ibid., 122; N. T. Wright, *Paul and the Faithfulness of God* (Philadelphia: Fortress Press, 2013), 21, 987.
[7] Richard J. Weymouth, "The Christ-Story of Philippians 2:6-11: Narrative Shape and Paraenetic Purpose in Paul's Letter to Philippi" (PhD, University of Otago, July 2015), 103–5, 61–3, 479.
[8] Cf. ibid., 17–18.
[9] Cf. Anthony C. Thiselton, "The Hermeneutics of Pastoral Theology. Ten Strategies for Reading Texts in Relation to Varied Reading-Situations," in *Thiselton on Hermeneutics: Collected Works with New Essays* (Grand Rapids: Wm. B. Eerdmans, 2013), 359; Stephen Crites, "The Narrative Quality of Experience," *Journal of the American Academy of Religion* 39, no. 3 (1971): 291–311.
[10] William S. Campbell, *Paul and the Creation of Christian Identity* (London: T&T Clark, 2008), 88–92; John M. G. Barclay, "Paul's Story: Theology as Testimony," in *Narrative Dynamics in Paul. A Critical Assessment*, ed. Bruce W. Longenecker (Louisville: Westminster John Knox Press, 2002), 146, 154n.40.
[11] David Horrell has pointed out that people's "conviction about the world" is essentially shaped by the mode of narrative thinking. See David G. Horrell, "Paul's Narrative or Narrative Substructure? The Significance of 'Paul's Story'," in *Narrative Dynamics in Paul. A Critical Assessment*, ed. Bruce W. Longenecker (Louisville: Westminster John Knox Press, 2002), 168–70, quoting G. Loughlin, *Telling God's Story: Bible, Church and Narrative Theology* (Cambridge: Cambridge University Press, 1999), 3–26; John Milbank, *Theology and Social Theory: Beyond Secular Reason* (Oxford: Blackwell, 2006), 330.

It is within these intellectual contours that I propose to use Ricoeur's narrative theory and Dunn's five levels of story model to investigate the identity formation of the Philippian community. Can a Ricoeurian narrative analysis enhance our understanding of Philippians as a contestation of narratives? Specifically, the research questions I plan to answer include: What temporal logics can we employ in further understanding the identity formation of the Philippian community? What specific functions does the story of Christ play within Paul's contestation? And in what temporal dimensions does Paul compete with his opponents for the identity-making of the Philippian community? With what attitudes should the Philippian community respond to this contestation? It is through the answering of these questions that I affirm that their "Christian identity" is indeed being shaped amid a contestation of narratives with divergent temporalities.

In this work, I argue that these competing narratives, which will be shown to comprise a double contestation of narratives and testimonies between Paul and his opponents (the political authorities and certain Jewish Christian leaders), are fundamental to the "Christian identity" formation of the Philippian community.[12] In particular, Paul is primarily engaging in an intra-Jewish contestation of testimonies with some Jewish Christian leaders regarding the experiences of his and the Philippian community's suffering. With divergent construals of time behind their respective stories (level four), Paul and these Jewish Christians compete for the right to narrate the suffering experiences of Paul and the Philippian community. Trapped in contestations of self-engaged narratives and testimonies in which no objectively verifiable evidence can be found, how could the Philippian community affirm Paul's testimony as truthful and reject those of his opponents? Within Paul's affirmation of God's revelation, and the Philippian community's affirmation of Paul's testimony, what kind of narrative logic can we discern?

After reviewing previous narrative-related scholarship, in the second chapter I will deal with various introductory issues that shape my approach to Philippians as a letter in context. These issues include (1) the compositional unity, (2) the role of suffering, (3) the identities of opponents, and (4) the imperial cult and pertinent exemption for the Jews. With my work focused on the investigation of the narrative dynamics of the identity-formation processes of the Philippian community, these issues can only be introduced briefly. I will then state my assumptions regarding them.

In order to rectify the foregoing shortcomings of previous scholarship and better analyze the narrative dynamics within Paul's identity-formation strategy within Philippians, I turn to Ricoeur's narrative theory in chapter three. According to Ricoeur, there is a universal correspondence between narrative and humans'

---

[12] I am well aware of the anachronistic nature of the label "Christian" when used to describe the early Christ-followers movement. Whether in terms of its relation to the Roman Empire and the Jewish people, its internal hierarchical formation, development of dogma, or endorsed tradition, it is far removed from the meaning this label acquired in later historical periods. This label "Christian," in particular when associated with the group "Jewish Christian leaders," thus serves only as a convenient way to refer to their general affiliation with the early Christ-followers movement. For details, see Bengt Holmberg, "Understanding the First Hundred Years of Christian Identity," in *Exploring Early Christian Identity*, ed. Bengt Holmberg (Tübingen: Mohr Siebeck, 2008), 3–5.

temporal experience.¹³ Drawing on Ricoeur's concepts and adapting selected ideas for my own project, I will analyze the interactions among the five levels of story within Paul's narrative world and deepen my understanding of its theology-generating role within Paul's discourse. Specifically, the threefold mimesis theory enables me to describe the state of the world of the Philippian community before they read Philippians (mimesis1), the emplotment process in which Paul puts together multiple groups' actions into a unified narrative configuration (mimesis2), and the Philippian community's refiguration process (mimesis3).¹⁴ Using Ricoeur's analysis of temporal dynamics (the dialectic of discordance and concordance,¹⁵ the dialectic of innovation and sedimentation,¹⁶ the dialectic of discontinuity and continuity,¹⁷ and the dialectic of external narration and internal conviction¹⁸), I will illuminate Paul's theologizing process within the context of double contestation of narratives.

Based on the concept of temporality as the distinguishing marker of a narrative or a text undergirded by a narrative, various temporal features of narrative will be introduced as expressions of this temporality, including structural units of "Beginning," "Middle," and "Ending," and an enduring temporal thought as its story theme. I will also introduce a model of nesting of stories, in which a current story resides upon a previous one in articulating the process of meaning creation between narratives.¹⁹ Through the analyses of multiple nested stories I will show how Paul blends the stories of his own and the Philippian community (levels four and five) with the stories of God, Israel, and Christ (levels one to three) in shaping the Philippian community's identity, sense of history, and experience of God.²⁰ Such reliance on Paul's own story leads to the problem of ascertaining his testimony. With the lack of objectively verifiable evidence, on what basis could the Philippian community affirm Paul's testimony as truthful and reject that of the Jewish Christian leaders as false? It is with respect to this challenge I introduce the concept of a truthfulness marked by a dialectic of subjective and objective "logic" within Paul's affirmation of God's revelation, and the Philippian community's discernment of Paul's testimony as coming from God.

One major application of this temporality concerns the formation of narrative identity for the Philippian community. According to Ricoeur, a person's narrative identity is made within her compliant reading of another's story and subsequent telling of her own in accordance with the temporality of another's story.²¹ However, due to

---

[13] Paul Ricoeur, *Time and Narrative* I (Chicago: University of Chicago Press, 1984), 52 (henceforth *T&N I*).
[14] Ibid., 52-6, 71, 81.
[15] Ibid., 4, 21-2, 31; Paul Ricoeur, *Time and Narrative* II (Chicago: University of Chicago Press, 1985), 4-5 (henceforth *T&N II*).
[16] Paul Ricoeur, "The Text as Dynamic Identity," in *Identity of the Literary Text*, ed. Mario J. Valdés and Owen J. Miller (Toronto: University of Toronto Press, 1985), 181-2.
[17] Ricoeur, *T&N I*, 80-1.
[18] Paul Ricoeur, "The Hermeneutics of Testimony," in *Essays on Biblical Interpretation*, ed. L. S. Mudge (Philadelphia: Fortress, 1980), 133-5.
[19] Cf. Ricoeur, *T&N I*, 28-30.
[20] Cf. ibid., 28-30.
[21] Paul Ricoeur, *Time and Narrative* III (Chicago: University of Chicago Press, 1988), 246-7 (henceforth *T&N III*); Paul Ricoeur, "Life: A Story in Search of a Narrator," in *A Ricoeur Reader: Reflection and Imagination*, ed. Mario J. Valdes (Toronto: University of Toronto Press, 1991), 437;

the open-ended and contested nature of narrative identity, each of the Philippian community members could always reinterpret her experience of suffering for the gospel. Then, how can we still rely on the storytelling of the Philippian community as a stable source of forming their "Christian identity"?[22] This brings us to the ethical dimension of such storytelling, which is marked by *a person's ethical response to another person in the form of a promise so that another can count on her over time.*[23] I argue that it is in light of this mode of "ethical identity" that the "Christian identity" of the Philippian community is shaped.

Based on these narrative concepts from Ricoeur and Dunn, I begin my exegetical analysis of Philippians, which will be divided into five units. In the exegesis of Phil. 1:3–2:4 (chapter four), I aim to show the nature and background of the exigency facing Paul as a double contestation of narratives between Paul and his opponents. Among many exegetical issues, I give close attention to the proper symbolic framework for interpreting πολιτεύομαι, the function of τῇ πίστει τοῦ εὐαγγελίου within believers' experience of assurance from God, and the meaning of ἔνδειξις (1:27-30). Contrasting receptions of Paul's testimony (1:12-18) will be looked upon as a contestation of truthfulness between Paul and his Jewish Christian opponents. The temporal logic of Paul's assurance amid doubt from other "God's followers" will be analyzed within his allusion to the story of Job (1:19-26). The exhortations of Paul in 1:3-11 will be examined as a call to shift the community's "viewpoint" to the imminent temporal horizon of the "Day of Christ Jesus," which is the end point of the story of Christ. I will then approach 2:1-4 as a contestation of ethical dispositions between true and false "Christ-followers."

In chapter five, I will disclose the temporal manners in which Paul's story fits itself with the paradigmatic story of Christ (Phil. 2:5-11, 3:17-21). I argue that Paul constructs a unique and temporally radical story of Christ (level three) to respond to his current contention about the manifestation of God's righteousness within believers' suffering for Him. Jesus's voluntary suffering and death are thus highlighted as His faithful response to God's plan of salvation.

Exaltation of Christ in 2:9-11 emphasizes not a universal worship of Christ from believers,[24] but God's vindicating response to Christ's earthly obedience, and Christ's upcoming judgment based on peoples' response to His suffering. Those who suffer for His gospel will be vindicated by Christ through the transfiguration of their humiliated bodies (3:20-21).

Paul Ricoeur, *Oneself as Another*, trans. Kathleen Blamey (Chicago: University of Chicago Press, 1992), 141–3.

[22] Cf. Ricoeur, *Oneself as Another*, 167–8.

[23] Paul Ricoeur, "The Hermeneutical Function of Distanciation," in *Hermeneutics and the Human Sciences: Essays on Language, Action and Interpretation* (Cambridge: Cambridge University Press, 1981), 133, 38.

[24] Richard R. Melick, *Philippians, Colossians, Philemon. An Exegetical and Theological Exposition of Holy Scripture*, NAC 32 (Nashville: Holman Reference, 1991), 107; Otfried Hofius, *Der Christushymnus Philipper 2, 6–11: Untersuchungen zu Gestalt und Aussage eines Urchristlichen Psalms* (Tübingen: Mohr, 1976), 37–40; Richard Bauckham, "The Worship of Jesus in Philippians 2:9–11," in *Where Christology Began: Essays on Philippians 2*, ed. Ralph P. Martin and Brian J. Dodd (Louisville: Westminster John Knox Press, 1998), 128, 32–3.

In chapter six, I argue that Paul sets up his own historical story (level four) as the exemplary story for the Philippian community to imitate. To show how this exemplar works, I approach 3:1-21 as a contrast between the temporal dimension of the testimonies of the Jewish Christian leaders and Paul. While the Jewish Christian leaders' testimony is marked by its past-oriented continuity with the "old" story of Israel, Paul's testimony is characterized by a future-oriented temporal dynamic installed by the "unfinished" story of Christ. Earthly suffering for the gospel has become the essential means of knowing Christ and experiencing His power of resurrection (3:10-11).

Nevertheless, a successful shaping of the community's "Christian identity" ultimately depends on each member's compliant reading and retelling of Paul's testimony. In chapter seven, I take Phil. 2:12-16a to be an epitome of Paul's intended story of the Philippian community (level five) and argue that Paul nests their story upon a historical trajectory of contested (or disputed) events within God's historical salvation timeline (Ps. 2:11, Ex. 15:22–17:7, Num. 14–17; Dan. 12:3). If each member rejects the narratives of Paul's opponents, and tells her own testimony in accordance with the temporality of Paul's testimony, her experiences of suffering will be transformed into the sources of God's grace (Phil. 1:29) and the means of knowing Christ (3:10-11). As the community members collectively hope for God's vindication of their sufferings, a collective "Christian identity" will be formed among them. Their understanding of history will follow the temporality of Paul.

Finally, in chapter eight, I integrate the above exegetical findings and map them onto three mimesis moments through which the collective identity formation of the Philippian community is analyzed. In the hope of Paul, after the community has compliantly read his letter (Philippians) and renewed the narrative configuration of their testimonies, the community would start to reshape their identity according to the temporality of his testimony. Along each member's identity-formation stages, I argue that each instance of the community member's narrative identity, which is composed of different dialectics of her preacquired traditions and her intentional resilience, evolves within the contestation of testimonies between Paul and the Jewish Christian leaders. At the end, I intend to show that the whole "Christian identity" formation process of the Philippian community is being shaped amid a contestation of testimonies with divergent temporalities.

Part I

Past Approaches to Philippians

1

Critical Review of Narrative Analyses of Philippians

This critical review of narrative analysis is divided into three parts. The first part pertains to a review of the general narrative methodology. This part is crucial to my work because it serves to build an overall picture of scholarly review for the narrative analysis of Pauline studies.

The second part is related to previous research on Philippians that has employed narrative methods of different kinds.[1] This part is vital in order to show this project's distinctiveness in the field of Philippians research. Finally, the third part will cover reviews of a particular application of narrative approach: identity formation.

1.1 Narrative Approach to the Pauline Letters

1.1.1 History of Research

Narrative analysis has been applied to Pauline studies for over thirty years.[2] Scholars have been applying different narrative theories to highlight the narrative aspects of Paul's theology, enhancing the view that Paul is a narrative theologian.[3] Through these theories, scholars hope to discover and unpack the ways of Paul's theological saying and thinking, which could not be seen before using traditional methodologies.[4] Vocabularies of "narrative," "story,"[5] "plot," "character" (disposition), "character"

---

[1] Along the thinking of Richard Hays and James Dunn, my proposal is not based on the text of Philippians itself as belonging to the genre of a "standard" narrative, nor the presence of narratives within the letter, but the existence of multiple levels of story within the narrative substructure "underneath" the text. See Hays, *The Faith of Jesus Christ*, 29–30; Horrell, "Paul's Narrative," 158.
[2] Bruce W. Longenecker, "The Narrative Approach to Paul: An Early Retrospective," *CBR* 1 (2002): 94–107.
[3] For references, see Norman R. Petersen, *Rediscovering Paul: Philemon and the Sociology of Paul's Narrative World* (Eugene: Wipf & Stock Pub, 2008), 1–42; Witherington III, *Paul's Narrative Thought World*, 1–10; Sylvia C. Keesmaat, *Paul & His Story: (Re)interpreting the Exodus Tradition*, JSNTSup 181 (Sheffield: Sheffield Academic, 1999), 15–53.
[4] Longenecker, "Narrative Approach," 94.
[5] It is important to note that scholars hold similar yet divergent meanings regarding many of the terms related to narrative. See H. Porter Abbott, "Story, Plot, and Narration," in *The Cambridge Companion to Narrative*, ed. David Herman (Cambridge: Cambridge University Press, 2007), 41–4. For a concise summary of scholars' various definitions of narrative, see Marie-Laure Ryan,

(personage), "frame," "intertextuality," "narrative dynamic," "temporality," "echo," and so on have become common in the circle of Pauline scholarship, offering fresh insights into Paul's persuasive strategies within his letters, pretextual components of his letters, and a more thorough understanding of the context of writing.

1.1.2 Discovery of Narrative Substructure (Richard Hays)

Among these efforts, one of the most prominent foci is to argue for the presence and influence of a narrative substructure "underneath" the writings of Paul. In his groundbreaking work *The Faith of Jesus Christ: The Narrative Substructure of Galatians 3:1–4:11* (1983), Richard Hays strives to prove the existence of a narrative substructure at the core of Paul's gospel in the epistle to the Galatians.[6] Focusing on the text Gal. 3:1–4:11, Hays argues that *the theological thinking of Paul grounds itself on top of a narrative structure*, which is a story of Jesus Christ.[7] Hays contends that it is neither a system of doctrines nor his personal religious experience but the "sacred story" of Jesus Christ that *constitutes the framework of Paul's thought* and plays a theology-generating role.[8] As Paul tackles various contingencies in churches, he "'theologizes' by reflecting upon this structure as an ordering pattern for his thoughts and experiences."[9] In other words, he sets his interpretations within the framework of this "sacred story," which is a story about Jesus Christ.[10]

One of Hays's central arguments is to validate that there is an organic continuity between the language of story and discursive language in the kind of discourse that Paul employs in the theological portions of his letters.[11] Based on the theories of Northrop Frye, Paul Ricoeur, and Robert Funk, Hays strengthens his position that a story can act as a constraint on the logic of an argument.[12] Thus, although we may only observe allusive and fragmentary expressions within the reflective discourse of Paul's letters, an "underneath" story is, in fact, governing the logic of the discourse in decisive ways.[13]

With the discovery of this story situated "underneath" Paul's discourse, scholars began to dig further to see more detailed differentiations of these narrative components. While Hays sees that there is one such layer of structure "underneath," Ben Witherington further divides Paul's fabric into three layers,[14] which is a view shared

---

"Toward a Definition of Narrative," in *The Cambridge Companion to Narrative,* ed. David Herman (Cambridge: Cambridge University Press, 2007), 22–35. See also Brian Richardson, *A Poetics of Plot for the Twenty-First Century: Theorizing Unruly Narratives* (Columbus: Ohio State University Press, 2019), 15–29; James Phelan and Peter J. Rabinowitz, "Time, Plot, Progression," in *Narrative Theory: Core Concepts and Critical Debates* (Columbus: Ohio State University Press, 2012), 71; Gerard Genette, *Narrative Discourse: An Essay in Method* (New York: Cornell University Press, 1980), 33–160. For a critique of Genette's approach, see Anthony C. Thiselton, "The Hermeneutics of Paul Ricoeur," in *Hermeneutics: An Introduction* (Grand Rapids: Wm. B. Eerdmans, 2009), 235–9.

[6] Hays, *The Faith of Jesus Christ*, 226.
[7] Ibid., 6.
[8] Ibid.
[9] Ibid.
[10] Ibid.
[11] Ibid., 21–2.
[12] Ibid., 21–8.
[13] Ibid., 22.
[14] Witherington III, *Paul's Narrative Thought World*, 6n.7.

by N. T. Wright.[15] No matter whether we take the view of a bipartite structure from Hays (substructure and reflective discourse) or a tripartite one from Witherington and Wright, most scholars have concluded that *stories or narratives no longer just serve as illustrations of beliefs but also generate thoughts themselves.*[16] As Longenecker says, "[These] narrative contours in the Pauline cognitive landscape are not simply the result of deeper theological processes but are themselves generative of theological articulations."[17] Thus, if we can better understand these narrative components, we would be granted more insight into the theology-making processes in the texts of Paul.

Hays's narrative theory and its application to understanding Paul's hermeneutics are not supported by all scholars. One particular scholar is Francis Watson. In his article "Is There a Story in These Texts?," Watson argues that Paul's "narrative substructure," if there is one, belongs to the "scriptural narratives relating to Israel's history with God."[18] Arguing against Hays's understanding of Paul as a "narrative theologian," Watson asserts that Paul is an interpreter or reader of the Torah, whose "construal of the Torah [as found in Galatians chapter three] requires only minimal intervention by Paul himself."[19] While Hays tends to see Paul as one who *revises* Israel's story through "the lens of the story of Jesus," Watson sees Paul's interpretation of Scripture as one that "always conforms to the 'semantic potential' of the texts."[20] According to Watson, "what Paul does not do is to incorporate his gospel into a linear story of creation and Israel as the end and goal of that story."[21]

An implicitly imposed dichotomy within Watson's argument is that narrative can accommodate only horizontal elements but not vertical.[22] With Paul's presentation of the gospel necessarily comprised of language of "divine incursion" from above, the Christ-event becomes "an absolute and unsurpassable event" that "does not exist on the same horizontal plane as the scriptural narrative(s)."[23] According to Hays, Watson's argument is right only if "we define 'narrative' *a priori* as limited to the ordinary plane of human agency, of finite cause and effect—that is, only if we decide before the fact that 'narrative' can describe only human actions, never God's action."[24]

---

[15] Wright, *People of God*, 123.
[16] Ibid., 38–44; Longenecker, "Narrative Approach," 93. "This narrative world is also distinguished from a copy of the historical setting behind the text. While the latter primarily relates to what happened, the former relates to "a fictional or reconstructed world created by Paul." See G. R. Osborne, "Hermeneutics/Interpreting Paul," in *DPL*, ed. Gerald F. Hawthorne and Ralph P. Martin (Leicester: InterVarsity Press, 1993).
[17] Longenecker, "Narrative Approach," 93.
[18] Francis Watson, "Is There a Story in These Texts?," in *Narrative Dynamics in Paul. A Critical Assessment*, ed. Bruce W. Longenecker (Louisville: Westminster John Knox Press, 2002), 232.
[19] Watson, "Is There a Story in These Texts?," 239; Francis Watson, *Paul and the Hermeneutics of Faith* (Edinburgh: T&T Clark, 2004), 517.
[20] Richard B. Hays, "Is Paul's Gospel Narratable?" *JSNT* 27, no. 2 (2004): 237; Barry S. Crawford, review of *Paul and the Hermeneutics of Faith*, by Francis Watson, *CBQ* 68 (2006): 560; Watson, "Is There a Story in These Texts?," 4, 163, 83.
[21] Watson, "Is There a Story in These Texts?," 234.
[22] Ibid., 232–3.
[23] Ibid., 234, 9.
[24] Hays, "Is Paul's Gospel Narratable?" 237–8. For a thorough critique of Watson's argument, see ibid., 236–9; Leslie Houlden, Review of *Paul and the Hermeneutics of Faith*, by Francis Watson, *JTS* 56 (2005): 555–8. For a defense of the capacity of narrative in incorporating "verticality" as well as

1.1.3 Five Levels of Story (James Dunn)

In his work *The Theology of Paul the Apostle*, James D. G. Dunn offers five "fluid but identifiable" levels of story interwoven and superimposed within Paul's letters (Figure 1).[25] Starting from the bottom, these five levels are:

(1) the story of God and creation—the deepest axiomatic level of Paul's theology;
(2) the story of Israel—the second level, where inherited presuppositions came under greatest strain from the revelation experienced by Paul;
(3) the story of Jesus—the third level and source of the transformation of Saul the Pharisee into Paul the apostle;
(4) the story of Paul—the transformative level, from his conversion onward;
(5) the story of Paul's churches—the surface level, at which the interaction between Paul and his churches is most immediately accessible through the letters Paul wrote to these churches.[26]

According to Dunn, none of these five levels of story stands on its own.[27] What is important is that as these stories interact and grind against each other, dissonances will arise and lead to questions of coherence or inconsistency in Paul's theology.[28] Dunn writes,

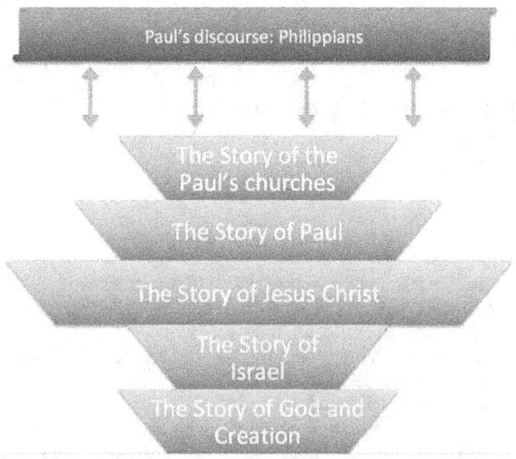

Figure 1 The five levels of story model from Dunn.

"horizontality," see Susan Stanford Friedman, "Spatialization: A Strategy for Reading Narrative," *Narrative* 1, no. 1 (1993): 12–23.
[25] Dunn, "Paul's Theology," 328.
[26] Ibid.
[27] Ibid.
[28] Ibid.

In fact, Paul's theology can be said to emerge from the interplay between several stories, his theologizing to consist in his own participation in that interplay . . . there are the complex interactions of Paul's own story with the stories of those who had believed before him and of those who came to form the churches founded by them.[29]

Thus, according to Dunn's model, in order to fully understand the narrative dynamics and hence theology of Paul in Philippians, more attention has to be paid to the interactions between all five layers of story. In particular, with the purpose of this book being the exploration of the identity-formation strategies used by Paul to shape the life of the Philippian community, the story of Paul on level four and the story of the community on level five are too important to be neglected. However, as the following review will show, despite narrative analyses in Pauline studies gaining momentum, no systematic effort has been paid to this aspect of Pauline theology in Philippians. When these two levels of story are excluded from the analysis, understanding of Paul's theological thinking is seriously limited.[30]

One basic but fundamental principle within my investigation of the narrative interplays between levels of story is the principle of narrative continuity, which is not a kind of linearity but rather, a coherence between stories. Within Paul's "conversion" (which rests on Paul's trust in the story that the crucified Jesus is indeed God's Messiah), the story of Christ (level three) throws Paul's understandings of the lower two stories (the story of God and the story of Israel) into confusion and reconfiguration, demanding a whole new way of building narrative continuities among the levels one through three.[31] Likewise, when we describe Paul's soteriology as grounded in a narrative, the stories of Paul and the Philippian community (upper level of stories) can be classified as compatible with, and hence faithful to, Christian soteriology only if they generate "narrative re-descriptions of the story of Jesus . . . that make it clear how it is the story of redemption."[32] Just as the story of Jesus Christ (level three) occurring κατὰ τὰς γραφὰς (according to the Scriptures) serves as a stimulus and governs the narrative imagination between level three and the lower levels, the story of Jesus guides the narrative continuities developing in the upper levels (four and five). In other words, Paul's letters are always in hermeneutical engagement, not only with Israel's story but also with the early "Christ-followers'" narrative of the εὐαγγέλιον (good news) of Jesus Christ.[33] Therefore, the adoption of this multi-level narrative substructure model from Dunn better equips us to further sharpen the differentiation of narrative components so that more insights can be gained into the theological thinking and identity-shaping strategy of Paul.

---

[29] Dunn, *Theology of Paul*, 18.
[30] James D. G. Dunn, "The Narrative Approach to Paul. Whose Story?," in *Narrative Dynamics in Paul. A Critical Assessment*, ed. Bruce W. Longenecker (Louisville: Westminster John Knox Press, 2002), 226; Dunn, "Paul's Theology," 327, 46.
[31] Dunn, "Paul's Theology," 337–8.
[32] Hays, "Is Paul's Gospel Narratable?," 234. What is assumed is that there exists a constant intertextual character of Paul's discourse among levels of narrative.
[33] Hays, "Is Paul's Gospel Narratable?," 237.

1.2 A Review of General Narrative Analyses of Philippians

While the work of Hays offers a ground-breaking narrative approach to Pauline studies, not many scholars have set the narrative analyses of Philippians as their priority. For example, in the book *Narrative Dynamics in Paul*, we see British-based scholars focus on Galatians and Romans while ignoring Philippians.[34] Having said that, there are a few scholars who have utilized various narrative theories in understanding Philippians. However, within their quest for understanding Paul's narrative logic in Philippians, each attempt has been hampered by shortcomings. In what follows, I briefly introduce these works and highlight their shortcomings and limitations.

1.2.1 N. T. Wright

In his lengthy monograph *Paul and the Faithfulness of God*, Wright develops a macro template of a reconstructed first-century Jewish storied worldview centered on Christ and applies it to Paul: "Paul's Jewish worldview, radically reshaped around the crucified Messiah, challenges the world of ancient paganism with the concrete signs of the faithfulness of God."[35] According to Wright, "Paul actually invents something we may call 'Christian theology'" and develops a "robust reappropriation of the Jewish beliefs—monotheism, election, and eschatology, all rethought around the Messiah and the spirit."[36] Based on this overarching framework of redefining covenant status, Wright looks at the relationship between the "Christ-Hymn" (Phil. 2:5-11) and Paul's "autobiographical" discourse in chapter three as one in which the faithful event of Christ redefines the pattern for membership in the covenant family.[37] What Paul offers in Philippians 3 is "exactly the same double-edged picture, even in the abbreviated form of Galatians."[38] The rejection of ἐμὴν δικαιοσύνην τὴν ἐκ νόμου (my own righteousness derived from the Law) in Phil. 3:9 points to the "new perspective" view of Paul, which understands Paul's efforts here not as "an attempt to add his own merit to the grace he had been given. They were an attempt . . . out of . . . obedience to Israel's God, the works *which would function as a sign in the present that he was part of the people who would be vindicated in the future* [Wright's own emphasis]."[39] Paul's agenda is not about earning the membership of God's Kingdom, but its demonstration. In the end, it is about receiving the "righteous status from God" in Christ.[40] On the other hand, Wright also reads an anti-imperial message in chapter three: "as I, Paul, have rethought my Jewish allegiance in the light of the crucified and risen Jesus, so you should rethink

---

[34] Longenecker, *Narrative Dynamics*, v–vi.
[35] Wright, *Paul and the Faithfulness of God*, 21.
[36] Ibid., xvi.
[37] Ibid., 987.
[38] Wright, *Justification*, 122. According to Wright, Phil. 3 is "in line with . . . Galatians 2:19–20," in which "*Paul has discovered in the Messiah the true-Israel identity to which his life under Torah had pointed but which it could not deliver, and he therefore warns the Philippians against being drawn in that false direction* [Wright's emphasis]." See ibid., 120.
[39] Ibid., 125. One of the typical views of the so-called "New Perspective of Paul" (NPP).
[40] Ibid., 128.

your Roman allegiance in the same light."[41] In a move which aligns with his broad framework of interpreting the ideology of Paul as against that of the pagan Roman Empire, Wright contends that Philippians 3, in a form of coded challenge, serves to remind the community not to "go along with the Caesar-cult that is currently sweeping the Eastern Mediterranean."[42]

Without pretending to have summarized all of Wright's points concerning Philippians,[43] what is inadequate in Wright's work is that his approach *does not fully allow the unique contingent situation of the Philippian community* to be taken into account. While his Christological reappropriation of the Jewish beliefs centering on the story of Christ as the Messiah has certainly enriched our understandings of Paul's theology, his subsequent approach toward Philippians as "an abbreviated form of Galatians" suffers from a huge oversight of the drastic differences between the contingent exigencies of Galatians and Philippians. With Wright's over-reliance on his overarching framework as the core hermeneutical key, he fails to pay enough attention to a unique kind of tension among diverse testimonies professed by Paul and his other more problematic set of opponents: some Jewish Christian leaders in Phil. 3:2 and other "Christ-followers" in Rome (Phil. 1:15-18) who try to hurt Paul deliberately. Galatians (and Romans), which largely represents Paul's concern regarding entry into God's Kingdom, becomes the chief interpretative key for Philippians. Polemics against the Roman Empire are wrongly assumed to be at the center of Paul's concern.

1.2.2 Michael Gorman

Another scholar who has not paid enough attention to the unique contingent situation of Philippians is Michael Gorman. Gorman sees Phil. 2:5-11 as the "master story" which contains many narrative patterns found in a story of Christ's death.[44] Taking into account the significance of religious experience and Paul's fondness of narrating that experience, Gorman argues that instead of searching for a static center of Paul's theology, "a narrative suggests action and movement, not merely around an immovable central feature but within the central phenomena of the story."[45] Thus, he proposes a theological expression which he calls "narrative spirituality" that means "a spirituality that tells a story, a dynamic life with God that corresponds in some way to the divine 'story.'"[46] With this "integrative narrative experience" of cruciformity, we can find the key to understanding Paul.[47]

---

[41] N. T. Wright, "Paul's Gospel and Caesar's Empire," in *Paul and Politics: Ekklesia, Israel, Imperium, Interpretation*, ed. Richard A. Horsley (Valley Forge: Trinity Press, 2000), 178.

[42] Wright, "Paul's Gospel," 178. For a critique of Wright's logic, see Seyoon Kim, *Christ and Caesar: The Gospel and the Roman Empire in the Writings of Paul and Luke* (Grand Rapids: Wm. B. Eerdmans, 2008), 11–16.

[43] Cf. N. T. Wright, *The Resurrection of the Son of God* (London: SPCK, 2003), 225.

[44] Michael J. Gorman, *Cruciformity: Paul's Narrative Spirituality of the Cross* (Grand Rapids: Wm. B. Eerdmans, 2001), 88–92; Michael J. Gorman, *Inhabiting the Cruciform God: Kenosis, Justification, and Theosis in Paul's Narrative Soteriology* (Grand Rapids: Wm. B. Eerdmans, 2009), 9–39.

[45] Gorman, *Cruciformity*, 370.

[46] Ibid., 4.

[47] Ibid., 371.

Just like Wright, Gorman has nicely employed narrative theology to offer insights on Pauline spirituality. However, his approach of identifying the story of Christ as a cruciformity of love, faith, power, and hope across all of Paul's letters seems to have imposed his own hermeneutical template onto the texts.[48] Besides covering Phil. 2:5-11, he does not offer much discussion of the situational specificity and radical contingency of Philippians.[49] The social realities in which the early "Christians'" identity formation takes place, in addition to the multiple dimensions of their human lives, are not being recognized. As Bengt Holmberg writes, "Any historical investigation of early Christian identity must start with, and give greater weight to, the earthy elements of identity, or in other words to its tangible dimensions."[50] Thus, Gorman's approach has again neglected the relationship between the story of Christ and those contingent narratives happening on levels four and five.

1.2.3 Richard Hays

Such a tendency of neglecting the radical contingencies within the narrative analysis of an epistle is also found in the approach of Hays, which has become more prominent with the emergence of Dunn's five levels of story model. When Hays focuses on validating the presence of one unified story "underneath," his direction of narrative interaction stretches only from level three (the story of Jesus) "downward" to the lower two levels (the story of God and the story of Israel). However, Graham Stanton cautions that Hays's approach has a tendency to produce text-immanent readings that are in danger of overlooking how the Pauline letters were actually heard "on the ground" in the first-century communities.[51] Stanton's criticism regarding Hays's approach is grounded in Hays's adoption of Greimas's narrative structure (the actantial model), which focuses solely on intratextual elements.[52] Similarly, Dunn also sees Hays as not having paid enough attention to the logic of assumed narrative structure in his later works.[53] As Dunn has emphasized, stories at levels four and five are also too important to be ignored in understanding the narrative dynamics of Paul in his theological writings.[54] Without a narrative structure which accommodates stories of Paul and the early churches, the analysis of narrative dynamics is incomplete.

To address this challenge, Stanton proposes that we need to be aware of contingent factors in the rhetorical environment such as the "stories of the Roman emperors." *We need an approach which accommodates those multiple fragmented, yet interrelated, stories of levels four and five, and their dynamic interactions with the stories on levels*

---

[48] Cf. ibid., 92–4; Kar Yon Lim, *'The Sufferings of Christ Are Abundant in Us': A Narrative Dynamics Investigation of Paul's Sufferings in 2 Corinthians*, LNTS (London: Bloomsbury T&T Clark, 2009), 22–3.
[49] Holmberg, "Understanding," 29.
[50] Ibid.
[51] Graham N. Stanton, "'I Think, When I Read That Sweet Story of Old'," in *Narrative Dynamics in Paul. A Critical Assessment*, ed. Bruce W. Longenecker (Louisville: Westminster John Knox Press, 2002), 131.
[52] Hays, *The Faith of Jesus Christ*, 82–94.
[53] Dunn, "Whose Story?," 218.
[54] Dunn, "Paul's Theology," 327.

one, two, and three. If Philippians represents primarily the story of Paul (level four), then a corresponding hermeneutical framework must be developed to investigate its interaction with the upper story (level five), and the lower ones (levels one, two, and three).

1.2.4 Richard J. Weymouth and Stephen Fowl

Another shortcoming of interpreters' previous narrative research into Philippians stems from their failure to recognize the narrative dynamics resulting from the interactions among the stories of Christ, Paul, and the Philippian community (levels three to five). As the following review will show, some interpreters tend to believe that the overall or major narrative logic of Paul's theological thinking in Philippians can still be properly discerned even when relatively little attention is paid to the passages outside the so-called "Christ-Hymn" (Phil. 2:6-11). As a result, not only do they fail to discern and delineate the various crucial dynamics among levels three to five but they also miss any narrative interactions between the upper levels (four and five) and God's previous works among the Israelites (levels one to two).

For example, in his PhD thesis *The Christ-Story of Philippians 2:5-11*, Weymouth sees Phil. 2:5-11 as a Pauline prose narrative and interprets it in terms of its "form, function, and content."[55] In his conclusion, Weymouth argues that the power of this story of Christ lies in its role as a shaper of other stories.[56] With its dual "exemplary-paradigmatic" nature, this story "models the mindset in thought and action that Paul desires to be reproduced in the lives of his status-obsessed hearers," and "functions to structure Christian existence in various ways and also invites participation in Christ."[57] Based on this method, Weymouth succeeds in recognizing the phenomenon of intersecting stories of Paul, the community, Christ, and others.[58] He has also taken the political background of the Roman Empire into account,[59] and argues that the story of Christ belongs to a kind of "counter-imperial narrative."[60] With his identification of "a modified narrative chiastic structure revolving around key narrative reversals in the story,"[61] the "Christ-Hymn" passage as a whole can be better understood.[62]

However, while Weymouth claims to endorse the significance of multiple intersecting narratives of Paul, the community, Christ, and others, he confines his work to Phil. 2:6-11 leaving the remaining text unanalyzed.[63] Speaking of a strict precedence and strong autonomy regarding the meaning of the "Christ-Hymn," Weymouth concludes that this "passage clearly deserves investigation on its own."[64]

---

[55] Weymouth, "Christ-Story," vii.
[56] Ibid., viii.
[57] Ibid., viii, 240–5, 481–2.
[58] Ibid., 103–5, 61–3, 479.
[59] Ibid., 8–10, 295–8, 424–9.
[60] Ibid., 313, 25–6, 36–7, 429.
[61] Ibid., 400, 70.
[62] Ibid., 482.
[63] Cf. ibid., 485.
[64] Ibid., 18.

Thus, the interpretation of the "Christ-Hymn" does not need to take into account Paul's own narrated autobiographical story in chapter three of the epistle.[65]

Weymouth may be correct to call Paul's life the "little story" compared to the "big story" of Christ, and in stating that Paul's story finds its meaning inside its relation to that of Christ.[66] Weymouth is also partially correct, in an implicit manner, to speak of the "Christ-Hymn" or the Cross as a "supergiant star," whose unparalleled gravitational pull virtually defines the meaning of every other story (or star, metaphorically) around it.[67] Weymouth's viewpoint, however, does not take into account the perspective that Philippians is a series of events described *by* the person Paul. All the intersecting stories within the epistle are of great significance for Paul. Instead of taking a bird's-eye view in which the supergiant star (Christ's story) and all the other smaller orbiting stars (e.g., Paul's story) are in sight, Philippians should better be understood as a "snapshot" taken by Paul "from his own star."

What is in view is thus not an objective panorama of the stars from somewhere "outside the universe" but a personal portrayal of what one has seen from one's own star (story) "inside the universe." Thus, phenomenologically speaking, the supergiant star, which metaphorically refers to Christ's story, should be viewed as "bound" or "attached" to the smaller star of Paul. *In order to determine the meaning of Christ's story in Philippians, one must incorporate the story of Paul.* In other words, these two stories (levels three and four) *must be considered together*. Only through both stories can we holistically grasp the narrative dynamics within the narrative substructure, and investigate its constraints on the logic of Paul's discourse in Philippians.

The failure to take the narrative dynamics from those upper stories into account is echoed in the work of Stephen Fowl. In his book *The Story of Christ in the Ethics of Paul*, Fowl argues that the story of Jesus Christ in Phil. 2:5-11, just like other similar hymnic materials, narrates "a story in which Christ is the main character ... (and) the foundation of the communities to which each epistle is written."[68] He suggests that Paul uses the story of Christ (2:5-11) to support the ethical demands of Phil. 1:27ff.[69] Concerning the particular relationship between the story of Christ and its influence on Philippians, Fowl stresses that to the Philippian community, the life of Jesus is their "exemplar," but not a model to imitate.[70] He derives this concept of "exemplar" from T. Kuhn in the learning and practice of science.[71] Based on Kuhn, Fowl explicates that an "exemplar" is not an "abstract law-like systematic generalisation" but "a concrete formulation or experiment which is recognized and shared by all scientists."[72] Its value lies in its capacity to be extended by analogy to offer solutions to particular problems by

---

[65] Ibid.
[66] Ibid., 17.
[67] Ibid., 18, 20, 398n.1, 503.
[68] Stephen E. Fowl, *The Story of Christ in the Ethics of Paul: An Analysis of the Function of the Hymnic Material in the Pauline Corpus* (Sheffield: JSOT Press, 1990), 199.
[69] Ibid., 77–101.
[70] Ibid., 92–101.
[71] Thomas S. Kuhn, *The Structure of Scientific Revolutions*, International Encyclopedia of Unified Science. Foundations of the Unity of Science, vol. 2, no. 2 (Chicago: University of Chicago Press, 1970), 186–208; Fowl, *The Story of Christ*, 92–3.
[72] Fowl, *The Story of Christ*, 93; Kuhn, *Scientific Revolutions*, 187.

someone who has the ability to see a similarity-in-difference between the "exemplar" and the particular problem.[73] Thus, Fowl sees this story of Christ not as "a concrete solution to a problem" but as an "exemplar" which can be adapted analogically to another concrete situation.[74]

Fowl's proposal regarding the relationship between the "Christ-Hymn" and exhortations in Phil. 1:27ff. has a few similarities with my approach. For example, in stating that the community draws its identity from the Christ-Hymn story as an acceptable interpretation of traditions about Christ, Fowl accommodates the active roles of Paul and the Philippian community within the identity-formation processes, which correspond to stories on levels four and five.[75]

However, there is one serious limitation to Fowl's approach, which stems from a lack of detailed explication on the "analogical" relation between the "Exemplar" of the "Christ-Hymn" and the particular historical situation facing the Philippian community. According to Fowl, due to the lack of a self-evident relation between the "Christ-Hymn" and the contingent situation of the community, Paul must take up the role of noting the "similarities-in-difference" between the two, which is a kind of analogical drawing.[76] Such a mode of reasoning represents a "language of ordered relationships . . . [which] is constituted by the distinct but similar relations of each analogue to some focal meaning, some prime analogue."[77] However, apart from giving a footnote to the work of David Tracy, Fowl does not offer much else in expounding the logic behind Paul's discourse.[78] With this broad-stroke style, it is not surprising to see Fowl end up just stating, without any explanation, that despite vast discrepancies between the models of scientific field and narrative ethics, Paul's mode of thinking can still be patterned after Kuhn's exemplar model.[79]

This work aims to go beyond such a vague explication and instead will elucidate the ways Paul's theological logic is influenced by the various narrative dynamics within the narrative substructure. In particular, this work will ask, how can the narrative relations among the stories of Christ and the Philippian community be more deeply explicated beyond analogy? How can the "focal meaning" or "prime analogue" be better substantiated so that we can further understand Paul's ethical logic? As the following methodological section will show, such narrative relations must be expounded by *delving into a specific "mode of ordering" when articulating the narrative logic within Paul's narrative substructure*, in addition to its subsequent constraints on the discourse of Philippians. Such a method will be presented using Ricoeur's narrative theory.

Similar to Weymouth, Fowl's argument is also weakened by his sidelining of the role of Paul's story within Paul's ethical exhortations to the Philippian community.[80] While

---

[73] Fowl, *The Story of Christ*, 93.
[74] Ibid., 93–5.
[75] Ibid., 199.
[76] Ibid., 94–5.
[77] Ibid., 92.
[78] Ibid., 202; David Tracy, *The Analogical Imagination: Christian Theology and the Culture of Pluralism* (New York: The Crossroad Publishing Company, 1998), 408.
[79] Fowl, *The Story of Christ*, 95.
[80] Mark Kiley, Review of *The Story of Christ in the Ethics of Paul: An Analysis of the Function of the Hymnic Material in the Pauline Corpus*, by Stephen E. Fowl, *CBQ* 54 (1992): 152–3.

Fowl may have had some success in proposing another model besides the relationship of imitation between the story of Christ and the lives of the Philippian community,[81] his work has overlooked the significance of Paul's own story within his ethical persuasion. As a result, Fowl relegates Paul to merely the "object" or the source of teaching in which the community should continue to become obedient.[82] Besides the role of *noting* the similarity-in-difference between the "exemplar" Christ story and the exigency within the Philippian community, Paul's own story in chapter three of the epistle is effectively diminished as mere illustration.[83] As a result, despite Fowl's observation of the absence of an analogous relationship between Paul's earthly spiritual experience (Phil. 3:10-11) and the exemplar of Christ, Fowl does not offer any in-depth investigation into the narrative relations between the story of Paul and those of Christ and the Philippian community.[84]

This diminishing of the significance of Paul's story has another consequence: an insensitivity to any dynamics resulting from competing narratives among the intersecting stories within Philippians. This particular weakness can again be discerned from the works of Fowl and Weymouth. In fact, when Fowl views the nature of the "Christ-Hymn" as an "exemplar" as defined by Kuhn, he seems to have assumed it to be a well-recognized, uncontroversial, and objective paradigm which allows Paul to draw consequential ethical applications from it.[85] In the eyes of Fowl, this "exemplar" is seemingly close to a physical law or a storied "shared norm."[86] However, it should not be difficult to accept the notion that the motivation of Paul's exhortation in Philippians is at least partly related to some kind of controversy regarding his personal experience of imprisonment among various "Christ-followers" (Phil. 1:12-19).[87] As my exegesis in the following will show, this assumption from Fowl *has neglected the contested nature and pertinent controversy within the composition of this particular version of the story of Christ, which is intimately related to the current disputed situation of Paul and the Philippian community.* What is being contested involves not only the composition of stories on level four (theology of Paul) and five (ethics of the Philippian community) but also a particular understanding of the story of Christ on level three. By no means should it be likened to any kind of physical law. Nor is it a kind of *readily* "shared norm" among various "Christ-followers" so that it can act as a foundation of firm tradition from which Paul can draw his arguments.[88]

Likewise, due to the story of Paul being virtually absent in Weymouth's work, specific processes of Paul's theological thinking have not been considered. While Weymouth admits that Paul may have refined certain theological concepts within his constitution of Christ's story, he dismisses the significance of this Pauline reflection as inaccessible

---

[81] Fowl, *The Story of Christ*, 80–95.
[82] Ibid., 96.
[83] Ibid., 93.
[84] Ibid., 99–100.
[85] Ibid., 93.
[86] Ibid., 93, 101.
[87] See chapter 4.1.1.2 for my challenge of Bradley Arnold's premise that all the Philippian community members will only be able to read from a Greco-Roman perspective.
[88] Ibid., 101. To be fair, Fowl also notes that this exemplar is a "specific interpretation of traditions about Christ," but he does not offer much explanation into this specific nature.

and claims that "the exact process by which Paul came to narrate the story of Christ in Phil. 2:6–11 remains beyond the limits of our knowledge."[89] With little value placed on the dynamics found within the story of Paul, Weymouth has severely limited his sensitivity to the competing dynamics between Paul's narration of the story of Christ and that of other "Christ-followers." The intersubjective dramatic foil, or competing narrative background, against which Paul writes, is identified only in the story of the Roman emperor.[90]

Such disregard of the significance of the story of Paul within the life-shaping of the Philippian community will be avoided in this work. In fact, due to the hints of rival responses among God's followers regarding the meaning of the current exigency of Paul, in which vicious intentions specifically directed against Paul are found within the preaching activities of the gospel (Phil. 1:12-18), it is highly possible that the core interest of Paul's writing to the Philippian community is closely mingled with his own defense against other "Christ-followers." Moreover, as the exegesis of Phil. 3:1-6 in the following will show, Paul could be competing for the authority in recognizing the identity of God's true people (3:1-6). Based on these preliminary observations, it should be safe to suggest that the theological reflective process within Paul's own story is likely constituted by competing judgments relevant both to Paul and the Philippian community, which could represent competing narrative representations of the story of Christ. Thus, we should look deeper into the constitutive process of Paul's own theological thinking, and investigate the presence and influence of competing claims within Paul's exigency.

1.2.5 A Brief Evaluation

As presented in the foregoing survey, the narrative approach has become widely accepted in the field of Pauline scholarship, which has resulted in a new wave of theological understanding regarding the theologizing of the apostle Paul. However, it is evident that previous narrative studies on Philippians have failed to fully address a number of narrative components, reflected in their neglect of the unique contingent situation of the Philippian community, the lack of attention to the interactions between the upper-level stories (four and five) and lower-level stories (one to three), and, most importantly of all, the failure to discern the dynamics of competing narratives on level four. In order to grasp a holistic and thorough picture of all major narrative dynamics within the narrative substructure beneath the discourse of Philippians, we cannot separate our understanding of the story of Christ (level three) from the stories of Paul and the Philippian community (levels four and five). While the meaning of the "little" story of Paul *comes from* the "big" story of Christ, the meaning of the story of Christ *comes through* the story of Paul, which is bound to the contingent concern of Paul in Philippians.

---

[89] Weymouth, "Christ-Story," 342n.3.
[90] Ibid., 318. According to Weymouth, the Christ story in Philippians is a counter-imperial narrative. See ibid., 326–37.

Therefore, instead of analyzing the story of Christ (level three) alone, it is necessary to investigate the believers' reception and representation of Christ's story in their own lives (levels four and five). How can we better articulate the relationship between Paul's earthly spiritual experience recorded in Philippians 3 and the implicit narrative logic found within the story of Christ? What mode of reasoning can allow us to obtain a more coherent understanding of the spiritual journey of Paul, which could have a profound impact on the earthly journey of the Philippian community? These questions would be better answered in narrative terms after I introduce the theories of Paul Ricoeur later.[91]

1.3 A Review of Narrative Studies on Identity Formation in Philippians

Having reviewed scholars' narrative studies on Philippians, I will now focus on the specific issue that this book is exploring: a narrative analysis of the identity-formation process in Philippians. But before we move on, perhaps we should ask ourselves one basic question: what exactly is identity? According to David Horrell, the concept *identity* has turned into a buzzword in studies of early Christianity and social science, rendering the notion difficult to define.[92] Quoting Anthony J. Blasi, Horrell explains the cause of such difficulty:

---

[91] Besides Ricoeur, many scholars have contributed to the link between narrative and the thinking about God, including David Tracy, Hans Frei, George Lindbeck, Stanley Hauerwas, Langdon Gilkey, and James McClendon. Generally speaking, scholars have categorized these narrative theologians or philosophers into two main camps: the Yale school and the Chicago school. While a complete comparison between them is beyond the scope of this book, it is worthwhile to pinpoint the edge that Ricoeur's theories, of which the Chicago school is comprised, bring to this investigation over the Yale school. In a work headlined by the theme of contestation of narratives, it is important for me to derive principles which shed insights on the processes of comparing and judging "offers" from different narrative *agencies*. In other words, I have to develop a methodology which differentiates different narrative configurations, and articulates the processes in which a person traverses over divergent narrative worlds. With this goal in mind, it is perhaps not difficult to see the inherent weakness of the Yale school, which, according to Sam Houston, tends to neglect "the plurality of narratives, doctrines, and symbols that constitute a community's self-understanding" (Houston, 170). While the emphasis of "the text . . . which absorbs the world, rather than the world [absorbs] the text" (Lindbeck, 118) seemingly reflects the Yale school's advantage of "upholding the priority and indispensability of the narrative shape of Scripture against any reductive approach" (Stiver, 142), a complete antithesis between the intra-scriptural and extra-scriptural overlooks a key phenomenon that the formation of "Christian identity" necessarily happens in a reality in which humans always "participate in many overlapping communities of discourse" (Houston, 171, quoting Pauw, 49). For details, see Sam Houston, "Narrative and Ideology: The Promises and Pitfalls of Postliberal Theology," *Religion & Theology* 23 (2016): 170–1; Gary L. Comstock, "Two Types of Narrative Theology," *Journal of the American Academy of Religion* 55, no. 4 (1987): 687–8; Dan R. Stiver, *The Philosophy of Religious Language: Sign, Symbol and Story* (Cambridge, MA: Blackwell Publishers, 1996), 134–62; Amy Plantinga Pauw, "The Word Is Near You: A Feminist Conversation with Lindbeck," *Theology Today* 50, no. 1 (1993): 49. Stiver adds the "California school" as the third category in his discussion. For details, see ibid., 154–62.

[92] David G. Horrell, "'Becoming Christian': Solidifying Christian Identity and Content," in *Handbook of Early Christianity: Social Science Approaches,* ed. Anthony J. Blasi, Jean Duhaime, and Paul-Andre Turcotte (Walnut Creek: AltaMira Press, 2002), 311.

> This is largely because a person's identity comprises a multiplicity of factors, or even a multiplicity of identities, not all of which are relevant, or salient, in every situation.
>
> One cannot therefore speak simply of someone's "identity" but must rather consider what aspects of identity are being considered and why these are relevant in a particular context.[93]

Thus, the question is that for each particular identity-formation inquiry, has the researcher considered those key and relevant aspects of the person/community and how they interact with each other? It is amid such a problem that certain scholars apply narrative theory in identity-formation analysis. For example, Thiselton avers that because human experience is essentially constituted from the organization and orientation of time, narrative, with its fundamental temporal dimension, is well suited for articulating not only the coherence, structure, and flow of human experience but also the elusive human identity. Similarly, Horrell, when discussing the capacity of narrative in shaping people's worldviews, character, and identity,[94] writes,

> If all modes of thought are regarded as story based, then Paul's story is competing on a somewhat more level playing field than might once have been thought. Instead of a mythological, ancient story being contrasted with the rational truths of science or economics, we see instead—if we follow Milbank and others—competing narratives about the world. We may then ask about how Paul's story and these other stories construct a sense of human identity and shape human interaction.[95]

According to my understanding of Horrell, if "every mode of thought is essentially a narrative" which shapes people's "conviction about the world," Paul's theological thinking can be seen as one of those "competing narratives seeking to outnarrate one another."[96] In other words, narrative is the chief mode of thinking through which we could and should analyze competing convictions on ethical issues of any discourse (e.g., the meaning of Paul's suffering for the gospel).[97] With its essential linkage to human agency *as the source of thinking and center of experience*, narrative should no longer be seen just as a "representational form or method of presenting social and historical knowledge"[98] but *the essential mode of thinking within the making of human identity*. It is within this intellectual context that we start our review of previous studies on the use of narrative theory to analyze the identity formation of Philippians.

---

[93] Ibid., 311; Anthony J. Blasi, "Symbolic Interactionism as Theory," *Sociology and Social Research* 56, no. 4 (1972): 453–65.
[94] Horrell, "Paul's Narrative," 168–70.
[95] Ibid., 170.
[96] Horrell, "Paul's Narrative," 168–70, quoting Loughlin, *Telling God's Story*, 3–26; Milbank, *Theology and Social Theory*, 330.
[97] Horrell, "Paul's Narrative," 170.
[98] Margaret R. Somers and Gloria D. Gibson, "Reclaiming the Epistemological 'Other': Narrative and the Social Constitution of Identity," in *Social Theory and the Politics of Identity*, ed. Craig Calhoun (Oxford: Wiley-Blackwell, 1994), 39.

1.3.1 James Miller

In the article "Communal Identity in Philippians," James C. Miller investigates the manner in which Paul's arguments function to shape the community's identity.[99] In the limited scope of thirteen pages, Miller guides us through three key components of communal identity and how they function in Philippians: "Perception of Similarity and Difference," "Sense of Continuity Through Time," and "Social Process." Making use of the Social Identity Theory (SIT) of Richard Jenkins, Miller illuminates the identity processes of the Philippian community with social scientific approaches such as model figures, exemplars, prototypes, routinization/institutionalization, group norms, and *communal narratives*.[100] Miller stresses that "collective identity involves a sense of place within an ongoing *story* of a group."[101] With a common past shared among them, a common self-understanding and shared narrative are informed for the present, creating a continuity of expectations into the future.[102] According to Miller, "such a narrative cannot be anything but an evaluative recounting of the story of what brought us to where we are in the present."[103] Miller's efforts are noteworthy for at least two reasons. First, his attention to the communal dimension of identity is precise, reminding us of the importance of the collective dimension of identity. Second, Miller is also correct in emphasizing the narrative and temporal aspect of collective identity, recognizing its "sense of continuity through time."[104]

However, due to Miller's primary reliance on SIT theories like "social interaction" and "group identification,"[105] few narrative categories are employed inside his concrete analysis. With heavy dependence on social theories instead of narrative ones,[106] Miller's subsequent analysis of the function of "communal narrative" almost fully neglects any specific aspects within the narrative mode of thought behind Paul's discourse. Regarding the constant negotiation, production, and re-production processes of the "communal identity" in each new situation, all Miller could provide are just "perceptions of similarities and differences" among "social positions of the various parties."[107] Ultimately, the narrative of Jesus in Phil. 2:6-11 becomes only an obedient pattern to practice.[108] The story or gospel in which Paul locates the Philippian community becomes just another label for the manner of life lived by Christ.[109] Instead of discerning relationships of coherence among the stories of Christ and the community (and Paul), a relation of linearity, which is best suited for describing objective logic, seems to come to the fore. In other words, what is found at the core

---

[99] James C. Miller, "Communal Identity in Philippians," *ASE* 27, no. 2 (2010): 11–23.
[100] Ibid., 12–24; Richard Jenkins, *Social Identity* (London: Routledge, 2004), 94, 133–6.
[101] Ibid., 14.
[102] Ibid.
[103] Ibid.
[104] Ibid., 13–15.
[105] Ibid., 13.
[106] This is not to assume that there exists a strict dichotomy between social analysis and narrative. For a differentiation of these two, see Somers and Gibson, "Reclaiming the Epistemological 'Other,'" 37–98.
[107] Miller, "Communal Identity," 15.
[108] Ibid., 18.
[109] Ibid., 19.

of Miller's communal narrative analysis is primarily social science based, and only remotely narratively constituted.

1.3.2 Sergio Nebreda

Another work (much longer than Miller's) which suffers from an inadequate narrative analysis of identity formation in Philippians is the book *Christ Identity: A Social-Scientific Reading of Philippians 2:5–11* written by Sergio R. Nebreda. Like Miller, Nebreda also bases his thorough research on SIT (of Henri Tajfel and John Turner), and tries to "assess the apostle's implicit strategies as well as to recognize his aims of creating a social identity based on Christ-orientation as displayed in Phil. 2:5–11, which Paul himself affirms he follows (3:12–13)."[110] While Nebreda does not see narrative as his main approach, on a number of occasions he highlights both the nature of the "Christ-Hymn" and the strategy of Paul's persuasion as belonging to the category of narrative, and expounds its function in the identity formation of the Philippian community.

For example, on the function of the "Christ-Hymn," Nebreda explains: "The rhetorical effect of the Philippian hymn is to establish the common vision that holds the church as a model for conduct ... responding to the tensions within the Philippian house church *with the invitation to place their own narrative with the narrative of Christ* [my emphasis]."[111] The magnitude and scope of the influence of this hymn cannot be underestimated, as it "evokes a narrative that shifts the emphasis from a power-based structure to a self-giving one that aims at reordering their symbolic universe. It is in following this radical re-categorisation of their context that the Philippian believers are included in the ingroup."[112] As such, Nebreda seems to incline himself to posit narrative at the foundational or ontological level, as he asserts that "theology and ethos can both be narrative."[113]

However, after stating these large notions of narrative, Nebreda does not offer much reflection with respect to the narrative mode of thinking. Narrative categories, such as human agency and temporal dimensions, receive little attention. Aside from a few occurrences of subsuming the power of narrative into social categories, the narrative approach receives little usage and thus offers little contribution in Nebreda's work.[114] In fact, considering the fact that Nebreda primarily uses the SIT approach, one of his hermeneutical tendencies would therefore be to favor structural and observable social behaviors such as interests and norms over human agency in trying to predict and control social behaviors against "systematic unpredictability" in human action. Despite Nebreda's position in not applying "law-like generalisations, but to approach the texts with some educated/tested questions in mind," predictions based on social

---

[110] Ibid., 28.
[111] Ibid., 283, quoting James W. Thompson, "Preaching to Philippians," *Interpretation* 61, no. 3 (2007): 306.
[112] Sergio Rosell Nebreda, *Christ Identity: A Social-Scientific Reading of Philippians 2.5–11* (Göttingen: Vandenhoeck & Ruprecht, 2011), 344.
[113] Ibid., 283.
[114] In a few places, Nebreda resorts to narrative to consolidate his arguments. See ibid., 339.

categories inevitably still dominate his "heuristic tool."[115] His minor applications of narrative reflect the tendency of social scientists to limit narrative to just a method of representing social knowledge.[116] Thus in his research, the "Christ-Hymn" (Phil. 2:5-11) can only represent a kind of narrative with rhetorical function to shape the conduct of the church.[117]

Just as the competing narrative dynamics between Paul and his opponents have been altogether missed by previous narrative researchers of Philippians, Nebreda has offered little analysis of the meanings created out of narratives composed by the human agencies of Paul and his opponents. Nebreda thus settles with abundant, yet general, typical, and categorical understandings of the first-century Roman Empire and Philippi as the exigency facing Paul and the Philippian community.[118] The contingent situation of Philippians, which I believe to involve multiple competing narrative dynamics, is overlooked. What is perceived becomes just a broad and categorically defined context in which "the Philippian believers are [already] included in the ingroup ... but still lack the exclusive focus (Christ-centred *Phronesis*) needed in order for the advance of the gospel."[119] The role of narrative is diminished to being a tool for the consolidation of social boundaries. No narrative dynamics are involved in the reconstruction of either the contingent situation or the subsequent transformative process. Narrative becomes just a rhetorical device, a static plot, a method of representation.

1.3.3 Robert Brawley and William Campbell

Another work which also deserves mentioning is the article "From Reflex to Reflection? Identity in Philippians 2:6-11 and Its Context" by Robert L. Brawley.[120] According to Brawley, the "Christ-Hymn" represents a "video of a common orientation on the screen" which "offers the briefest of allusions to Jesus' way of life."[121] Attributing this "video" to be a kind of narrative concept, Brawley writes, "in Phil. 1.27-30 Paul plays just such a video in which the Philippians are characters whose story of suffering is recounted, although elliptically."[122]

Within his reconstruction of the situation of the Philippians, it is the disruptive sufferings caused by the imperial system which provokes Paul to write. With the identities of the opponents restricted to the authorities, Brawley proceeds to develop an exegesis for the Christological Hymn (Phil. 2:5-11) and analyzes its influence upon the Philippians' identity.[123] The reading of an anti-Judean contention or polemic in

---

[115] Ibid., 45.
[116] Ibid., 243; Somers and Gibson, "Reclaiming the Epistemological 'Other,'" 3.
[117] Nebreda, *Christ Identity*, 283.
[118] For example, "Honor and Shame" on pp. 91-8; "Romanisation" on pp. 147-60; "Slavery conditions in the societies of Greece and Rome" on pp. 189-98.
[119] Ibid., 344.
[120] 120 Robert L. Brawley, "From Reflex to Reflection? Identity in Philippians 2.6-11 and Its Context," in *Reading Paul in Context: Explorations in Identity Formation: Essays in Honour of William S. Campbell*, ed. Kathy Ehrensperger and J. Brian Tucker (New York: T&T Clark International, 2010), 135-41.
[121] Ibid., 137, 41.
[122] Ibid., 135.
[123] Ibid., 137-41.

which the "dogs" are identified as the Jewish people has been displaced.[124] In Brawley's words, "it is more productive to find correspondences between Paul's warning about dogs and deities such as Diana, Cybele and Hecate ... who were blended into imperial religion to legitimate citizenship under Caesar's lordship."[125]

Here, what will receive scrutiny is Brawley's stand in arguing that there is an intrinsic connectedness between Paul's Israelite identity and his newly developing theological identity of being in Christ. Regarding the relation between the stories of Christ and Paul, Brawley argues that even though Paul's identity in Christ clearly takes precedence in Phil. 3:4-8, he does not reject or dismiss his ethnic identity, or make any "vicious parody on Israelite circumcision."[126] This interpretation of Brawley puts him alongside scholars such as William Campbell and J. Brian Tucker, who both tend to *locate the early Christian identity as arising from the existing identities (Jewish and gentile)*.[127]

According to Campbell, the way Paul writes in Phil. 3:4-8 should lead us to the conclusion that all things should be viewed in *relativization* to Christ, thus stressing the *continuity* between the new identity in Christ and the old Jewish identity of Paul. Paul's encounter with Christ is actualized through *a process of rethinking his value system within his existing contexts*.[128] It is precisely through the "radical relativization" of Paul's previous boasting as dung that the supremacy of being in Christ is prioritized.[129] In terms of Dunn's five levels of story model, what becomes prominent is *the continuous transforming of believers' life stories on levels four and five*. Thus, such new self-understanding will not obliterate any of Paul's social and historical categories.[130] Looking at this issue with the lens of a more futuristic eschatology against the hazard of over-realized eschatology, Campbell cites Horrell to support his view of "a reconfiguration of the history and identity of those in Christ rather than simply the obliteration of their past," highlighting the transformation of Paul and distinct believers in Christ within a contextual and prolonged identity formation.[131]

With such *ethnic continuity* emphasized, "no new people are being birthed and ... the Christ-movement is described in the context of their existing ethnic and social identities."[132] Ethnic "horizontality" of identity formation between the contextual situation of Paul and his subsequent transformation in time is highlighted. In other words, belief in an abrupt and discontinuous creation of an early universal "Christian

---

[124] Ibid., 142; Mark D. Nanos, "Paul's Reversal of Jews Calling Gentiles 'Dogs' (Philippians 3:2): 1600 Years of an Ideological Tale Wagging an Exegetical Dog?" *Biblical Interpretation* 17, no. 4 (2009): 458. It is noteworthy that Brawley bases his conclusion on the work of Mark Nanos.
[125] Brawley, "From Reflex to Reflection?," 146.
[126] Ibid., 130, 44. Nebreda published his book in 2011, which shares a similar strategy to that of Brawley.
[127] Campbell, *Paul and the Creation*, 91–2; Anthony C. Thiselton, *The First Epistle to the Corinthians* (Grand Rapids: Wm. B. Eerdmans, 2000), 547.
[128] Campbell, *Paul and the Creation*, 88.
[129] Ibid., 88–9.
[130] Ibid., 88. According to Campbell, we cannot "pit the God of creation and Israel's election against the God of apocalyptic deliverance." See ibid., 145–6; Douglas Harink, "Paul and Israel: An Apocalyptic Reading," *Pro Ecclesia* 16, no. 4 (2007): 372.
[131] Campbell, *Paul and the Creation*, 91; Horrell, "Paul's Narrative," 168.
[132] J. Brian Tucker, *Remain in Your Calling: Paul and the Continuation of Social Identities in 1 Corinthians* (Eugene: Wipf & Stock Pub, 2011), 62–8.

identity" should be replaced by a processual and continuous transformation in Christ by different communities.

The approach held by Brawley and Campbell deserves credit for its accommodation of Paul's story within the core of identity formation of the Philippian community. With Campbell's approach focusing on the "reconfiguration of the history and identity of those in Christ," it is adequate to address the contingent conditions that the Philippian community were facing, thus fully accommodating the contesting stories on levels four and five and their pertinent interactions with the story of Christ on level three.[133]

However, a serious drawback of Campbell's line of reasoning is that his logic features a diminishing of the concreteness of an early historical "Christian identity." When Campbell argues that the respective groups in Rome (so too in Philippi) actually "continue to live within that same culture but under the transforming influence of Christ," Christianity is then just "a transformation of a (mainly) Pharisaic Judaism, from which it borrows and affirms some motifs while rejecting others."[134] In this manner, theological constructions are seen only to solve problems within a predefined identity, which is first and foremost *ethnic*.[135] Not only does theological identity in Christ not break from ethnic identity, it also "follows after." No genuine overriding flesh-and-blood theological identity occurs for the early "Christian identity."[136] Such emphases of "horizontality" and continuity within the "Christian identity" formation of the Philippian community do not seem to have successfully covered all the identity-formation conceptual spaces and processes of those early "Christian" communities.

What is even more troubling is the futility of discerning the meaning of God's work with respect to human experiences. This may not be something welcomed by Campbell, but if different people groups could quite "freely" transform and evolve themselves from around their "social existence" into differing "Christian" cultures and identities,[137] and if Paul is too "Jewish" to embody the ideal paradigm of a certain "Christian identity" for the *gentile* Philippian community,[138] where is the foundation for Paul to demand the community to follow his version of the story of Christ and reject others'? How could Paul still ask the Philippian community to join in imitating him (Phil. 3:17)? What is the point for different "Christ-followers," who, for practical reasons, could not share all sets of culture, ethnic origin, tradition, language, educational background, and so on, in engaging in theological debate regarding the *right* mode of thinking and behavior for another unique person, let alone another community? The preaching of one's own theology or testimony necessarily amounts to imposing one's biased opinion upon the lives of others. If Christ is essentially just one of many other cultural forces, is it legitimate to still frame the resultant non-stop process as a "Christian identity" formation? Rather than calling it a contestation for the formation of a true "Christian identity," it is better to name it a quarrel among different social, ethnic, or political groups with certain "Christian" traditions.

---

[133] Cf. Campbell, *Paul and the Creation*, 87–9.
[134] Ibid., 1, 102.
[135] Ibid., 52.
[136] Cf. Holmberg, "Understanding," 18.
[137] Campbell, *Paul and the Creation*, 165–6.
[138] Cf. ibid., 88.

1.3.4 Ben Meyer and John Barclay

There are some scholars who take a very different approach toward the identity-making of early "Christians." In his book *The Early Christians: Their World Mission & Self-Discovery*, Ben Meyer stresses the aspects of verticality and discontinuity by highlighting the uniqueness of the Christ-event and its subsequent domineering influence on the formation of a "Christian identity." Such "discontinuity" is upheld to support the notion of a common transcendent foundation within the formation of a universal communal "Christian identity" across different ethnicities and social profiles. According to Meyer, while various concrete self-definitions are allowed for different Christ-follower communities in light of their unique cultural situations, *a common core identity for all "Christians"* is already well secured by kerygma and confessions from the early "Christ-followers," which is fostered out of a radically reorienting "Easter experience."[139] A "permanent residue" of this encounter is to "bear witness to the supreme fulfilment event of human history."[140] As this witnessing experience is nurtured in the community through rites and behavior patterns, thus the original founding experience will be embodied by the community and becomes accessible to later generations.[141] In this way, later generations of "Christians" are empowered to reflect upon their situations, recount the story of Jesus, and change their self-understanding. Recurring reflections from later hearers of the gospel story likewise appropriate the original experience through a "fusion of horizons," bringing about a learning process through loops of feedback.[142]

Meyer's methodology should be applauded particularly for his emphasis on the founding "Easter experience," which leads to successive appropriations in each subsequent generation despite different cultural situations. By linking and likening early "Christians'" witnessing of the original radical experience with the reflections of subsequent generations, Meyer seemingly presents us with a picture that accommodates the narrative re-presentations of the story of Christ on levels four and five. There is also an early genesis of a universal "Christian identity" across Christ-follower communities of different cultures and ethnicities.

However, I believe there is one serious weakness in Meyer's approach that relegates the theologizing processes in different communities to mere self-definition or a "way of living and manifesting this identity."[143] Along this line of reasoning, *all stories on levels*

---

[139] Ben F. Meyer, *The Early Christians: Their World Mission & Self-Discovery* (Wilmington: M. Glazier, 1986), 48, 173; Holmberg, "Understanding," 24–6.

[140] Meyer, *The Early Christians*, 48.

[141] Concerning the function of ritual in confirming Christian identity, see Horrell, "Becoming Christian," 333.

[142] Meyer, *The Early Christians*, 173; Holmberg, "Understanding," 24–7. Similarly, Holmberg examines the problem from the angle of historical accessibility, referencing Horrell to conclude that belonging together in Christ is an idea that has already started to "change very much in people's practiced social identity." This view eliminates the doubt that a universal Christian identity is just a theological belief of the future. See ibid., 19–20; David G. Horrell, "'No Longer Jew or Greek': Paul's Corporate Christology and the Construction of Christian Community," in *Christology, Controversy and Community: New Testament Essays in Honour of David R. Catchpole*, ed. David G. Horrell and Christopher M. Tuckett (Leiden: Brill, 2000), 321–44.

[143] Meyer, *The Early Christians*, 173; Holmberg, "Understanding," 25–6.

four and five, which pertain to the identity-making experiences of Paul and the Philippian community, are totally excluded from the constitution of believers' own "Christian identity." The interaction of narratives among the stories in levels three to five, as in the case of Philippians, becomes peripheral to the "Christian identity" formation of the Philippian community. What is left within this "Christian identity" is *a separate and finished core identity represented by the level three story of Christ* (or levels one to three). In other words, the "Christian identity" of the community exists irrespective of their unique behaviors, values, and ethics. Contestations of specific problems and the pertinent theological understandings within Philippians are, strictly speaking, relevant only to their specific situation, which does not constitute any of the core nature of a universal "Christian identity." The contesting narrative dynamics between Paul and his opponents becomes something *irrelevant* to the formation of "Christian identity." No common "Christian" formation processes can be gleaned from it.

Such a line of reasoning concerning the identity-making of early "Christian" communities may have found its support from the viewpoint of John Barclay. Based on a unique under-standing of the logic and structure of time, Barclay argues that there exists a disparate gap of significance between the stories of Christ and Paul.[144] According to Barclay, a certain degree of radical break (otherness) in human history has been instigated by the Christ event.[145] Since then, "neither Paul, nor Israel, nor the church have any stories of significance before God except those that are fractured by the cross of Christ."[146] As such, Paul's own story should be identified no longer as a continuation or relativization of his past Jewish story[147] but a story purely defined by the "radical grace of God."[148] What is implicit in Barclay's affirmation of the centrality of "the apocalypse of Jesus Christ" is his skepticism concerning seeing the grace of God in terms of a linear salvation timeline (*Heilsgeschichte*).[149] Both the "Christian identity" of Paul and of the Philippian community should involve "a complete reconception of the self,"[150] *"Christian identity" of the Philippian community, just like that of Paul, is thus solely created by the invasive action of Christ.* In terms of Dunn's five levels of story model, what becomes prominent is a unique story of Christ, comprised of His death and resurrection, now radically puncturing and interrupting all other levels of story. With this transcendent origin of identity, the "verticality" of identity formation

---

[144] Cf. ibid., 154n.40, in which Barclay rejects N. T. Wright's understanding on the Jewishness of Paul's story as recorded in Philippians 3.
[145] Ibid., 146; Campbell, *Paul and the Creation*, 140; J. Louis Martyn, *Galatians* (New Haven: Yale University Press, 2004), 349.
[146] Barclay, "Paul's Story," 146.
[147] Ibid., 154.
[148] Ibid., 154–5.
[149] Ibid., 154; Horrell, "Paul's Narrative," 159–63. According to Barclay, such emphasis of continuity with human historiography would lead to "the normal criterion that the smaller plot fits within the larger," which would make Christ's story become just one of many events in a linear timeline. Regarding the limitation of this linear sense of time in representing believers' participation in Christ, Barclay references the article of David F. Ford. See David F. Ford, "System, Story, Performance: A Proposal about the Role of Narrative in Christian Systematic Theology," in *Why Narrative? Readings in Narrative Theology*, ed. Stanley Hauerwas (Eugene, OR: Wipf & Stock Pub, 1997), 208. While a complete response to Barclay's concern is beyond the scope of this book, I see Ricoeur's concept of time as a potential "solution" to this query. For relevant discussions, see footnote 92 on p.57.
[150] Barclay, "Paul's Story," 149.

is affirmed, but ethnic "horizontality," which highlights the contextual situation, is completely negated.

1.3.5 A Brief Evaluation

One of the main sources of discrepancy between the approaches of Campbell and Barclay lies in their underlying convictions regarding the *structure of time* within the identity-making of the early "Christians," and the corresponding *form of interaction* between the story of Christ on level three and the stories of believers on levels four and five. When Campbell's approach endorses a linear historical time which grounds all the stories of Christ, Paul, and the early "Christian" community, the corresponding identity-formation process of the Philippian community features a manner of life transformation close to the *assimilation* of the story of Christ (level three) into believers' existing life stories (levels four and five). There is no punctuation or invasion of time from another temporal dimension within the making of a "Christian identity."[151]

On the other hand, according to Barclay's understanding, with the existence of a radical break between the "paradigm of Christ crucified" and the stories of Paul and the Philippian community,[152] the interaction between them becomes one in which the Christ-event "punctures other times and other stories not just as a past event recalled but as a present event," which does *not* cohere with human telling of stories or account of history.[153] The corresponding identity-formation processes of believers would probably be best articulated by a radical temporal dynamic in which the "story" of Christ crucified "weaves its own independent patterns in history."[154]

It is beyond the scope of this book to give a full critique of the positions of Campbell and Barclay, and a comprehensive review of the issues of discontinuity and continuity within Paul's theological thinking. But perhaps it suffices to say that this issue has a serious bearing on not only Paul's own spiritual transformation in Christ (the dynamics between stories on levels three and four) but also his identity-formation strategies toward the Philippian community (the dynamics among stories on levels three, four, and five). While both phenomena of discontinuity and continuity seem to have considerable prominence within the formation of a "Christian identity," *each of the approaches illustrated earlier as epitomized by Brawley and Campbell, and Meyer and Barclay, cannot accommodate such a kind of paradox in Paul's shaping of early "Christian identity" and hence the Philippians' own identity formation*. In Barclay's approach, while

---

[151] Cf. ibid., 146. Except for "punctuation," Barclay offers little attention to the *reception processes* and narrative nature of this revelation, which necessarily happen within the time of human history. Toward this, Horrell has provided a systematic critique. According to Horrell, there is no necessary contradiction between the supremacy of Christ's story and its enactment in history. For details of his arguments, see Horrell, "Paul's Narrative," 157–71. For relevant critiques of the kind of methodology deployed by Barclay, see also Michael Root, "The Narrative Structure of Soteriology," in *Why Narrative? Readings in Narrative Theology*, ed. Stanley Hauerwas (Eugene, OR: Wipf & Stock Pub, 1997), 274.

[152] The phrase "paradigm of Christ crucified" is suggested by Horrell in his reading of Barclay's article, which serves as a contrast to Hays's narrative substructure approach concerning the *story* of Christ. See Horrell, "Paul's Narrative," 159; Barclay, "Paul's Story," 134n.6.

[153] Ibid., 146.

[154] Ibid.

the distinctiveness of Christ's story is preserved, subsequent contingent situations of the community, as well as the prominence of believers' dedicated efforts, are altogether neglected.[155] While Barclay seems to accept that believers connect themselves to God's grace "because their lives have adopted, and continue to adopt, that pattern of death to the world and self-giving in love," he insists that what counts is not any "human causation" but God's interruption.[156] However, as Dunn and Silva have insightfully noted, Paul's theology in Philippians does not seem to deny the fundamental significance of believers' efforts.[157] In Campbell's approach, while the processual and situational conditions are well considered, the foundation of an early transcendental and theologically universal "Christian identity" is shattered. The originality and invasive uniqueness of the story of Christ is dismissed.[158] The formation of a supposedly transcendental "Christian identity" becomes the enrichment of a "Christian" tradition to an existing ethnic, social, or political identity.

Based on Ricoeur's narrative theory, I argue that these phenomena of discontinuity and continuity actually reflect parts of a more holistic dynamic in which *the story of Christ interacts with other levels of story*.[159] While I agree with Horrell that "the fundamental story of God's gracious dealings with humanity reach their zenith in the Christ event, itself the generative centre of this story," I argue that within the story of Christ in Philippians there exists an *incomplete storyline* between the "Easter experience" and the Parousia (Phil. 2:5–11, 3:20–21) which demands believers' "filling in."[160] Within the chronological time correlated with this incomplete storyline, believers' faith experience inherently comes from a dialectic of the radical story of Christ's death and resurrection (what Barclay sees as the source of discontinuity), and the contextual stories of believers in which life transformation is seen (what Campbell sees as the source of continuity). Hence, I aver that a more complete picture of the Philippian community's identity-formation process can be revealed if we can utilize a hermeneutical approach which could include and adapt perspectives from both camps. With Campbell highlighting the contextual situation ("horizontality"), and Barclay highlighting the transcendental origin ("verticality"), the potential insight brought forth by a dialectic of the approaches of Campbell and Brawley, and Barclay and Meyer, will be helpful in developing a more rigorous approach in examining the identity formation of the Philippian community.

---

[155] Cf. James D. G. Dunn, "Philippians 3.2-14 and the New Perspective on Paul," in *The New Perspective on Paul* (Grand Rapids: Wm. B. Eerdmans, 2007), 489; Moisés Silva, *Philippians*, 2nd ed., BECNT (Grand Rapids: Baker Academic, 2005), 118–21. Talking about believers' response to God's call in Christ Jesus, Dunn writes, "That the dedicated effort of the believer was also necessary was evidently neither inconsistent with nor a threat to the God-givenness and the Christ-centredness of the end result." Similarly, Moisés Silva writes, "The striking verbal correspondence between 1:6 and 2:13 suggests strongly that the two verses reflect a common, and profound, conceptual link. But the only concept that fits both passages is the paradoxical engagement of human and divine activity in the total work of salvation—a concept that recurs elsewhere in Philippians (notably 3:7–14)." See ibid., 120–1. The prominence of believers' initiative and dedicated efforts are found in Phil. 1:27–30, 2:12–15, 3:12–14, 4:4–6, 12–13.
[156] Barclay, "Paul's Story," 139, 54–5.
[157] See footnote 150 on this page.
[158] Ibid., 154–5.
[159] For details of this argument, see pp. 47–51ff. and subsequent applications of Ricoeur's concepts.
[160] Cf. Horrell, "Paul's Narrative," 168.

Can we find a narrative approach which can both support the concern of Campbell over the processual and evolutionary side, and the concern of Barclay over the punctuated and radical side? Can we develop a hermeneutical approach which honors both the capacity of human agencies in continuously making transformative narrative meanings, and the supremacy of Christ's story in setting the radical framework (or "grid," to use Barclay's own word) within which identities of Paul and the Philippian community are created?[161]

I propose that this paradox can be "solved" through an investigation of the narrative dynamics arising from the interaction among the stories as depicted by Dunn's five levels of story model. My introduction of Ricoeur's theory below will introduce a hermeneutical approach in which the contingent situation of the Philippian community will be taken into account. The narrative dynamics involving levels four and five will be fully discerned. Instead of applying a text-immanent approach which considers only the intratextual narrative elements, I will reconstruct the exact extra-textual contingent world from which Paul the author of the theological discourse on level four plots a "narrative world," acts inside as one of the main characters, relates to the extra-textual world through this narrative, and finally uses it as the bedrock of his recapitulated writing.

In order to address the dynamics of competing narratives on level four, narrative will not be just a representational method exemplified by a static plot, but a kind of dynamic plot process with considerations of epistemological reflection, theology generation, and identity formation.[162] Time will not be just an aspect of social phenomena, but "incorporated into the core conception of identity."[163] In particular, a specific structure of time and its pertinent operations within the identity-making of a person will be introduced. The identity of the Philippian community, being a relational and social one, will not primarily arise from constraints or antagonism from multiple social forces, but from the dynamic plot processes driven by relevant human agencies.

Last but not least, if the aggregate formation process conjoined by the above two paradoxical aspects can be considered as representing the comprehensive whole, validation of the presence of a contestation of narratives within each of these two could consequently help prove the idea that the identity formation of the Philippian community indeed happens in the midst of a contestation of narratives.

1.4 Conclusion

I have reviewed previous narrative-related scholarship, including general narrative approaches to the Pauline letters, narrative analyses of Philippians, and narrative studies on the identity formation in Philippians. I have addressed various shortcomings of previous scholarship in particular, and shown that no specialized narrative study has been devoted to the identity-formation processes in Philippians. Previous

---

[161] Barclay, "Paul's Story," 134.
[162] Somers and Gibson, "Reclaiming the Epistemological 'Other,'" 2, 5.
[163] Ibid., 5. Cf. Nebreda, *Christ Identity*, 28–9.

applications of the narrative method are often relegated to forms of representing social identity theories. The unique contingent situation of the Philippian community has been neglected. In terms of Dunn's five levels of story model, there has been a lack of attention to the narrative dynamics involving stories on levels four and five and their interactions with levels one to three. As a result, the theme of the contestation of narratives regarding the identity formation of the Philippian community is neglected by previous scholarship. It is my agenda in this work to take this competing narrative dynamic into account and explore its influence upon the identity formation of the Philippian community.

2

Brief Review of Introductory Issues

Before I shift my attention to the methodology of this work, let me introduce a few assumptions. There are certainly a lot of other areas of research to which this study is related. The scope of this book is limited to the investigation of the narrative dynamics of the identity-formation processes and the theme of the contestation of narratives. As such, I can only give a rather brief review of the following areas of research and state my assumptions without providing a full examination of these controversial issues.

2.1 Compositional Unity

The first assumption concerns the debate regarding the literary integrity of Philippians. One of the traditional understandings of the current form of this epistle to the Philippians is that it originally comprised two to three separate letters.[1] While they were all authentically written by Paul over a short span of time, they were later put together by someone unknown resulting in this current form.[2] However, this "partition theory" has been largely rejected by a lot of researchers.[3] In fact, as Garland has observed, there are multiple thematic resonances ("humility and self-abasement," "acceptance of suffering," "struggle for progress in the Christian life," "joyful confidence in the congregation") and parallel vocabulary usages (μορφή and σύμμορφος, σχῆμα and μετασχηματίζω, ταπεινόω and ταπείνωσις, etc.) throughout the whole epistle.[4] Moreover, both of the narratives of Christ and Paul closely relate to the theme of suffering. Thus, it is fair to claim that the probability that the epistle to the Philippians was composed as one whole far exceeds that of it being composed from several epistles. This is the position from which this investigation works.

---

[1] For a list of scholars who support this hypothesis, see D. E. Garland, "The Composition and Unity of Philippians: Some Neglected Literary Factors," *Novum Testamentum* 27 (1985): 141n.3; Robert Jewett, "The Epistolary Thanksgiving and the Integrity of Philippians," *Novum Testamentum* 12, no. 1 (1970): 41–4.

[2] James L. Blevins, "Introduction to Philippians," *RevExp* 77, no. 3 (1980): 316.

[3] To know more of their arguments, see Garland, "Composition," 144–57; Jewett, "Epistolary Thanks-Giving," 41; Loveday Alexander, "Hellenistic Letter-Forms and the Structure of Philippians," *JSNT* 37 (1989): 96–8; Gordon Fee, *Paul's Letter to the Philippians*, NICNT (Grand Rapids: Wm. B. Eerdmans, 1995), 21–2.

[4] For details, see Garland, "Composition," 157–60, esp. 158n.62; Alexander, "Hellenistic Letter-Forms," 99.

2.2 The Role of Suffering

The meaning of suffering in the letters of Paul has been treated by Christian thinkers in various ways, including Christ-Mysticism by Albert Schweitzer, Martyrology by Ernst Lohmeyer, "Dying and Rising" with Christ by Robert Tannehill, "Weakness and Power" by Scott Hafemann, and Cruciformity by Michael J. Gorman.[5] Some other scholars are more interested in identifying the frames of reference for these sufferings, which could help explain Paul's specific purposes in each of his contingent suffering experiences.[6]

For example, Fitzgerald contends that there exists a strong sense of similarity between Paul's categories of suffering and those of the contemporary Stoics.[7] However, Fitzgerald's interpretation is rejected by K. T. Kleinknecht and S. J. Hafemann, who both identify the OT and the theme of the faithful suffering servant of traditional Judaism as Paul's main sources of inspiration.[8] I generally share this perspective of Hafemann.

Another key perspective of my work on Paul's suffering is that it comes from a situation of persecution. This view is doubted by L. A. Jervis. According to Jervis, the suffering situation of Paul is precisely "in Christ" and nothing more.[9] What matters is the doubt in the minds of the Philippian community members, which are answered through theological discourse.[10] The social background and contextual situation of Paul and the Philippian community are minimized in Jervis's study. My research direction is very different from that of Jervis. While Paul's concern is ultimately theological, a dichotomy between theological issue and contextual rivalries among Paul and his opponents is seen as succumbing to theological reduction, which overlooks the nature of the specific theological issue in Philippians as necessarily constituted by a contestation of narratives between Paul and his opponents. Underestimating the oppression faced

---

[5] For a concise summary of these perspectives, see Naomi Noguchi Reese, "The Pauline Concept of Suffering in Phil 3.10–11" (ThM, Biola University, 2003), 4–12. See also Albert Schweitzer, *The Mysticism of Paul the Apostle*, trans. W. Montgomery (London: A. & C. Black, 1912), 116; Ernst Lohmeyer, *Die Briefe an die Philipper, an die Kolosser und an Philemon* (Gottingen: Vandenhoeck & Ruprecht, 1964), 52, 58; Robert C. Tannehill, *Dying and Rising with Christ: A Study in Pauline Theology*, BZNW 32 (Berlin: Topelmann, 1967), 127; Gorman, *Cruciformity*, 18; Scott Hafemann, "Suffering," in *DPL*, ed. Gerald F. Hawthorne and Ralph P. Martin (Leicester: InterVarsity Press, 1993).

[6] Charles H. Talbert, *Learning through Suffering: The Educational Value of Suffering in the New Testament and in Its Milieu*, Zacchaeus Studies. New Testament (Collegeville: Liturgical Press, 1991), 11–21; Susan R. Garrett, "The God of This World and the Affliction of Paul: 2 Cor 4:1–12," in *Greeks, Romans, and Christians: Essays in Honor of Abraham J. Malherbe*, ed. David L. Balch and Everett Ferguson (Minneapolis: Fortress, 1991), 99–117; John T. Fitzgerald, *Cracks in an Earthen Vessel: An Examination of the Catalogues of Hardships in the Corinthian Correspondence*, SBLDS 99 (Atlanta: SBL, 1988), 47–116; L. Gregory Bloomquist, *The Function of Suffering in Philippians*, JSNTSup 78 (Sheffield: Sheffield Academic, 1993), 18–34; L. Ann Jervis, *At the Heart of the Gospel: Suffering in the Earliest Christian Message* (Grand Rapids: Wm. B. Eerdmans, 2007), 48–9, 55, 73–4; Hafemann, "Suffering"; K. T. Kleinknecht, *Der Leidende Gerechtfertigte: Die Alttestamentlich-Jüdische Tradition vom 'Leidenden Gerechten' und ihre Rezeption bei Paulus*, WUNT, vol. 2/13 (Tübingen: Mohr Siebeck, 1988).

[7] Fitzgerald, *Cracks*, 47–116.

[8] Hafemann, "Suffering," quoting Kleinknecht, *Der Leidende Gerechtfertigte*; C. G. Kruse, "Afflictions, Trials, Hardships," in *DPL*, ed. Gerald F. Hawthorne and Ralph P. Martin (Leicester: InterVarsity Press, 1993).

[9] Jervis, *At the Heart*, 49.

[10] Ibid., 44–5.

by the Philippian community is also inconsistent with the martyrological approach largely emphasized by the early Church.[11] To investigate Paul's identity-formation strategies toward the Philippian community, we need to fully take into account the confrontational nature of Paul's suffering.

2.3 The Identities of Opponents

Scholars disagree regarding the identities of Paul's opponents in Philippians, in addition to the questions of "where," "how many," and the nature of their conflicts.[12] In his work *St. Paul's Opponents and Their Backgrounds*, John J. Gunther summarizes that there have been eighteen different proposals concerning the identity of Paul's opponents in Philippians 3.[13] Throughout the entire letter, opponents are thought to be present in Phil. 1:15-17, 1:28-29, 2:15, 3:2, 3:18-19. As Paul does not mention the exact identities of his opponents or the pertinent conflicts, it is not surprising to see scholars wrestling to reach a consensus. Some scholars have even questioned the existence of these opponents.[14] The identities of Paul's opponents will be seriously addressed in this book. Following Mikael Tellbe, I argue that the identities of various opponents in Philippians have to be understood in their sociological context.[15]

2.4 The Imperial Cult and Exemption for the Jews

NT scholars typically tend to downplay the religious nature and hence the influence of the imperial cult on the early "Christian" communities' formation.[16] The relationship between the "heavenly" Paul and the "earthly" political authorities thus becomes

---

[11] Cf. Bloomquist, *Function of Suffering*, 18–34.
[12] Demetrius K. Williams, *Enemies of the Cross of Christ: The Terminology of the Cross and Conflict in Philippians*, JSNTSup 223 (Sheffield: Sheffield Academic, 2002), 26–7, 346; Chris Mearns, "The Identity of Paul's Opponents at Philippi," NTS 33 (1987): 200–2.
[13] John J. Gunther, *St. Paul's Opponents and Their Background: A Study of Apocalyptic and Jewish Sectarian Teachings* (Leiden: Brill, 1973), 3.
[14] David A. deSilva, "No Confidence in the Flesh: The Meaning and Function of Philippians 3:2–21," *Trinity Journal* 15 (1994): 31–2; Davorin Peterlin, *Paul's Letter to the Philippians in the Light of Disunity in the Church*, NTSupp 79 (Leiden: Brill, 1995), 90–2; Bloomquist, *Function of Suffering*, 49, 138, 96–7.
[15] Mikael Tellbe, "The Sociological Factors behind Philippians 3.1–11 and the Conflict at Philippi," *JSNT* 55 (1994): 97–121; Mikael Tellbe, *Paul between Synagogue and State: Christians, Jews, and Civic Authorities in 1 Thessalonians, Romans, and Philippians* (Stockholm: Almqvist & Wiksell Intl, 2001), 261–7. Scholars have failed to reach a consensus about the place and date of the writing of Philippians. This investigation follows the stand of Gordon Fee, who proposes that Paul was imprisoned in Rome and wrote Philippians in the early 60s CE. See Fee, *Paul's Letter*, 34–7; Silva, *Philippians*, 5–7; John Reumann, *Philippians*, The Anchor Yale Bible Commentaries (New Haven: Yale University Press, 2008), 8–18.
[16] Pieter J. J. Botha, "Assessing Representations of the Imperial Cult in New Testament Studies," *Verbum et Ecclesia* 25 (2004): 16.

insignificant.[17] Believers should submit to the earthly political leaders, whose authority has been given by God.[18] With the rise of "Pietism," "Christian Faith" became increasingly treated as a kind of personal moral belief.[19] Paul's teachings are then understood as theological declarations and ethical codes which fit across all times and cultures.[20] The "political inclination" of Paul is one which essentially urges submission to the governing authorities.

However, this trend of neglecting Paul's political dimensions was somewhat reversed around the end of the last century.[21] In particular, many scholars have paid attention to the unique relationship between the city Philippi and the rise of the Roman Empire.[22] In relation to scholars' recent research on Philippians, for example, Gordon Fee argues that the Philippian community suffered because they refused to participate in the imperial cult of the empire.[23] Mikael Tellbe contends that the gospel of Paul ideologically runs in an opposite direction to that of the empire.[24] Likewise, Joseph H. Hellerman suggests that it is within the "rites and honors associated with the [imperial] cult" that the social classes in Philippi were differentiated into different strata.[25] An even more "anti-imperial" approach is found in the work of Erik M. Heen, who avers that with a technique of "hidden transcript" Paul uses his praise of the obedience of Christ to deprecate the "self-aggrandizement" of the emperors in grasping after the honor of equality with God.[26]

This trend of understanding Paul is not without its opponents. In his rejection of the connection between the rhetorics of the "Christ-Hymn" (Phil. 2:5-11) and the contemporary imperial cult,[27] Christopher Bryan argues that the function of the hymn is not to contrast Christ and Caesar, but to encourage unity among the believers.[28] The

---

[17] Cf. Paula Fredriksen, "Christians in the Roman Empire in the First Three Centuries CE," in *Companion to the Roman Empire*, ed. David Porter (Oxford: Blackwell, 2006), 589-90; Steven J. Friesen, *Twice Neokoros: Ephesus, Asia, and the Cult of the Flavian Imperial Family*, RGRW 116 (Leiden: Brill, 1993), 73-4, 146-52; Simon R. F. Price, *Rituals and Power: The Roman Imperial Cult in Asia Minor* (Cambridge: Cambridge University Press, 1984), 8-9.

[18] John Calvin, *The Epistles of Paul the Apostle to the Romans and to the Thessalonians*, ed. David W. Torrance and Thomas F. Torrance, trans. Ross Mackenzie (Grand Rapids: Wm. B. Eerdmans, 1960), 281-2.

[19] Tim Gorringe, "Political Readings of Scripture," in *The Cambridge Companion to Biblical Interpretation*, ed. John Barton (Cambridge: Cambridge University Press, 1998), 67.

[20] Magnus Zetterholm, *Approaches to Paul: A Student's Guide to Recent Scholarship* (Minneapolis: Fortress Press, 2009), 60-3.

[21] James B. Rives, "Graeco-Roman Religion in the Roman Empire: Old Assumptions and New Approaches," *CBR* 8 (2010): 249-52; Price, *Rituals*, 2, 8-14; Friesen, *Twice Neokoros*, 26-8, 73-4, 146-52.

[22] Lukas Bormann, *Philippi: Stadt und Christengemeinde zur Zeit des Paulus*, NovTSup 78 (Leiden: Brill, 1995), 41-4; Peter Pilhofer, *Philippi. I. Die Erste Christliche Gemeinde Europas*, WUNT 87 (Tübingen: Mohr Siebeck, 1995), 42; Beth Severy, *Augustus and the Family at the Birth of the Roman Empire* (New York: Routledge, 2003), 34, 133-4.

[23] Fee, *Paul's Letter*, 31-2, 197.

[24] Tellbe, *Paul between Synagogue and State*, 250-9.

[25] Joseph H. Hellerman, "The Humiliation of Christ in the Social World of Roman Philippi, Part I," *BibSac* 160 (2003): 331-2.

[26] Erik M. Heen, "Phil 2:6-11 and Resistance to Local Timocratic Rule: Isa Thed and the Cult of the Emperor in the East," in *Paul and the Roman Imperial Order*, ed. Richard A. Horsley (New York: Trinity Press, 2004), 138-9.

[27] Christopher Bryan, *Render to Caesar: Jesus, the Early Church, and the Roman Superpower* (Oxford: Oxford University Press, 2005), 86-8.

[28] Ibid., 86-8.

logic behind the uses of the word-group πολιτεύ- in 1:27 and 3:20 is *a fortiori*: just as the believers have submitted to Caesar, they should likewise submit to Christ.[29] There is thus no anti-imperial message in Philippians.[30] Likewise, Peter Oakes argues that Paul's theologies of Christology and Eschatology are only indirectly related to Rome's rule and the imperial cult.[31] An anti-imperial message could at most be an implication, but not the explicit core of Paul's concern.[32]

It is beyond the scope of this book to give a thorough assessment of the foregoing contrasting viewpoints. In this work, based on the multiple allusions to the OT (LXX) texts, I argue that a subtle polemic against Caesar is not without possibility. However, even if the Philippian community's rejection of the imperial cult was one of the chief sources of their suffering, I do not see Paul's *primary* message in Philippians as an anti-imperial polemic. Instead, the contestation of narratives between Paul and the political authorities, as important as it is, serves only as *the key backdrop* to the contestation of testimonies between Paul and the Jewish Christian leaders. In other words, while there could be an anti-imperial message in Philippians, it is of *secondary importance* in relation to the contention between Paul and his fellow "Christ-followers."

To understand this backdrop, some historical background is needed. While there are occasions of anti-Jewish events and literature,[33] it has been generally accepted that the Romans viewed the practices and religion of traditional Judaism in positive terms.[34] Due to a "respect for ancestral tradition," multiple scholars have pointed to the phenomena of Jews being given special concessions by the Roman authorities for the practice of their ethnic traditions and monotheistic religion during the early decades of the first century,[35] including temple tax,[36] the Sabbath,[37] dietary laws,[38] the exemption from military service,[39] and the exemption from participating in the imperial cult.[40] This last exemption is the one concession that is highly significant to this investigation.[41]

---

[29] Ibid., 84.
[30] Ibid., 83–7.
[31] Peter Oakes, "Re-Mapping the Universe: Paul and the Emperor in 1 Thessalonians and Philippians," *JSNT* 27 (2005): 314–15.
[32] Oakes, "Re-Mapping," 315. Cf. Kim, *Christ and Caesar*, 10–23; Denny Burk, "Is Paul's Gospel Counterimperial? Evaluating the Prospects of the 'Fresh Perspective' for Evangelical Theology," *JETS* 51 (2008): 321–2.
[33] Jeremy Punt, "Paul's Jewish Identity in the Roman World. Beyond the Conflict Model," in *Paul the Jew: Rereading the Apostle as a Figure of Second Temple Judaism*, ed. Gabriele Boccaccini and Carlos A. Segovia (Minneapolis: Fortress Press, 2016), 266n.53.
[34] Shaye J. D. Cohen, "Crossing the Boundary and Becoming a Jew," *HTR* 82, no. 1 (1989): 15; Richard A. Horsley, *Paul and the Roman Imperial Order* (New York: Continuum, 2004), 8.
[35] Fredriksen, "Christians," 595; Punt, "Paul's Jewish Identity," 252. Cf. Tacitus, *Hist.* 5.4–5; Josephus, *Ant.* 14.267.
[36] Ben Witherington III, *The Paul Quest: The Renewed Search for the Jew of Tarsus* (Downers Grove: InterVarsity Press, 1998), 180.
[37] Tellbe, *Paul between Synagogue and State*, 44; Josephus, *Ant.* 14.226, 242, 245, 258, 261, 263–4; 16.163, 168.
[38] Ibid., 45; Josephus, *Ant.* 4.226.
[39] Ibid., 45; Josephus, *Ant.* 14.223–40.
[40] Oskar Skarsaune, *In the Shadow of the Temple: Jewish Influences on Early Christianity* (Downers Grove: InterVarsity, 2002), 58; Amnon Linder, *The Jews in Roman Imperial Legislation* (Wayne State University, 1995), 103–7, 20–4; Josephus, *Ant.* 19.280–5, 19.304–5.
[41] For opposing perspectives, see Tessa Rajak, "Was There a Roman Charter for the Jews?" *JRS* 74 (1984): 107–23. For a critique of Rajak's viewpoints, see Tellbe, *Paul between Synagogue and State*,

2.5 Conclusion

I have reviewed a few areas of research to which this work is connected, including the compositional unity of the epistle, the role of suffering, the identities of opponents, and the imperial cult and pertinent exemption for the Jews. With the scope of my work limited to the investigation of the narrative dynamics of the identity-formation processes of the Philippian community and the theme of the contestation of narratives, I have stated my assumptions regarding these controversial issues. With these assumptions, I now shift my attention to the methodology of this work.

47, 56–7. See also John M. G. Barclay, *Jews in the Mediterranean Diaspora: From Alexander to Trajan* (Berkeley: University of California Press, 1996), 274–8.

Part II

Theoretical Framework

3

Ricoeur's Narrative Theory

Contestation of Temporalities, Identities, and Testimonies

Paul Ricoeur (1913–2005) was a French philosopher who contributed many ideas to the fields of phenomenology, hermeneutics, and biblical exegesis. Of all the diverse topics on which he has written, one of the most influential areas is his theorization of narrative, which has generated an immense impact on theories of both textual interpretation and identity formation. It is my desire in the limited space that follows to concisely introduce a few of his various concepts and highlight those that will be instrumental to my investigation of the formation of the Philippian community's identity.

I am not the first one to make use of Ricoeur's theories in understanding Paul's making of identity. In the book *Paul in Israel's Story: Self and Community at the Cross*, John L. Meech sets out to "correlate the ontology of the self in community [as developed by Ricoeur] with Paul's communal self."[1] After addressing the inadequacy of Rudolf Bultmann's account of Paul's anthropology, Meech employs Ricoeur's ontology of the self in community and dialectic of selfhood and otherness to articulate "the kerygma as the story of Israel and an ontology of the self in community."[2] Meech then correlates his Ricoeurian understanding of the self, community, and the transcendental Other with Robert Jenson's theological account of the Spirit in a community, and contends that "Paul can address us again in our interpretations because we live with him in the community of the living and dead in Christ, and because the Spirit of Christ speaks in our community's conversation."[3] While both Meech and I employ Ricoeur's theories to delineate Paul's writings, our research differs in terms of goal and approach. As Meech seeks to disclose the role of the community inside Paul's ontology of the self and provides the ground that Paul can use to address us in our interpretations, his approach is marked by a mix of philosophical and theological discussions.[4] In contrast,

---

[1] John L. Meech, *Paul in Israel's Story: Self and Community at the Cross* (New York: Oxford University Press, 2006), 129.
[2] Meech, *Paul in Israel's Story*, 51–3, 55, 125–8, 32.
[3] Ibid., 137; Robert Jenson, *Systematic Theology*, 2 vols (New York: Oxford University Press, 1997–9), 2:181.
[4] Meech, *Paul in Israel's Story*, 129. "First, how can the ontology help us to understand Paul? Second, how can the ontology help us to let Paul address us again?"

with my goal set to show that the "Christian" identity formation of the Philippian community happens amid a contestation of narratives with different construals of time, my approach is characterized primarily as exegetical and secondarily as philosophical. If Meech engages more with other philosophers and theologians (e.g., Bultmann and Jürgen Moltmann), I engage more with the actual text of Paul.[5]

3.1 Threefold Mimesis

In *Time and Narrative* (*T&N*, 3 vols., 1984–8), Ricoeur proposes a universal correspondence between humans' temporal experience and narrative:

> My basic hypothesis [is] that between the activity of narrating a story and the temporal character of human experience there exists a correlation that is not merely accidental but that presents a transcultural form of necessity. To put it another way, *time becomes human to the extent that it is articulated through a narrative mode, and narrative attains its full meaning when it becomes a condition of temporal existence.*[6]

In other words, time becomes *humanly intelligible time* when it is presented in a narrative mode, and narrative is structured around humans' temporal experience.[7] Similarly, in a previously published article, *Narrative Time*, Ricoeur writes,

> My first working hypothesis is that narrativity and temporality are closely related ... Indeed, I take temporality to be that structure of existence that reaches language in narrativity and narrativity to be the language structure that has temporality as its ultimate referent. Their relationship is therefore reciprocal.[8]

Thus, narrative has the unique capacity of *bringing the temporality of our human experience into language.*[9] In this investigation, I argue that this reciprocity will allow me to *make use of Ricoeur's understanding on narrative and its various temporal dynamics to analyze the interactions among the five levels of story within Paul's narrative world*. If these narrative interactions or dynamics are by themselves generative of theological articulations, a deeper understanding of them would bring much insight to Paul's theologizing and the way he shapes the temporal experience of the Philippian community.[10]

---

[5] Cf. Luke Timothy Johnson, Review of *Paul in Israel's Story: Self and Community at the Cross*, by John L. Meech, *JTS* 69 (2008): 435.
[6] Ricoeur, *T&N I*, 52.
[7] Ibid., 2; Paul Ricoeur, "Narrative Time," *Critical Inquiry* 7, no. 1 (1980): 169.
[8] Ricoeur, "Narrative Time," 169.
[9] James Fodor, *Christian Hermeneutics: Paul Ricoeur and the Refiguring of Theology* (Oxford: Oxford University Press, 1995), 198.
[10] David Pellauer, "Narrated Action Grounds Narrative Identity," in *Paul Ricoeur in the Age of Hermeneutical Reason: Poetics, Praxis, and Critique*, ed. Roger W. H. Savage (Lanham: Lexington Books, 2015), 71; Longenecker, "Narrative Approach," 93.

In elaborating this reciprocal relationship, Ricoeur makes use of Augustine's threefold present and Aristotle's concept of mimesis and produces the threefold mimesis moments: a reader's prefigured way of understanding things before her reading of a text (mimesis1), an emplotment process exemplified by a configuration of actions (mimesis2), and the refiguration of a reader's experience within her reading of the text (mimesis3).[11] With the mimesis2 serving as the pivotal point of creation, the "mediating role of emplotment between a stage of practical experience that precedes it and a stage that succeeds it" comes to the fore.[12]

3.1.1 Prefiguration (Mimesis1): Diverse Traditions toward Suffering for the Gospel of Christ

Generally speaking, mimesis1 represents the "general narrative background or preunderstanding of human action" supposed by the narrative composition in mimesis2.[13] It belongs to the category of traditions, the "taken-for-granted forms to be found in new experience."[14] It is the assumed ways to make sense of upcoming events.[15] According to Dan Stiver, it refers to "the preunderstanding that one brings to writing or reading a text."[16] Specifically for this work, mimesis1 on the one hand relates to the Greco-Roman society's mainstream understanding of someone suffering for her conviction at the hands of the authorities. On the other hand, it refers to the traditions or preunderstanding of one particular person (or group) from which she enters into the process of narrating the suffering experiences of Paul and herself. In this case, one specific prominent part of this mimesis1 belongs to the preunderstanding of the Philippian community on suffering with Paul before they read Paul's letter (Philippians). *It is with respect to the subsequent transformation of this preunderstanding that Paul and his opponents are competing against one another.* Implied in this competition is the

---

[11] Ricoeur, *T&N I*, 52–6, 71, 81; Ricoeur, "Hermeneutical Function," 140–2.
[12] Concerning mimesis (μίμησις), I am not the first one who applies this class of ancient Greek concepts to the exegesis of the Philippians. For example, in her journal article, Susan Eastman refers to Plato's writings on mimesis and gives a "theatrical reading" to the "Christ-Hymn." But her choice of Plato and tendency in seeing life transformation as based on "virtue ethics" makes her study drastically different from my reference to Ricoeur, who develops his mimesis theory more in relation to Aristotle than Plato. See Susan G. Eastman, "Philippians 2:6–11: Incarnation as Mimetic Participation," *JSPL* 1, no. 1 (2011): 1–22; Jo-Ann A. Brant, "The Place of Mimēsis in Paul's Thought," *Studies in Religion* 22, no. 3 (1993): 285–300. For a concise summary of the difference between concepts of mimesis from Plato and Aristotle, see Ricoeur, *T&N I*, 34; Karl Simms, *Paul Ricoeur*, Routledge Critical Thinkers (New York: Routledge, 2003), 62–5. For a differentiation between Ricoeur's concept of ethics from the tradition of "virtue ethics," see Mark S. Muldoon, "Ricoeur's Ethics: Another Version of Virtue Ethics? Attestation is Not a Virtue," *Philosophy Today* 42, no. 3 (1998): 301–9.
[13] Keith D'Souza, "Ricoeur's Narrative Development of Gadamer's Hermeneutics: Continuity and Discontinuity" (PhD, Marquette University, 2003), 126; Ricoeur, *T&N I*, 62.
[14] Oliver Mallett and Robert Wapshott, "The Challenges of Identity Work: Developing Ricoeurian Narrative Identity in Organisations," *Ephemera* 11, no. 3 (2011): 278.
[15] It pertains to the "knowledge arrived at through prior experience." See Mallett and Wapshott, "Challenges of Identity Work," 278.
[16] Dan R. Stiver, *Theology after Ricoeur: New Directions in Hermeneutical Theology* (Louisville: Westminster John Knox Press, 2001), 66. "It is akin to Gadamer's 'prejudices' (*Vorurteil*) that shape our approach to a text."

existence of a variety of different preunderstandings of this issue of suffering with Paul, resulting from a spectrum of variegated narratives with diverse ethical values.[17]

In this investigation, the essence and shaping of this preunderstanding is mediated by what Ricoeur calls "temporality."[18] "Temporality" (*Innerzeitigkeit*), defined by Ricoeur as the "pre-narrative quality of human experience,"[19] concerns the intrinsic *temporal structure* within the making of each narrative.[20] According to Ricoeur, it concerns "the way in which everyday praxis orders the present of the future, the present of the past, and the present of the present in terms of one another."[21] In this work, it revolves around how various actions of the past, future, and present are ordered together into a narrative that gives meaning to the suffering experiences of Paul and the Philippian community.

3.1.2 Configuration (Mimesis2): Narrative Dynamics of Paul's Narrative World amid a Contestation of Narratives

Prior to engaging the text through to the engaging via reading, mimesis2 concerns the emplotment process by which various human actions are configured into a narrative whole. According to Ricoeur, a plot is "the intelligible whole that governs a succession of events in a story ... A story is *made out of* events to the extent that plot *makes* events *into* a story."[22] Building upon the Aristotelian notion of *muthos* and *mimesis*, Ricoeur stresses that this emplotment process behind a narrative is not just an imitation of action, but a *creative organizing* of human action into a unique whole.[23] Instead of translating *muthos* and *mimesis* as nouns of organization and imitation, they should be seen as "an activity: *muthos*, the act of organising events into a system; and *mimesis*, the act of imitating or representing." Contrary to the notion of a passive and static plot structure, emplotment is a dynamic and active structuration process.[24] What is significant to the theme of contestation of narratives is that *out of the same set of suffering events of Paul and the Philippian community, multiple different plots, which give different verdicts to Paul's sufferings, can be organized.*[25] Considering the dimension of ethical judgment within each verdict, a person's telling of a story is necessarily accompanied by the persuasion of her own endorsed ethical principles.[26] Thus, an emplotted narrative is not an exact replica of the events, but a selective, self-involved,

---

[17] Cf. Ricoeur, *T&N I*, 53; Stiver, *Theology After Ricoeur*, 67.
[18] Ricoeur, *T&N I*, 54–63; Fodor, *Christian Hermeneutics*, 211; D'Souza, "Gadamer's Hermeneutics," 128, 52–3.
[19] Ricoeur, "Life," 434; Crites, "Narrative Quality," 291–311. Such a kind of temporal characteristic is similarly proposed by Stephen Crites as the "narrative quality of experience."
[20] Ricoeur, *T&N I*, 59–61. Ricoeur bases his analysis of temporality (*Innerzeitigkeit*) on the work of Heidegger, which refers to the concept of human being within time. Cf. Martin Heidegger, *Being and Time*, trans. John Macquarrie (Oxford: Basil Blackwell, 1978), 38.
[21] Ricoeur, *T&N I*, 60.
[22] Ricoeur, "Narrative Time," 171.
[23] Ricoeur, *T&N I*, 33.
[24] Ibid., 48.
[25] Seymour Benjamin Chatman, *Story and Discourse: Narrative Structure in Fiction and Film* (New York: Cornell University Press, 1978), 43.
[26] Ricoeur, *OAA*, 163–4.

and ethically engaged organization.[27] The contestation of narratives between Paul and his opponents thus hinges on the contestation of emplotment processes. In order to understand the narrative dynamics that arise from this contention, it is necessary for us to go into the operational details of this emplotment.

3.1.2.1 Discordant Elements Are Joined into a Concordant Plot

First, the most basic operation of an emplotment is that heterogeneous and discordant elements are joined into a concordant and unified plot. Within an emplotment, contingent incidents are being selected, woven together, and assimilated into a concordant plot, forming what Ricoeur calls a "discordant concordance."[28] Thereafter, an event is no longer just an individual occurrence, but *a narrative event* that contributes to the configuration and progress of a single story either as its "Beginning," its "Middle," or its "Ending."[29] The emplotted story is not just an enumeration of successive incidents, but an intelligible and unified organization of events.[30]

3.1.2.2 The Dialectic of Time as Sequence and Configuration

Second, one of the temporal logics of an emplotment may be described as a dialectic between time as sequence and time as configuration, in which "composing a story is, from the temporal point of view, drawing a configuration out of a succession."[31] On the one hand, each narrative features a temporal aspect of a chronological succession. Along this, there can be *unceasing* sets of questions and answers in the form of "and then what?" and "then something happened, and then . . . ."[32] Theoretically, an indefinite series of future episodes can be added to the story.[33] In short, *it refers to the iteration of what things happened in the manner of a temporal sequence.*

On the other hand, there is another temporal aspect of an enduring structure as discordant events are *shaped into a nonchronological configuration.*[34] When a person arranges her story episode by episode into a sequence, she is already engaging herself in reflecting the meaning of all the previous episodes by forming successive configurations of time which *encompass all episodes that she has traversed and provide successive evaluations of traversed episodes and expectations of coming episodes.*[35] As this "reflective act" runs to the end of a story, there will arise an enduring configuration of

---

[27] Ibid., 163–8; Anthony C. Thiselton, *New Horizons in Hermeneutics* (Grand Rapids: Zondervan, 1992), 355.
[28] Ricoeur, *T&N I*, 66. These elements include goals, causes, discoveries, surprises, conflicts, interactions, agents, chance, unintended circumstances, etc.
[29] Cf. Pellauer, "Narrated Action Grounds Narrative Identity," 78.
[30] Paul Ricoeur, "Life in Quest of Narrative," in *On Paul Ricoeur: Narrative and Interpretation*, ed. David Wood (London: Routledge, 1992), 21.
[31] Ricoeur, "Life in Quest," 22. Ricoeur writes, "If we may speak of the temporal identity of a story, it must be characterized as something that endures and remains across that which passes and flows away."
[32] Ricoeur, *T&N I*, 67.
[33] Kenneth Sheppard, "Telling Contested Stories: J. G. A. Pocock and Paul Ricoeur," *History of European Ideas* 39, no. 6 (2013): 888.
[34] Ricoeur, "Narrative Time," 178.
[35] Ricoeur, *T&N I*, 66–7; Ricoeur, *T&N II*, 21–7. It is this temporal dialectic of chronological time and configurational time that Ricoeur sees as being overlooked by many historians and literary critics.

time (temporality) *of the whole sequence*,³⁶ which is characterized by *how evaluations and expectations embedded in previous episodes have all been guided to the conclusion of the story*.³⁷ Certain previously assumed ways to make sense of events and pertinent ethical principles of the reader or the society's mainstream understanding may have been affirmed or changed. In short, *it refers to why something happened in the mode of reflective evaluation*.

The formation and perception of this temporality can be illustrated briefly with a Philippian community member's reading experience of a portion of Paul's story within Philippians. At the "Beginning," having participated in Paul's fruitful ministry for some time, she is alarmed with the news of Paul's chains and upcoming trial. During the "Middle," as she focuses on what will happen next for Paul and the ministry, she reflects on the meaning of Paul's *past* evangelistic effort, his *future* fate considering the authorities' antagonistic attitude to the newly formed "Christian" communities, and his present state of mind inside the prison. Just as worry begins to creep into her mind, at the "Ending" she is *surprised* by the "fact" that Paul and the ministry have been blessed by this imprisonment (Phil. 1:12-14).³⁸ With this closure, an enduring temporal thought of God's guidance, protection, and sovereignty has been absorbed throughout Paul's whole journey of *past* evangelistic effort, *present* situation, and *future* fate. This enduring temporal configuration has registered itself as the intrinsic identity of this particular episode of Paul's story.

According to Ricoeur, the identity of a narrative is thus essentially linked to its temporality, which can be *created, perceived, and understood only by "following" its episodes from the beginning to the end*.³⁹ The chronological sequence in which one synthesizes one's various life episodes into a single story *becomes the "birth-place" of* the temporality of one's story. In the case of a contestation of testimonies in which Paul contends that his story is the legitimate narrative reappropriation of Christ's story, he is fundamentally arguing that *the temporality created out of his own chronological sequence best resonates and fits with the temporality of the story of Christ*.⁴⁰ What has implicitly become essential is the dialectic between the chronological sequence of Paul's story upon which he recapitulates within the discourse of Philippians, *and the temporality of Christ's story with which Paul aligns. Within the formation of a "Christian identity," without a chronological sequence of a believer's own story, the temporality of Christ's story simply cannot exert its effect on her. Without the temporality of Christ's story, the chronological sequence of a believer has no reference with which she can resonate and*

    History is then severed from storytelling, and narrative study becomes an analysis of surface grammar.

³⁶ Ricoeur, *T&N I*, 67. "To understand the story is to understand how and why the successive episodes led to this conclusion, which, far from being foreseeable, must finally be acceptable, as congruent with the episodes brought together by the story."

³⁷ Ricoeur, *T&N I*, 66-7.

³⁸ This significance of the interaction between the text and the reader is also recognized by scholars of rhetorical narratology. Cf. Phelan and Rabinowitz, "Time, Plot, Progression," 58.

³⁹ Ricoeur, "Text," 177.

⁴⁰ Regarding this resonance, it will be modeled by the structure of the nesting of stories to be covered in p.57ff. in articulating Paul's theologizing process. Regarding this "fitness," it will be shown by a comparison of the demarcations of time within the testimonies of the Jewish Christian leaders and Paul on p.193ff.

fit. As the following explanation will show in more detail, it is on the basis of such temporal logic that I approach the temporality of a narrative as the primary identifier in differentiating the narrative of Paul from those of his opponents, and the core essence of a person's narrative identity.

3.1.2.3 *The Dialectic of Discordance and Concordance*

Another dialectical phenomena peculiar to this emplotment process is the dialectic of discordance and concordance.[41] According to Ricoeur, our experience of time is not reducible to either pure discordance or concordance.[42] On the dimension of discordance, as contingent occurrences are continuously admitted into our previously configured narrative, our "expectations created by the prior course of events" are constantly being thwarted, and the temporal theme (identity) of our story is continuously being challenged.[43] On the dimension of concordance, as every contingent occurrence is accepted into the story, it is instantly transformed into a further advancement of the flow of the story. The story is then granted the order and coherence of a unified narrative arrangement.[44] In other words, a contingent occurrence, which could have happened in whatever manner, is *given a particular meaning retrospectively* within the ever-continuous cycles of discordances and concordances. It is *within this continuous story-making of a person* that each "meaningless" occurrence acquires its *necessary* meaning as a "narrative necessity."[45]

Two fundamental principles useful to this investigation can be drawn from this dialectic of discordance and concordance. First, while Paul's suffering may mean nothing at all to certain people, for those who care, *such a "meaningless" occurrence has been creatively inverted into a necessary, significant, and teleological event within their emplotment processes*. The contestation of the meaning of Paul's chains thus arises from a contestation of *self-created* narrative logics of life. No social, universal, or objectively verifiable principle can supplant the agencies of Paul and Paul's opponents as the sources of meaning of their own narratives.

Second, within the ever forward-moving journey in which contingencies are always waiting, a person's fragile and discordant experience can continuously be governed or regulated by the enduring temporal thought (concordance) of a narrative.[46] Based on this regulative capacity, I am going to analyze Paul's reflection of his own spiritual journey and the Philippian community's reception of Paul's testimony. Specifically, this work will address the following questions: What kind of theological thinking can we discern from Paul's situation of an unknown trial result, which could potentially bring death as a discordant blow? Due to the suffering that lies ahead of the Philippian

---

[41] The concept of discordance and concordance is first suggested by Ricoeur in *T&N* in connection with emplotment. See Ricoeur, *T&N I*, 4, 21–2, 31; Ricoeur, *T&N II*, 4–5.
[42] Ricoeur, *T&N I*, 71–2.
[43] Ricoeur, *OAA*, 142.
[44] Ricoeur, *T&N II*, 23; Ricoeur, *OAA*, 141.
[45] Ricoeur, *OAA*, 142. Ricoeur calls this this dialectic "the inversion of the effect of contingency into an effect of necessity." See Ricoeur, *T&N I*, 67.
[46] Mark Currie, *The Unexpected: Narrative Temporality and the Philosophy of Surprise* (Edinburgh: Edinburgh University Press, 2013), 46.

community, what kind of challenges can we perceive within their perseverance in supporting Paul?

3.1.2.4 The Dialectic of Sedimentation and Innovation

Another temporal dialectic is one of sedimentation and innovation. While every narrative is always creatively produced, it is also "connected in one way or another to the paradigms of a tradition."[47] In fact, if every action is symbolically mediated (not controlled) by and interpreted through contemporary cultural conventions,[48] every narrative can be identified by placing it within a certain *living* tradition.[49] In the case of a narrative mode of thought (mimesis2) which follows its tradition (mimesis1) rather strictly, a stable or sedimented mode of narration continues without any shift of plot, exhibiting no deviance from the temporality of its tradition. However, for one whose plot deviates notably from its tradition, what comes forth instead is an innovative narrative whose intrinsic temporal identity has undergone an obvious change from its prefigurative tradition. The assumed conventions and belief within a person's interpretation of the past, present, and future have been evidently altered.[50] For every new narrative, the dialectic of sedimentation and innovation reflects different proportions of sedimentation and innovation.[51]

As Ricoeur has argued, while the more formal and universal features of narrative could be described as a dialectic of discordance and concordance, each individual narrative by itself creates an order of events with causal relations, which could then be sedimented into a stable schema of interpreting daily life events.[52] These sedimented types of interpretation are themselves created and governed by a dialectic of historical tradition and peoples' productive imagination, which Ricoeur also categorizes as an interplay of sedimentation and innovation.[53] Instead of being bound by the formal features of the paradigm of narrative which spans across all times and culture, in this book I deal with the particular interplay of sedimentation (or tradition) and innovation with respect to the narrative theologizing of Paul's suffering experience, and the Philippians' subsequent reading experience.

As the following exegesis will show, the way Paul suffers for the gospel embodies a theological story which involves an innovation from his Jewish tradition. Simultaneously, *the causal relations among the stories of God, Israel, Christ, Christ-followers, and himself (levels one to five) are being rewritten.* I argue that the "grinding" of stories within Paul's narrative world beneath Philippians[54] occurs when Paul

---

[47] Ricoeur, "Text," 182.
[48] Ricoeur, *T&N I*, 58; Ricoeur, "Life," 434.
[49] Ricoeur, "Text," 181–2.
[50] Ibid., 183.
[51] Henry I. Venema, *Identifying Selfhood: Imagination, Narrative, and Hermeneutics in the Thought of Paul Ricoeur* (Albany: State University of New York Press, 2000), 114.
[52] Ricoeur, *T&N I*, 69.
[53] Ibid., 67–8.
[54] Dunn, "Paul's Theology," 328. Dunn elaborates his views on the interaction among levels of story within Paul's theological making process: "none of these stories stands on its own. It is the interaction between them that makes Paul's theology so fascinating, puzzling, and frustrating by turns, and that has provided the grist to the mills of ongoing debate. It is the dissonance

modifies the relations revolving around a generally preaccepted Jewish tradition—the application of physical circumcision to attain God's blessing. It is exactly in the midst of Paul's innovation of this tradition that some Jewish Christian leaders arise to challenge his testimony, and intend to keep this tradition.

3.1.2.5 The Dialectic of Discontinuity and Continuity

Another dialectic is one of discontinuity and continuity. As previous stories are creatively narrated, something "new" is produced. The newly formed narrative "takes the place of" the "old" stories that are referred to.[55] An element of discontinuity thus exists between the traditional stories and the newly narrated story.[56] However, paradoxically, an element of continuity continues to exist, as it is the "same" thing that is talked about before and after the narration. This dialectic of discontinuity and continuity will be useful in explaining the relationship between various stories within Paul's narrative world. In particular, how should we judge the relationship between Paul's previous life story (Phil. 3:4-6) and his new one in Christ (Phil. 3:9-11)? What is the relation between the story of Israel and the story of Christ, and how does this affect the identity formation of the Philippian community?

3.1.3 Refiguration (Mimesis3): Transformative Reading amid a Contestation of Horizons

While there is an enduring temporal thought within the narrative configuration (mimesis2) beneath any discourse, this temporal structure, as a paradigm of human experience, will only be "completed" after it has been taken up through an act of reading, refiguring the temporal experience of the reader regarding her practical world (mimesis3).[57] Instead of "projecting oneself and one's own beliefs and prejudices" into the text, there is a "confrontation between the world of the text and the world of the reader."[58] As a reader reads and understands oneself in front of the text, she is invited to live her life according to the implicit ethical principle of the text.[59] However, a reader

---

between the stories that raises the question of the coherence or inconsistency of Paul's theology. Alternatively expressed, it is the *grinding* of the different levels against each other that has caused the earthquakes both in Paul's theology itself and in modern attempts to come to grips with that theology."

[55] Pellauer, "Narrated Action Grounds Narrative Identity," 77.

[56] As narrative "grafts new temporal elements" to the preexisting reality, the meaning of an event or action is augmented, bringing about an "increase" in meaning. See Pellauer, "Narrated Action Grounds Narrative Identity," 72, 77. Ricoeur names this increment of meanings toward an event as an "iconic augmentation," which is similar to the semantic innovation in metaphors. See Ricoeur, *T&N I*, 80–1.

[57] Ricoeur, "Life," 431. In a middle ground where neither the text nor the reader has total control, mimesis3 marks the space where the world of the text and the world of the reader intersect, producing what is called by Gadamer the "fusion of horizons." See Hans-Georg Gadamer, *Truth and Method* (London: Sheed and Ward, 1975), 301–2; Ricoeur, *T&N I*, 70–88; Ricoeur, *T&N III*, 166–79. For a nuanced critique of the concept of "fusion of horizons," see Paul Ricoeur, *From Text to Action: Essays in Hermeneutics, II* (Evanston: Northwestern University Press, 1991), 70–4, 280–5.

[58] Ricoeur, *T&N II*, 5.

[59] Ricoeur, "Hermeneutical Function," 143; Ricoeur, *OAA*, 163–8.

is not a passive receiver, and there is no guarantee that she will become compliant to the text.[60] Regarding the pertinent ethical issue, the reader probably would have already exposed herself to multiple different narratives. Actions narrated in the text often have already been narrated with other ethical principles embedded in other proposed narrative worlds. In other words, ethical principles based on other narrative configurations would be brought into the mind of the reader during her reading. Thus, different ways of narrating the actions and events as referred to by a text are always part of a contentious reading process.[61] No text or tradition can control the response of the reader. However, this uncertainty does not rule out that there are certain ways in which a narrative text will have effects upon the reader. In fact, with narrative being the privileged mode for articulating the human experience of time, understanding the dynamics within the reading of a narrative becomes very important in explaining how one's temporal experience can possibly be transformed.[62] In what follows, I will explore these temporal processes.

When a reader engages herself with a narrative by following the plot *for the first time*, she will enter into a forward-moving temporal experience parallel to that of the character found within the story. As the reader moves through contingencies with the character, the reader, before reaching the end of the story, will likely experience the episodes in the "Middle" *according to the preunderstanding (mimesis1) of herself or the mainstream culture*.[63] However, as the reading reaches the end, the reader, along with the character, will "simultaneously" come to recognize the organizing perspective of the enduring temporal thought.[64] She finally gains the point of view of the narrator who has put all the previous episodes into a whole, which invites her to see those previous episodes with the new understanding provided by the narrator.[65]

This reading experience gains further significance when a reader *rereads or retells* the story. Quoting Louis O. Mink, Ricoeur comments, "it is really in the case of re-telling a story—reading the story backwards from its conclusion to its beginning—that we understand things had to 'turn out' as they did."[66] With the ending of a story known to the reader, the element of surprise is reduced.[67] But there is another new kind of temporal dimension arising within this rereading:[68] each episode is now read *in light*

---

[60] W. David Hall, *Paul Ricoeur and the Poetic Imperative: The Creative Tension between Love and Justice* (New York: State University of New York Press, 2008), 43.
[61] Cf. William C. Dowling, *Ricoeur on Time and Narrative: An Introduction to Temps et Récit* (Notre Dame: University of Notre Dame Press, 2011), 14.
[62] Ricoeur, *T&N I*, 2.
[63] The mimesis1 here stands for the commonly accepted rules of a society in understanding the ethical issue addressed by the story.
[64] Dowling, *Ricoeur on Time and Narrative*, 51.
[65] While Aristotle and modern semioticians like A. J. Greimas analyze the structure of narrative in strictly spatial terms, Ricoeur understands narrative primarily in temporal terms.
[66] Ricoeur, *T&N I*, 207.
[67] According to Ricoeur, even though readers have known the result of a plot, within their following of a story they could still taste the common expectation and hence sudden reversals as experienced by the characters within a story. See Ricoeur, *T&N I*, 240n.26.
[68] Ibid., 67.

of its progression toward a well-known conclusion provided by the "invisible" narrator. Ricoeur writes,

> As soon as a story is well known—and such is the case with most traditional and popular narratives as well as with the national chronicles of the founding events of a given community—retelling takes the place of telling. Then following the story is less important than apprehending the well-known end as implied in the beginning and the well-known episodes as leading to this end. Here again, time is not abolished by the teleological structure of the judgment which grasps together the events under the heading of 'the end.'[69]

In other words, the story now not only provides an organizing principle *by* its conclusion known at the end of the story, but also a teleological forward movement in which successive events are *instantly* seen by the reader as moving toward a definite and anticipated closure.[70] According to Ricoeur, while Mink tends to abolish most if not all the temporal reading experience of first reading by the retrospective dimension in second reading, Ricoeur observes that "the same structure of narrative, namely, the dialectic between contingency and order, episode and configuration, discordance and concordance" actually continues to exert its influence within the rereading processes.[71] In other words, the temporal emplotment dynamics analyzed in mimesis2 would endure into mimesis3 and avail themselves as the space in which readers are invited into a life-configuring process. The theology-generating dynamics discovered in mimesis2, and the rhetorical impact of the letter upon the community, are thus intrinsically connected.

Two opposite senses of time have emerged within this rereading. On the one hand, the reader can still situate herself within the *limited* horizon of the character,[72] who inside the *forward* direction of the story *remains in a condition of partial knowledge* regarding the ultimate consequences of her actions, moves *forward* as an active volitional agent, and engages in making ethical choices for her actions.[73] According to Ricoeur, the reader could still perceive what the character sees and feels within the character's limited horizon as if the reader did not know the final outcome of the story. In the context of this investigation, when each Philippian community member rereads Philippians, she is still able to perceive what Paul (the character) and she herself might have felt during her first reading.

On the other hand, paradoxically, the reader is already aware of the point of view of the narrator, who "gazes" *backward* from a vantage point "above" the sphere of the

---

[69] Ricoeur, "Narrative Time," 179.
[70] Ricoeur, "Life," 431.
[71] Ricoeur, *T&N I*, 158.
[72] Regarding the theory of limited horizon or partial knowledge for a volitional agent, see Dowling, *Ricoeur on Time and Narrative*, 48–9, 97.
[73] What Ricoeur emphasizes is that the character is not just a passive attribute of the story, but an *active agent*. See Glenda Ballantyne, *Creativity and Critique: Subjectivity and Agency in Touraine and Ricoeur* (Leiden: Brill, 2007), 133, 49–50. For a defense of the effect of this temporality on readers' rereading temporal experience, see Ricoeur, *T&N I*, 158–60.

characters,[74] and confers ethical meaning to the episodes of the story.[75] As a result, *along the rereading the reader will see how her previous perception of each episode is being turned toward those ethical meanings and pertinent emotions as proposed by the narrator.* In the context of this work, I argue that as each community member rereads Paul's story, she is "invited" by the "invisible" narrator to give up her previous perception of Paul's suffering, perceive God's surprising guidance of Paul through his adversities, and understand each suffering episode as progressing toward the foreseen ending of glory for Paul (1:11b, 2:16, 3:20-21). In this manner, each community member *will enter into a horizon where the experience of her practical world will be narrated with the same temporality of the story of Paul.* Just as those unexpected and discordant events of Paul will progress toward the foreseen ending of Paul's story, discordant realities *in the practical world* of each Philippian community member, within her imaginative horizon, will unfold in the same temporal manner.[76] Events of her own past, present, and future will be joined together in accordance with the temporal structure of Paul's story. She will then "successfully" imitate Paul (Phil. 3:17).

However, when it comes to shaping the suffering experiences of the Philippian community, Paul's opponents have also offered other narratives and hence contesting

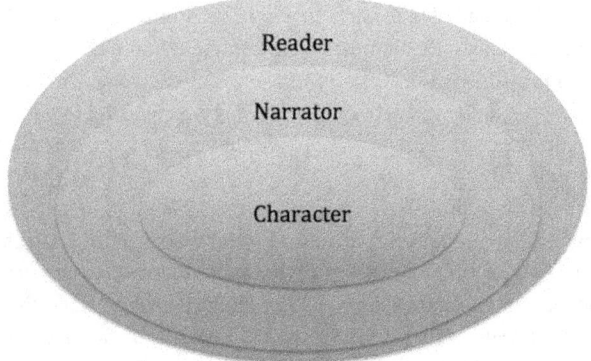

Figure 2 Three concentric spheres of narrative consciousness.

---

[74] Ricoeur, *T&N I*, 157; Dowling, *Ricoeur on Time and Narrative*, 97–8. Based on *T&N I*, Dowling argues that we may visualize such relationships of within and without as *three concentric spheres of narrative consciousness* (see Figure 2), where the characters as volitional beings operate in the innermost sphere, the narrator in the middle, with the reader the most peripheral. These spheres find a lot of resonances with the concepts of Phelan's multileveled communication in James Phelan and Peter J. Rabinowitz, "Narrative as Rhetoric," in *Narrative Theory: Core Concepts and Critical Debates*, (Columbus: Ohio State University Press, 2012), 3, in which rhetorical narrative theorists Phelan and Rabinowitz emphasize the importance of the *purposive* aspect of narrative: "We are interested in the ways in which the elements of any narrative (e.g., character, setting, plot structure) are shaped in the service of larger ends. The focus on narrative as *multileveled communication* means that we are interested not simply in the meaning of narrative but also in the experience of it."

[75] In a single grasping together of heterogeneous events, the narrator connects all the successive moments of time (within the story) according only to her comprehension. This vantage point of the narrator from the "exterior" of the story is what Ricoeur calls *totum simul*, which means the grasping of the whole at once, in analogy to the manner of God's knowledge of the world. Ricoeur references this concept from Louis O. Mink and Boethius. See Ricoeur, *T&N I*, 159–60.

[76] Venema, *Identifying Selfhood*, 113.

reading experiences to the Philippian community. Among these narratives, multiple *characters* of Paul, Christ, and God have been created in playing out contesting narrative sequences. Divergent ethical meaning and emotions can be felt when each community member tries out and follows each of the stories from Paul and his opponents. *It is exactly in this contesting of horizons of viewing Paul's suffering*, constituted by negative evaluations from Paul's opponents and a positive one from Paul, that multiple reading processes unfold in the minds of the Philippian community members.[77] Will they believe in Paul's narrative and see the "invisible" narrator of his narrative as guided by God, the ultimate master of human history?

In light of this contestation of narratives, in which multiple self-engaged judgments clashing with each other are offered to the Philippian community, the relation between narrative and rhetoric inside mimesis3 could receive more attention. However, due to the limitations of space, I cannot offer a full analysis here.[78] What suffices here is that there are at least two sets of criteria from which we can gauge the rhetorical effectiveness of a narrative construction. First, to successfully argue against other perspectives, the golden principle for classical rhetorics is to transfer "the agreement granted to premises onto conclusions."[79] In other words, successful persuasion *begins from* "the set of shared beliefs that bring together audiences and rhetors."[80] We have to identify the *doxa* (common belief or popular opinion) from which we can recognize "the conventions of a community as the foundation for shaping persuasive discourse."[81] In contrast to this conventional mode of persuasion is narrative, whose creative dimension "stirs up the sedimented universe of conventional ideas which are the premises of rhetorical argumentation."[82] Thus, the set of assumptions considered true *by most people*, called by Aristotle in *Topics* the *endoxa*, can not only be kept relatively stable but also be changed and expanded by creative or imaginative dimensions of narrative.[83]

---

[77] Cf. Ricoeur, *T&N I*, 77–80.

[78] To know more about previous scholars' investigations on this issue, see Paul Ricoeur, "Between Rhetoric and Poetics: Aristotle," in *The Rule of Metaphor* (Toronto: University of Toronto Press, 1977), 9–43; Paul Ricoeur, "Rhetoric – Poetics – Hermeneutics," in *From Metaphysics to Rhetoric*, ed. Michel Meyer (Dordrecht: Springer Netherlands, 1989), 137–49 (henceforth "RPH"); Eugene E. White, *The Context of Human Discourse: A Configurational Criticism of Rhetoric* (Columbia: University of South Carolina Press, 1992), 3–43; Michal Beth Dinkler, "New Testament Rhetorical Narratology: An Invitation toward Integration," *BibInt* 24, no. 2 (2016): 203–28; Andreea Deciu Ritivoi, *Paul Ricoeur: Tradition and Innovation in Rhetorical Theory* (New York: State University of New York Press, 2006), 49–94; Christopher D. Stanley, *Arguing with Scripture: The Rhetoric of Quotations in the Letters of Paul* (New York: T&T Clark International, 2004), 1–74.

[79] Ritivoi, *Tradition and Innovation in Rhetorical Theory*, 14, quoting Ricoeur, "RPH," 139.

[80] Ritivoi, *Tradition and Innovation in Rhetorical Theory*, 49.

[81] Ibid., 14. Ritivoi is careful to point out the presence of two different concepts of *doxa* from classical rhetoric and contemporary rhetoric: "In contemporary rhetorical theory we can distinguish two meanings of the classical term doxa. The first is more faithful to the classical heritage; it therefore stems from an epistemic perspective grounded in the contrast between certainty and probability. The second unfolds along a social and cultural dimension and is concerned with sets of beliefs widely espoused by particular audiences." See ibid., 50.

[82] Ibid., 14, quoting Ricoeur, "RPH," 143.

[83] Ritivoi, *Tradition and Innovation in Rhetorical Theory*, 14–15; Otfried Höffe, *Aristotle*, ed. Anthony Preus, trans. Christine Salazar (New York: State University of New York Press, 2003), 35. While categories of Aristotelian rhetoric like *logos, pathos*, and *ethos* have been useful in scholars' previous analyzing of Paul's persuasion strategy, they would not receive attention in this book.

Second, my analysis of the underlying temporality of Paul's text enables me to explain and elaborate Eugene White's rhetorical theory within the context of mimesis3, in which the Philippian community are invited to follow a forward teleological structure.[84] Specifically speaking, the analogies between the text (e.g., The Epistle to the Philippians) and the readers' concern and promotion of "further movement toward closure" will be articulated by an emplotment process whose configurative operation produces a structure that invites the readers to join its teleological movement.[85] Successful promotion from the outset *toward* the closure/ending of any one narrative would then attest that particular narrative's rhetorical impact as prevalent over others'. In this work, this impact would be decided upon the best concordance (a narrated continuity) proposed among the Philippian community's previous *seeing* of Paul's evangelistic efforts (Phil. 1:30, Acts 16:11-40), their current hearing of Paul's imprisonment (Phil. 1:30, 1:12-18), and their memory of the ongoing suffering arising from their refusal to participate in the local imperial worship since their reception of the gospel (Phil. 1:3-8). The concordance will be evaluated and validated by how well the "grand" historical trajectory, of which the recent story of Christ is comprised, best coheres with the Philippian community's "little" narrative.[86]

3.2 Temporality and the Making of Identity

One feature which permeates all of the components of the threefold mimesis is the concept of temporality.[87] The application of this temporality starts with the temporal manner by which heterogeneous and contingent incidents are selected and ordered together into a whole,[88] producing units of "Beginning," "Middle," and "Ending."[89] It is the identity marker of a narrative, or a text undergirded by a narrative.[90] As a

---

[84] White, *The Context of Human Discourse*, 216. "To begin persuading, an advocate must meet readers and listeners where they are at the outset of the communication. He or she must provide them with language and ideas that will enable them to perceive analogies between what is being said and some aspect of their own relevant knowledge, beliefs, values, attitudes, and behaviors. . . . To promote further movement toward closure, the persuader must enable his or her readers/listeners to enlarge and reinforce the initial beachheads of identification and to perceive fresh areas of identification."

[85] Cf. Ricoeur, *T&N I*, 132–42; Abbott, "Story, Plot, and Narration," 43; Dowling, *Ricoeur on Time and Narrative*, 40–1.

[86] In order to restore the concordance of a religious narrative (testimony), the narrator must be able to incorporate both the "grand narrative" of God, which deals with His cosmological plan of salvation across epic time scales, and those "little narratives" of people, which deal with their daily life stories and life plans. See Ricoeur, *T&N I*, 29–30; Ricoeur, *OAA*, 175; Anthony C. Thiselton, "The Hermeneutics of Doctrine as a Hermeneutic of Temporal and Communal Narrative," in *The Hermeneutics of Doctrine* (Grand Rapids: Wm. B. Eerdmans, 2007), 66.

[87] Conceptually speaking, regarding the aspects of theology and philosophy, temporality (*Zeitlichkeit*) refers to the kind of foundation upon which we study concepts of truth, revelation, narrative, time, death, promise, hope, and identity. See Ricoeur, *T&N I*, 61.

[88] Ricoeur, *T&N II*, 23; Ricoeur, *OAA*, 141–2.

[89] Pellauer, "Narrated Action Grounds Narrative Identity," 77.

[90] Within the field of Ricoeurian study, Pol Vandevelde has offered us a good summary of how Ricoeur develops the relation between a text (writing down) of human actions and the phenomenon of narrative. According to Vandevelde, through qualifying human lives and actions as having a prenarrative structure, Ricoeur not only builds an intrinsic correlation between text and action, but

distinguishing theme, temporality is known for its enduring temporal thought, which is to be received by a person as the paradigm of her own experience of life. As a nonchronological temporal structure, temporality is also characterized as a teleological and layered structure through which a reader can interact with the stories of her own and others (to be explained later).

3.2.1 Assessing the Degree of Coherence across Narratives

This concept of temporality will be applied to this work in a few ways. First of all, it allows us to assess the degree of coherence across multiple narratives.[91] One method for testing if two narratives share the same temporality is to identify the meaning they assign to an individual occurrence. If the conferred meanings are the same in both, then it is more likely that they share the same temporally configured thought. The more of such tests they pass, the more likely that they share the same temporality. Among them there exists a coherent relationship. On the contrary, if the conferred meanings differ and even contradict each other, their temporally configured thoughts would likely be different and thus probably compete against each other. They are then marked as incoherent to one another. This capacity of comparing and contrasting temporally configured thoughts forms my basis in showing the coherency between the stories of Christ and Paul, and the incoherency between the stories of Christ and Paul's opponents.

3.2.2 Nesting of Narratives: Articulating the Processes of Paul's Theological Thinking

Besides assessing the similarity and difference between narratives, the temporality of a narrative can be used to mark the shaping of meaning from one narrative to another. If I read Ricoeur correctly, building on the similarity between human time and its limit (eternity) within a person's engagement with the eternal story of God, a person's response to God can be explicated through a *continuous nesting of structures of time*, in which she either approaches or withdraws from God's eternal plan.[92] Our relationship

---

also the narrative quality within the writing (objectification) of meaningful actions. Texts of human actions are thus narrated actions. For details, see Pol Vandevelde, "The Challenge of the 'such as it was': Ricoeur's Theory of Narratives," in *Reading Ricoeur*, ed. David M. Kaplan (New York: SUNY Press, 2008), 141–7; Ricoeur, *T&N I*, 58–60, 74; Ricoeur, *From Text to Action*, 152.

[91] One particular challenge intrinsic to the issue of the NT use of the OT is the discernment and hence validation of correspondence or echo between particular NT and OT passages. Hays has proposed seven tests to cope with "varying degrees of certainty in our efforts to identify and interpret intertextual echoes." See Richard B. Hays, *Echoes of Scripture in the Letters of Paul* (New Haven: Yale University Press, 1989), 29–32. For a revised version of Hays's tests, see Leroy A. Huizenga, *The New Isaac: Tradition and Intertextuality in the Gospel of Matthew* (Leiden: Brill, 2012), 63–5. See also G. K. Beale and D. A. Carson, *Commentary on the New Testament Use of the Old Testament* (Grand Rapids: Baker Academic, 2007), xxiv–xxvi.

[92] "The third way in which the dialectic of time and eternity affects the interpretation of the *distentio animi* is no less important. At the very heart of temporal experience, it produces a hierarchy of levels of temporalization, according to how close or how far a given experience approaches or moves away from the pole of eternity." See Ricoeur, *T&N I*, 28.

with the eternity one fundamentally consists in a temporal hierarchization which is best articulated through a structure of levels of stories.[93] Our experience of God is then necessarily mediated by a continuous nesting of stories, in which *the meaning of a previous story blends with that of a current one.*[94] It is with this particular nested or stacked nature of the interplaying stories that I will approach the articulation of Paul's theological thinking. Specifically, this investigation will show that the making of Paul's narrative world is characterized by processes of nesting episodes from a particular level of story on top of episodes from another level. As the following exegesis will show, a majority of these nesting stories in Philippians involve a blending of meanings through a kind of "creative resonance" between passages from the NT and the OT (graphically speaking, a story of Paul nested on top of a story of OT).[95] Regarding this nesting process, there are five aspects to be analyzed.

First, regarding the kind of resonance between Paul's own story and the alluded OT stories, the logic of Hays would be a good starting point.[96] Relying on John Hollander's work, Hays articulates the allusive echo as a trope of metalepsis or transumption (metaphorical transference).[97] According to Hays, metalepsis is "a rhetorical and poetic device in which one text alludes to an earlier text in a way that evokes resonances of the earlier text beyond those explicitly cited. The result is that the interpretation of a metalepsis requires the reader to recover unstated or suppressed correspondences between the two texts."[98] When an NT passage alludes to an earlier OT passage, "the figurative effect of the echo can lie in the unstated or suppressed (transumed) points of resonance between the two texts."[99] In contrast, in this work I argue according to Ricoeur's narrative theories explicated in temporal and teleological terms. In particular, it is along pair(s) of parallel trajectories of upper and lower-level stories, which share sets of dialectic of discordance and concordance, sequence and configuration, sedimentation and innovation, discontinuity and continuity, that new meanings on the level of Paul's story are created over those lower levels of story. What is common, though, is that the scope of echo or resonance considered within the allusion

---

[93] Ibid., 28–30, 84–5.
[94] Cf. Ricoeur, *T&N I*, 28–30; Thiselton, "Hermeneutic of Temporal and Communal Narrative," 66; Bishop of Hippo Saint Augustine, *The Confessions of St. Augustine*, trans. E. B. Pusey (Oak Harbor, WA: Logos Research Systems, Inc., 1996), 11:29:39, 30.40.
[95] A similar effort has been made by J. Gerald Janzen. Based on the work of Richard Hays (*Echoes of Scripture in the Letters of Paul*), Janzen approaches resonance as a kind of intertextual overtone operating between specific earlier OT texts and later Pauline texts. See J. Gerald Janzen, "Toward a Hermeneutics of Resonance: A Methodological Interlude between the Testaments," in *When Prayer Takes Place: Forays into a Biblical World*, ed. Brent A. Strawn (Eugene: Wipf and Stock Publisher, 2012), 244.
[96] Not all scholars support Hays's approach. For critiques of Hays's approach, see Bryan D. Estelle, *Echoes of Exodus: Tracing a Biblical Motif* (Downers Grove: InterVarsity Press, 2018), 28–60; Paul Foster, "Echoes without Resonance: Critiquing Certain Aspects of Recent Scholarly Trends in the Study of the Jewish Scriptures in the New Testament," *JSNT* 38, no. 1 (2015): 108–9; David A. Shaw, "Converted Imaginations? The Reception of Richard Hays's Intertextual Method," *CBR* 11 (2013): 234–45.
[97] Hays, *Echoes of Scripture*, 20–4; John Hollander, *The Figure of Echo: A Mode of Allusion in Milton and After* (Berkeley: University of California Press, 1981), ix.
[98] Richard B. Hays, *The Conversion of the Imagination: Paul as Interpreter of Israel's Scripture* (Grand Rapids: Wm. B. Eerdmans, 2005), 2.
[99] Ibid., 20.

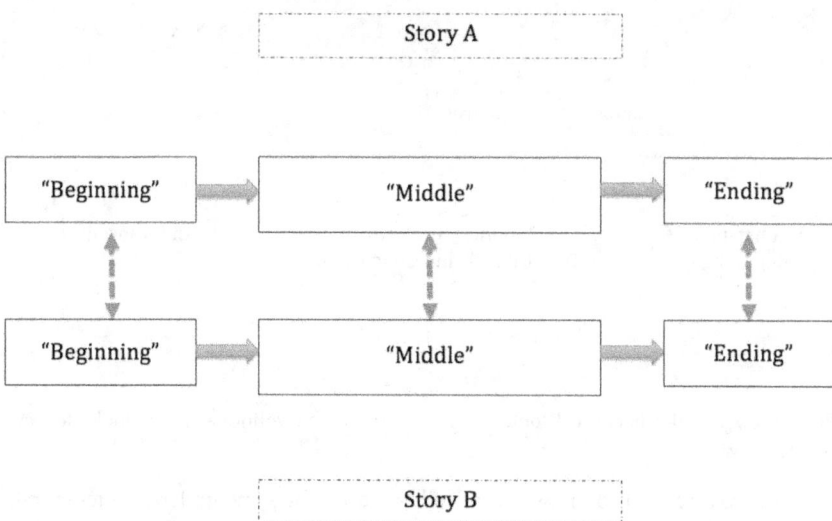

Figure 3 Three hooked moments inside the nesting of narratives.

will go beyond the alluded OT verse into its immediate literary context. Regarding the scale of the literary context of the cited OT passage, each allusion would be decided individually.[100]

Second, just as each story is constituted by units of a "Beginning," a "Middle," and an "Ending," nested episodes will be interconnected between these three units, marking the three key nodal points.[101] In other words, the "Beginning" of story "A" will be hooked to the "Beginning" of story "B," the "Middle" of story "A" will be hooked to the "Middle" of story "B," and the "Ending" of story "A" will be hooked to the "Ending" of story "B" (see Figure 3).[102]

Third, while demarcations between these continuous units of time are bound to be fuzzy in nature, categorizing them into such a framework will not only help uncover the alignment and key resonances between respective units of the stories,[103] but also enable the subsequent analysis of the nested stories according to various temporal categories. Such categories may be the forward-looking approach of a volitional agent, the backward-looking nature of a narrator, and the dialectic of concordance

---

[100] Cf. Lyn Nixon, "New Testament Quotation at the Reader-Author Intersection: Evoking Story for Transformation" (PhD, Middlesex University, 2015), 28; L. Hartman, "Scriptural Exegesis in the Gospel of St. Matthew and the Problem of Communication," in *L'Évangile selon Matthieu: Rédaction et théologie*, ed. M. Didier (Gembloux: Duculot, 1972), 151–2, in which Lyn Nixon quotes the work of L. Hartman and addresses the scale of the cited OT literary context.

[101] J. Gerald Janzen, "Creation and New Creation in Philippians 1:6," *Horizons in Biblical Theology* 18, no. 1 (1996): 34–7. According to Janzen, many stories in the Bible are embedded into larger narratives by attaching their own points of starting and ending to those of the larger narratives. Regarding these points, he calls them "nodal points of a narrative pattern."

[102] Within this web of multiple allusions and connections, each pair of alluded points or episodes within a single pair of stories or among pairs of stories does not operate independently. Instead, each alluded relation must relate coherently to the whole web of relations.

[103] For previous discussions of the nature of this resonance, see p.71f.

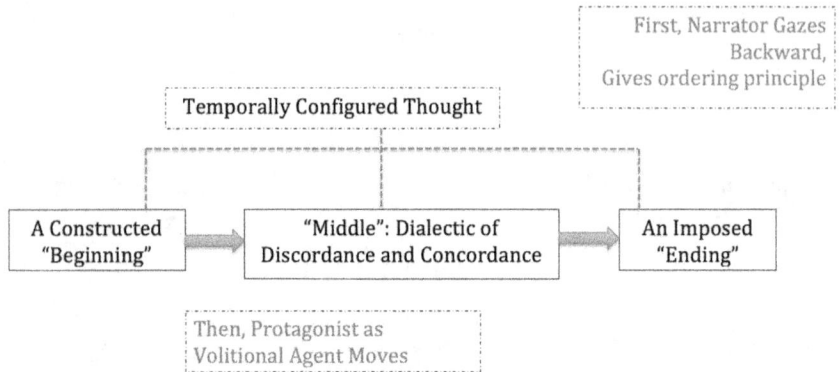

Figure 4 After the backward-looking of a narrator, the volitional agent looks forward accordingly.

and discordance, and so on, which are all based on the same underlying temporally configured thought (see Figure 4).[104] In particular, the "Beginning" of this structure identifies the opening stage of a temporal sequence;[105] the "Middle" contains the temporal phase in which discordant contingencies or sudden reversals of circumstances (from good to bad) arise, demanding choices, explanations, concordance, and meaning;[106] and the "Ending" marks the point of closure in which judgment is made, giving meaning to the narrated actions, rendering a concordant unity.

Fourth, while the understanding of each set of nested stories is not characterized in a mechanical way of one story strictly following another, I argue that *Paul puts these stories together with a clear agenda: to strengthen his case as he contests against his various opponents that his story (level four) is the legitimate narrative representation of the story of Christ (level three)*.[107] With this particular bearing, the story of Christ will *always* take theological precedence in providing the temporally configured thought in its nesting with other stories.[108] In other words, stories on levels one, two, four, and five

---

[104] These expressions, together with the demarcations, are all part of a narrative time which is constituted by a dialectic of physical (cosmological) time and psychological (phenomenological) time. While none of these expressions can exhaustively express the underlying temporally configured thought, what is significant is that they refer to the same temporally configured thought coherently encompassing themselves. Thus each one of them can be used to represent or epitomize the underlying temporal identity of the narrative. See Ricoeur, *T&N II*, 4–5.

[105] Ricoeur writes, "What defines the beginning is not the absence of some antecedent but the absence of necessity in the succession." See Ricoeur, *T&N I*, 38.

[106] Ricoeur, *T&N I*, 38–9, 73, 207; Ricoeur, *T&N II*, 25; Ricoeur, "Life in Quest," 32; Currie, *The Unexpected*, 37. Reflecting the work of Ricoeur, Currie comments, "These reversals of fortune, which Aristotle called *peripeteia*, and might include chance occurrences or conscious choices, are the umbrella under which literary critics have discussed events which turn things upside down in a narrative."

[107] According to Ricoeur, this production of meaning belongs to a kind of productive imagination, similar to the semantic innovation he talks about in *The Rule of Metaphor* and *T&N I*. See Paul Ricoeur, *The Rule of Metaphor: Multi-Disciplinary Studies of the Creation of Meaning in Language*, University of Toronto Romance Series (Toronto: University of Toronto Press, 1981), 5–6, 125, 310; Ricoeur, *T&N I*, ix–x, 68–76.

[108] There will *not* be any transition to another era of God's salvation in the future. Such *terminal* nature of this story of Christ means that suffering on behalf of Christ has become the *ultimate* manner

will be interpreted in a direction according to the temporality of the story of Christ (level three). Even for the nested structures of stories not directly involving the story of Christ (e.g., a story of Paul nested over a story of Job as level four over two), the hermeneutics of this nested structure will unfold according to such an agenda.

Lastly, while it is common to see people making sense of their present story by nesting it over one from the past story of God, not every nesting represents a truthful narrative representation of the story of God.[109] In fact, I argue that it is within a contestation of representing the stories of God, Israel, and Christ on levels one to three that Paul, on level four, contends against the Jewish Christian leaders. A truthful reception and articulation of God's revelation is one that nests these levels of story according to God's situational demand (His righteousness).[110] There is thus an implicit yet intrinsic dimension of controversy of "truthfulness" (ἀλήθεια) within each nesting of stories.[111] There is a bifurcation within each nesting of one's own story with God's previous ones, which does not necessarily align oneself and others to the intended appropriation of the story of God. According to Ricoeur, through this nesting of stories one has a capacity to "approach" or "move away from" God's eternal plan.[112]

3.2.3 "Alluded Stories": Serving Paul's Agenda in Contestation

Another corollary of this agenda regarding the hermeneutics of the nesting structure is that all the "alluded stories" in Paul's narrative world are not copies of objectively available stories, as if their meanings are universally accepted, readily available, and impartial "commentaries" on those stories. Instead, all the pieces of Paul's "alluded story," including the stories of Job, Isaiah, Jeremiah, Psalms, Exodus, Numbers, Daniel, and even the story of Christ, emerge as Paul's engaged, tailor-made, and creatively synthesized version of those stories, which *function primarily to serve his present agenda*. However, it is important to note that even with new meanings beyond the original context being created within Paul's allusion, the original meaning of the various OT passages is not excised.[113]

---

of believers' participation in God's master plan of salvation (cf. Gal. 1:8-9). In other words, the Lordship of YHWH is now on its way of being fulfilled *eschatologically* in Christ. This story of Christ has taken on the supremacy from which all other levels of story must follow.

[109] Cf. Ricoeur, *T&N I*, 28.

[110] Instead of meaning a state of righteousness as granted from God the Judge, the righteousness here means more of God's practical action of redemption which demands people's rightful response and narration. See BDAG, s.v. "δικαιοσύνη," 247. For more details on the meaning of δικαιοσύνη in Philippians as understood by this work, see note 62 on p.149, and p.159.

[111] Cf. Martin Heidegger, "The Origin of the Work of Art," in *Poetry, Language, Thought*, trans. Albert Hofstadter (New York: Harper Perennial Modern Classics, 2013), 49; Sophie Vlacos, *Ricoeur, Literature and Imagination* (New York: Bloomsbury Publishing, 2014), 78; Josef Bleicher, *Contemporary Hermeneutics: Hermeneutics as Method, Philosophy and Critique* (London: Routledge, 1980), 117. Ricoeur's approach to knowledge treats the issue of *Aletheia* or truth in a Heideggerian sense. The concept highlighted does not belong to an objective or absolute one, but something that points to the disclosure of an ontological world.

[112] Ricoeur, *T&N I*, 28–30; *Confessions* 11:29:39, 30.40; Alice Bennett, *Afterlife and Narrative in Contemporary Fiction* (Hampshire: Palgrave Macmillan, 2012), 49–50.

[113] In a work that analyzes the relationship between the concept of intertextuality and NT use of OT, Leroy A. Huizenga expounds Stefan Alkier's model of intertextuality and leans toward an

Concerning this manner of understanding Paul's allusion of OT in which new meanings beyond the original context are read, DiMattei has suggested that rather than identifying Paul's logic as according to some post-Pauline hermeneutical antithesis of typology against allegory,[114] there exists a new "extrabiblical story" inside Paul's reading which the OT biblical details function as exegetical linchpins.[115] In other words, with Paul's own context as the new story, the OT storyline has been *extended* to incorporate elements found not in the OT but in the NT.[116] DiMattei's analysis fits quite nicely with my methodology. One clear difference would be that the way I see Paul "extend" the OT story is through a hierarchy or nesting of Paul's own story over a creatively alluded story of the OT passage.[117]

Specifically, it is with respect to the temporality and its pertinent narrative sequence of each "alluded story" that Paul finds it useful to connect the stories of his own and the Philippian community so that events of his time could be narrated according to him. Instead of restricting a fixed or mechanical relation between the alluded OT story and Paul's NT story, the function of each nesting of narratives will be evaluated on a case-by-case basis.[118] Formally speaking, it is within the resonance of both similarity and difference, along the temporal trajectory, that I analyze Paul's narrative dynamics and

understanding of NT use of OT in which both the OT original context and NT context are taken into consideration. Huizenga writes, "Interpretation, then, is both dynamic and constrained: constrained, because interpreting a particular text involves examining its particular relations to the appropriate encyclopedia (['the cultural framework in which the text is situated and from which the gaps of the text are filled']) from which it was produced, but also dynamic, because texts have infinite potential connections to other texts and cultures, even those which do not yet exist." See Leroy A. Huizenga, "The Old Testament in the New, Intertextuality and Allegory," *JSNT* 38, no. 1 (2015): 19; Stefan Alkier, "Intertextuality and the Semiotics of Biblical Texts," in *Reading the Bible Intertextually*, ed. Richard B. Hays, Stefan Alkier, and Leroy A. Huizenga (Waco: Baylor University Press, 2015), 8. Cf. Hays, *Echoes of Scripture*, 19, in which Hays's reliance onHollander's theory seems to have provided a foundation for paying attention to both the "old voices" and "new acoustical environments."

In other words, while Paul has not confined himself to the "original" or "identical" meaning of the OT passages, his allusion still bears senses of continuity and coherence with the original contexts and hence reflects his prudent consideration in the allusions. In this work, by means of the model of the nesting of stories, I intend to show the alluded story as a *depicted* version of the original passage, with which Paul's own story now resonates. Cf. Stanley, *Arguing with Scripture*, in which Stanley argues that Paul's OT quotation strategies "manipulate[d] both the source text and the audience" (p.36), cited the OT "without regard for their original context" (p.100), and potentially hurt his trustworthiness and rhetorical effectiveness. For a critique of Stanley's viewpoint, see Steve Moyise, review of *Arguing with Scripture: The Rhetoric of Quotations in the Letters of Paul*, by *JSNT* 27 (2005): 86.

[114] DiMattei is careful to distinguish the *exegetical principle* typology from the typological *use* of the OT. See Steven DiMattei, "Biblical Narratives," in *As It Is Written: Studying Paul's Use of Scripture*, ed. Stanley E. Porter and Christopher D. Stanley (Atlanta: SBL, 2008), 62n.12.

[115] Ibid., 91.

[116] Ibid., 87.

[117] To know more about DiMattei's analysis of the relationship between the OT and the NT story, see ibid., 90–3.

[118] A complete review of the relationship between Paul's hermeneutical practice and his contemporary Jewish custom is beyond the scope of this book. What suffices here is that this investigation emphasizes the "Jewishness" of Paul's hermeneutical principles with the view that Paul was someone whose theologizing originates from an innovating of his Jewish tradition. Paul indeed imparts his current situational challenges as the "extra" framework in bringing out the alluded meaning of the various OT passages. Such approach is in line with his contemporary Jewish exegetical practices. To know more about Paul's Jewish hermeneutical practices, see ibid., 77; Watson, *Paul and the*

rhetorical strategy.[119] Practically speaking, I argue that the temporality and in particular the teleology of these "alluded stories" provide the basis of coherence with which Paul's own story resonates so that the Philippian community could be persuaded to see Paul's story not only as *a truthful and eschatological extension* of these OT stories but also of God's and their own. Thus, instead of seeing Paul's own story as a natural or static commentary on these past "alluded stories," these "alluded stories" on the contrary serve to illuminate the temporally configured thought of Paul's current story, which is about his contestation of the meaning of his suffering for the gospel.[120]

3.2.4 The Narrated Event of Christ's Death: A Christocentric Earthly Upper Limit of Time

Inspired by divergent attitudes of Augustine and Heidegger on humans' earthly upper limit of time—death—Ricoeur avers that humans, being finite creatures, will confer to themselves different ways of *narrating one's own future death*. Each of these narrations will consequently incorporate a unique understanding of the meaning of time after death—eternity—and time before death—life.[121] This upper limit of time marks the "Ending" or event of closure within each person's life narrative toward which all previous life episodes progress and receive meaning. In this work, this upper limit will not only correspond to believers' own future point of *death*, but also find its expression in the narrated event of Christ's *death* as a *Christocentric upper limit of time*. Different ways of narrating *death* become not only the chief manner of disclosing the disparity between the temporal logics of the stories of Paul and his opponents, but also the kind of historical trajectory in which the Philippian community are invited to identify. The influence of Christ's death on the meaning of suffering and resurrection within the lives of Paul and the Philippian community will also be discussed.

Hermeneutics of Faith, 1; Craig A. Evans, "Jewish Exegesis," in *DTIB*, ed. Kevin Vanhoozer (Grand Rapids: Baker Academic, 2005), 380–4.

[119] Cf. Richard B. Hays and Joel B. Green, "The Use of the Old Testament by New Testament Writers," in *Hearing the New Testament: Strategies for Interpretation*, ed. Joel B. Green (Grand Rapids: William B. Eerdmans, 1995), 228, in which Green writes, "one might inquire into how a NT writer like Paul has worked deliberately to invite his audience into a kind of echo chamber so as to hear in the current text reverberations of other texts. We can thus see him inscribing himself into the tradition, grounding his theological efforts in the solid granite of Israel's past. Hence, as we seek to understand a Pauline text we can ask: On what OT texts is this Pauline text built? This is not to say, however, that via the phenomenon of intertextuality a NT writer simply agrees with and builds on an earlier writing. Rather, his engagement with the OT might be parodic, repeating an old pattern or echoing ancient metaphors to signal difference at the very heart of similarity."

[120] The "alluded story" pertains only to the scope of a story *created out of* the story alluded, whose meaning is seen by Paul as useful to his concern. While it is easy to characterize the scope of this "alluded story" as a subset of the original whole story, with the *augmented meaning* within Paul's allusion (see p.75), I see this simple logical relation as inappropriate.

[121] Ricoeur, *T&N I*, 86; Heidegger, *Being and Time*, 372–4. Ricoeur writes, "The most serious question this work may be able to pose is to what degree a philosophical reflection on narrativity and time may aid us in thinking about *eternity and death* [my emphasis] at the same time." For a philosophical reflection of Ricoeur's understanding on "limit," see David E. Klemm, "Philosophy and Kerygma. Ricoeur as Reader of the Bible," in *Reading Ricoeur*, ed. David M. Kaplan (New York: SUNY Press, 2008), 54–5.

3.2.5 Narrative Identity of a Storyteller Acquired from the Narrative Told

Another narrative dimension crucial to my methodology is the relation between the identity of a text and that of the storyteller. According to Ricoeur, as a story unfolds, the identity of the character is constructed in correlation with the configuration of the plot.[122] The temporal dynamics within the narrative configuration of the story (mimesis2), for example, its dialectic of discordance and concordance, are transferred from the plot to the character, who is playing the role of a volitional agent, making decisions and advancing the story.[123] In the case of *a storyteller telling a story about herself*, she not only creates a narrative with a plot, but also a character with which she identifies herself as her own narrative identity.[124] As Ricoeur says, "subjects recognize themselves in the stories they tell about themselves."[125] In other words, *it is through the telling of a story that a person acquires the narrative identity which corresponds precisely to the told story's temporally configured thought.*[126]

It should not be difficult to discern the significant difference between my approach and narrative-related scholarship reviewed earlier: the source of identity. While the work of Weymouth and Nebreda employs narrative only to support the formation of a social identity structured around social categories, here the origin of a person's identity is argued to arise first and foremost from the narrative told by a person, which is structured around a person's self-interpreted temporal experience. The contestation of narratives between Paul and his opponents thus becomes a contestation of temporal structures upon which the Philippian community members would build in interpreting their temporal experiences.

3.2.6 From Narrative Identity to Ethical Identity: Character and Self-Constancy

However, there is an inherent "weakness" inside the formation of narrative identity: it is always fragile, incomplete, and open-ended.[127] In every instant of the creation of a narrative identity, there is an intrinsic nature of partiality concerning what

---

[122] Ricoeur, *OAA*, 141–3; Hall, *Paul Ricoeur and the Poetic Imperative*, 56. Ricoeur says, "The narrative constructs the identity of the character, what can be called his or her narrative identity, in constructing that of the story told. It is the identity of the story that makes the identity of the character." See Ricoeur, *OAA*, 147–8.

[123] Ricoeur, *OAA*, 143; Valérie Nicolet, *Constructing the Self: Thinking with Paul and Michel Foucault* (Tübingen: Mohr Siebeck, 2012), 130.

[124] See Ricoeur, *OAA*, 121–2, 140–51; Ricoeur, "Life," 437.

[125] Ricoeur, *T&N III*, 246–7.

[126] Ricoeur himself writes that narrative identity "rests on a temporal structure that conforms to the model of dynamic identity arising from the poetic composition of a narrative text." See Ricoeur, *T&N III*, 246. Anthony Thiselton also notes that among many different models of theorizing personal identity, Ricoeur selects a narrative approach so as to utilize its intrinsic temporal logic as his foundation to investigate a primary trait of a person: temporality." See Anthony C. Thiselton, *Interpreting God and the Postmodern Self: On Meaning, Manipulation and Promise* (Edinburgh: Wm. B. Eerdmans, 1995), 73–5.

[127] Ricoeur, *T&N III*, 207.

heterogeneous elements will be included, and to what ending the story will reach.[128] Just as the same set of events can be synthesized into different narratives, a person's narrative can allow unlimited incidents to be continuously added to it and arrive at different endings. A person's narrative identity is thus never stable and always subject to change.[129] What is perhaps more troubling is that there exists "no definitive criterion to arbitrate between the competing plots."[130] Incorporating controversial events into one's narrative, which necessarily involves the granting of meaning, results in a serious contestation of plots within the identity-formation process. Ricoeur thus suggests that *reading, and the subsequent imaginative identification with the character of a narrative, does not amount to completion of one's identity formation as proposed by that narrative.*[131] No matter how deeply one has grasped the theme of a narrative, or how many times one has read over the story, identity formation for a person cannot be assumed even though one has comprehended and sympathized with the narrative identity of a text or a story.[132]

According to Ricoeur, the formation of a person's "ethical identity" actually penetrates into *the interpersonal and teleological zone of the reader's physical world* (as opposed to the imaginative space offered by a narrative).[133] Relying on the work of Emile Benveniste on discourse as an *event* of language, Ricoeur argues that each structured work is *originally* constituted by "a series of sentences whereby someone says something to someone about something."[134] A compliant reading of a discourse is then *an ethical response to another person within the reader's physical world and life timeline*. For a reader to develop her identity which incorporates this ethical dimension, she must reject other competing narratives and make a decision to bind herself to the ethical demand of one narrative, which *allows another person to count on her continuously*.[135] A reader's response to the ethical dimension of a narrative becomes *her promise to another one, as she is held accountable for her self-endorsed responsibilities over time*.[136] Living her life in full compliance with this promise becomes her life vision and aim of a "good life."[137] Her identity is thus constructed within the promise and

---

[128] According to Ricoeur, our minds possess the capacity of running different narrative configurations for the same set of events. As we go through the temporal processes we can foretaste how the lives would be and reflect on the pertinent ethical values. We can then experiment ourselves with the "judgments of approval and condemnation" involved in each narrative configuration. It is in this manner that we understand Ricoeur who suggests that narrative serves as a laboratory for moral thought experiments. See Ricoeur, *OAA*, 115, 21–2, 40, 48.

[129] Sheppard, "Telling Contested Stories," 888.

[130] Just as there are multiple ways of joining heterogeneous events into respective narratives, there are multiple ways of configuring one's narrative identity. See Ricoeur, *T&N III*, 248; Boyd Blundell, *Paul Ricoeur between Theology and Philosophy: Detour and Return* (Indiana: Indiana University Press, 2010), 103.

[131] Ricoeur, *OAA*, 163.

[132] Ibid., 114–15, 52–68. With respect to the actualizing of identity transformation between a narrative and the reader, the best a story or a narrative-laden literature can offer is an *imaginative space* in which a reader can experiment by substituting and recognizing herself with the narrative character.

[133] Ibid., 163–8.

[134] Ricoeur, "Hermeneutical Function," 133, 38; Stiver, *Theology after Ricoeur*, 89–90; Pellauer, "Narrated Action Grounds Narrative Identity," 72–3.

[135] Ricoeur, *T&N III*, 249; Ricoeur, *OAA*, 151–2, 65–7.

[136] Ibid., 165–6.

[137] Ibid., 172.

moral commitment made before another person.[138] She recognizes herself as a "subject of imputation" within a particular promise.[139] As Ricoeur comments, "Here I am!"[140]

It is *specifically with respect to the formation of this ethical identity* that Ricoeur discusses two specific modes of narrative identity.[141] According to Ricoeur, every phenomenon of narrative identity is always *a dialectic of two continuances of human personal identity (idem and ipse)*.[142] Practically speaking, every instance of the narrative identity of a Philippian community member consists of a dialectic of her preacquired traditions/dispositions and her intentional resilience. First, there is an aspect of identity marked with its physically reidentifiable facets, continuities to established traditions, habits, and lasting dispositions.[143] Ricoeur names this *idem* (sameness), which represents the more "objective" attributes of the self over time. The second refers to the less empirically observable personal identity which relates to itself and others, makes conscious efforts and intentional resiliency in orientating the self, commits itself to ethical intentions, changes the plot, and abides by a promise.[144] Ricoeur names it *ipse* (selfhood), which represents a kind of dynamic selfhood that involves change. In a spectrum of various narrative identities, two specific modes (character and self-constancy) reside at two extreme ends.

3.2.6.1 "Pole" of Character: Lasting Dispositions of Habits, Identifications, Values, Heroes

The first mode of narrative identity is found at the "pole" of character (disposition), which is characterized with a set of lasting (*not* static) dispositions, including stable habits, acquired identifications, values, heroes, and so on.[145] Often found in the case of fairy tales for young children, this mode of narrative identity basically undergoes no change across time.[146] As the story unfolds, no shift of temporal theme is involved in the narrative configuration.[147] The character (personage) engages nothing unexpected or discordant in her emplotment, and stays the "same" by living a steady way of life with lasting dispositions. What is readily seen is continuity in her own habits and lasting dispositions in staying true to another person.

---

[138] Ibid., 165.
[139] Ibid., 167.
[140] Ibid.
[141] Ibid., 118, 65.
[142] Ibid., 140–51. Just as Ricoeur in *T&N* utilizes the temporal dimension of narrative to poetically "solve" the paradox between chronological time and phenomenological time, in *OAA* he employs the anthropological and existential dimensions to "solve" the dilemma between two kinds of personal identity: *idem* and *ipse*. Narrative identity is thus characterized by a dialectic of sameness (*idem*) and selfhood (*ipse*), which is neither an incoherent succession of occurrences as constituted only by *ipse* nor an immutable substance incapable of changing as constituted only by *idem*.
[143] Ibid., 116–24.
[144] Ibid.
[145] Ibid., 148. According to Ricoeur, in the case of a fairy tale where the protagonist experiences virtually no discordance of life, the narrative identity can be identified by a virtual overlapping of *idem* and *ipse*. This type of identity can be said to be located at one end of the spectrum of manifestations of narrative identity.
[146] Ibid., 148.
[147] In the words of threefold mimesis, no discrepancy is found between her stages of preunderstanding (mimesis1) and refiguration (mimesis3) within her continuous emplotment processes (mimesis2).

But these dispositions are by no means static and atemporal because they are acquired *over time*.[148] In the realm of human existence, it designates the habits *formed* and *sedimented* throughout a person's life.[149] It consists of previously *acquired* identifications including "values, norms, ideals, models, and heroes in which the person or the community [*intentionally*] recognizes itself."[150] Through these processes, a person progressively turns such qualities into part of her character (disposition).[151] Eventually, as she keeps engaging herself with the same qualities, she internalizes these traits into her lasting character. *Virtually no conscious effort or creative resilience is required to sustain them.*[152] The temporal experiences of her narrated past, present, and future *have all been transformed nearly perfectly* according to her professed narrative configuration. Metaphorically speaking, the personal identity (*ipse*) responsible for making conscious efforts for changing the plot and acquiring new habits and values, has been "covered up" by *a steady figure marked with a lasting character and stable narrative configuration*.[153] In the words of Ricoeur, her *ipse* has been "hidden behind" her *idem*.[154]

Such a narrative identity finds its best embodiment in the case where a person has kept her promise to another without any discordant disruptions of her professed narrative configuration. As the following exegesis will show, it is especially useful in describing the identity of the Philippian community during their long and stable time of suffering *financially* with Paul until the arrival of a set of discordant events: Paul's imprisonment, the heightened persecution of the community by Philippi's local authorities, and the reception of a divergent testimony from the Jewish Christian leaders regarding the meaning of Paul's suffering.

3.2.6.2 *"Pole" of Self-Constancy: Keeping One's Words without Support from Lasting Dispositions*

Then, in keeping her commitment to another person, what should a person do when unexpected and discordant events happen in her worldly life, which seem unable to be fitted into her previous narrative configuration? This brings us to what Ricoeur calls the "pole" of self-constancy (another end of the spectrum),[155] which is useful in analyzing the experience of sustaining one's words in a promise *amid unfavourable circumstances and contesting narratives.*

In this keeping of her promise, instead of relying on her sedimented habits and lasting disposition, a person *intentionally takes the initiative* to stay faithful to another

---

[148] Ibid., 120.
[149] Every habit begins under the initiative of *ipse*, and then slowly cements itself into part of *idem*. Ibid., 121.
[150] Ibid., 121.
[151] Ibid.
[152] Ibid., 118–25.
[153] Ibid., 122.
[154] Harry Kunneman, "Ethical Complexity," in *Complexity, Difference and Identity: An Ethical Perspective (Issues in Business Ethics)*, ed. Paul Cilliers and Rika Preiser (London: Springer, 2010), 142.
[155] Ricoeur, *OAA*, 119, 65.

person.[156] Although she could be worn down by various unrelenting challenges over time, and many unfavorable circumstances threaten her promise, she still makes herself dependable for that person.

Such fidelity can become seriously challenged when a severe degree of discordance is introduced. While the life story at the "pole" of character is marked by the phenomenon in which every new event is *readily* absorbed to consolidate the "same" narrative identity, for the life story at the "pole" of self-constancy such readiness has been seriously disturbed. *Without renewed habits, identifications, or heroes which help explain the unexpected discordances, a person's narrative configuration cannot be refreshed or modified to undergird her thinking in coping with the new adverse situation.* Without an updated narrative configuration, previous concordance and pertinent conviction is weakened. The previous *doxa* endorsed by a person (or community) no longer best fits and explains her new situation. The stronger the discordance she has faced, the more confusion or disorientation she could feel.

She is forced to live a life and pattern of behavior constituted by an altered narrative world whose temporal dynamics are very different from the world she previously acknowledged.[157]

The bigger the discrepancy between her previously embraced temporality and the one forced into her life, the bigger the challenge for her to keep her promise to another one. In other words, the bigger the discrepancy, the stronger intentional resilience would be required to keep her fidelity to another one.

Facing this situation, she can no longer rely on her previous stable habits and dispositions resulting from her lasting narrative configuration. In fact, new dispositions, which run against her promise, could have already emerged due to the new and discordant experiences.[158] For her to keep her promise to another, she must *intentionally withstand* new tensions evoked from these conflicting tendencies, which would lead to other narrative configurations and identities with divergent ethical values.[159] Without much support from a continuity to past traditions (*idem*), what becomes prominent is then not a steady figure of lasting dispositions, but a personal figure of conscious resilience or perseverance (*ipse*) that intentionally constructs a constancy to "hold firm" to her words against other competing narratives.[160] The

---

[156] For references, see ibid., 16, 167.
[157] Ibid., 320. Narratives not only enable us to articulate and evaluate the actions we act, but also the actions we receive from other people.
[158] Even though these dispositions may not have sedimented themselves to the point of lasting ones. See Kunneman, "Ethical Complexity," 143. Here Kunneman gives an example to illustrate the introduction of such new dispositions: "Such a form of self constancy, as exhibited for instance in the constancy of friendship or the constancy of other intimate relations, do indeed embody a different form of permanence in time, because a promise to be faithful can lead to great tensions and even conflicts with specific dispositions embodied in *idem* identity, for example, a disposition to be thrilled by new erotic experiences and the concomitant tensions with a promise to be faithful to a partner."
[159] Ricoeur, *OAA*, 167–8; Mallett and Wapshott, "Challenges of Identity Work," 274–5. Ricoeur writes, "Between the imagination that says, 'I can try anything' and the voice that says, 'Everything is possible...' a muted discord is sounded. It is this discord that the act of promising transforms into a fragile concordance: 'I can try anything,' to be sure, but 'Here is where I stand!'"
[160] Metaphorically speaking, her *ipse* has "emerged" out of the "shadow" of her *idem*, causing a "gap" between them. See Ricoeur, *OAA*, 122; Kunneman, "Ethical Complexity," 142.

bigger the discrepancy between a person's previously embraced temporality and the one forced into her life, the bigger the tension that arises.[161]

Such a narrative identity finds its exemplary embodiment in the case where a person keeps her promise to another amid serious discordances. As the following exegesis will show, it is useful in analyzing the identity of the Philippian community during the time when they respond to the various discordant events (Paul's imprisonment, the heightened persecution toward the community by Philippi's local authorities, and the reception of a contesting testimony of the Jewish Christian leaders) that occur in their lives. How can Paul renew the community's habits, identifications, and heroes that could help them face these challenges? How can Paul refresh their narrative configuration that could undergird their thinking within the new adverse situation? What could the community members do if they have not perfectly developed the trait of suffering for the gospel into their character?

With these two modes of narrative identity mentioned above, my research should be able to separate the community's identity-formation process into multiple temporal stages. While scholars tend to oversimplify the "spiritual" condition of the Philippian community into one simple state,[162] along each member's identity-formation stages I argue that each instance of the community member's narrative identity, which is comprised of different dialectics between a member's preacquired traditions/dispositions and intentional resilience, evolves within the contestation of testimonies between Paul and the Jewish Christian leaders. A more rigorous analysis of the temporal logic and roles of the community members' traditions and intentional agencies will be provided.

3.2.7 Applying the Threefold Mimesis and Temporality Models to the Narrative Dynamics of Philippians

This sums up my introduction to the theories of threefold mimesis and temporality from Ricoeur. Based on the reciprocity between narrative and the temporal experience of humanity, I hope I have shown the potential of employing narrative theory to analyze and elucidate the temporal experiences of Paul and the Philippian community. With the soon-to-be-constructed prereading situation (mimesis1), the temporally analyzed theologizing process (mimesis2), and the corresponding temporal reading experience (mimesis3), I argue that Ricoeur's threefold mimesis, along with its concept of temporality and the formation of identity, can indeed enable us to thoroughly investigate Paul's identity-shaping strategies toward the Philippian community. Specifically, these tools will be used to disclose and explicate the theme of contestation of narratives, which is seen to be the defining phenomenon in this work.

To complete my coverage of Ricoeur's theory and its pertinent application, in the section that follows I will summarize Ricoeur's philosophical reflection on a person's

---

[161] Ricoeur, *OAA*, 122.
[162] For example, Weymouth equates the state of the community with the general mainstream culture of Philippi society and calls the community some "status-obsessed hearers." For details of Weymouth's research, see p.33ff.

experience of God: testimony. What is noteworthy is that a person's interpretation of God's actions will also influence her own self-understanding, changing the narrative in which she looks both at God and herself.[163] A person's self-understanding or identity is thus closely predicated on her perception of God. It is with such significance that I begin to introduce this philosophical reflection, and explore its corollaries on the theme of the contestation of testimonies.

3.3 The Hermeneutics of Testimony

One of the central arguments of my work is that the narratives contesting with one another in Philippians are not just interpretations of historical events, but also theological claims that speak about an understanding of God.[164] When we pay attention to the proposed contingent situation of Philippians, the controversy of ascertaining one's revelatory experience of God comes clearly to the fore. However, previous narrative scholarship on Philippians has largely ignored the epistemological dimension within one's reception and confirmation of the transcendent revelation from God. What has been overlooked pertains to *the justification and falsification of the self-engaged testimonies of God's revelations among believers as to which is the genuine representation of the story of Christ*. It is regarding the epistemology of one's revelatory experience that we analyze *Paul's story as a response to the call of God, and as a witness to the Philippian community*. What needs to be explored are the dynamics within these unique relationships, and how they will contribute to our understanding of the identity formation of the Philippian community inside a contestation of religious narratives.

3.3.1 Dialectic of External Narration and Internal Conviction

In the essay "The Hermeneutics of Testimony" (HT), Ricoeur avers that within a witness's reception of revelation, there is always a dialectic of an "external" narration of events ("quasi-empirical") and an "internal" confession of conviction.[165] On the "external" side, within her narration (mimesis2) of a set of contingent events, the witness has "observed" and identified certain actions of God.[166] On the "internal" side, she has found this interpreted narration coherent with her usual criterion of the discernment of God's actions (Ricoeur calls it the "criteriology of the divine").[167] As

---

[163] Ricoeur, "HT," 147–53; Hall, *Paul Ricoeur and the Poetic Imperative*, 78.
[164] Cf. George W. Stroup, *The Promise of Narrative Theology* (Atlanta: Wipf & Stock Pub, 1997), 193.
[165] Ricoeur, "HT," 133–5.
[166] Testimony is also comprised of an emplotment process as described by the mimesis process. Thus, every making of a testimony is marked by its creative process of organizing heterogeneous incidents into a unified whole. Out of the same set of events, multiple different testimonies can be made. Thus, the narrative world of the testimony is not an exact replica of the events, but a self-involved and ethically engaged organization.
[167] Ricoeur, "HT," 131–4; Stiver, *Theology after Ricoeur*, 200. According to Ricoeur, this "criteriology of the divine" comes through a person's self-understanding when she allows herself "to be governed by what is manifested and said" from her own narration. See Paul Ricoeur, "Toward a Hermeneutic of the Idea of Revelation," in *Essays on Biblical Interpretation*, ed. L. S. Mudge (Philadelphia: Fortress, 1980), 97.

Ariaan Baan similarly comments: "Testimony is not a report about observed facts but an exterior, visible action attesting to an interior and invisible conviction or faith."[168]

What is significant to the theme of contestation is that testimony is always found in a "quasijuridical" lawsuit setting in which parties argue against each other for their claims.[169] When Paul, the original witness, proclaims his testimony, the Philippian community must take the role of a judge to decide on the authenticity of the testimony: "does the narration of the Paul fit our understanding of God?"[170] In this manner, an *interpreted* testimony from the source (Paul) becomes the *object of interpretation* to the hearers (the Philippian community), who in turn will interpret and judge the narration against their own "criteriology of the divine."[171] By checking its coherency with their professed theological traditions, they will produce their own narration of the original event, giving rise to a never-ending chain of interpretations.[172] Should the Philippian community trust Paul's testimony, or that of his opponents?

3.3.2 The Self-Engaged Nature of Testimony

One of the implications of the above theories is that *self-engagement* is essential in testimony to receive the revelation from God. Based on Ricoeur, Bauckham thus asserts that an "eyewitness ... offers us engaged interpretation, for in testimony fact and meaning co-inhere."[173] An engaged witness "sees" something disclosed in what just happened.[174] *Quasi-empirical narrations of historical and external "facts," and engaged interpretations out of theological and internal convictions co-inhere.*[175] The quasi-empirical aspect and the confessional aspect of a testimony are always inseparable (but not indescribable).[176] Paul's testimony is ultimately an account of his *self-engaged experience* of the Lord, not a lecture of theological proposition.[177] The whole reception process of testimony is characterized by *a knowledge of the probable*, rather than an objectively verifiable certainty.[178]

3.3.3 Contestation of Convictions: Truthfulness of a Testimony

With this engaged and unverifiable nature, it is not surprising to find that testimony, especially the kind that involves a deviation from the traditional way of understanding

---

[168] Ariaan W. Baan, *The Necessity of Witness: Stanley Hauerwas's Contribution to Systematic Theology* (Eugene: Pickwick Publications, 2015), 110.
[169] Ibid., 108; Ricoeur, "HT," 128.
[170] Ibid., 133–4.
[171] Ibid., 133–4, 40, 45; Jean Greisch, "Testimony and Attestation," in *Paul Ricoeur: The Hermeneutics of Action*, ed. Richard M. Kearney (New Delhi: Sage Publications, 1996), 82.
[172] Ricoeur, "HT," 123, 33–46.
[173] Richard Bauckham, *Jesus and the Eyewitnesses: The Gospels as Eyewitness Testimony* (Grand Rapids: Wm. B. Eerdmans, 2008), 487–508.
[174] Bauckham, *Jesus and the Eyewitnesses*, 507.
[175] Ibid., 404.
[176] Ibid., 505; Ricoeur, "HT," 136–47. We simply cannot understand testimony as disengaged observer.
[177] Ricoeur, "Idea of Revelation," 111.
[178] Ricoeur, "HT," 125–7.

God,[179] is always found in a contentious situation in which the witness asks to be believed among contesting testimonies: "I was there... believe me!"[180] The contestation of testimonies becomes simultaneously a contention of convictions, a contention of internal "criteriology of the divine," and even a contestation of dogmas, in which fellow "Christians" debate with one another on the proper formulae of discerning God's actions or simply, Himself.[181] Within this contestation, what can be relied upon *does not come from arguments on purely objective terms*. On what basis then can we develop criteria to differentiate a good testimony from a bad one?[182] In other words, how can Paul himself and the Philippian community come to *affirm their own testimonies as truthful, and differentiate them from the false one of his opponents*?

Here, I propose that it is precisely within this lack of objective certainty and verifiable evidences that *a mode of truthfulness marked by a dialectic of subjective and objective logic becomes the epistemological function whereby the original witness, Paul, "assures" his knowledge and conviction of God's guidance*.[183] In particular, it is based on Ricoeur's various explanative and "structural" engagements within the pursuit of the understanding of humans' personal (and collective) identity that "scientific 'explanation' and phenomenological 'understanding' converse and converge."[184] According to Ricoeur, while testimony, as a remembrance of the past, refers to an empirical account of what has happened,[185] it also bears witness to "something that cannot be seen or fully articulated."[186]

While many events of the past can be *legitimately* narrated differently, *a truthful testimony of God's revelation deserves a truthful or faithful remembrance from the future*,[187] in which the original witness and even the subsequent hearers have been *held*

---

[179] See p.73ff.
[180] Paul Ricoeur, *Memory, History, Forgetting*, trans. David Pellauer and Kathleen Blamey (Chicago: University of Chicago Press, 2004), 164–5.
[181] Such rightful discernment of God's actions (Phil. 3:9) will be one of the cornerstones of my explanation of Paul's strategy within his contestation with his fellow "Christ-followers."
[182] Ricoeur, "HT," 133–4; Bauckham, *Jesus and the Eyewitnesses*, 5.
[183] Cf. Ricoeur, "HT," 130. "The engagement of the witness in testimony is the fixed point around which the range of meaning pivots. It is this engagement that marks the difference between the false witness and the faithful and true witness."
[184] Cf. Richard M. Kearney, *On Paul Ricoeur: The Owl of Minerva: Transcending Boundaries in Philosophy and Theology* (Burlington: Ashgate Pub. Ltd., 2004), 4. Quoting Ricoeur, Kearney writes, "[Ricoeur] aimed to show how the text is the exemplary level at which (a) the 'structural explanation' of the scientific approach and (b) the 'hermeneutic understanding' of the phenomenological approach confront one another: 'It was then necessary, however, to expand the hermeneutical project . . . to the dimensions of the problem posed by the passage from the structure immanent in every text to its extra-linguistic aim (*visée*) - the aim or reference which I sometimes designate by other related terms: the matter of the text, the world of the text, the being brought to language by the text.'" See ibid., 20; Paul Ricoeur, "A Response by Paul Ricoeur," in *Hermeneutics and the Human Sciences*, ed. John B. Thompson (Cambridge: Cambridge University Press, 1981), 35.
[185] Examples of this kind are like queries or the mention of dates or places that describe something in the past: "When did Britain declare war toward Germany during World War II?"
[186] David Leichter, "The Dual Role of Testimony in Paul Ricoeur's Memory, History, Forgetting," in *Phenomenology 2010, volume 5: Selected Essays from North America. Part 1: Phenomenology within Philosophy*, ed. Lester Embree, Michael Barber, and Thomas Nenon (Bucharest: Zeta Books, 2010), 373–4. "The meaning of the past, as bearing witness, cannot be exhausted by a narrative account of what happened."
[187] Ricoeur, *MHF*, 12–13. This is not to rule out the many variegated forms of the meaning of this revelation for different people.

accountable by God in rightfully discerning His ethical demands. The affirmation of this truthful testimony is not marked by something objectively verifiable, but *something which relates to a witness's desire to be truthful to an interpreted past, and a conviction of God's active guidance.*[188] A person's truthful testimony in the past, which incorporated her ethical commitment to God *with the form of a promise*, would *rightfully* "demand" her future faithfulness and fidelity. Inside his reflection, what Paul (the *present* writer of Philippians) must ask is whether the testimony given from the "previous" Paul, the original witness of the *past*, is worthy of being trusted?[189] Do his narration of events and its intrinsic understanding of God, together with the person who gave the testimony, all deserve his trust now? Does that narration still provide a memory which coheres with Paul's current horizon so that a "sensible" history can be seen? It is amid this *processual cycle of self-questioning and affirming* that Paul assures and prolongs his conviction, and presents his testimony to be the object of interpretation to the Philippian community.[190]

Instead of developing an objective certainty, what Paul has relied upon then is a sustained duration of being truthful to God, within which his initial reception of God's revelation, and his subsequent keeping of the testimony, are found. This category of truthfulness has become the chief "logic" within the affirmation of his seeking of God's revelation, and the foundation of conviction in persuading the Philippian community. The more Paul stays truthful, the more he affirms God's guidance. The more he affirms, the more convicted he is and the more persuasive he becomes to the Philippian community. It is in this unique manner that a mode of being truthful to God, oneself, and even other people becomes the critical parameter within the seeking of truth and assessing the trustworthiness of a witness.[191]

Would this mode of conviction degrade our seeking of truth into a purely subjective and psychological state of affairs? I reject this notion. While truthfulness belongs to the subjective category of what a witness believes, it is also recognized by her *faithful, whole-hearted, and persevering attitude* toward that truthful interpretation *from her past*. There are thus multiple forms of *historical* life in which we can observe and attest the truthfulness of a witness. In what follows, I will introduce four life forms from

---

[188] Ricoeur develops a category of truthfulness based on a dialectical process of objective and subjective, in which a more truthful interpretation of God's guidance can be continually validated and achieved through explanative moments, which subsequently turn into moments of refined understanding of God. Cf. Paul Ricoeur, *Freud and Philosophy: An Essay on Interpretation*, trans. Denis Savage (New Haven: Yale University Press, 1977), 342; Leichter, "The Dual Role of Testimony," 374.

[189] Ricoeur, *OAA*, 21. Ricoeur calls this the concept of attestation (or the expression "I believe-in"). "It thus links up with testimony, as the etymology reminds us, inasmuch as it is in the speech of the one giving testimony that one believes." Such certitude introduces a notion of truth that is not based on verifiable objective knowledge, but in phenomenological terms, a probable truth opens to be revised. Contrary to truthfulness, a false witness lacks a truthful commitment to what she believes and even intends to mislead and deceive the audience. No truthful concordance is found. For further references, see Leichter, "The Dual Role of Testimony," 382–3; James Carter, *Ricoeur on Moral Religion: A Hermeneutics of Ethical Life* (Oxford: Oxford University Press, 2014), 111ff.

[190] Ricoeur, "HT," 133–4, 40, 45. The above-mentioned process from Paul will be repeated within the Philippian community in order to authenticate Paul's truthful testimony from the false one of his opponents.

[191] Ricoeur, *MHF*, 4, 12–13, 21, 57.

which a person's truthfulness can be seen, and the notion of collective history in which collective identity is formed.

3.3.3.1 The Pervasive Form: The Narrative Unity of a Life Reinforces Truthfulness

First, a truthful witness is one who can show the *pervasiveness* of her testimony in covering all aspects of her life, resulting in what Ricoeur calls the "narrative unity of a life."[192] A truthful witness is one with no hidden stories that involve personal interests or selfish ambitions which disguise her real cause. The testimony she subjectively engages is one perceived with pure motive to honor God. There is thus an inner coherence across different facets of her life.[193] In this manner, the witness becomes a person whom she herself and the recipients of the testimony can trust, whose judgment concerns not only the accuracy of the claim, but also an appraisal of the moral character of the witness herself.[194]

3.3.3.2 The Refreshing Form: The Renewal of Testimony Restores Truthfulness

Truthfulness takes a different form when some discordant events spring up and "seemingly" cannot mesh perfectly with one's sedimented conviction. With a lack of concordance between one's understanding of God and the recent contingent events, alternative ways of narrating that recent "God-experience" are bound to arise, triggering a chain of contested understandings of God. To restore this conviction, the witness must *refresh* her own narrative with a *renewed* story that fits coherently with God's salvation plan, the recent discordant events happening in her daily life, and her future outlook on life.[195] The previous *doxa* endorsed has to be deconstructed and reconstructed. In this investigation, these discordant events primarily consist of Paul's imprisonment and the escalating oppression facing the Philippian community. How can these be seen not as setbacks, but instead as meaningful experiences leading to God's salvation? Is Paul's recent imprisonment something congruent with God's actions toward the fulfilment of His Kingdom? Can those "ordinary" Philippian community members really embody Paul's testimony in their lives, and experience their daily suffering as something valuable and meaningful? How can Paul update the *doxa* of the Philippian community and compete against the *endoxa* of his opponents? These would be challenges Paul must address within his contestation against the Jewish Christian leaders.

3.3.3.3 The Persevering Form: The Reiteration of Testimony Attests Truthfulness

With the "winner" of the contestation being disclosed only at the eschatological end time of Christ's *parousia* (a *cosmological* upper limit of time), a truthful witness must

---

[192] Ricoeur, *OAA*, 157–63.
[193] Ibid., 157, 78.
[194] Ricoeur, *MHF*, 164–5; Leichter, "The Dual Role of Testimony," 381–2.
[195] Cf. Ricoeur, *T&N I*, 29–30; Ricoeur, *OAA*, 175; Anthony C. Thiselton, "Dialectic in Hermeneutics and Doctrine: Coherence and Polyphony," in *The Hermeneutics of Doctrine* (Grand Rapids: Wm. B. Eerdmans, 2007), 127.

persevere in keeping her fidelity to her own testimony for her whole life journey. In other words, a truthful witness must be able to reiterate her declaration, which refers not to one who could replicate word-for-word what she previously said, but one who can *stay steadfast about her testimony over time*.[196] This attests to the presence of a genuine hope or desire for the *Aletheia* of God.

3.3.3.4 The Sacrificial Form: Dying for Testimony Reaches Truthfulness' Limit

Last but certainly not least, a witness can reinforce her testimony by a "sacrificial form" through which she chooses to suffer and even die for her conviction.[197] In this case, with the situation often found in political persecution, a witness dies for her testimony with the effect of winning the heart of her hearers. While such an action is not proof of her testimony, reaching the limit of death certainly pushes her conviction to the utmost.[198] A witness of this magnitude of conviction has identified herself with the humiliated prophets in the OT, who also died for their fidelity to the Lord.[199]

3.3.3.5 The Formation of Collective Identity and History with the Same Temporality

Finally, testimony relates also to the formation of a collective religious identity.[200] Such formation hinges on at least two issues. The first one is the relationship between collective identity and personal identity. According to Ricoeur, collective identity basically shares the same narrative structure and formation process as a person's individual identity.

Ricoeur writes, "The notion of narrative identity also indicates its fruitfulness in that it can be applied to a community as well as to an individual. We can speak of the self-constancy of a community, just as we spoke of it as applied to an individual subject."[201] The formation of the collective identity of a religious group thus depends primarily on the testimonies told by each of its members. When multiple individuals from a community commit to living a life of truthfulness to their shared testimonies, an intersubjective solidarity among the members will be built (Ricoeur calls it the "natural institution").[202]

The second issue concerns the sharing of a common history among the community members. Throughout his life, Ricoeur often grapples with problems of the "past," including memory and history. A complete review of the development of Ricoeur's

---

[196] Ricoeur, *MHF*, 165; Esteban Lythgoe, "Ricoeur's Concept of Testimony," *Analecta Hermeneutica* 3, no. 1 (2011): 15. In other words, the meaning and temporal identity embedded in one's narration of the past continue to endure in one's narration of the present and the future.

[197] Ricoeur, "HT," 129.

[198] Ibid.

[199] Ibid., 132.

[200] Ricoeur, *MHF*, 165.

[201] Ibid., 94; Dieter Teichert, "Narrative, Identity and the Self," *Journal of Consciousness Studies* 11.10–11 (2004): 184–5. For an in-depth analysis on the role of intersubjectivity regarding Ricoeur's concept of collective identity and memory, see David J. Leichter, "Collective Identity and Collective Memory in the Philosophy of Paul Ricoeur," *Ricoeur Studies* 3, no. 1 (2012): 117–26.

[202] Ricoeur, *MHF*, 165–6.

understanding of the past is beyond the scope of this book.[203] What matters to this work is that the memories and histories shared by a community again share many of the epistemological dynamics of narrative.[204] In both of the articles *Narrative Time* and *The Narrative Function*, Ricoeur aims at showing "mutual clarification of historicality and narrativity" within the making of communal history.[205] In the case of a double contestation of testimonies over the meaning of Paul's suffering, the meaning of the past of Paul and the Philippian community becomes one of, if not the most contested "battlefields" among Paul and his opponents. Only by adopting the configuration of Paul's testimony could the Philippian community forget (in the sense of neglect) "their" shameful history as told by the political authorities and the Jewish Christian leaders.

While Ricoeur's degree of analysis of the past reaches far beyond the scope of this work, at this juncture, it suffices to notice that the logic of recognizing truthful memory and history overlaps a lot with the manner of proving the veracity of testimony.[206] To raise the truthfulness of his testimony, Paul must demonstrate that his story resonates with those immediate experiences of himself and the Philippian community, and the "ancient" history within God's sovereign history. It is with respect to *this rhetorical purpose that multiple allusions to the OT (LXX) have been read, proposing a renewed history of God*. It is this *narrated continuity with the past that serves as the ultimate rhetorical strategy* in inviting the Philippian community to accept Paul's testimony as a truthful representation of God's action. In short, the understanding of the Philippian community's own history bears seriously on the success of Paul's identity formation strategy.

Following this, it has become clear that it is only when the Philippian community altogether witness their experiences with God with the same temporally configured thought, that their memories of God's past work will contribute to the development of a shared history and community identity.[207] A self-perpetuating and intersubjective hermeneutical process of reading and life change would result.[208] The Philippian

---

[203] For an introduction of Ricoeur's development with respect to his understanding of memory, see Angelos Mouzakitis, "From Narrative to Action: Paul Ricoeur's Reflections on History," *Rethinking History* 19, no. 3 (2015): 393–408.

[204] See Paul Ricoeur, "The Narrative Function," in *Hermeneutics and the Human Sciences*, ed. John B. Thompson (Cambridge: Cambridge University Press, 1981), 275–7, in which Ricoeur analyzes the origin of analytical philosophy's negligence on the narrative character of history.

[205] Ricoeur, "Narrative Time," 187. Ricoeur writes, "It is always a community, a people, or a group of protagonists which tries to take up the tradition—or traditions—of its origins. It is this communal act of repetition, which is at the same time a new founding act and a recommencement of what has already been inaugurated, that 'makes history' and that finally makes it possible to write history. Historiography, in this sense, is nothing more than the passage into writing and then to critical rewriting of this primordial constituting of tradition. The naive forms of narration are deployed between this constituting of tradition and the writing of history (for example, legends and chronicles). And it is at the level of this mediation, where the writing of history is preceded by something already recounted, that historicality and narrativity are confounded and confused." See Ricoeur, "Narrative Time," 189. Cf. Ricoeur, "The Narrative Function," 278–80.

[206] David Pellauer, *Ricoeur: A Guide for the Perplexed* (London: Continuum, 2007), 110–26.

[207] Cf. Ricoeur, *T&N III*, 113.

[208] Ricoeur, *MHF*, 165, 71. A community member's compliant reading of a text (mimesis3) will of course transform her subsequent way of figuring things out regarding the subject matter of the text, and the expectation she brought to her next reading of the text (mimesis1). For a community in which members have been used to sharing stories, norms, and behaviors, such a compliant reading

community will continue to draw their collective identity from their reception of this letter as their "sacred text."[209] There will be shared norms, habits, traditions, heroes. As their narratives converge into one, a collective identity with the same temporality will be formed.

3.3.4 Applying Truthfulness to Analyze the Religious Identity of the Philippian Community

In this section, I have explicated the narrative epistemology of one's revelatory experience. With the lack of objective verification in testimony, a category of truthfulness, marked by a dialectic of subjective and objective, has been singled out as the unique mode of conviction formation through which we assess the trustworthiness of a witness. To help the Philippian community differentiate his truthful testimony from the false testimony of his opponents, Paul has to demonstrate his testimony by living the life forms of the pervasive, the refreshing, the persevering, and even the sacrificial. Most important of all, he must show that his narrative provides the best concordance in which the Philippian community's *recent and little memory* fits with *the grand historical trajectory* of which the stories of God, Israel, and Christ are comprised.[210] In the exegesis that follows, I will show how these forms of conviction formation could provide insights into Paul's theologizing and his ways of exhorting the Philippian community to imitate him in suffering for the gospel.

3.4 Conclusion

In conclusion, the theories introduced above have provided tools for analyzing the narrative dynamics within Paul's theologizing process. First, the threefold mimesis theory has illuminated the temporal relations between a writer and a reader. The concept of temporality and its pertinent dialectical expressions have expanded our understandings of the dynamics within Paul's rhetorical and identity-formation strategies. Finally, the hermeneutics of testimony has provided us with the epistemology within a person's affirmation of God's revelation.

While Dunn's five levels of story model has proved to be useful in providing an infrastructure of Paul's narrative substructure, I argue that Ricoeur's narrative theories outlined earlier can better allow us to disclose the temporal dynamics and narrative logic involved within the identity-making process of the Philippian community. This claim

---

by one could also lead to a similar change of expectation for other members regarding the text. In other words, the preunderstanding which the mimesis3 would follow, could be shaped by a reader's own refigurative act, and others' previous readings. The mimesis process thus involves what Venema calls a process of "intersubjective knowledge." See Henry I. Venema, "Paul Ricoeur of Refigurative Reading and Narrative Identity," *Symposium* 4, no. 2 (2000): 243–4.

[209] Ricoeur, *T&N III*, 248; Paul Ricoeur, "The 'Sacred Text' and the Community," in *Figuring the Sacred: Religion, Narrative, and Imagination* (Minneapolis: Fortress Press, 1995), 68–72.

[210] Cf. Ricoeur, *T&N I*, 29–30; Ricoeur, *OAA*, 175; Thiselton, "Hermeneutic of Temporal and Communal Narrative," 66.

is predicated on two things. The first is the usefulness of various temporal categories and dialectics introduced in analyzing the temporal dynamics of the "Christian identity"–formation processes of Paul and the Philippian community. The second is the conceptual continuity between the temporal analysis of Paul's narrative world and the formation of narrative/ethical identity for Paul and the Philippian community. Based on my proposed hermeneutical framework, I can not only address the temporal dynamics between the multiple stories in Paul's narrative world but also construct the identity of the storyteller from whom the story is told. Dynamics from the intratextual narrative analysis are transposed to the extratextual identity-making of Paul himself.

Guided by the same temporality, Paul plots the narrative world of Philippians, acts inside this narrative as a character, and relates to the exigency within his own extra-textual world. As Paul the "narrative theologian" generates his thoughts from the level four of his own narrative world, he shapes the identity of himself and the Philippian community.

But Paul is not the only "narrative theologian" here. As the following exegesis will show, when Paul wrote Philippians, he was primarily contesting with a group of Jewish Christian leaders (Phil. 3:2) who have given a different testimony regarding the meaning of his imprisonment. Based on another narrative world *with drastically different interactions between the multiple stories*, these Jewish Christians take on a similar theologizing role to that provided by Paul and try to shape the story of the community in a different way.

Thus, there are at least two different ways of grasping together the "grand" historical trajectory of God's salvation and the "little" memory of the Philippian community's recent experience.

The dynamics involved in the identity-making of the Philippian community go beyond the interplays between stories within one single substructure. There are thus *severe tensions between two active narrative worlds in the making* which compete with each other in representing the story of Christ (level three) and shaping the lives of the Philippian community (level five). To better explain *the phenomenon of a contestation of narratives between two level four "theologians,"* multiple dialectics of Ricoeur's theories will be instrumental.

To gauge my point of analysis alongside the agencies of Paul and the Jewish Christian leaders, I have to align my hermeneutical viewpoint at the level four of the substructure. It is in this alignment with Paul's contention of the reappropriation of God's work in Christ and the shaping of the identity of the Philippian community that Ricoeur's narrative theory will be used. With these tools of Ricoeur, not only will the various shortcomings of previous scholarship be addressed, but the theme of the contestation of narratives or testimonies will be shown to be a key aspect of the identity-formation process of the Philippian community.

Part III

Exegetical Analysis

Before proceeding with the exegesis of Philippians, it is perhaps useful to introduce the exegetical layout and the reasons for the epistle's division. I have partitioned the epistle in a way best able to show the narrative dynamics behind the identity-making process of the Philippian community. Based on Dunn's five levels of story model, the epistle is partitioned into exegetical chapters, one for the story of Christ (level three), one for the story of Paul (level four), and one for the story of the Philippian community (level five).[1] The division also relies on the implicit boundaries hinted by the wrapping around of a few explicit narrative passages (1:12-26, 2:5-11, 3:4-11, 20-21), and the general epistolary flow within Paul's overall argument.

It is with these considerations in mind that I have divided the exegetical section into five chapters so that Paul's flow of thought can be mapped out and examined. Chapter four is largely concerned with the exegesis of chapter one of the epistle (Phil. 1:3–2:4), which defines the nature and introduces the background of the problem at large--a double contestation of narratives between Paul and his opponents. Chapter five deals with the story of Christ (2:5-11, 3:17-21), which will be shown to be the guiding narrative within Paul's narrative world. The story of Paul (3:1-21) will be examined in chapter six, in which Paul figures himself as the ideal exemplar for the identity formation of the Philippian community. Following this, in chapter seven, we see Paul's intended story of the Philippian community (2:12-16a), in which its collective identity will be formed only if each community member, amid a double contestation of narratives, voluntarily retells Paul's testimony. Finally, in chapter eight, I will integrate the exegetical findings and map them onto several stages of the identity formation of the Philippian community. The aim of this work is to show that the "Christian identity" of the Philippian community is shaped amid a contestation of testimonies with divergent temporalities.

---

[1] While each of the stories of God (level one) and the Israelites (level two) would not take up a single or separate passage unit, their presence would be readily "felt" in tension with stories on levels three to five.

4

Nature and Background of the Problem: Double Contestation of Narratives (Phil. 1:3–2:4)

The focus of this current chapter is to introduce and define the nature of the problem facing Paul and the Philippian community. Constituted by the rather long passage of Phil. 1:3–2:4, it is necessary to further demarcate it into a few exegetical units. Having taken into account scholars' proposals on the layout of this text, I divide this chapter into four units: 1:3-11, 12- 26, 27-30, 2:1-4.[1] The first passage to receive attention is Phil. 1:27-30. The reasons for framing these four verses into a single unit are not too difficult to understand. While Paul in 1:12-26 recalls and evaluates his experience regarding his current imprisonment in Rome, in 2:1-4 he exhorts the community with a list of moral instructions. There is thus a "natural" demarcation of Phil. 1:27-30. Also, having compared it with examples of ancient rhetoric many scholars regard this unit as the *propositio* of the whole epistle, which means that we can locate Paul's central proposition of his message in Philippians here.[2] In this work, such a unit will be looked upon as a theological snapshot of the challenges facing Paul.

Besides this theological snapshot unit, each of the other three units in this chapter reflects Paul's specific concern as related to the exigency of a contestation of narratives. In Phil. 1:12-26, not only will we see Paul narrate the historical and "external" incidents of his conflict, but will also discern the embedded meaning and his understanding of God ("internal criteriology of the divine") within the historical incident of his contestation of narratives with his opponents.[3] The next unit is Phil. 1:3-11, which has been commonly identified as a section of epistolary thanksgiving and prayer.[4] Due to multiple mentions of ἡμέρας Χριστοῦ (Ἰησοῦ), and the presence of a few other temporal markers (ἐνάρχομαι, ἐπιτελέω, ἀπὸ τῆς πρώτης ἡμέρας ἄχρι τοῦ νῦν) in Phil.

---

[1] Cf. Fee, *Paul's Letter*, 3; Silva, *Philippians*, 15–17; Ralph P. Martin, *Philippians: An Introduction and Commentary*, TNTC 11 (Downers Grove: InterVarsity Press, 1987), 57–8; Reumann, *Philippians*, 6.
[2] Duane F. Watson, "A Rhetorical Analysis of Philippians and Its Implications for the Unity Question," *Novum Testamentum* 30 (1988): 59; Timothy C. Geoffrion, *The Rhetorical Purpose and the Political and Military Character of Philippians: A Call to Stand Firm* (Lewiston: Mellen Biblical Press, 1993), 23–5; Edgar M. Krentz, "Military Language and Metaphors in Philippians," in *Origins and Method: Towards A New Understanding of Judaism and Christianity: Essays in Honour of John C. Hurd*, ed. John Coolidge Hurd and Bradley H. McLean (Sheffield: JSOT Press, 1993), 112–13.
[3] See p.100ff.
[4] Fee, *Paul's Letter*, 72–105.

1:3-11, the temporal dimension of Paul's narrative world, in which stories of different levels have been nested together, will be analyzed. Lastly, Phil. 2:1-4 is a unit in which ethical values within the testimonies of Paul and his opponents will be contrasted.

4.1 Persecution from Political Authorities and Theological Debate with Other "Christ-Followers" (1:27-30)

1:27-30 is a unique passage because it succinctly defines the nature of the problem Paul is facing in Philippians. This passage will be scrutinized in four segments, each one representing a key aspect around the theme of this book: a double symbolic context for πολιτεύομαι (27a- e), a practical manual for battle (27f-28a), the contesting evaluations of the suffering experiences of the community (28b-29d), and a shared historical and temporal context between Paul and the Philippian community (30a-c). The original Greek text of 1:27-30 now follows,[5] arranged according to my understanding of the sentence structure.

27a	Μόνον ἀξίως τοῦ εὐαγγελίου τοῦ Χριστοῦ πολιτεύεσθε,
27b	ἵνα
27c	εἴτε ἐλθὼν καὶ ἰδὼν ὑμᾶς
27d	εἴτε ἀπὼν ἀκούω
27e	ἀκούω τὰ περὶ ὑμῶν,
27f	ὅτι στήκετε ἐν ἑνὶ πνεύματι,
27g	μιᾷ ψυχῇ συναθλοῦντες τῇ πίστει τοῦ εὐαγγελίου
28a	καὶ μὴ πτυρόμενοι ἐν μηδενὶ ὑπὸ τῶν ἀντικειμένων,
28b	ἥτις ἐστὶν αὐτοῖς ἔνδειξις ἀπωλείας, ὑμῶν δὲ σωτηρίας,
28c	καὶ τοῦτο ἀπὸ θεοῦ
29a	ὅτι ὑμῖν ἐχαρίσθη
29b	τὸ ὑπὲρ Χριστοῦ,
29c	οὐ μόνον τὸ εἰς αὐτὸν πιστεύειν
29d	ἀλλὰ καὶ τὸ ὑπὲρ αὐτοῦ πάσχειν,
30a	τὸν αὐτὸν ἀγῶνα ἔχοντες,
30b	οἷον εἴδετε ἐν ἐμοὶ
30c	καὶ νῦν ἀκούετε ἐν ἐμοί.

4.1.1 Controversy on the Understanding of Πολιτεύομαι (27a-e)

This section demonstrates that the nature of the problem that Paul faces in Philippians pertains to the nature of a contestation of political allegiance in the Greco-Roman context, and to the nature of a theological dispute over the right of representing God according to Jewish tradition. This is achieved through confirming a double symbolic context for the word πολιτεύομαι. As the following exegesis will show, these two

---

[5] The version of the text is Novum Testamentum Graece, NA 28th Edition, Accordance 12.2.7.

symbolic contexts correspond to the double contestation of narratives facing Paul in his current exigency.

As shown earlier, across the four verses of 1:27-30 there is only one main clause in the original Greek text as shown in 27a: Μόνον ἀξίως τοῦ εὐαγγελίου τοῦ Χριστοῦ πολιτεύεσθε. Its main verb πολιτεύεσθε (πολιτεύομαι) has been translated differently by scholars. Being the only verb in this main clause, πολιτεύομαι probably stands as the chief command among Paul's many in the epistle. Additionally, Paul has placed μόνος ("only") at the very beginning of this clause, further highlighting the preeminence of this command. Thus, its meaning is highly significant for a correct understanding of both this passage and the whole epistle. Almost all translations of English Bibles tend to understand πολιτεύομαι as denoting a kind of "general" lifestyle exhortation.[6] However, these translations may have failed in accurately grasping Paul's idea by not paying attention to the symbolically mediated networks (mimesis1) from which πολιτεύομαι draws its meaning. Notably, this is the only time Paul uses πολιτεύομαι in all his epistles. In most other cases of urging believers to live a good life because of their faith, the word he uses is περιπατέω.[7]

According to Ricoeur, all human actions are symbolically mediated, which necessarily situates interpretation of sentences rich in symbols within a specific temporal, spatial, and cultural context (mimesis1).[8] In order to access the meaning of πολιτεύομαι, we must inquire after the symbolic cultural network(s) from which πολιτεύομαι obtains its signs, rules, and norms. If one finds the Greco-Roman context to be the sole framework, then all the subsequent interpretation on the configuration process (mimesis2) will have to be confined to this Greco-Roman context, rather than the context of Jewish traditions. Conversely, if the Jewish tradition is found to be the primary context, Greco-Roman interpretations should be sidelined, if not neglected altogether.

While scholars tend to perceive πολιτεύομαι as belonging to either the Jewish or Greco-Roman framework, I aver that the meaning of πολιτεύομαι relates to symbolic contexts of *both* Greco-Roman and Jewish backgrounds.[9] In regard to the Greco-Roman context, the word's association is related to the idea of citizens having a sole allegiance to a city, and the scenes of military battles. A Jewish context would render the word symbolic of the theological reflection of the Israelites' collective identity in the midst of oppression from other nations.

---

[6] NASB95, NIV, and NET all have it translated as "conduct yourselves"; ASV and ESV render it as "let your manners of life"; NRSV and HCSB perceive it as "live your life."

[7] Rom. 6:4, 8:4, 13:13, 14:15; 1 Cor. 3:3, 7:17; 2 Cor. 4:2, 5:7, 10:2-3, 12:18; Gal. 5:16; Phil. 3:17-18; 1 Th. 2:12, 4:1, 12. For references, see Stephen E. Fowl, "Philippians 1:28b, One More Time," in *New Testament Greek and Exegesis: Essays in Honor of Gerald F. Hawthorne*, ed. Amy M. Donaldson and Timothy B. Sailors (Grand Rapids: Wm. B. Eerdmans, 2003), 169-70; Joseph H. Hellerman, "The Humiliation of Christ in the Social World of Roman Philippi, Part II," *BibSac* 160 (2003): 422-3; *NIDNTT*, s.v. "πολιτεύομαι," 800.

[8] Ricoeur, *T&N I*, 58.

[9] According to Bradley Arnold, the meaning of πολιτεύομαι comes only from its Greco-Roman background. See Bradley Arnold, *Christ as the Telos of Life: Moral Philosophy, Athletic Imagery, and the Aim of Philippians* (Tübingen: Mohr Siebeck, 2014), 160-71.

As the following exegesis will show, this phenomenon of a double-situated symbolic context for πολιτεύομαι has a direct bearing on our understanding of Paul's situation as a double contestation of narratives against two different groups of opponents.

4.1.1.1 Greco-Roman Context: Contestation of Political and Military Allegiance

Political: Exercise Your Citizenship

The symbolic association of πολιτεύομαι with the Greco-Roman political context is not difficult to discern. First, due to its association with the cognate noun πόλις (city), the most general and literal meaning of πολιτεύομαι is to be a citizen (πολίτης) in a city with its political quality as compared to resident aliens and slaves.[10] Depending on the particular instance, πολιτεύομαι can be employed to deliver meanings with a few different nuances.[11] To grasp the meaning of πολιτεύομαι in Philippians, we have to reconstruct the probable challenges facing Paul in his particular situation.

Situated beside the Egnatian Way, the city of Philippi was a key battle site when Octavian fought his way to become emperor as Augustus Caesar.[12] After the civil wars, being a city chosen to settle a large group of veteran soldiers, Philippi was honored as a Roman military colony and named after Octavian's daughter as "*Colonia Augusta Julia Philippensis.*"[13] When Paul visited the colonial city in c. 49 CE (Acts 16:11-15), Philippi had even acquired the distinguished status of *ius italicum* (Italian legal system), bestowing the Roman citizens there with virtually identical rights as those in Rome.[14] Most of the archaeological evidence from the city of Philippi, whether buildings, inscriptions, or ritual relics, points to the fact that the city was strongly influenced by the culture of the Roman Empire.[15] Although we cannot be exact on the proportion of Roman citizens in Philippi, it is quite probable that more than a few of its populace possessed Roman citizenship.[16] Quantitatively speaking, these citizens might not be the largest group in the city. But with their power in determining the social honors, values, and statuses, they were most likely the "ideological majority."[17] Due to their respect for the empire, local authorities of Philippi would shape their local political

---

[10] H. Strathmann, "πόλις κτλ," *TDNT* 6:516–35.

[11] According to *TDNT*, generally speaking πολιτεύομαι can refer to meaning: a. "of life as a citizen"; b. "of life in a specific political order, like living with freedom"; c. "of political action, e.g., acting publicly"; d. "of the direction of politics, e.g., the control and use of political power"; e. "of the sense 'to rule' or 'to discharge an office.'" See Strathmann, *TDNT* 6:516–35.

[12] Krentz, "Military Language," 111–12; Lawrence Keppie, *The Making of the Roman Army: From Republic to Empire* (Norman: University of Oklahoma Press, 1998), 104–5.

[13] Craig S. de Vos, *Church and Community Conflicts: The Relationships of the Thessalonian, Corinthian, and Philippian Churches with Their Wider Civic Communities* (Atlanta: SBL, 1999), 235; L. M. McDonald, "Philippi," in *DNTB*, ed. Craig A. Evans and Stanley E. Porter (Downers Grove: InterVarsity Press, 2000).

[14] de Vos, *Church and Community Conflicts*, 246; Krentz, "Military Language," 112. With this privilege, Philippi was recognized as part of the Italian territory, which represents a much-distinguished location as compared to other eastern cities of the empire.

[15] Hellerman, "Humiliation, I," 336; de Vos, *Church and Community Conflicts*, 250.

[16] Fee, *Paul's Letter*, 25. Concerning scholars' debate on the proportion of Roman citizens in Philippi, see de Vos, *Church and Community Conflicts*, 236, 41.

[17] Hellerman, "Humiliation, I," 327–30.

structure according to the typical Roman pattern.[18] Evidence of this extraordinarily strong Roman cultural influence is apparent in Paul's referring to the community by its Latin form (Φιλιππήσιοι) in Phil. 4:15.[19]

Thus, it is safe to assume that the community of the Philippian Christ-followers would be very aware of these cultural norms that each of them should live out, and honor as if they were all citizens of the Regime.[20] Living within this world of preunderstanding things and values (mimesis1), the general public would "naturally" describe and prescribe their actions according to this highly regarded allegiance, and see it as the "ethical norms" of the city.[21] Loyalty to the Roman Empire, as the core element of being a citizen, becomes the governing "root metaphor" or "guiding narrative" of all other thoughts and behaviors.[22]

Because of this, perhaps we should not be surprised to see the definition of πολιτεύομαι in Spicq: "Such a citizenship carries with it rights and privileges but also obligations and responsibilities. Each one is then required to 'live as a citizen' (πολιτεύομαι), i.e., according to the laws and the spirit of this city, conformably to its statutes."[23] Thus, the semantic meaning of πολιτεύομαι is specifically related to the constitution of a political group as its members live out a way of life that is loyal to their political group leader. Based on BDAG, Timothy Geoffrion further argues that the correct translation of πολιτεύομαι in 27a should be "exercise your citizenship."[24] In short, πολιτεύομαι in Philippians refers not only to personal conduct but to how people should comply with the constitution of a political group they belong to, living out their expected behaviors and being loyal to their political group leader.

Military: Contestation of Allegiance

However, this political sense of πολιτεύομαι may not have exhausted its meaning in Philippians. Scholars have noted that military conflict may be another symbolically mediated network that Paul alludes to in πολιτεύομαι. In Phil. 3:20, πολίτευμα (another *hapax legomenon* in NT) clearly forms an *inclusio* with πολιτεύομαι in 1:27.

---

[18] Peter Garnsey and Richard Saller, *The Roman Empire: Economy, Society and Culture* (Berkeley: University of California Press, 1987), 107–25; de Vos, *Church and Community Conflicts*, 245–7.

[19] Acts 16:12; Hellerman, "Humiliation, II," 421–2. Notice that in Luke's record of Paul, among those eight colonial cities that Paul visited, only in the city of Philippi did Luke introduce it with the title κολωνία. Thus, the Philippi City was indeed intimately related to the empire in its culture, language, and economic and social class structure, achieving a more intimate relationship than other general colonial cities. See Barbara Levick, *Roman Colonies in Southern Asia Minor* (Oxford: Oxford University Press, 1967), 161; de Vos, *Church and Community Conflicts*, 245–7.

[20] G. Walter Hansen, *The Letter to the Philippians* (Grand Rapids: Wm. B. Eerdmans, 2009), 94–5.

[21] Coupled with this thinking would be the general phenomenon of promoting one's own social status according to that Roman pattern of life. For details, see Pilhofer, *Philippi*, 42; Hellerman, "Humiliation, I," 336. For other perspectives, see Joseph A. Marchal, "Military Images in Philippians 1–2: A Feminist Analysis of the Rhetorics of Scholarship, Philippians, and Current Contexts," in *Her Master's Tools? Feminist and Postcolonial Engagements of Historical-Critical Discourse*, ed. Caroline Vander Stichele and Todd Penner (Atlanta: SBL, 2005), 11–13; Keppie, *Making*, 106–7, 21–9.

[22] Paul Ricoeur, *Interpretation Theory: Discourse and the Surplus of Meaning* (Fort Worth: Texas Christian University Press, 1976), 64.

[23] *TLNT*, s.v. "πολιτεία, κτλ," 124–33.

[24] Geoffrion, *Rhetorical Purpose*, 23–5; Raymond F. Collins, *The Power of Images in Paul* (Collegeville: Liturgical Press, 2008), 54; Peter Orr, *Christ Absent and Present: A Study in Pauline Christology* (PhD, Durham University, 2011), 82n.251; BDAG, s.v. "πολιτεύομαι," 846.

Paul not only has alerted readers to the importance of this πολιτεύ- word-group as the probable "root metaphor" of understanding the whole epistle, but he also adds a "military flavor" to its meaning with a severe tone in 3:17-21. Edgar Krentz, in arguing that military language rather than athletic language colors the text of Philippians, avers that πολιτεύομαι and the language of 1:27–4:2 resembles the kind of speeches made by generals to troops.[25] Based on the distinct Roman culture and Philippi's status as a colony of Rome, Raymond Brewer argues that the meaning of πολιτεύομαι should be read against the backdrop of a conflict of allegiance between Christ and Nero as the Philippians are forced to join the imperial worship.[26] Such a theme of military contestation is also supported by Geoffrion, indicating that the deliberative rhetoric "topos" of Philippians belongs to a popular category of *territory defense* in warfare of the Greco-Roman period.[27]

However, not all scholars agree with such a reading. For example, Christopher Bryan argues that the logic of Paul using πολίτευμα in Phil. 3:20 is actually an *a fortiori* argument: just as the Philippian community had been loyal to the empire, similarly they should be even more obedient to Christ's Kingdom.[28] Similarly, Walter Hansen claims that when Paul exhorted the community to "shine like stars in the midst of their crooked and depraved generation," he was hoping that believers should behave properly in Roman society.[29] No contestation of allegiances is then perceived in Philippians. Following this approach, the hidden structure of thought to be disclosed in the metaphorical expression "ἡμῶν γὰρ τὸ πολίτευμα ἐν οὐρανοῖς ὑπάρχει" (3:20) would be that the Roman citizens guard themselves against the threat of amalgamation by the culture of foreigners among whom they live. The Christ-followers in Philippi should then overcome the threat of surrounding pagan Roman culture and focus their ultimate destiny on the city in heaven.[30] The sphere of cultural context to which this metaphor alludes would then be that Roman citizens should live a life complying with the customs of their empire, rather than being amalgamated by cultures of *non*-Roman citizens.[31]

Due to its complex relations with the issue of imperial worship and the identity of the opponents, a complete response to the debate concerning the overtone of military contestation within πολίτευμα is beyond the scope of this book. But perhaps what stands out as the strongest textual evidence against the view of Bryan and Hansen is the structure of thought found within the scenario of Phil. 3:17-21, in which an eager hope for a savior has been enveloped by polarized lifestyles. Within the immediate literary context of 3:17-21, Paul speaks with an extraordinarily severe tone regarding the

---

[25] Krentz, "Military Language," 113–14; de Vos, *Church and Community Conflicts*, 278–9; Raymond Hubert Reimer, "'Our Citizenship is in Heaven': Philippians 1:27-30 and 3:20-21 as Part of the Apostle Paul's Political Theology" (PhD, Princeton Theological Seminary, 1997), 144–6.
[26] Raymond Rush Brewer, "The Meaning of Politeuesthe in Philippians 1:27," *JBL* 73, no. 2 (1954): 76–83; Geoffrion, *Rhetorical Purpose*, 45–6.
[27] Ibid., 36.
[28] Bryan, *Render to Caesar*, 84.
[29] Hansen, *Philippians*, 94–5.
[30] Justin P. Rossow, "Preaching the Story behind the Image. A Narrative Approach to Metaphor for Preaching" (PhD, Concordia Seminary, 2009), 77.
[31] Ibid., 77–82, 272–7.

contrasting destinies of the "enemies of the cross" and those who look forward to the transformation of their *humiliated bodies* (τὸ σῶμα τῆς ταπεινώσεως ἡμῶν). It is only after this that Paul narrates the metaphorical expression ἡμῶν γὰρ τὸ πολίτευμα ἐν οὐρανοῖς ὑπάρχει in 3:20. What specific sphere of context would posit such a metaphor of Roman citizens crying for the destruction (ἀπώλεια) of their enemies while hoping for their own rescue?[32] What kind of a situation would require a Roman citizen to be eagerly longing (ἀπεκδέχομαι) for a savior?[33] As Justin Rossow comments, "Citizens paying taxes, voting, even living distinctive lives do not wait for salvation with eager expectation."[34] Sticking to a lifestyle compliant with the customs of the empire does not mesh convincingly with the structure of thought found within the text.

In contrast, the cultural scene of Roman citizens being threatened by foreign noncitizens in a Roman territory and looking forward to the military intervention of the empire as their rescuer would fit nicely with the structure of thought in Phil. 3:17-21.[35] Only in such a cultural context does the textual structure of thought find correspondence with the hope of being rescued from enemies by a savior.[36] From this perspective, the message disclosed would be that just as Roman citizens eagerly await rescue and salvation by the empire from the threat of *non*-Roman people, the Christ-followers in Philippi should eagerly wait for the eschatological *parousia* when Jesus Christ will save them from the enemies of the cross, whose god is the bellies of their bodies. Based on this metaphor, a clear theme of military conflict is thus brought to the fore. The element of contestation of allegiance between parties becomes prominent. As such, the foundation for understanding Paul's exhortation to the Philippian community as a kind of contestation of lordships is built. What remains to be shown is *the identity of this competing lord with which the Lordship of Christ will be compared, and the role of this particular contestation within the identity-formation process of the Philippian community.*

4.1.1.2 Jewish Context: A Dispute over Who Could Represent God

Having introduced the symbolic context (mimesis1) from Greco-Roman culture, I will shift to the domain of Jewish tradition. Similar to what I have found in Greco-Roman culture, scholars have noted that in the Septuagint, πολιτεύομαι refers not only to alternative lifestyles, but also actions with political connotations.[37] The *Additions to Esther* likely arises from a historical situation where Jews in the diaspora experienced

---

[32] Relying on a modified "actantial model" from Greimas and metaphor theory from Roger White, Justin Rossow investigates how an implicit narrative structure from a source domain maps itself to a target domain and thus helps determine the true meaning of a metaphor. For details, see ibid., 58–9, 78–80, 273–4; Roger M. White, *The Structure of Metaphor: The Way the Language of Metaphor Works* (Oxford: Wiley-Blackwell, 1996), 78–80, 94–5.
[33] Rossow, "Preaching," 140.
[34] Ibid., 80.
[35] Ibid., 272–7.
[36] Ibid., 77–82, 272–7.
[37] Markus Bockmuehl, *The Epistle to the Philippians* (London: A & C Black, 1997), 97. Oakes objects to reading πολιτεύομαι from a political standpoint, but Vos has already given comprehensive critiques on his viewpoints. See Peter Oakes, *Philippians: From People to Letter* (Cambridge: Cambridge University Press, 2001), 199; de Vos, *Church and Community Conflicts*, 282.

political conflicts with native peoples. The author thus reflects on the narrative of Esther where Jews are under the threat of annihilation from Haman the Agagite, and writes to affirm the unique identity of Jews in relation to a mighty God.[38] Similarly, in 2 Maccabees 6:1, the author reflects on one particular episode of the Maccabaean history, in which the Jews were forced to depart from the laws of God when their temple was being profaned by Antiochus.[39] In both cases, there are strong indications that πολιτεύομαι is used to express how certain (not all) Jewish people, while being threatened by enemies, fulfilled their loyalty to God through upholding the law and their collective identity.[40]

Similarly, in his research on the use of πολιτεύομαι in the LXX and Jewish literature earlier to and contemporary to Paul, Ernest Miller argues that the sense of πολιτεύομαι conveys something beyond civic obligation and thus also indicates that Jews should "fulfill their 'Jewishness'" as a collective identity through fidelity to the Torah of God.[41] For example, in 3 Maccabees 3:4 while *defending their separation from hateful others regarding their food laws*, the narrator emphasizes that those particular Jews, not all Jews, do this out of their worship to God and His Law (σεβόμενοι δὲ τὸν θεὸν καὶ τῷ τούτου νόμῳ πολιτευόμενοι).

In the light of these examples, we may infer that πολιτεύομαι was used to affirm the fulfillment of particular Jewish people groups' *fidelity to God in the midst of disputes over theology and politics*. In other words, the political connotation of πολιτεύομαι has been repeatedly employed by Jewish writers in the self-understanding and shaping of their collective identity amid external oppositions and theological dispute.[42] Through this, they can affirm that they have been chosen by God to be rightfully called His people, and His true representatives.

While Miller argues that Paul takes up this tradition and employs πολιτεύομαι to signify that the Church has somewhat replaced the Jews as God's people, I would argue that Paul takes up this *tradition of dispute* and makes use of πολιτεύομαι to highlight the controversy involved in the judgment of his testimony. As the following exegesis shows, the core notion within Paul's testimony is that suffering for the gospel of Christ is something from God, and so people truthfully doing so should be considered His representatives. A compliant reception of Paul's testimony will then serve as the definite boundary marker for the collective identity of the Philippian community.[43] As such, *the*

---

[38] R. H. Charles, *The Apocrypha and Pseudepigrapha of the Old Testament* (Oxford: Clarendon Press, 1913), Additions to Esther, 8:15-16: "[Jews] . . . are no evil-doers, but govern themselves with the most righteous laws, and are sons of the Most High, Most Mighty, Living God" (Ἰουδαίους εὑρίσκομεν οὐ κακούργους ὄντας, δικαιοτάτοις δὲ *πολιτευομένους* νόμοις. ὄντας δὲ υἱοὺς τοῦ ὑψίστου μεγίστου ζῶντος θεοῦ).

[39] Charles, *Apocrypha*, 2 Maccabees 6:1: "Shortly after this the king sent an old Athenian to compel the Jews to depart from the laws of their fathers, and to cease living by the laws of God." (Μετ' οὐ πολὺν δὲ χρόνον ἐξαπέστειλεν ὁ βασιλεὺς γέροντα Ἀθηναῖον ἀναγκάζειν τοὺς Ἰουδαίους μεταβαίνειν ἀπὸ τῶν πατρίων νόμων καὶ τοῖς τοῦ θεοῦ νόμοις μὴ πολιτεύεσθαι.)

[40] Fowl, "Philippians 1:28b," 170.

[41] Ernest C. Miller, "Politeuesthe in Philippians 1:27: Some Philological and Thematic Observations," *JSNT* 15 (1982): 87.

[42] Ibid., 86-96; Geoffrion, *Rhetorical Purpose*, 47.

[43] Miller, "Politeuesthe," 91. According to Miller, the way Paul writes in Phil. 1:27 has a lot of similarity to those in the Book of the Maccabees. He writes, "The adverbial phrase ἀξίως τοῦ εὐαγγελίου τοῦ Χριστοῦ modifying πολιτεύεσθε functions just as θεοῦ νόμοις or τῷ τούτου νόμῳ for the

theme of contestation of testimonies in relation to the identity-making of the Philippian community, is at least coherent with the Jewish usage of πολιτεύομαι *at the time of Paul.*

However, there is recent scholarship which rejects the Jewish background of πολιτεύομαι. In his book *Christ as the Telos of Life: Moral Philosophy, Athletic Imagery, and the Aim of Philippians*, Bradley Arnold argues that the essence of πολιτεύομαι in Phil. 1:27 is to encourage the community to live "virtuously as members of an alternative polis."[44] Seeking to illuminate the logic of Paul's arguments by a correlative pattern of thought in moral philosophy, Arnold denies the militaristic sense of πολιτεύομαι (and στήκω) and promotes its athletic connotations.[45] Based on a somewhat conjectural social demography of Philippi by Peter Oakes, Arnold insists that most of the Philippian Christ-followers are poor non-Roman citizens, which he claims would then justify the reception of Paul's message within the framework of moral philosophy in the Greco-Roman context.[46] Arnold thus contends that the conceptual background to which πολιτεύομαι alludes should strictly be the "Greek connotation of living as a citizen of a polis" alone, and not the "Jewish connotation of living as the new Israel" at all.[47] As the Philippians' suffering experiences are relegated to economic sanctions resulting from the rejection of cults other than the imperial worship, moral formation becomes the single focus of the epistle.[48] The common ἀγών between Paul and the community collapses into pursuing one's ultimate life goal through living virtuously in the face of difficulties.[49]

Arnold's research on the correlative relationship between Paul's thought in Philippians and his contemporary Greco-Roman moral philosophy is illuminating, though I am not in a position to fully review his work. But the foundation of his denial of the "Jewishness" of Paul's thought in Philippians is open to serious doubt. Given

---

Maccabean writers. To Jews acquainted with the LXX literature such an alteration of phraseology would stand out starkly."

[44] Arnold, *Christ as the Telos*, 164.

[45] Ibid., 51–4; Reumann, *Philippians*, 287; Geoffrion, *Rhetorical Purpose*, 44–5, 56, 60, 63. Referencing the work of John Reumann, who contends that the verb στήκω is historically too new to be ascribed an established usage, Arnold quickly dismisses Geoffrion's detailed argument on the military sense of στήκω. However, in terms of Ricoeur, denying the existence of a sedimented tradition or prefigured habit of a military sense of στήκω is one thing; judging one of its particular meanings in the context of a military city (Philippi), and within the literary context filled with political and military metaphors, is another thing.

In fact, while the usage of ἵστημι in Herodotus (who lived in the fifth century BC) and Xenophon (who lived mainly in the fourth century BC) as observed by Geoffrion cannot be used to ascertain the military sense of στήκω here, they at least attest to the likelihood or tendency of στήκω, which, being a later form of ἵστημι, could be used in a similar manner. In other words, instead of unreasonably magnifying one's doubt on the continuity between ἵστημι and στήκω, the usage of ἵστημι could reasonably contribute positively to our understanding of στήκω. Unfortunately, these considerations are altogether dismissed by Arnold. Moreover, finding other senses of στήκω as employed by Paul also cannot deny the possibility of a specific military sense here.

Lastly, Arnold's understanding of Paul's usage of στήκω to "exhort believers to remain committed to the gospel" seems to reflect an antithetic cleavage between his understanding of the nature of the gospel and the contingent context in which the gospel is experienced by the believers. For the historical linkage and synonymity between ἵστημι and στήκω, see W. Grundmann, "στήκω, ἵστημι," *TDNT* 7:636–53; M. Wolter, "στήκω," *EDNT* 3:275.

[46] Oakes, *Philippians*, 60; Arnold, *Christ as the Telos*, 39–41.

[47] Ibid., 161.

[48] Ibid., 41–2; Oakes, "Re-Mapping," 312–14, 319.

[49] Arnold, *Christ as the Telos*, 169–70.

the importance of the double symbolic network behind the meaning of πολιτεύομαι in this investigation, it is necessary for me to address Arnold's perspective. Here I will summarize three key aspects that lead me to doubt his preference for the Greco-Roman over the Jewish context. Hopefully, we will be able to see a more evident picture of a double cultural framework from Greco-Roman and Jewish cultures, and its implication for the theme of the contestation of narratives.[50]

First, it has long been observed that unlike other Pauline texts, the epistle to the Philippians does not seem to contain any explicit discussion of OT scriptures.[51] However, as Moisés Silva comments, it would be a grave mistake to overlook Paul's indirect but heavy dependence on the Jewish scriptures.[52] For example, Fowl in a fairly recent work has argued that there are at least three passages in Philippians (1:19, 2:10-11, 2:12-18) where the OT "scriptural texts are either cited or stand in the very near background."[53] Although these allusions to the Jewish Scriptures come through the Greek LXX, we cannot deny their Jewish background. While many of these allusions are fragmented expressions rather than full quotations, my methodology takes into account the interactions between the story of Israel and the story of Paul and thus we can properly discern the presence of pertinent Jewish stories (level two) beneath Paul's reflective discourse.[54] We should then be able to differentiate and extract stories from within Paul's narrative substructure so as to understand how those Jewish stories of the past would contribute to the identity-making of the Philippian community in the present. The Jewish cultural framework thus becomes indispensable within our understanding of πολιτεύομαι and Paul's whole narrative world. In fact, based on Ricoeur's mimesis theory, it is perfectly feasible that heterogeneous elements from both cultures of Greco-Roman and Jewish contexts become synthesized into a unified whole.[55] If we neglect the presence and significance of these Jewish stories, we will miss invaluable narrative dynamics among the levels of the story and subsequently undermine our understanding of Paul's message in Philippians. Can we discern the theme of the contestation of testimonies within Paul's various allusions to OT? And how do these OT allusions contribute to the case of Paul in his contestation with other "Christ-followers"? Such questions will be answered later as I address the various OT allusions.

[50] Regarding the perspective of taking both the Greco-Roman culture and the early Judaism context as the interpretative frameworks of the early "Christianity," Susan Docherty writes, "no longer is any great chasm envisaged separating early 'Judaism' from early 'Christianity', or 'midrashic' from 'Christological' exegesis.
    The challenge for commentators moving forward will be to balance this important perspective with an appropriate appreciation of the larger Graeco-Roman culture in which both early Judaism and early Christianity were formed." See Susan Docherty, "'Do You Understand What You Are Reading?' (Acts 8.30): Current Trends and Future Perspectives in the Study of the Use of the Old Testament in the New," *JSNT* 38, no. 1 (2015): 122.
[51] Stephen E. Fowl, "The Use of Scripture in Philippians," in *Paul and Scripture: Extending the Conversation*, ed. Christopher D. Stanley (Atlanta: SBL, 2012), 164–5; Moisés Silva, "Philippians," in *Commentary on the New Testament Use of the Old Testament*, ed. G. K. Beale and D. A. Carson (Grand Rapids: Baker Academic, 2007), 835.
[52] Ibid., 835–6.
[53] Fowl, "Use of Scripture," 164.
[54] Hays, *The Faith of Jesus Christ*, 22; Osborne, "Hermeneutics/Interpreting Paul."
[55] Cf. Ricoeur, *T&N I*, 66.

Second, Arnold's premise that all the Philippian community members will only be able to read from a Greco-Roman perspective is highly doubtful. Scholars have generally agreed that we are largely ignorant of exactly how Paul's letters were received by the so-called "original audiences."[56] According to Fowl, "no one can speak authoritatively about the ways in which the actual first recipients of Paul's letters engaged with those epistles or the Old Testament over time."[57] While it is reasonable to assume that not all of the "original audience," the Philippian community, would have acknowledged the Jewish allusions on first hearing, there is still the possibility that over time certain individuals discovered such allusions and circulated these interpretations alongside further study of the relevant Hebrew passages.[58] We can safely conjecture that over a period of diligent reading, the "Jewishness" of various passages would be discerned.[59] These "alluded OT stories" (level two), which will prove to be key elements within Paul's emplotment, would further enrich the Philippian community into a deeper understanding of Paul's storied thinking, and further shape their testimonies and experiences into conformity with those of Paul (Phil. 3:17).[60]

Third, there is a misconstrued understanding of the nature of "Jewishness" within Arnold's dismissal of the Jewish nature of πολιτεύομαι. After setting up an antithesis between "the Greek connotation of living as a citizen of a polis" and "the Jewish connotation of living as the new Israel," Arnold avers that evidence of the former

---

[56] Fowl, "Use of Scripture," 163–4; J. Ross Wagner, *Heralds of the Good News: Isaiah and Paul "in Concert" in the Letter to the Romans* (Boston: Brill, 2012), 33–6; Harry Y. Gamble, *Books and Readers in the Early Church: A History of Early Christian Texts* (New Haven: Yale University Press, 1997). There are simply too many factors within this particular reception, such as levels of literacy, access to LXX, nature of oral transmission, number of hearings, competency of studying allusions, etc.

[57] Fowl, "Use of Scripture," 164.

[58] Ibid., 168–9. Fowl writes, "It is clear that by the early third century Origen had clearly noted the connection between Isa 45:23 and Phil 2:10-11 . . . there is evidence of a developed theological culture within which at least some Christians are able to recognize, appreciate, and even develop further the sorts of allusions, references, and connections that Paul is able to make. . . . One can assume that churches from Paul's day to Origen's began to develop this theological culture over time."

[59] Given that Paul himself is a Hellenistic Jew, Arnold's way of identifying Paul's thought as exclusively either Jewish or Hellenistic is methodologically doubtful. In fact, one of the defining characteristics of Paul's vocation is to be a Jewish apostle to the gentiles. Hans Hermann Henrix comments on Paul's special role, "he proclaimed the gospel to the Gentiles as an 'Israelite.' He did this in 'Jewish categories.'" Setting up an antithesis between allusions to Greco-Roman and Jewish contexts simply cannot do justice to the calling of the Jewish Paul and to the identity formation of the gentile Philippians. See Acts 13:48-49, Isa. 49.6; S. J. Hafemann, "Paul and His Interpreters," in *DPL*, ed. Gerald F. Hawthorne and Ralph P. Martin (Leicester: InterVarsity Press, 1993); Hans Hermann Henrix, "Paul at the Intersection between Continuity and Discontinuity: On Paul's Place in Early Judaism and Christianity as well as in Christian-Jewish Dialogue Today," in *Paul and Judaism: Crosscurrents in Pauline Exegesis and the Study of Jewish-Christian Relations*, ed. Reimund Bieringer and Didier Pollefeyt (London: Bloomsbury T&T Clark, 2014), 199.

[60] Arnold's treatment of πολιτεύομαι overlooks Paul's current imprisonment as the key to unlocking his message. As Holloway points out, in Philippians Paul responds with a renewed assessment of suffering that involves the continual progress of the gospel despite his imprisonment, and his boldness in the face of death as "the things that really matter" (Phil. 1:10). Dismissing the influence of such a unique and contingent crisis evidently seems to go against Paul's flow of thought. See Paul A. Holloway, Review of *Philippians: From People to Letter*, by Peter Oakes, *The Journal of Religion* 82 (2002): 435–6; Hellerman, "Humiliation, I," 331–6; Joseph H. Hellerman, *Reconstructing Honor in Roman Philippi: Carmen Christi as Cursus Pudorum* (New York: Cambridge University Press, 2005), 189n.73; Pilhofer, *Philippi*, 42; Bormann, *Philippi*, 32–67.

option should naturally bring the rejection of the latter, which would then rule out the presence of any Jewishness behind πολιτεύομαι.⁶¹ However, as my discussion of Miller's work has shown, there is more than one interpretation of the Jewish nature of πολιτεύομαι.⁶² Objection to the interpretation of πολιτεύομαι as seeing the new "Christian" communities replacing Israel does not amount to a total dismissal of the Jewish perspective on πολιτεύομαι.⁶³ Instead, in what follows I intend to show that there was a Jewish tradition of contestation among the Israelites in discerning the actions of God, to which Paul's current contestation also belongs. Based on Ricoeur's mimesis theory, the meaning of the current contestation of testimonies between Paul and other "Christ-followers" is presented by an emplotment in which various contingent contestations of testimonies among previous generations of God's people (stories of Israel) are fabricated by Paul into a concordant unity. Such is the importance of the Jewish nature of πολιτεύομαι.

In order to fully understand Paul's identity-formation strategies in Philippians, we must involve both the Greco-Roman and Jewish framework.⁶⁴ Thus far, I have demonstrated that no matter whether we look at πολιτεύομαι from the background of the Greco-Roman (e.g., Brewer) or the Jewish (e.g., Miller) perspective, we would arrive at the conclusion that there is a well-attested tradition of confrontation and even military conflict between parties in dispute. I have also introduced three crucial symbolic contexts or traditions (mimesis1) regarding the meaning of πολιτεύομαι: political, military, and theological. Although these dimensions may come from different backgrounds or have different semantic emphases among them, I will show that *they all conflate to form a particular framework of interpretation in articulating Paul's narrative world*. Such a conflation of three symbolic frameworks will prove appropriate for the phenomenon of a contestation of narratives within Paul's shaping of the collective identity of the Philippian community.

4.1.2 The Contestation of Allegiance between Caesar and Christ (27f-28a)

27f ὅτι στήκετε ἐν ἑνὶ πνεύματι,
27g   μιᾷ ψυχῇ συναθλοῦντες τῇ πίστει τοῦ εὐαγγελίου
28a   καὶ μὴ πτυρόμενοι ἐν μηδενὶ ὑπὸ τῶν ἀντικειμένων,

---

⁶¹ Cf. Arnold, *Christ as the Telos*, 161.
⁶² See p.124ff.
⁶³ Cf. Miller, "Politeuesthe," 91.
⁶⁴ Bonnie B. Thurston and Judith Ryan, *Sacra Pagina: Philippians and Philemon* (Collegeville: Michael Glazier, 2009), 88. Regarding the "Christ-Hymn" (Phil. 2:6-11), Bonnie B. Thurston and Judith Ryan write, "the Philippian hymn exemplifies what I have called elsewhere Paul's 'dual purpose vocabulary.' Paul had a genius for choosing language that had connotations in both Jewish and Hellenistic ideational worlds. . . . Paul either composes or chooses a hymn that has material that can be recognized both by those who know Jewish thought and by those familiar with Hellenistic thought." See also Troels Engberg-Pedersen, "Introduction: Paul beyond the Judaism/Hellenism Divide," in *Paul beyond the Judaism/Hellenism Divide*, ed. Troels Engberg-Pedersen (Louisville: Westminster John Knox Press, 2001), 1–4.

According to the Greek sentence structure, the meaning of πολιτεύομαι in 27a is illustrated by these three verbs: στήκετε, συναθλοῦντες, πτυρόμενοι. Being the main verb of the subordinate clause, στήκετε means "to be firmly committed in conviction or belief" or "stand,"[65] with its antonym being φεύγω, which means "flee," "eluding danger."[66] According to Karl Donfried, "stand firm" is a well-established theme of tradition in the context of persecution.[67] In this sense, "standing firm in one spirit" (στήκετε ἐν ἑνὶ πνεύματι) represents the form of their exercising of "heavenly citizenship."

The general semantic meaning of συναθλοῦντες (συναθλέω) is "contend/struggle along with," which appears only here and in Phil. 4:3 in the NT.[68] Scholars are largely divided concerning its interpretation. Some scholars emphasize the military sense and Jewish background of συναθλέω and argue for its connotation of summoning soldiers in a standard battle line during military warfare.[69] For example, Martin Brändl asserts that while there is a paradigmatic function of inviting the Philippians to imitate Paul from the athletic imagery, the usage of συναθλέω here primarily arises from the Jewish tradition of the suffering righteous and the early-Jewish apocalyptic tradition in 4 Maccabees 17:11-16, in which the martyrs will be rewarded with eternal life for their faithful suffering against Antiochus IV Epiphanes.[70] The exercising of "heavenly citizenship" (πολιτεύομαι) is thus further qualified by the Jewish tradition of the suffering righteous.

However, some scholars look at συναθλέω from other angles.[71] For example, Arnold insists that despite a lack of archaeological evidence for athletics in Philippi, a majority of the Philippian Christ-followers would have been preoccupied with such Greek heritage.[72] Without offering solid refutations to Brändl's arguments, Arnold again resorts to the social composition of Philippi construed by Oakes to dismiss the Jewish tradition outlined earlier as problematic.[73] Abundant archaeological evidence of imperial worship in Philippi, which would have brought out ramifications of forced worship, the contestation of allegiance between Caesar and Christ Jesus, and even senses of confrontation between the Philippian community with the authorities, is

---

[65] BDAG, s.v. "στήκω," 944.
[66] BDAG, s.v. "φεύγω," 1052.
[67] Karl P. Donfried, *Paul, Thessalonica and Early Christianity* (London: A & C Black, 2003), 56, referencing E. G. Selwyn, *The First Epistle of St Peter, the Greek Text with Introduction, Notes and Essays* (London: Macmillan & Co, 1955), 454-8.
[68] BDAG, s.v. "συναθλέω," 964; E. Stauffer, "ἀθλέω, κτλ," *TDNT* 1:167-8; Collins, *Power*, 56. The other two verbs συναθλοῦντες and πτυρόμενοι are participles, so grammatically they serve as explications of στήκω.
[69] Krentz, "Military Language," 120; Reimer, "Our Citizenship Is in Heaven," 147-9; de Vos, *Church and Community Conflicts*, 277-8.
[70] 4 Macc. 17:15-16: "θεοσέβεια δὲ ἐνίκα τοὺς ἑαυτῆς ἀθλητὰς στεφανοῦσα. τίνες οὐκ ἐθαύμασαν τοὺς τῆς θείας νομοθεσίας ἀθλητάς; τίνες οὐκ ἐξεπλάγησαν." See also Martin Brändl, *Der Agon bei Paulus: Herkunft und Profil Paulinischer Agonmetaphorik* (Tübingen: Mohr Siebeck, 2006), 289-305, 318-19, 52.
[71] For a list of interpreters who understand συναθλέω as according to the Greco-Roman context, see Arnold, *Christ as the Telos*, 48-51.
[72] Ibid., 105.
[73] Ibid., 48.

largely dismissed by Arnold.⁷⁴ Based on the foregoing discussions, I argue that it is the former meaning of συναθλέω that is the more probable one. As the following exegesis shows, it is more than probable that Paul has alluded to Jewish traditions of the suffering righteous and faithful martyrs in his justification of suffering for the gospel of Christ.⁷⁵

Similar confrontational tradition can also be found in the use of πτυρόμενοι (πτύρω), which is generally denoted as "to let oneself be intimidated."⁷⁶ What is noteworthy is that Paul has not stuck to his common usage of φοβέω or φόβος, but chooses to use this *hapax legomenon*. According to *LSJ*, πτύρω is "used on occasion in classical Greek of timid horses that shy upon being startled at some unexpected object."⁷⁷ Likewise, Geoffrion provides two more observations: first, Plutarch, a Greek historian and Roman citizen living contemporaneously with Paul, uses πτύρω to describe the way a horse on the battlefield unexpectedly trembles and causes a consul of Rome to fall, emphasizing the crippling of fighting capacity due to fear.⁷⁸ Second, the way that Plutarch employs πτύρω with concepts of "adversaries, fear, divine signs, salvation and disaster/destruction" in his political and military context prompts us to consider the possibility of a similar setting in Philippians.⁷⁹ There may be no horses in Philippians, but it is quite plausible that there is trembling and fear among the Philippian community in light of the coming oppression, which might weaken their unity and ability to exercise their citizenship for Jesus Christ.⁸⁰

What is the identity of these ἀντικειμένων (28a)? What kind of people can potentially cause trembling in the community? Who has brought "the same" (τὸν αὐτὸν, 30a) suffering to Paul and the community? Who would alert Paul to the degree that he needs to use the political and military metaphor of πολιτεύομαι/πολίτευμα to engage the community? Based on the immediate literary context and my earlier analysis, I argue that *the best probable identity of ἀντικειμένων belongs to the local political authorities of the Roman Empire*.⁸¹

Based on my analysis of the symbolic frameworks (mimesis1) behind πολιτεύομαι, it is reasonable to suggest that in Philippians there exists a contestation of allegiance between Caesar and Christ. In this confrontation with the authorities, the particular contestation concerns whether Caesar or Christ is the true Lord and Savior who alone embodies εὐαγγέλιον, de-serves absolute allegiance, and merits the obedience of His citizens. If Caesar of the empire represents the true savior who brings peace to the world, the Philippian community really should not follow the path of Paul, whose way of preaching the gospel has led to his imprisonment and even potential martyrdom. In this sense, the meaning of πολιτεύομαι encompasses the political context in which

---

⁷⁴ Hellerman, "Humiliation, I," 331–3; Bormann, *Philippi*, 32–67; Brawley, "From Reflex to Reflection," 143.

⁷⁵ For a discussion on the concept of martyrdom in the writings of Paul, see John S. Pobee, *Persecution and Martyrdom in the Theology of Paul* (Sheffield: JSOT Press, 1984), 93–106.

⁷⁶ BDAG, s.v. "πτύρω," 895.

⁷⁷ LSJ, s.v. "πτύρω," 1341; Hansen, *Philippians*, 98.

⁷⁸ Geoffrion, *Rhetorical Purpose*, 67.

⁷⁹ Ibid., 66–8.

⁸⁰ Ralph P. Martin, *Philippians: Based on the Revised Standard Version* (Marshall: Morgan & Scott, 1976), 84.

⁸¹ For a list of different proposals for the identities of these opponents, see Reumann, *Philippians*, 278–9.

the Philippian community lives, one in which people are accustomed to giving sole allegiance to Caesar. A clash of lordships is on the horizon.

4.1.3 A Manual for Battle: Assurance of the Gospel (27g)

27g μιᾷ ψυχῇ συναθλοῦντες τῇ πίστει τοῦ εὐαγγελίου

Facing such an adverse situation, what can the Philippian community count on? It is with such a question that we approach another *hapax legomenon* phrase, τῇ πίστει τοῦ εὐαγγελίου in 27g. Most scholars interpret τῇ as a kind of dative of interest (or dative of advantage), which means Paul expects the believers to fight for "the faith which belongs to, and which comes from, the hearing of the gospel."[82] However, I argue that there exists another option for interpreting this τῇ: a dative of instrument, which implies that believers should fight *through* something.[83] Based on the definition of πίστις in *LSJ* and Donald Robinson's analysis on the semantic meaning of πίστις,[84] I aver that τῇ πίστει τοῦ εὐαγγελίου should be translated as "the *assurance* of the gospel," which emphasizes *the positive consequences from the present toward the ultimate future of the believers as promised by God.* This interpretation is preferable because the collective function of 27fg and 28a should be a kind of "manual" (practical advice) for the exercising of their citizenship.[85] Within the immediate literary context, as Paul substantiates his admonition in 27f by giving two principles in 27g (μιᾷ ψυχῇ συναθλοῦντες) and 28a

---

[82] Victor C. Pfitzner, *Paul and the Agon Motif: Traditional Athletic Imagery in the Pauline Literature* (Leiden: Brill, 1967), 116. See also I-Jin Loh and Eugene A. Nida, *A Translator's Handbook on Paul's Letter to the Philippians (Helps for Translators)* (New York: United Bible Societies, 1977), 40.

[83] Ian G. Wallis, *The Faith of Jesus Christ in Early Christian Traditions* (Cambridge: Cambridge University Press, 2005), 122. For a list of different interpretations on the nature of the genitive of εὐαγγέλιον, see Mark Jennings, "'Make My Joy Complete': The Price of Partnership in the Letter of Paul to the Philippians" (PhD, Marquette University, 2015), 121n.321. The current investigation takes it as a subjective genitive, which is also supported by Victor C. Pfitzner. See Pfitzner, *Paul and the Agon*, 116.

[84] *LSJ*, s.v. "πίστις," 1408; Donald W. B. Robinson, "Faith of Jesus Christ: A New Testament Debate," *RTR* 29, no. 3 (1970): 76; Paul Foster, "Πίστις Χριστοῦ Terminology in Philippians and Ephesians," in *The Faith of Jesus Christ: Exegetical, Biblical, and Theological Studies,* ed. Michael F. Bird and Preston M. Sprinkle (Peabody: Non Basic Stock Line, 2010), 99. In *LSJ* definition II.1, πίστις is understood as "assurance, pledge of good faith, guarantee." And regarding the meaning and usage of πίστις, Donald Robinson writes, "the predominant use of pistis in ordinary Greek was not to indicate what we indicate by the word 'Faith' or 'trust' directed to someone, but rather what we indicate by the word 'reliability' or 'fidelity,' or, in a more concrete way, an 'assurance' or 'pledge.' The Septuagint, for example, probably never uses pistis in our sense 'Faith' or 'trust.' So at least we can say that pistis by itself could not primarily suggest the idea of 'Faith' or 'trust.'" See Robinson, "Faith of Jesus Christ: A New Testament Debate," 76.

[85] Interpreting τῇ πίστει as a dative of interest suggests that during the course of his practical advice, Paul suddenly reverts back to reminding them of the purpose of their striving. However, Paul has already stated this purpose very clearly in 27a: Μόνον ἀξίως τοῦ εὐαγγελίου τοῦ Χριστοῦ.
In fact, according to research on the normative usage of the dative of interest, it is mostly found as relating to people but only rarely to a thing. In contrast, when it comes to the dative of instrument, the standard convention is that the dative noun should be something impersonal and concrete, serving as "the means or instrument by which the verbal action is accomplished." Thus, Paul in 27g should be urging the Philippian community to fight in one mind "by means of" (τῇ) "an assurance" specifically intrinsic to a particular dimension of his understanding of the gospel, which concerns the necessity and meaning of suffering for the gospel. See Daniel B. Wallace, *Greek Grammar beyond the Basics: An Exegetical Syntax of the New Testament with Scripture, Subject,*

(μὴ πτυρόμενοι ἐν μηδενὶ ὑπὸ τῶν ἀντικειμένων), the community are reminded that they have to fight side by side in a standard battle line metaphorically. They can stand firm together only as long as they are not frightened by the opponents and continue to strive together *through the assurance of the gospel*. While these opponents could hurt them (even bodily), their positive future has been guaranteed. With such assured hope and blessing, the Philippian community can be better equipped for their particular battle.

4.1.4 Contestation of the Meaning of the Philippians' Suffering (28bc)

28b ἥτις ἐστὶν αὐτοῖς ἔνδειξις ἀπωλείας, ὑμῶν δὲ σωτηρίας,
28c καὶ τοῦτο ἀπὸ θεοῦ
29a ὅτι ὑμῖν ἐχαρίσθη
29b τὸ ὑπὲρ Χριστοῦ,
29c οὐ μόνον τὸ εἰς αὐτὸν πιστεύειν
29d ἀλλὰ καὶ τὸ ὑπὲρ αὐτοῦ πάσχειν,

After giving some practical advice for the battle, Paul reflects on the meaning of this battle in theological terms. The significance of this theological input cannot be overstated. Even after the Philippian community has received Paul's battlefield guidance, one critical question still remains unanswered for the community: Is it true that the recently escalated suffering (and that of Paul) is from God? While the Philippian community has been a willing partner of Paul's ministry, practically speaking, most of their previous participation may have been in financial terms only (Phil. 4:14-16, 2 Cor. 8:1-5). However, it is probable that with the local authorities promoting imperial worship as a citywide norm, the community could have been placed under more severe oppression and subjected to worse persecution than before. Their previous narrative configuration, together with its habits and identifications, can no longer undergird their thinking in facing such heightened challenges. The community have thus been forced to live a life and behavior pattern constituted by an altered narrative world whose temporality is very different from their previously acknowledged one. It is essential for Paul to renew his narrative world with updated habits and heroes and even with a renewed understanding of God ("criteriology of the divine"). It is only after their recently updated situation of heightened conflicts with the authorities is illuminated with a theological perspective that their subsequent transformation will be real and long-lasting.

It is from this perspective that I contend that the unit 28b-29d primarily functions to serve as a kind of theological "footnote" on suffering and even the possibility of martyrdom in this particular historical and temporal context (30a-c).[86] In terms of

---

and Greek Word Indexes, 4th rev. ed. (Grand Rapids: Zondervan, 1996), 142, 62; Loh and Nida, *Translator's Handbook*, 41.

[86] Gerald F. Hawthorne, *Philippians*, ed. Ralph P. Martin, rev ed., WBC 43 (Waco: Thomas Nelson, 2004), 168.

the Greek sentence structure, 28b is the relative clause to 27fg and 28a. Its function is thus coordinated toward this practical battle advice. Meanwhile, from 28c to 29abcd we observe that there exists a few (direct and indirect) references to God or Christ packed closely together. With 28b and 28c joined together as a parallel structure by a καί, we may see 28bc and 29abcd as one unit with a common motif. However, there are two exegetical issues in 28b. First, what is the antecedent of the pronoun ἥτις in 28b? Second, what elements should we supplement to the "elliptical sentence" ὑμῶν δὲ σωτηρίας to make its meaning complete?[87]

Most western scholars accept the interpretation that faith demonstrated by the community in sufferings is a "sign" (ἔνδειξις) that these opponents (the antecedent of αὐτοῖς is ἀντικειμένων in 28a) are going to be destroyed (αὐτοῖς ἔνδειξις ἀπωλείας, 28b).[88] According to Fee, there is a "Christian eschatological framework" within this translation.[89] When the end time comes, these opponents will be destroyed (ἀπωλεία) and the Philippian community will be saved (σωτηρία). Such an interpretation is based on the frequent understandings of ἀπωλεία and σωτηρία in other parts of the Bible, in which their meanings are usually associated with people's contrasting fates in the end time.[90]

However, this kind of import from other contexts is questionable because it may have omitted the contingent context of Philippians.[91] To understand the correct meaning of ἔνδειξις, we have to examine the word ἔνδειξις in its immediate context.[92] According to BDAG, there are two possible meanings for ἔνδειξις: first, it can refer to "sign/omen." Second, it can denote "demonstration/proof."[93] The former meaning is close to another word often employed by Paul: σημεῖον.[94] When scholars interpret that these opponents are going to be destroyed eschatologically, their understanding of ἔνδειξις belongs to this kind.[95] Yet, Paul has not used the common word σημεῖον but rather chosen this relatively rare word ἔνδειξις.[96] Overviewing his other three uses of ἔνδειξις, Paul always

---

[87] Hansen, *Philippians*, 99. With those two pronouns in 28b belonging to two different cases (αὐτοῖς as dative, ὑμῶν as genitive), this supplementation has become more complicated. See Hawthorne, *Philippians*, 168.
[88] Fowl, "Philippians 1:28b," 172–5; Fee, *Paul's Letter*, 168; Bockmuehl, *Philippians*, 101. In fact, most English Bible translations convey this meaning. See NASB95, RSV, NRSV, NIV, TNIV, HCSB, and ESV.
[89] Fee, *Paul's Letter*, 168.
[90] Cf. *NIDNTT*, s.v. "σωτηρία," 205.
[91] Relying on the research of F. F. Bruce, Moisés Silva argues that concept of Phil. 1:28 can be found also in 2 Thess. 1:4-8. If Paul in Thessalonians emphasizes the salvation of the end time, likewise ἀπωλείας and σωτηρίας should be interpreted in the same way in Philippians. See Silva, *Philippians*, 90; F. F. Bruce, *1 & 2 Thessalonians*, WBC 45 (Waco: Word, 1982), 149.
[92] In fact, even a single word may refer to different things in a single letter. We cannot even assume the meanings of ἀπωλεία and σωτηρία in Phil. 3:19-20 to be the same here in 1:28. Similarly, while Paul in 1:19 has probably used σωτηρία to express his potential release from prison, in the Bible and other contemporary Greek literature ἀπώλεια is often used to refer to natural and physical destruction, instead of destruction at the end time. See BDAG, s.v. "ἀπωλεία," 127.
[93] BDAG, s.v. "ἔνδειξις," 332.
[94] BDAG, s.v. "σημεῖον," 920. Paul has used σημεῖον altogether eight times in Rom. 4:11, 15:19, 1 Cor. 1:22, 14:22, 2 Cor. 12:12 (twice), 2 Thess. 2:9, 3:17.
[95] Fee, *Paul's Letter*, 169n.55.
[96] Among all the Pauline letters, ἔνδειξις has appeared four times, whereas σημεῖον has appeared eight times.

sticks to the latter meaning.⁹⁷ Thus, without denying the future end time consequences of God's righteousness for the world, Paul's typical usage of ἔνδειξις attests to a pattern of something that has already been demonstrated and is "observable" in the *present*, instead of waiting for something to be seen in the future end time.

Without putting the present effect and future consequence into direct antithesis, I argue that the appropriate connotation of ἔνδειξις should be more akin to a *present demonstration* instead of a future sign. In the words of BDAG: it is "something that compels acceptance of something mentally or emotionally."⁹⁸ However, it is simply unreasonable to assume that these opponents, who most probably are the political authorities in Philippi,⁹⁹ will perceive their (coming) destruction after seeing the suffering of the Philippian community.¹⁰⁰ In fact, it is close to impossible for anyone to perceive a *present demonstration* of the destruction of the authorities. What kind of a logic can justify Paul's usage of ἔνδειξις here?

4.1.4.1 Emplotment of the Authorities: Suffering Points to an End of Destructive Death

Such logic is best explained by Ricoeur's notion of narrative as a "dynamic structuration."¹⁰¹ With such a creative emplotment process of organizing incidents into a unified whole, the same set of events can be organized by different people into multiple different plots.¹⁰² What is created are two self-involved and ethically engaged configurations made possible by emplotment.¹⁰³ What Paul is trying to convey in 28b are contradictory evaluations of his recent imprisonment made by himself and the authorities. As far as the political authorities are concerned (αὐτοῖς),¹⁰⁴ the defeat and perseverance within the Philippian community's suffering are all *present demonstrations* of their coming destruction (ἀπωλεία), which probably could mean death.¹⁰⁵ Giving allegiance to a crucified man instead of to Caesar is deemed to be both unacceptable and nonsense to the authorities, which could lead to persecution, bodily suffering, and even death for the Philippian Christ-followers. Instead of perceiving such suffering as

---

⁹⁷ Rom. 3:25, 26; 2 Cor. 8:24. In Romans 3:25-6, Paul writes εἰς ἔνδειξιν τῆς δικαιοσύνης αὐτοῦ . . . πρὸς τὴν ἔνδειξιν τῆς δικαιοσύνης αὐτοῦ ἐν τῷ νῦν καιρῷ, which means that God has demonstrated/proven His righteousness in this present time. In 2 Corinthians, Paul again writes, τὴν οὖν ἔνδειξιν τῆς ἀγάπης ὑμῶν . . . ἐνδεικνύμενοι, which means "demonstration/proof of your love" in this present world.

⁹⁸ BDAG, s.v. "ἔνδειξις," 332.

⁹⁹ Only the local authorities are powerful enough to cause not only trembling to the Philippian community, but also potential bodily damage to them.

¹⁰⁰ Fowl, "Philippians 1:28b," 174, quoting Hawthorne, *Philippians*, 72–5. See also Hansen, *Philippians*, 100.

¹⁰¹ Mara Rainwater, "Refiguring Ricoeur: Narrative Force and Communicative Ethics," in *Paul Ricoeur: The Hermeneutics of Action*, ed. Richard M. Kearney (New Delhi: Sage Publications, 1996), 99; Ricoeur, *T&N I*, 48.

¹⁰² Chatman, *Story and Discourse*, 43.

¹⁰³ Thiselton, *New Horizons*, 355.

¹⁰⁴ A more proper interpretation of αὐτοῖς in 28b should belong to a kind of "ethical dative," which helps carry a perspective from someone on some actions in the present. The fitting translation would be "as far as the opponents are concerned." For further discussions on the meanings of this dative, see Wallace, *Greek Grammar*, 146–7; *The NET Bible* Phil. 1:27n.47.

¹⁰⁵ Fowl, "Philippians 1:28b," 175; Hansen, *Philippians*, 100.

courage or faith from God, the authorities would just dismiss the sufferers as "a mark of stubbornness."[106]

Within this narrative of the authorities, the imprisonment event of Paul and anyone sharing his action are woven into a concordant unity marked by a coherence with the overwhelmingly palpable power of the empire well observed in the recent past and foreseeable future. As the general public of the city of Philippi engages in reading the suffering of the Philippian community, nothing other than the meaning of "destructive end" (death) to the bodies of Paul and the Philippians could be found. In short, suffering for the gospel of the crucified Jesus points to the destiny of a *destructive* and shameful death. The notion of suffering for the gospel as an initiative of God is just too discordant to be integrated into their narratives. Suffering for a crucified slave is too absurd to be recognized as coherent with their internal "criteriology of the divine."[107] Thus, Paul's original witness of the manifestation of God's action is easily rejected by the authorities and the like-minded. If suffering should reflect any action from God, it should be disapproval and repudiation from Caesar, not salvation from the crucified Jesus.

4.1.4.2 Emplotment of Paul: Suffering Points to an End of Glorious Death

In contrast, the same set of suffering events (the imprisonment of Paul and the escalating oppression of the Philippian community) has been organized by Paul into another narrative with totally disparate cause and effect relationships. If the local authorities' narrative is guided by a coherence within its alignment with a story that features the triumphant and oppressive Caesar as the true lord of the world, Paul's narrative has been guided by a narrative that features his suffering for the gospel of Christ as part of the salvation plan of God (ὑμῶν δὲ σωτηρίας, 28b).

Based on Ricoeur's concept of the upper limit of time, these divergent narrations could be explained by their disparate attitudes in narrating the upper limit of their own life (timeline): death.[108] As the roles of death differ within the layered structures of time of both the authorities and Paul, different teleological perceptions of death and bodily suffering have emerged.

While for the authorities any suffering or death should be avoided, for Paul the meaning of suffering and death has been Christocentrically modified:[109] with the believers' death "pegged" to the narrated event of the obedient death of Christ (to be explicated later), suffering for the gospel now points to *the closure of a glorious death*. An assurance of the promise in the gospel (τῇ πίστει τοῦ εὐαγγελίου, 1:27g) has been granted.[110]

---

[106] Fowl, "Philippians 1:28b," 175.
[107] See p.101ff. for the discussion of the "criteriology of the divine."
[108] Ricoeur, *T&N I*, 27–30; Anthony C. Thiselton, *The Two Horizons: New Testament Hermeneutics and Philosophical Description* (Grand Rapids: Wm. B. Eerdmans, 1980), 171–9.
[109] For a discussion on Ricoeur's concept of the upper limit of time, see p.91f.
[110] Cf. Ricoeur, *T&N I*, 27–30; Ricoeur, *T&N III*, 66–7; Thiselton, "Hermeneutic of Temporal and Communal Narrative," 66.

This experience of the assurance of salvation amid suffering is not something the Philippian community can passively obtain. The particular ἔνδειξις for them involves a kind of co-inherence of narration and meaning, which makes it impossible to prove objectively that these sufferings are from God.¹¹¹ According to Ricoeur's concept in HT, within a person's self-engaged perception of God's revelation, a mode of conviction called truthfulness from each of the community members is necessary for her to feel assured that her suffering for the gospel is indeed approved by God. In the exegesis of the story of Paul that follows, this logic will be characterized by a self-engaged logic of ongoing hope as a response toward a future glorious coming of Christ, in contrast to a kind of logic that comes mainly from the past or the present.

4.1.4.3 Two Parallel Perceptions of Reality: The Contestation of Narrative Worlds for the "Dwelling" of the Philippian Community

In short, two parallel perceptions of reality have been created by Paul and the authorities. The same occurrences of the suffering of Paul and the community have been transformed into two sets of disparate narrative events, which respectively contribute to the configuration and progress of two different realities.¹¹² Such demonstration (ἔνδειξις) of realities is not achieved through a kind of objective and impersonal knowledge,¹¹³ but self-engaged, narrative interpretations. These realities thus "function" not by references to an objective logic from the physical world, but through refiguration of the experiences of the Philippian community by unfolding a narrative world in which the community members are invited to "dwell."¹¹⁴ The Philippian community have thus been presented with two competing narrative worlds within which they can simultaneously test and taste the experiences of two different identities from two disparate narrative worlds. Two different versions of their recent memories with Paul have been proposed.

4.1.5 The Contestation of Testimonies between Paul and the Jewish Christian Leaders (29a-d)

If 28bc represents Paul's concern with the contestation of narratives between the authorities and himself, here in 29a-d he shifts his attention toward an even deeper dimension of the contestation: theological debate with other "Christ-followers." In 29a, Paul elaborates his theological annotation: ὅτι ὑμῖν ἐχαρίσθη. Most interpreters translate ὅτι as "for/because/since," which means that 29a can provide more support

---

[111] Cf. Ricoeur, "HT," 133–4; Bauckham, *Jesus and the Eyewitnesses*, 5.
[112] Ricoeur, *T&N I*, 60; Pellauer, "Narrated Action Grounds Narrative Identity," 78; Xavier Lakshmanan, "Narrative and Ontology: Paul Ricoeur's Hermeneutic Philosophy as a Guide to Theological Method" (PhD, Charles Sturt University, 2013), 212–13.
[113] The type of knowledge that assumes the position of a human self sitting outside time as an objective, detached, and stable being. See Ricoeur, *T&N I*, 60; Kevin Aho, *Existentialism: An Introduction* (Malden: Polity Press, 2014), 35.
[114] Cf. Ricoeur, *T&N I*, 70–88.

for the notion in 28c that sufferings (and the situation of contestation) are from God.¹¹⁵ As Paul emphasizes, this suffering is a kind of grace. Following this, in 29b we have an awkward structure τὸ ὑπὲρ Χριστοῦ, which can be understood and translated in three different ways.¹¹⁶ First, if we translate ὑπέρ as "because of," the connection between 28c and 29ab would be that it is because of Christ that the community receives this kind of grace, which is grammatically and theologically possible. But then Christ, rather than God the Father, would be seen here as the source of grace. Another translation would be "for the sake of Christ." However, such a translation would create an awkward connection between 29b and 28c-29a, for it would mean that the sufferings of believers should not only be viewed as grace but also seen as a sacrificial action to Christ, benefiting Him. Neither would it be sensible to connect 29b to 29cd, for this would mean our suffering for Christ is for the benefit of Christ. Finally, we may consider translating ὑπὲρ Χριστοῦ as "on behalf of Christ." Again, it does not make sense to connect 29b to 28c-29a, for it seems awkward to juxtapose the idea of believers suffering in place of Christ with it being a grace from God.

A totally different kind of picture is seen when we connect 29b to 29cd. First, it is apparent that 29b and 29d share a common structure (τὸ ὑπὲρ . . .). In 29b we have τὸ ὑπὲρ Χριστοῦ, in 29d we have τὸ ὑπὲρ αὐτοῦ πάσχειν.¹¹⁷ Based on this similarity between 29b and 29d, we may suggest that the force of ὑπὲρ Χριστοῦ should be primarily connected to πάσχειν in 29d.¹¹⁸ It is plausible that Paul originally wanted to write τὸ ὑπὲρ Χριστοῦ πάσχειν in the place of 29b.¹¹⁹ But in order to emphasize its rhetorical force regarding suffering, Paul interrupted himself and inserted 29c with the form of a οὐ μόνον . . . ἀλλὰ καὶ (not only . . . but also), highlighting suffering as an essential and irreplaceable element of believing. With this insertion, the emphasis is put on suffering *on behalf of* Christ, underscoring the idea that believers who are suffering for the gospel of Christ stand as the legitimate and truthful representative of Christ's πολίτευμα.¹²⁰

What Paul wants to say is that his story of suffering on behalf of Christ (level four) is indeed a legitimate narrative representation of the story of Christ (level three). This narrative is not only self-engaged but also *initiated and graciously given by God*: ὑμῖν ἐχαρίσθη (29a). The third translation is thus preferred over the previous two. It is best supported by the text, and it also highlights the assessment of suffering as the key to demonstrating one's identity as being in Christ, which fits with my perspective that suffering for the gospel of Christ is treated as a *non-negotiable theological mark* of being in Christ.

However, Paul's theological assessment of his suffering is not well received by some other "Christ-followers" (Phil. 1:15-18). Based on my understanding of the identity of the opponents in Philippians, the "Jewish Christian leaders" alluded to in 3:2-3

---

¹¹⁵ J. Harold Greenlee, *An Exegetical Summary of Philippians*, 2nd ed. (Dallas: SIL International, 2008), 78. See also NASB95, ESV, NET, HCSB, TNIV, NRSV, ASV.
¹¹⁶ BDAG, s.v. "ὑπέρ," 1030.
¹¹⁷ In the middle of it (29c) we have οὐ μόνον τὸ εἰς αὐτὸν πιστεύειν.
¹¹⁸ Greenlee, *Exegetical Summary*, 79.
¹¹⁹ Fee, *Paul's Letter*, 171.
¹²⁰ For the tradition of using πολιτεύομαι to convey a sense of contestation in denoting who has been chosen by God to have the legitimate right to be called His people, see Miller, "Politeuesthe," 86–96.

probably could belong *ideologically* to the same group of people as referred to by Paul in 1:15-18, who could not acknowledge Paul's testimony as coming from God. Similar to the truthful prophets in OT who condemned false prophets, the opponents may be of the view that God is punishing Paul via his imprisonment.[121] They might have difficulties in trusting Paul's aggressive evangelistic efforts as favorable to the development of the gospel (1:15-17, 2:20). As I will explain more in detail later, to protect the Philippian community from unnecessary confrontation with the empire, they have probably offered circumcision as a kind of Jewish social identity marker so that the community can gain an exemption from imperial worship (3:2-3).[122] Thus, the contestation between Paul and these Jewish Christians does not revolve around the necessary criteria of being accepted as a "Christian" as found in Galatians. The controversy here is the necessity and hence normative meaning of suffering for the gospel as displayed by Paul.

Compared to the narrative of Paul, which seemingly promotes suffering for its own sake, the suggestion by these "Jewish Christian leaders" actually makes more sense with respect to the "present ordinary reality." Based on Ricoeur, if we take this "reality" as representing the assumed ways to make sense of upcoming events (mimesis1), it is not difficult to see the "genius" of the Jewish Christian leaders. After all, there is no clear evidence that relying on their well-accepted and proven historical heritage to avoid suffering from the empire is incoherent with their commitment to Jesus Christ as their "spiritual" Lord.[123] If one can keep her loyalty to the Lordship of Christ without being persecuted, why not?

How could Paul justify his self-engaged testimony as representing an authentic revelation from God, and promote a theology of suffering for the gospel of Christ? While the previous confrontation with the authorities points to a contestation of allegiances between Caesar and Christ, here against the "Jewish Christian leaders," the issue of contestation concerns the validity of the theology of suffering for the gospel as an exemplary pattern of life for the Philippian community, if not for all "Christians." While certain scholars who understand Paul as conveying confrontational messages

---

[121] Cf. 1 Kgs 18-22; Jer. 27-28. See also Ricoeur, "HT," 119-20.

[122] Tellbe, *Paul between Synagogue and State*, 263-78. Further details of Mikael Tellbe's arguments can be found on p.38ff., 172ff. of this work.

[123] E. P. Sanders has put together a study categorizing into four stands the typical responses of Jews to oppression in the first century. Apart from (1) those who are ready to take up arms and fight for the nation, there are those who would (2) die passively rather than transgress the law, and there are also some (3) who are willing to fight but would rather have an intervention from God. Finally, there are those (4) who would just wait, pray, and hope for the best.

Concerning the last of these four stands, Sanders believes that supporters of this category could also have a theology like this: "If God wanted things to change, he would see to it. If he did not, there was no point in doing anything." So, it is not impossible to guess that of those Jewish people who have been converted to the movement of Jesus Christ, they might prefer a meeker approach when it comes to clashing with the Roman authorities and find it uncomfortable to preach the gospel in an overly aggressive manner like Paul. After all, even Flavius Josephus may have switched from stand three to four. See E. P. Sanders, *Judaism: Practice and Belief, 63 BCE—66 CE* (Minneapolis: Augsburg Fortress, 2016), 459-73. Similarly, Paul Middleton argues that even within the period of the Maccabees, there were already some traditions that prefer life over death. "Death was not always preferred to life." See Paul Middleton, *Martyrdom: A Guide for the Perplexed* (London: T&T Clark International, 2011), 133.

would therefore understand Philippians primarily as anti-imperial political literature, in this work I argue that Paul's core concern, in fact, arises as *a defense of his testimony against other followers of God* that suffering for the gospel is something from God (τοῦτο ἀπὸ θεοῦ, 1:28) and in Christ (ἐν Χριστῷ, 1:12-14). In other words, anti-imperialism, or the contestation of allegiance between Caesar and Christ, becomes more of a "supporting actor" or a "contextual backdrop" in which the contestation of testimonies between Paul and the Jewish Christian leaders takes place. As I am going to show in the following, Paul's use of πολιτεύομαι here echoes the tradition of a dispute of theology and collective identity found in the Jewish tradition, where different Jewish people groups "fight" with each other over the interpretation of scripture, and the legitimacy of representing the Lord.[124] It is within this trajectory of theological controversy and contestation of testimonies that Paul highlights suffering as an indispensable element of believing.

In short, Phil. 1:28b-29d provides a summary of the phenomenon of the contestations of narratives in the whole epistle. Based on Ricoeur's notion of temporality, we can say that Paul's political and "Christian" opponents have incorporated Paul's imprisonment event with drastically disparate temporalities to Paul, which results in a contestation of allegiance regarding the testimony of suffering for the gospel. Facing rejection from the political authorities and the "Jewish Christian leaders," Paul has to argue against both fronts in a single epistle. What I intend to argue is that it is out of these contestations that the Philippians develop their own collective identity. From this we will see divergent allegiances, views of death, uses of the body, aims of life, narratives, and ultimately identities.

4.1.6 The *Same* Suffering of Paul and the Philippian Community (30abc)

30a τὸν αὐτὸν ἀγῶνα ἔχοντες,
30b   οἷον εἴδετε ἐν ἐμοὶ
30c   καὶ νῦν ἀκούετε ἐν ἐμοί.

After providing a "manual" for the battle in 27f-28a and a theological explanation in 28b- 29d, in 30a-c Paul backs up his claim with the pertinent historical and temporal context within which his identity-making of the community takes place. It is *this particular recent and shared temporal context as narrated by Paul* that Paul expects the community to incorporate into their narrative and recent history. The most critical exegetical issue centers on the meaning of ἀγῶνα (ἀγών) in 30a, which can either mean "an athletic contest in the moral and spiritual realm with the goal of a virtuous life" or "a struggle against opposition, struggle, fight."[125] Based on Oakes's understanding of a predominantly gentile composition of the Philippian community, Arnold again argues

---

[124] Miller, "Politeuesthe," 86–96; Geoffrion, *Rhetorical Purpose*, 47n.50.
[125] BDAG, s.v. "ἀγών," 17; E. Stauffer, "ἀγών," *TDNT* 1:134–40; Arnold, *Christ as the Telos*, 119. There are numerous pieces of evidence for both of these usages in ancient Greco-Roman literature. For details, see Krentz, "Military Language," 126; Pfitzner, *Paul and the Agon*, 114–18.

that ἀγών should be interpreted strictly within the context of athletics from the Greco-Roman world.[126]

However, there are at least three reasons for favoring the second sense (not necessarily excluding the first). First, according to Paul Holloway, we cannot detach our understanding of Philippians from Paul's current imprisonment as a scenario of oppression.[127] In his review of Oakes's *Philippians: From People to Letter*, without denying Oakes's emphasis on the economic side of the persecution, Holloway comments,

> But Oakes surely errs when he dismisses the contribution that Paul's own suffering (imprisonment) made to the Philippians' distress. Indeed, in 1:25-26 Paul explicitly states that the Philippians' current discouragement is due precisely to his imprisonment, and he implies as much in 1:27 and 2:17-18.[128]

Holloway argues that Paul's assessment of his imprisonment is exemplary for the Philippian community, as in Phil. 1:10 Paul prays for them: εἰς τὸ δοκιμάζειν ὑμᾶς τὰ διαφέροντα.[129] In other words, Paul's assessment of his suffering is something he hopes the community can follow. The same (τὸν αὐτὸν) ἀγῶνα should then refer to a type of suffering or struggle within the setting of an opposition.

Second, according to the foregoing analysis (28b-29d), Paul is framing his discourse in a contestation of narratives with respect to suffering (πάσχω, 29d). Importantly, both the antagonist offering an opposing narrative against that of Paul, and the persecutor causing Paul's imprisonment or potential martyrdom, belong to the same people group: the political authorities.

The role of this contentious opponent is just too prominent and critical to be dismissed. Striving toward Christ as the τέλος of life by living virtuously in difficult circumstances is conceptually compatible with Paul's argument in Philippians, but the context of contestation and suffering with respect to an antagonistic opponent is at least equally true.

The third reason for favoring the reading of ἀγών as "struggle or fight" lies in the probable historical situations referred to by Paul in 30bc. After portraying the Philippian community and himself as experiencing the *same* struggle (τὸν αὐτὸν ἀγῶνα) in 30a, Paul provides two contingent historical scenarios as examples of this *same* type of ἀγών. In 30b, Paul describes a shared memory of himself and the community, in which they witnessed (ὁράω) with their own eyes an incident of Paul's "struggling."[130] While it is impossible for us to ascertain the historical likelihood of this event, there is one event in the memory of Paul and the community that fits neatly with Paul's discourse here: the serious beating and subsequent imprisonment event recorded in Acts 16:11-40 (probably

---

[126] Arnold, *Christ as the Telos*, 49–51.
[127] Holloway, Review of *Philippians*, 435.
[128] Ibid.
[129] Ibid.
[130] BDAG, s.v. "ὁράω," 719–20; Wallace, *Greek Grammar*, 502.

attested by Paul in 1 Thess. 2:2).¹³¹ What is strikingly similar between this event and Paul's current suffering being heard now (νῦν ἀκούετε, 30c) by the community is that both incur serious imprisonment, bodily hardship, and even a contention of true lordship and allegiance between Caesar and Christ Jesus within Paul's course of gospel sharing. In short, as narrated by Paul, the present suffering of the Philippian community *bears the same nature* as the sufferings of Paul in the past and present.

Admittedly, the community are not experiencing the *same* sufferings that Paul suffered or continues to suffer. Nor do they share the same ethnic backgrounds, cultural traditions, and the pertinent unique challenges of Paul's apostolic calling. So on what basis or logic can Paul say that the community is experiencing the *same* suffering as him?¹³² Based on Ricoeur's concept of temporality as the identity of a narrative, this *sameness* is marked by the same temporality or temporally configured thought among the narratives told about one's life *in accordance with* (not identical to) the temporality of the narrative of Christ (Phil. 2:5-11, 3:17-21). Despite many of the obvious differences between Paul and the Philippian community, they suffer *with a shared temporal identity* in their relationships to the story of Christ.

Such shared temporality between the suffering of Paul and the community does not come "naturally" or "externally," as if they belong to some objectively identifiable attributes or empirical criterion of a human event. This shared identity comes into being only through the making of a specific type of narrative/ethical identity created by their own choices.¹³³ It is only through the ethical intentions in abiding by the promise of suffering on behalf of Christ that such a temporal identity comes into being. In this assessment of the "same" (τὸν αὐτὸν), what Paul could realistically hope is that with the community's unique ethnic and cultural background, they would intentionally engage in creating and telling testimonies of their own *after the temporality of his testimony*, so that their identities would be configured and recognized in the "same" way. Paul's articulation of this narrated sameness thus serves as a productively imagined memory, inviting the Philippian community to remember and identify it as their collective history. It is based on such invitation of remembering and identifying that Paul has set himself up as the ideal exemplary Christ-follower for the Philippian community, persuading the Philippian community to follow Paul in suffering with Christ.

4.1.7 Conclusion

In light of the foregoing analysis of a text filled with symbols and metaphors alluding to the traditions of Greco-Roman imperial politics and military warfare, as well as Jewish heritage, it is reasonable to define the nature of the problem in Philippians as the contestations of narratives regarding the meaning of Paul's suffering for the gospel within the context of the identity formation of the Philippian community. How did Paul run into such a situation of double contestation with the political authorities and

---

[131] Joseph H. Hellerman, "Vindicating God's Servants in Philippi and in Philippians: The Influence of Paul's Ministry in Philippi upon the Composition of Philippians 2:6–11," *BBR* 20, no. 1 (2010): 85–102.
[132] Cf. Campbell, *Paul and the Creation*, 88.
[133] Cf. Ricoeur, *OAA*, 116–18.

the "Jewish Christian leaders"? To answer this, we need to look at the passage of 1:12-26 as a contingent controversy that brings Paul to write the epistle.

4.2 Contrasting Receptions of Paul's Testimony among Christ-followers (1:12-18)

According to Ricoeur's HT, within each reception of a revelation from God there is a co-inheritance of quasi-empirical narrations of historical and external "facts," and engaged interpretations out of theological and internal convictions.[134] In Phil. 1:12-18, Paul introduces the particular "birthplace" of this theologizing. I argue that this passage serves not only to report his recent news to the Philippian community but also attests to his unique understanding of the contingent imprisonment exigency, which ultimately triggers his participation in this contestation of testimonies regarding the meaning of his suffering.

Paul begins his narration by alerting his audience to the seriousness of the following passage in 1:12: Γινώσκειν δὲ ὑμᾶς βούλομαι, ἀδελφοί. Paul is compelled to alert the community to pay special attention to something. Based on Paul's repeated mentioning of the influences of his δεσμός in 1:13-14, τὰ κατ' ἐμὲ (1:12) should point to his recent imprisonment, which is seen by him as a kind of suffering experience as explicated in 1:27-30. With Paul having received a gift from the Philippian community through Epaphroditus (4:18), the community has clearly been well informed of Paul's recent imprisonment. What else does Paul come to see as the most pressing message that needs to be communicated to them?

4.2.1 Paul's Understanding of His Chains Deviates from the Philippian Community's Expectation

The most pressing point is the narrated "fact" that his recent imprisonment experience has *surprisingly* turned out to bring progress to the gospel (μᾶλλον εἰς προκοπὴν τοῦ εὐαγγελίου ἐλήλυθεν, 1:12). According to BDAG, there are two possible meanings for μᾶλλον: "to a greater degree" or "rather."[135] If Paul was imprisoned for his preaching of the gospel, then logically speaking the advance of the gospel would have been hindered. However, according to what Paul mentions in 1:13-14, not only has the advance not been prevented, but it has gained extraordinary "momentum." Thus, the more probable meaning of μᾶλλον here should be "rather," which highlights the surprising and extraordinary result with respect to the previously assumed way of narrating (mimesis1) of the Philippian community. Such progress is not supposed by the community's assumed way of understanding Paul's ministry. What has been

---

[134] Bauckham, *Jesus and the Eyewitnesses*, 404.
[135] BDAG, s.v. "μᾶλλον," 614.

perceived by the Philippian community as a blow to the advance of the gospel now receives a drastically opposite narration (mimesis2).[136]

Paul supplies further details of this extraordinary reversal in 1:13-14, where we encounter another difficult exegetical issue: the awkwardness of the word order in ὥστε τοὺς δεσμούς μου φανεροὺς ἐν Χριστῷ γενέσθαι.[137] Generally speaking, there are three possible ways to render the meaning of this clause. First, as explained by Silva, if we link up τοὺς δεσμούς μου with ἐν Χριστῷ first, then the meaning would be close to the translation of NASB95: "my imprisonment in the cause of Christ has become well known."[138] Coupled with the following phrase ἐν ὅλῳ τῷ πραιτωρίῳ καὶ τοῖς λοιποῖς πᾶσιν, such an approach emphasizes the extensive spreading of an understanding that Paul's imprisonment has a categorical linkage to something of Christ (possibly His crucifixion). While this interpretation is logically possible, it does not complement the function of the preceding ὥστε, which is Paul's explication of the surprise. In fact, if we agree that 1:12 comes as a surprise to the Philippian community, it seems reasonable to expect that the dependent clause 1:13 should provide some relevant information for the surprise in 1:12.[139] In fact, based on Paul's style of writing, scholars have expressed doubt regarding the suggestion that Paul would put the predicate adjective φανεροὺς in between two syntactically linked phrases.[140] Thus, this translation is less than satisfactory.

Another slightly different option is to render the meaning of the clause as following the word order. As NIV translates: "it has become clear throughout the whole palace guard and to everyone else that I am in chains for Christ," which highlights that Paul's personal motivation for his imprisonment is for the sake of (or because of) Christ.[141] However, Silva suggests that if Paul wanted to convey this particular sense, he would most probably resort to his favored phrase ὑπὲρ Χριστοῦ.[142] Again, this translation is not very satisfactory.

How can we understand Phil. 1:13 in a way that relates the pertinence of a surprise, attests to Paul's desire for the transformative effect of the gospel, and respects the word order of Paul's composition? Here I contend for a third way of understanding 1:13. First we must honor the existing word order, which would link τοὺς δεσμούς μου with φανεροὺς. With these two units belonging to a syntax structure of predicate accusative, the clause will be rendered by predicating φανεροὺς (an accusative adjective) on the accusative substantive τοὺς δεσμούς μου. What remains to be explained is the meaning

---

[136] The mimesis2 here refers to the emplotment from which Paul's current imprisonment has been narrated and thus given meaning. Cf. L. Gregory Bloomquist, "Subverted by Joy: Suffering and Joy in Paul's Letter to the Philippians," *Interpretation* 61 (2007): 275–6.
[137] Fee, *Paul's Letter*, 112; Silva, *Philippians*, 62.
[138] Ibid.
[139] It is dubious that Paul would set the spreading of the *cause* of his imprisonment in apposition to the advance of the good news itself. With Paul's zeal for the transformation of people's lives through receiving the gospel (εὐαγγέλιον), it is doubtful that he will be excited in just raising the awareness of the cause.
[140] Silva, *Philippians*, 62; M. R. Vincent, *A Critical and Exegetical Commentary on the Epistles to the Philippians and to Philemon*, ICC (Edinburgh: T&T Clark, 1897), 16.
[141] This is the only time in all his letters that Paul mentions the elite soldier group πραιτώριον.
[142] Silva, *Philippians*, 62.

of the phrase ἐν Χριστῷ, and the pertinent theological implication found in the word φανερός.

Generally taken to mean something "visible, exposed to view, apparent, clear, and public,"[143] one of the common Pauline uses of φανερός is to denote something readily seen outwardly by all eyes.[144] However, Paul also uses φανερός to express something more theological and epistemological about God. In Rom 1:19, within the discourse of the revealing (ἀποκαλύπτω) of God's righteousness and wrath, he writes διότι τὸ γνωστὸν τοῦ θεοῦ φανερόν ἐστιν ἐν αὐτοῖς· ὁ θεὸς γὰρ αὐτοῖς ἐφανέρωσεν to refer to the revealing of God Himself even to the ungodly and unrighteous men (ἐπὶ πᾶσαν ἀσέβειαν καὶ ἀδικίαν ἀνθρώπων, Rom. 1:18). What is manifested is something beyond outward appearances. Alerted by Paul's typical theological overtone in φανερός, P.-G. Müller avers that "φανερός appears in the NT in theologically significant contexts where Paul uses it . . . in the context of specific revelatory terminology."[145] So, does Paul also employ φανερός to deal with the manifestation and perception of theological revelation in Phil. 1:13?[146]

When we pair up τοὺς δεσμούς μου with φανεροὺς in a predicate accusative structure with the infinitive γενέσθαι, a syntactical structure of φανερὸς γίνομαι comes to the fore. As scholars have observed, apart from the general Pauline usage of making something "come to light" or "become known," Paul on occasion uses φανερὸς γίνομαι to refer to a kind of "eschatological manifestation."[147] In fact, no matter whether from the category of "general usage" or specific "eschatological manifestation," what is foundational to both is that there is a kind of clarification or justification of certain people's stand with respect to their relationship to God. In other words, what is disclosed and then perceived is not something confined to empirical and objective observation, but a kind of previously hidden God-human relationship which became disclosed and perceived by certain people.

Therefore, when Paul in 1:13 writes ἐν Χριστῷ, he is probably writing something beyond his personal willingness to suffer for God.[148] In compliance with my analysis of 1:27-30, I argue that this clause articulates Paul's reception of a "Godly-disclosed" revelation that his chains (τοὺς δεσμούς μου) are actually "in Christ" (ἐν Χριστῷ) and ordained by God (καὶ τοῦτο ἀπὸ θεοῦ, 1:28c).[149] In other words, Paul is talking about some newly perceived way of understanding his relationship with God, which arises from God's initiative in disclosing a revelation around his imprisonment event.

According to Ricoeur's HT, every testimony involves a co-inheritance of quasi-empirical narrations of external "facts" and engaged interpretations out of internal

---

[143] P.-G. Müller, "φανερός," *EDNT* 3:412–13; BDAG, s.v. "φανερός," 1047.
[144] Rom. 2:28.
[145] P.-G. Müller, *EDNT* 3:412–13.
[146] Three other non-Pauline occurrences of φανερός with such an implication can be found in Mark 3:12, 4:22, 6:14 and Acts 4:16.
[147] R. Bultmann and Dieter Lührmann, "φανερός," *TDNT* 9:1–10.
[148] He would have written ὑπὲρ Χριστοῦ.
[149] As Fee suggests, the phrase ἐν Χριστῷ probably points to something about Paul's "understanding of the *nature* of discipleship": "I am in chains because I am a man *in Christ*." See Fee, *Paul's Letter*, 113, quoting Fritz Neugebauer, *In Christus: Eine Untersuchung zum Paulinischen Glaubensverständnis* (Göttingen: Vandenhoeck & Ruprecht, 1961), 121.

convictions. Within his own self-engaged testimony, Paul has preliminarily disclosed (φανερός) that his recent jailing by the authorities represents not a setback for the gospel nor a defeat or mistake by himself, but *rather* a glorious manifestation of Christ's saving activity. This in turn has brought about a further spread of the gospel *plus* personal discipleship to Paul himself.[150] In other words, Paul is not just giving some consolation to the Philippians. *He is also not saying that the gospel will continue to thrive despite his current adversity.*[151] *He is saying that his current adversity of suffering for the gospel has turned out to be instrumental to the progress of the gospel.*

If what Paul has perceived concerns himself only, the controversy incurred among communities of "Christ-followers" would be further diminished. This is not the case, however. Within Paul's testimony of his imprisonment, what is more important (and hence controversial) for himself and the Philippian community is the discernment of a new "criteriology of the divine," which concerns the (normative) way God's salvation works on earth and His manifestation. What Paul has disclosed thus deviates not only from the preunderstanding (mimesis1) of his close partners, the Philippian community, but also that of a significant portion of the early "Christian" communities. Based on Ricoeur's dialectic of innovation and sedimentation, it is due to the serious deviance from the temporality of the traditional mode of narrating his imprisonment that contesting testimonies, which necessarily consist of contesting convictions and judgments, have come forth from certain "Christian" leaders (Phil. 1:15-17, 3:2).

This contestation between Paul and other "Christian" leaders becomes increasingly serious when Paul cites further testimonies from others to elicit support for his case, as this revelation of God has been well received by many others: ἐν ὅλῳ τῷ πραιτωρίῳ καὶ τοῖς λοιποῖς πᾶσιν (1:13). If J. B. Lightfoot is right that the best possible meaning of πραιτώριον is "the soldiers composing the imperial regiments,"[152] then these soldiers guarding Paul could be Caesar's own troops in Rome.[153] Based on the contesting relation between Paul and the authorities, it is probable that Paul may have implied a flavor of the "triumph" of Christ over Caesar.[154] By emphasizing that even the closest imperial guards to Caesar have come to share a belief, Paul has further strengthened his testimony by providing "evidential facts" that his imprisonment has attested not only to the gospel's advance but also to Christ's sovereignty over Caesar.[155] Based on Ricoeur's understanding of testimony, Paul has spread his contestation of theological conviction among the "Christian" circle to the much "wider" (in the sense of public)

---

[150] Cf. Fee, *Paul's Letter*, 113; Bauckham, *Jesus and the Eyewitnesses*, 404.
[151] Silva, *Philippians*, 62.
[152] J. B. Lightfoot, *Saint Paul's Epistle to the Philippians* (London: Macmillan, 1913), 88; Fee, *Paul's Letter*, 113.
[153] Fee, *Paul's Letter*, 113. It is probable that when Paul wrote the letter to the Philippians, the community of Christ-followers in Rome may have already spread to many sectors of the city, even in the imperial palace. See Lightfoot, *Paul's Epistle*, 32. For references of scholars' discussions on the place of Paul's imprisonment, see Fee, *Paul's Letter*, 34-7; Martin, *Philippians*, 20-39.
[154] Fee, *Paul's Letter*, 114.
[155] As if the evidence presented by the "seeing" of these guards is not enough, such sense of Christ's triumph over Caesar is further upheld when we see Paul write μάλιστα δὲ οἱ ἐκ τῆς Καίσαρος οἰκίας (4:22) at the end of the letter, intensifying the theme of Caesar's defeat, that even certain emperors' household members have identified themselves as the saints or people of God in Christ Jesus (ἅγιον ἐν Χριστῷ Ἰησοῦ).

contestation of political allegiance, thus further *affirming the pervasiveness and hence truthfulness of his testimony* in covering all aspects of his life, even in his relation to the empire![156] Knowing that even those imperial guards have confessed Jesus rather than Caesar as their true κύριος, the Philippian community would be encouraged to pay their allegiance to Christ over Caesar.[157] Their confidence in the truthful nature of Paul's testimony would be strengthened.

4.2.2 A Contrast of Truthfulness between Paul and the Jewish Christian Leaders

While we cannot ascertain the place of Paul's imprisonment, the exact number of guards within the "entire" (ὅλος) imperial guard, and to what degree these people have "seen" this enlarged theological horizon,[158] what matters here is that in Phil. 1:15-17 the testimony of Paul has been received and witnessed ("produced") in contrasting ways depending on people's motivation toward the gospel. According to Ricoeur's HT, the trustworthiness of a testimony is highly dependent on the presence of truthfulness within its construction. I argue that these divergent and even contesting receptions of Paul's testimony attest to the presence and absence of truthfulness among the community of Christ-followers in Rome. Whereas those brothers in the Lord (τῶν ἀδελφῶν ἐν κυρίῳ), in truthfulness, receive Paul's testimony and produce testimonies of their own out of love (ἐξ ἀγάπης) and good will (δι' εὐδοκίαν), some, without truthfulness, deny Paul's testimony and produce a type of testimony that proclaims Christ only out of jealousy and strife (διὰ φθόνον καὶ ἔριν). While the testimony of the former group is trustworthy, that of the latter is not.

We are not told explicitly why this group of preachers from Rome thinks (οἴομαι) that it can add distress (οἰόμενοι θλῖψιν ἐγείρειν, 1:17) to Paul through proclaiming Christ.[159] Some scholars treat it primarily as a kind of theological dispute between Paul and one particular group of his opponents. For example, Lightfoot argues that this group belongs to the *same* kind of Judaizers that Paul faced in Colossae and Galatia, though with a different contingent historical background.[160] However, considering the drastically different ways Paul reacts to the Judaizers in Galatia and this group in Phil. 1:15-17, Lightfoot's proposal is probably inadequate.[161] Another option has been produced by T. Hawthorn: this group tried to stir up strife between Rome and Paul so that they could speed up the martyrdom of Paul and the *parousia* of Christ.[162] Such a view is firmly rejected by Richard Melick as anachronistic.[163] Additionally, driven by the chiastic and parallel structure of 1:15-17, some scholars even treat it as an excursus

---

[156] See p.105.
[157] Fee, *Paul's Letter*, 114.
[158] For further discussion among scholars on the place of Paul's imprisonment and the meaning of πραιτώριον, see ibid., 114; Lightfoot, *Paul's Epistle*, 99–104; Silva, *Philippians*, 5–7.
[159] For a list of various proposals, see Hawthorne, *Philippians*, 47–8.
[160] Lightfoot, *Paul's Epistle*, 88–9.
[161] Cf. Silva, *Philippians*, 64–5; Fee, *Paul's Letter*, 123.
[162] T. Hawthorn, "Phil. 1:12–19 with Special Reference to vv. 15, 16, 17," *ExpTim* 62 (1950): 316–17.
[163] Melick, *Philippians*, 175.

or a stand-alone unit, which means there is no necessary connection between this unit and the immediate literary context.[164]

Based on the apparently antithetical pairs of relational terms, other scholars bracket this contestation into a kind of personal rivalry (ἔρις), which involves no doctrinal questions at all.[165] The contention becomes detached from the theological domain and reduced to just an ethical issue. The joy that Paul finds (1:18) *apparently* from these malicious preachers' work further shows that the content preached is fine and even the same as that of Paul, suggesting a split between the subjective motive of the preachers and the objective substance of their preaching.[166] While we may not conclude that Paul is addressing the general relation between the work of evangelism and the motive of a preacher, such dichotomy would suggest that Paul favors the achievement of evangelism irrespective of the evangelist's intention,[167] which clearly contradicts the list of vices (φθόνος, ἔρις, ἐριθεία) and vicious intention (οὐχ ἁγνῶς, οἰόμενοι θλῖψιν ἐγείρειν τοῖς δεσμοῖς μου) Paul deliberately ascribes and imputes to these preachers.[168] In fact, as Silva has argued, it is inadequate to think that this group of "Christ-followers" can proclaim Christ with no theological deviance from Paul. How can you hurt Paul if you preach like Paul?[169] *A dichotomy between theological issues and personal rivalry* is not convincing.

A better explanation to this controversy can be offered if we understand Paul's reflection in 1:18 as referring to the preaching of Christ *from both pure and impure motives* (εἴτε προφάσει εἴτε ἀληθείᾳ).[170] The thing that Paul highlights, in which he rejoices (ἐν τούτῳ χαίρω), is not the preaching of the malevolent preachers, but *the contentious situation in which Christ is preached and he is trapped*. Paul's joy here arises primarily not from the fact that some people hear the gospel message despite vicious intention. Taking the immediate literary context (1:12-26) into account, the more probable source of his joy actually stems from his conviction that the divergent responses to his testimony among "God's followers" would not hinder the advancement of the gospel, and more importantly, God's continuous guidance of *him* (1:19-26).

It is with respect to this situation of contesting responses that we explore the attitude of those who support Paul with an intention marked with εὐδοκία (1:15).[171] One critical hermeneutical issue is whether εὐδοκία refers to a person's attitude or God's will. According to Gottlob Schrenk, when we survey usages of εὐδοκία in the

---

[164] Cf. Martin, *Philippians*, 77; Silva, *Philippians*, 64.
[165] Ibid., 64–5; BDAG, s.v. "ἔρις," 392.
[166] Cf. Martin, *Philippians*, 80–1; Hawthorne, *Philippians*, 48.
[167] Cf. Fee, *Paul's Letter*, 124–5, in which Fee suggests that Paul's passion for Christ and the gospel led him to see everything in light of the bigger picture of Christ's salvation and discipleship. While this interpretation is theologically correct, I argue that it has not paid enough attention to the immediate literary context of Phil. 1:12-18.
[168] Cf. Hawthorne, *Philippians*, 48.
[169] Silva, *Philippians*, 64–5.
[170] Jerry L. Sumney, *Philippians: A Greek Student's Intermediate Reader* (Grand Rapids: Baker Academic, 2007), 24. "The γάρ indicates that the question relates back to the preceding statement about some preaching Christ from pure motives and others from impure motives."
[171] Most English translations understand εὐδοκία as representing the good intention of those believers who support Paul. See NASB95, NET, ESV, HCSB, NIV, KJV.

Septuagint, *Jesus Sirach*, and rabbinic writings,[172] despite occurrences that convey a person's emotion or disposition, the predominant meaning is always "pleasure, grace or will of God."[173] Based on this predominant usage, Schrenk argues that the εὐδοκία in Phil. 1:15 should not be translated as "of good intention or sincere purpose," which is improperly controlled by a cursory understanding of an antithesis between εὐδοκία and διὰ φθόνον καὶ ἔριν in strictly ethical terms.[174] Instead, a better rendering would be "of a good mind in the sense of good will," which highlights the convergence of Paul's mind with God's will found in the gospel.[175]

Thus, perhaps a strict dichotomy between God's will and a human's active intention is not necessary. Just as *Sir.* 35.3, 16 employs εὐδοκία to imply both aspects in a context of admonition, where a person should choose one's action according to God's pleasure, I contend that *Paul is using εὐδοκία here to express such double participation from both sides.*[176] What is noteworthy is that in another occurrence of εὐδοκία in Phil. 2:13, we see exactly this double participation from God and humans.[177] It is in the midst of the working of God (θεὸς γάρ ἐστιν ὁ ἐνεργῶν ἐν ὑμῖν καὶ τὸ θέλειν καὶ τὸ ἐνεργεῖν, 2:13), *and* the working of the community (τὴν ἑαυτῶν σωτηρίαν κατεργάζεσθε, 2:12), that both the goodwill of God *and* the wilful desire of the community is fulfilled. Thus, the primary cause behind the antithesis in 1:15-17 stems from *a contrast between a truthful testimony to God's revelation and a deceitful one*. In particular, it is a contrast in terms of the truthfulness which two contesting groups have with respect to their stance on Paul's current suffering. While the opponents do it out of human fleshly jealousy and strife (φθόνον καὶ ἔριν, 1:15), those who accept Paul's ministry do it out of God's divine pleasure. While both have witnessed, only the latter do it in compliance with God's will.

There are two implications for this double participation. First, an initiative participation of will and work from Paul is completely endorsed by God. Fulfilling the goodwill of God necessarily involves a self-engaged participation of a person. Paul's defense of God's actions (εἰδότες ὅτι εἰς ἀπολογίαν τοῦ εὐαγγελίου κεῖμαι, 1:16) thus necessarily runs through Paul's self-engaged defense of his own actions. Based on Ricoeur's dialectic of external narration and internal conviction, such a defense occurs specifically *when Paul witnesses how the newly narrated story of Christ has impacted his internal understanding of God ("criteriology of the divine")*. This testimony encompasses not only an apology (ἀπολογία) of God's active involvement within his recent suffering, but also the normative way of God's self-manifestation through the suffering of His followers.

Second, it is within this entanglement of God's will and human will that the discernment of God's action becomes highly challenging and contentious. According to Ricoeur's analysis on the self-engaged nature of testimony, there are simply no objectively reliable measures in differentiating the will of God from human will. Thus,

---

[172] G. Schrenk, "εὐδοκέω, εὐδοκία," *TDNT* 2:738-51.
[173] Often taken to translate the Hebrew word רצון, εὐδοκία in the Septuagint implies the "sacrifice which is pleasing to God" or a "divine favor" a man receives from God. And out of the fifty-six occurrences of רצון in OT, only sixteen are used to refer to the disposition of a human. For references, see *Sir.* 11:17, 39:18, 41:4; G. Schrenk, "εὐδοκία," *EDNT* 2:75-6.
[174] G. Schrenk, *TDNT* 2:738-51; Bockmuehl, *Philippians*, 78-9.
[175] Schrenk, *TDNT* 2:746.
[176] Cf. *Sir.* 35:3: "εὐδοκία κυρίου ἀποστῆναι ἀπὸ πονηρίας, καὶ ἐξιλασμὸς ἀποστῆναι ἀπὸ ἀδικίας."
[177] G. Schrenk, *TDNT* 2:738-51.

it is not surprising to find that certain "Christians" not only reject Paul's understanding of God but find his understanding of God "contaminated" with his personal will (and vice versa). It is thus "natural" to see that both parties highlight the moral issues of each other, which would undermine each's "narrative unity of life" and hence truthfulness.[178] *The contestation of theological issues necessarily becomes a contestation of personally engaged truthfulness.* Both dimensions of theology and personal rivalry are necessarily involved as key aspects of a contestation of narratives between Paul and a group of Christ-followers in Rome.[179]

4.2.3 The Contestation of Testimonies between "Christ-followers"

Based on the foregoing, the reason for Paul to include this quarreling from Rome in Philippians has become clearer. Not only do they both encounter sufferings as incurred by political authorities, but they also run into a kind of struggle which involves a contestation of testimonies with fellow Christ-followers.[180] What is peculiar is that this group of "Christ-followers," marked by the intention of ἐξ ἐριθείας and οὐχ ἁγνῶς, intends to add to the misery of Paul *through proclaiming the gospel* (τὸν Χριστὸν καταγγέλλουσιν, 1:17). What kind of preaching could bring more distress to Paul?[181] Would it be one that could bring a higher likelihood of the martyrdom of Paul? If we take notice of how Paul talks about death in 1:20-21, it does not seem plausible that physical death itself can distress him.

In contrast, what Paul really cares about (cf. κατὰ τὴν ἀποκαραδοκίαν καὶ ἐλπίδα μου, 1:20), and hence potentially could become troubled by, is whether his current chains and the result of the upcoming trial would be seen as *bringing Christ glory* (μεγαλυνθήσεται Χριστὸς, 1:20). What is more likely to bring misery to Paul is a negative reception of his testimony by the believers in Rome, rendering Paul's testimony as something only from himself. Again, a contestation of narratives or testimonies regarding Paul's imprisonment is at the heart of the matter. Apart from a contestation of allegiance to the true lord in a "political" manner, there is a contestation of testimony regarding Paul's suffering in a theological manner.

With this contestation of testimonies in mind, I investigate how Paul responds to the opposing group. Trapped in this entanglement of theological thinking and personal rivalry, apart from describing them as bearing impure and insincere intentions (οὐχ ἁγνῶς),[182] Paul sees their proclamation of the gospel as motivated by ἐξ ἐριθείας. Commonly translated as "selfish ambition," "contention," or "rivalry,"[183] a deeper sense of this ἐριθεία may be discerned when we consult its usage and its cognates in Aristotle (*Politics*) and Philo (*To Gaius* 68). In Aristotle's Πολιτικά 5.3.1302ᵇ4 and 1303ᵃ14, ἐριθεία and its cognate verb ἐριθευόμενοι are used to convey "a self-seeking pursuit

---

[178] Cf. Ricoeur, *OAA*, 157–63.
[179] Cf. Ricoeur, "HT," 131–4, 20; Paul Ricoeur, *The Course of Recognition*, trans. David Pellauer (Cambridge, MA: Harvard University Press, 2005), 92. See also p.101ff.
[180] Cf. Fee, *Paul's Letter*, 123–4.
[181] Cf. 2 Cor. 2:17.
[182] BDAG, s.v. "ἁγνῶς," 13–14.
[183] BDAG, s.v. "ἔρις," 392; *TLNT*, s.v. "ἐρεθίζω, κτλ," 2:70; F. Büchsel, "ἐριθεία," *TDNT* 2:660–1.

of political office by unfair means" or by "illegal manipulation."[184] In Philo's *On the Embassy to Gaius* 68, the cognate adjective ἀνερίθευτος is used to describe the only right government as one "without strife and intrigue" (ἡγεμονία δὲ ἀφιλόνεικος καὶ ἀνερίθευτος ὀρθὴ μόνη).[185] What is common in these examples is that apart from acquiring personal interests, ἐριθεία (and its cognates) is affiliated to the gaining of *political* position through dubious means.

It may be overly ambitious to rely on these parallel uses to ascertain the function of ἐριθεία. However, based on the conflated symbolic contexts of the Jewish tradition of striving to be God's chosen people and the Greco-Roman political metaphor of πολιτεύομαι/πολίτευμα as explicated earlier (1:27-30), it is possible that Paul employs ἐριθεία to *allude* to the intrigue of his rivals in contesting with him for the *position* of interpreting his suffering in God's πολίτευμα.[186] Just as Paul tries to install suffering for the gospel of Christ as *the core constitution* of Christ's πολίτευμα, his "Christian" rivals are lobbying other Christ-followers to reject Paul's testimony. As they create another version of Christ's πολίτευμα which excludes suffering for the gospel, they marginalize and hurt Paul. While it is false to assume Paul is vying for some prominent "position" or "office" in Christ's πολίτευμα or among the "churches," it is probable that he and his opponent group in Rome are "jockeying" for the critical position of interpreting his recent imprisonment, and even the normative way of discerning God's involvement in suffering. In this manner, while ἐριθεία probably should still be understood as "selfish ambition," less emphasis should be placed on the gaining of personal advantage, and more on a malicious contending of the position of Paul out of his rivals' failure in acknowledging the work of God.

4.2.4 Conclusion

Following this understanding of ἐριθεία, we have taken a closer look at the way Paul differentiates himself from his "Christian" rivals in Rome. In particular, it is within a contestation of truthfulness that Paul and the Jewish Christian leaders contend against each other for the "truth" of Paul's chains. While it is true that Paul has wholeheartedly identified himself with the gospel of Christ through his service,[187] if both he and his rivals were making self-engaged testimonies based on their "inner criteriology of the divine,"[188] where can Paul find his foundation of assurance to offer such seemingly

---

[184] 1302ᵇ4: ἔτι δὲ ἄλλον τρόπον δι' ἐριθείαν, 1303ᵃ14: διά τε τὰς ἐριθείας . . . ὅτι ἡροῦντο τοὺς ἐριθευομένους. See Aristotle, *Aristotle's Politics (Greek)*, ed. W. D. Ross (Medford, MA: Clarendon Press, 1957), 5.1302b.1-4; BDAG, s.v. "ἔρις," 392; *TLNT*, s.v. "ἐρεθίζω, κτλ," 2:72; F. Büchsel, *TDNT* 2:660-1. According to the translation of H. Rackham, both of these ἐριθεία mean "election intrigue." See Aristotle, *Aristotle in 23 Volumes*, ed. W. D. Ross, trans. H. Rackham, 21 (Medford, MA: Harvard University Press, 1944), 5.1302ᵇ4, 5.1303ᵃ14.

[185] Philo, *Philo: On the Embassy to Gaius (Greek)*, trans. F. H. Colson, X (London: William Heinemann Ltd, 1962), 68; *TLNT*, s.v. "ἐρεθίζω, κτλ," 2:72.

[186] Cf. de Vos, *Church and Community Conflicts*, 282; Brawley, "From Reflex to Reflection," 136n.36; Miller, "Politeuesthe," 86-96.

[187] Fee, *Paul's Letter*, 121.

[188] See p.101ff.

"malicious" comments regarding those who disagree with his theology?[189] On what terms could Paul justify that he was acting ἁγνῶς, while these opponents in Rome were acting out of selfish intention? After all, is it not Paul who is more susceptible to personal interest within his narration of his own predicament? To justify Paul's trustworthiness in his shaping of the Philippian community, we have to look for a kind of foundation of assurance that best supports the advantage of his theological viewpoint over his opponents. Based on Ricoeur's understanding of truthfulness in HT, I will explore this issue in the next section.

4.3 Assurance amid Doubt: Narrative Logic within Allusion to Job (1:19-26)

Divided by a double use of χαίρω in Phil. 1:18, Paul shifts his attention to the anticipation of his imminent future.[190] What stands out in this anticipation is a display of confidence and assurance that Christ will be magnified (μεγαλυνθήσεται Χριστὸς, 1:20) and Paul will be released from prison (1:22-26). As Ricoeur's theories suggest, there exists no objective logic to prove or disprove the arguments involved in a contestation of testimonies. How can Paul then provide any grounds for his hope and confidence? It is in the direction of this question that we find Paul alluding to the story of Job.

4.3.1 Similarity and Difference between Job and Paul

At the start of this passage (1:19) there is an exact *verbatim replica* of LXX Job 13:16: τοῦτό μοι ἀποβήσεται εἰς σωτηρίαν. While scholars agree that Paul consciously copies this verse from Job, they disagree in their interpretations as to why.[191] Indeed, there are similarities between the situation of Job and Paul: Both are facing some kind of suffering which is reported to be "from God." Both are looking for σωτηρία which most probably includes rescue from their current predicament. And even more importantly, both are instructed by their "religious and wise companions" that they themselves should take blame for their suffering. For Job, it is the "pious homilizers" of wisdom; for Paul the other preachers of Christ.[192] Thus, both were looking for vindication from God.

However, besides these similarities, their situations are obviously different. While Job suffers from physical illnesses, the deaths of family members, and the loss of wealth

---

[189] Cf. Ricoeur, "HT," 131-4. For the explanations of the pejorative nature of Paul's discourse here, see Fee, *Paul's Letter*, 121n.22.
[190] Fee, *Paul's Letter*, 106n.3.
[191] Cf. Hays, *Echoes of Scripture*, 21-4; Fowl, "Use of Scripture," 173; Fee, *Paul's Letter*, 130-2. However, a few scholars still hesitate about the allusion here. See Reumann, *Philippians*, 233; J. Hugh Michael, "Paul and Job: A Neglected Analogy," *Expository Times* 36, no. 2 (1924): 67.
[192] John Reumann, "The (Greek) Old Testament in Philippians 1:19 as Parade Example," in *History and Exegesis: New Testament Essays in Honor of Dr. E. Earle Ellis on His Eightieth Birthday*, ed. Sang-won Son and S. Aaron Son (New York: Bloomsbury T&T Clark, 2006), 195.

in a rather passive manner, Paul suffers imprisonment and potential martyrdom out of his active zeal for the gospel of Christ. While their sufferings are both "from God," their reasons for suffering are very different. While Job suffers out of a heavenly debate between Satan and God, in which Job has no active participation, it is fair to say that Paul does contribute to his own imprisonment by the political authorities through his evangelistic efforts. While the challenge to Job from his friends is clearly about the theological tradition of retribution (Job 4:7-9, 33:8-21; 34:5-20), Paul's rivals in Rome (and also in Philippi) object to Paul probably because of the practical consideration of avoiding unnecessary suffering.[193] While Job is determined to prove his innocence regarding his suffering, Paul is determined not to be shamed (ἐν οὐδενὶ αἰσχυνθήσομαι, Phil. 1:20) by proving his testimony comes from God. While Job occasionally laments and questions God, Paul rejoices with assurance from God.[194] While God sometimes appears as an adversary to Job, He always appears as the defender of Paul.[195] While death looms as darkness for Job, to Paul this is a gain (κέρδος, Phil. 1:21).

4.3.2 Interpretive Issues within Allusion to Job

With the foregoing similarities and discrepancies in mind, we are ready to ask a few interpretive issues critical to my work. First, what is the meaning of σωτηρία? Is Paul talking about his imminent release from prison, or is he talking about his ultimate future salvation from God? According to Gerald Hawthorne, σωτηρία in 1:19 represents Paul's desire of his release from prison.[196] As opposed to the meaning of an "ultimate cosmic saving act of God" at the end time, Hawthorne sees the vindication that Paul hoped for as similar to God's saving of Job from his current troubles. However, many scholars have strong doubts about such an explanation. For example, based on his understanding of Job's vindication as pointing to some heavenly deliverance, Lohmeyer argues that the σωτηρία here does not refer to Paul's being delivered from prison, but to his ultimate vindication.[197]

On the other hand, Silva notes that Paul "ties in his adversity with his deliverance" in a peculiar way.[198] When Paul writes τοῦτό μοι ἀποβήσεται εἰς σωτηρίαν, its meaning is really not that Paul will be delivered from his suffering. Rather, the best translation should be "his adversity *will result* in his deliverance."[199] Understanding that his current situation mentioned in 1:12-18 (τοῦτο) will turn into his release simply does not make sense. Neither can we interpret Paul's line of thought as if he is saying that things will be fine *despite* suffering.[200]

---

[193] For a related discussion on a spectrum of stands from the Jews on rising against the opposition, see note 123 of this chapter.
[194] Cf. the meaning of τῇ πίστει τοῦ εὐαγγελίου in Phil. 1:27 in chapter 4.1.3.
[195] Hays, *Echoes of Scripture*, 22; Fowl, "Use of Scripture," 172.
[196] For further details of Hawthorne's logic, see Hawthorne, *Philippians*, 49–50.
[197] Lohmeyer also references 2 Tim. 4:8 as evidence of such assurance. See Lohmeyer, *Die Briefe an die Philipper, an die Kolosser und an Philemon*, 50–1; Silva, *Philippians*, 70.
[198] Silva, "Philippians," 836.
[199] Ibid.
[200] According to Silva, when Paul writes "this will turn into salvation" in 1:19, he is perhaps implying a conceptual parallel with his previous saying in 1:12: just as the things against me (τὰ κατ᾽ ἐμὲ) will

4.3.3 Nesting the Story of Paul upon the Story of Job

To correctly understand Paul's understanding of σωτηρία in 1:19 and his pertinent concern, I suggest we have to take the "alluded story" of Job into account. According to LXX Job 13:13-18, it is not difficult to see that Job is actually dealing with something more than a release from his current earthly trouble.[201] It is alleged by his friends that it was his hidden sin and wickedness that led to his suffering (an attack of his "narrative unity of a life"). Thus, Job is eager to vindicate himself not only from his current predicament but also his own *spiritual standing before God*.[202] Within Job's hope of being vindicated by God, while those deceitful people (δόλος) would not be able to come before God (ἐναντίον αὐτοῦ, Job 13:16), his salvation would arrive through his coming before God.[203]

When Paul compares his current situation to that of Job, he is not quoting from Job to merely express confidence amid trying circumstances, something that the words mean literally.[204] Between these analogous circumstances of suffering, the particular dynamic within Paul's narrative world that undergirds his written discourse in 1:19-26 can be well modeled by applying the structure of the nesting of stories that I derive from Ricoeur,[205] in which a particular aspect of Paul's own story in Philippians is nested upon an "alluded story" of Job (Job 13:12-18). Using this particular episode of Job (level two), Paul has *creatively* synthesized and identified certain temporal thoughts as beneficial to the development of his own story (level four).[206]

4.3.3.1 "Beginning": Suffering Righteous Accused by Unwise "God-followers"

At the "Beginning" of this nested structure, what is common to both volitional agents exceeds the fate of suffering.[207] Between them, there is a resonance of a "suffering righteous" person being accused by "ungodly God-followers." Both are trapped in a

---

turn into (μᾶλλον ... ἐλήλυθεν) progress of the gospel, this situation (τοῦτό) will similarly *turn into* (ἀποβήσεται εἰς) my salvation (μοι ... σωτηρίαν). See Silva, *Philippians*, 70.

[201] Job's response here belongs to a larger literary context of responding (Job 12:1ff.) to the Σωφαρ ὁ Μιναῖος (Zophar the Naamathite), who challenges Job (11:1ff.) that he should repent for his sin to stop God from further punishing him.

[202] For accusations on Job's hidden sin, see Job 4:7-11, 5:5-7, 8:3-4, 11:6, 15:3-5, 18:5-21, 20:4-29. For his "great wickedness," see Job 22:5-9. See also Silva, *Philippians*, 70.

[203] Fee, *Paul's Letter*, 131.

[204] Hays, *Echoes of Scripture*, 23. According to Fee, such allusion can "echo" not only language but also the setting of a certain OT passage, and refit them into the new setting of Paul. The OT passage then should be understood according to the new setting of Paul in an analogous way. See Fee, *Paul's Letter*, 130-1.

[205] For a definition of the "alluded story" in this work, see chapter 3.2.3. What is important to note is that while such a nested structure is essential to the formation of meaning here, the understanding of Paul's story here by no means just follows the story of Job in a mechanical way. Instead, it follows after Paul's specific way of structuring his arguments within this passage of Philippians, which reflects the recapitulation of his synthesized stories. See Ricoeur, *The Rule of Metaphor*, 5-6, 125, 310; Ricoeur, *T&N I*, ix—x, 68-76.

[206] Cf. Ricoeur, *T&N I*, 58. See also Hays, *Echoes of Scripture*, 23.

[207] For Job, the suffering consists of illness, deaths of family members, and loss of wealth. For Paul, it is his imprisonment by the earthly Roman Empire. For details related to the concept of "volitional agent," see chapter 3.1.3.

contestation regarding their right to interpret their suffering experiences *theologically*. Just as Job suffers as an innocent figure being accused of his own hidden sin, Paul suffers as an enthusiastic and zealous preacher being challenged for his radical testimony and probably his aggressive style in evangelism.[208] While Job's earthly sufferings are extremely severe, what really matters to him is that he can see the face of God and be proved righteous against the accusations from his "pious and wise" friends.[209] Likewise, facing accusations that his imprisonment is not part of God's plan, Paul is adamant to show that no matter whether he lives or dies, he (his body) will still be an instrument of Christ's exaltation (μεγαλύνω) and will be vindicated by God. In short, in both of their cases, the core challenge does not lie in physical sufferings or their being delivered out of them. Instead, the heart of the issue is that the suffering righteous person will be vindicated and proved "right" with regard to his viewpoints regarding his spiritual standing before God and those who accuse him. Just as Job and his "friends" contest for the right to interpret Job's sufferings, Paul and his fellow Christ-followers are fighting for the interpretation of his chains.[210]

Not every scholar agrees with such an interpretation along the tradition of the "suffering righteous."[211] For example, Fee views it through the lens of the "poor man" who appears in Psalms, which then figures Job as an ideal prototype of the sufferer.[212] Along with this strand of interpretation, what is highlighted is the *lamenting feeling* of the sufferer as unfortunate and poor (e.g., Ps. 34:3-6) who awaits God's *mercy*.

However, with the tradition of the "suffering righteous" I am emphasizing the sufferer's *craving for a righteous verdict from God*.[213] Job does suffer, but what Fee has overlooked is that Job is a rich man, who, instead of lamenting for God's mercy as a sufferer or poor man, is actively protesting his *innocence* as related to his spiritual standing before God (Job 6:24-30; 10:1-7).[214] In his detailed review of many proposals concerning such allusion, Reumann inclines to approve the perspective of German scholar K. T. Kleinknecht, who avers that Job should be read with the Jewish tradition of the "suffering righteous."[215] In this tradition, God is often understood as One who will eventually prove right (vindicate) His righteous servants.[216] Likewise, Paul, who has been challenged by other Christ-followers with respect to his testimony as a

---

[208] Cf. ibid.
[209] Job 16:20b-21a, 19:25-27; Reumann, "The (Greek) Old Testament," 199.
[210] Richard Jacobson, "Satanic Semiotics, Jobian Jurisprudence," in *Semeia 19: The Book of Job and Ricoeur's Hermeneutics*, ed. John Dominic Crossan (Chico, CA: SBL, 1981), 69.
[211] On the view pertaining to "suffering righteous," see Kleinknecht, *Der Leidende Gerechtfertigte*, 308; Reumann, "The (Greek) Old Testament," 198–9.
[212] Fee, *Paul's Letter*, 130–1. Cf. Hays, *Echoes of Scripture*, 22; Bockmuehl, *Philippians*, 85.
[213] Cf. Reumann, "The (Greek) Old Testament," 196–201.
[214] Ibid., 197.
[215] Kleinknecht, *Der Leidende Gerechtfertigte*, 308; Reumann, *Philippians*, 232–3; Reumann, "The (Greek) Old Testament," 199.
[216] Traditions of the "suffering righteous" usually rely on a few OT and Jewish texts, such as Ps. 22:8, Wis. 2:12-20. There, the suffering righteous is identified as the Son of God and vindicated by Him. As K. L. Onesti and M. T. Brauch write, "there is a coupling of the motif of the suffering righteous with the traditional Hebrew understanding of God as One who vindicates (Ps. 26, 31:14-18)." See K. L. Onesti and M. T. Brauch, "Righteousness, Righteousness of God," in *DPL*, ed. Gerald F. Hawthorne and Ralph P. Martin (Leicester: InterVarsity Press, 1993).

legitimate narrative representation of the story of Christ, has his heart firmly on his interpretation being vindicated by God.

4.3.3.2 "Middle": Confidence of Righteousness before God Irrespective of Release

In the "Middle" of the nested stories,[217] the resonance arises from the character and action of the volitional agent: a determined and confident Job and Paul. Admittedly, there have been different interpretations regarding Job's state of faith.[218] Over the span of the whole Book of Job, there are indeed mixed states of hope and despair (e.g., Job 9-10). However, despite these ups and downs, what cannot be neglected in this particular episode (Job 13:12-18) is his response to the sudden reversal of fortune: *Job firmly believes his vindication will eventually come.*[219] As Robert Alden writes, "The larger context of this speech (chaps. 12-14) and all of Job's responses are more negative than positive, but there is no reason to eliminate those glimmers of hope and those flashes of faith that punctuate these otherwise depressing chapters."[220] Only those who are confident of their cases would press for trial in court.[221] In fact, according to Hebrew Law, Job's determination of seeking vindication even *in the face of God*, which would inevitably put him in the danger of being killed by God (Job 13:15), actually *attests to his confidence* of his righteousness before God (e.g. Ps. 9:3-4, 68:2-3).[222]

Likewise, in Philippians, we have a determined and confident Paul. With complete boldness (ἐν πάσῃ παρρησίᾳ, 1:20) Paul introduces his heartfelt desire and hope in his response to the sudden reversal of his circumstances (imprisonment and looming death). Such similarity between Job and Paul is also observed by Kleinknecht, who highlights the similarity between Job and Paul's *confidence* of participating in "God's demonstration of righteousness (צְדָקָה) that frees one from sufferings."[223] Thus, I argue

---

[217] "Middle" stands as the temporal phase in a narrative in which discordant contingencies or sudden reversals of circumstances are encountered by the character. For a detailed explanation of this process, see chapter 3.2.2 and note 106 of chapter 3.

[218] One of the most popular views on Job's lack of faith is from David J. A. Clines, who proposes an antithesis between Job's faith in God and in himself. According to Clines, Job is a figure of hopelessness who suffers from self-doubt. See David J. A. Clines, *Job 1-20*, WBC 17 (Waco: Thomas Nelson, 1989), 313-14.

[219] Michael, "Paul and Job," 69; Job 13:13-15, 18, 23:10-12, 27:5-6, 29:12-17, 31:1-40.

[220] Robert Alden, *Job: An Exegetical and Theological Exposition of Holy Scripture*, NAC 11 (Nashville: Holman Reference, 1994), 160.

[221] Hays, *Echoes of Scripture*, 22.

[222] John E. Hartley, *The Book of Job*, NICOT (Grand Rapids: Wm. B. Eerdmans, 1988), 223; Francis I. Andersen, *Job: An Introduction and Commentary* (London: InterVarsity Press, 1976), 179-80. Cf. Exo. 33:20; Judg. 6:22-23, 13:22. What matters here is that even though Job may be seen as challenging God, his determination to seek vindication from God shows that he is a man of faith. Such a position does not rule out that Job has his own shortcomings in his dealings with God.

[223] "*so konvergieren beide Texte doch in der im zitierten Satz zum Ausdruck kommenden Zuversicht des Leidenden, der von den Leiden befreienden צְדָקָה-Erweise Gottes teilhaftig zu werden.*" See Kleinknecht, *Der Leidende Gerechtfertigte*, 308; Reumann, *Philippians*, 232-3. Instead of meaning a state of righteousness as granted from God the Judge, the righteousness here means "God is right" over His choice and manner of working within His plan of redemption. See BDAG, s.v. "δικαιοσύνη," 247. For more details on the meaning of δικαιοσύνη in Philippians as understood by this work, see chapter 5.3.2.

that it is regarding this kind of confidence that Paul nests his story upon an "alluded story" of Job.

While Paul's confidence of righteousness before God emerges ultimately from the nesting of his story with the story of Christ, a key dimension of Paul's confidence of his σωτηρία comes *with a horizon irrespective of his upcoming physical release*. Just as Job confidently hopes for his ultimate vindication from God without knowing when or how God will remove his earthly sufferings, Paul appeals for the community to trust that Christ can be magnified through him *whatever* the outcome of his trial. No matter whether he will live or die after the trial, they should still understand that his current suffering has been ordained by God. In other words, a physical release of Paul and a martyrdom for Paul are both potential manifestations of Paul being saved by God.

While Kleinknecht and Reumann argue that the inclusion of both physical release and future salvation has its basis in a broad spectrum of God's righteousness (צדקה), this investigation will count on Ricoeur's narrative logic for a more nuanced analysis.[224] Here I argue that the σωτηρία that Paul hopes for is constituted by a structure of temporal logic best articulated by *an emplotment that allows different discordant events to be incorporated into a concordant story with an ultimate eschatological end*.[225] According to Ricoeur, just as one single event can be integrated into different narratives leading to different temporal themes, for a narrative with a definite temporal theme and ending, the narrator can admit different discordant events into the "Middle" of the narrative and still keep the narrative in concordance with the same temporality.[226] Caught in chains, Paul has found himself in this kind of temporal process.

Within the battle of testimonies with his rivals, this dialectical nature of σωτηρία has to a degree bothered Paul. Paul is concerned about his immediate physical release and also the ultimate justification from God. But the challenge he is facing involves more than a false dichotomy of judging σωτηρία as either upcoming physical release or ultimate vindication.

What he hopes for in fact involves a continuously (ὡς πάντοτε καὶ νῦν) *ever-refreshing testifying* of his gospel,[227] which is based on an indefinite result of his trial before the tribunal of Caesar in the *near future*, and a definite vindication before the tribunal of God in the *ultimate future*. Regardless of the manner or order in which heterogeneous and discordant elements (like the possible verdicts of his trial, different durations of his imprisonment, timings of his physical release, future salvation from God, and even his martyrdom) are grouped together, Paul truthfully believes that these variegated forms of little narratives should *all* be understood as part of the σωτηρία,[228] and will *all* lead to (ἀποβαίνω, 1:19) the known ending of the grand narrative of his own—his ultimate vindication from God. Just as Job looks forward to his ultimate vindication no matter what immediate contingencies are lying ahead of him, Paul truthfully testifies that he is going to be vindicated by God no matter the result of his trial.

---

[224] Kleinknecht, *Der Leidende Gerechtfertigte*, 312; Reumann, "The (Greek) Old Testament," 199.
[225] Ricoeur, "Life in Quest," 21–2; Sheppard, "Telling Contested Stories," 888.
[226] Ricoeur, *T&N I*, 67; Ricoeur, *T&N II*, 23.
[227] For previous discussions of the refreshing nature of a truthful testimony, see chapter 3.3.3.2.
[228] Cf. Kleinknecht, *Der Leidende Gerechtfertigte*, 309.

While Job and Paul might share a similar temporal logic of their salvation, the source from which Paul acquires his conviction does not primarily stem from Job. Notwithstanding a strong resonance between them (Job and Paul), or that Paul may have earned some comfort from Job, no "narrative necessity" can be derived from the story of Job as the source of a truly confident Paul in the light of his challenge.[229] Based on Ricoeur's dialectic of discordance and concordance, I argue that Paul's conviction is primarily made possible because of *the regulative capacity of an enduring temporal thought provided by another story*: the story of Christ. Paul's experience of conviction is primarily predicated on the narration of the story of Christ whose enduring temporal thought and ultimate end time have become the cosmological paradigm with which all other stories must cohere. Only in this story of Christ can Paul locate the ultimate ending from which his own predicament will be vindicated.

While Job hopes (and dares) to seek the face of God directly, the trajectory of Paul's confidence of vindication is not directly between himself and God but through Christ: "even now as always, Christ will be exalted in my body, whether I live or die" (1:20). His "state of righteousness" depends on the exaltation of Christ.[230] In other words, Paul's righteous standing before God is necessarily mediated by the story of Christ, which leads us to a significant insight into Paul's theological thinking: a Christological centering of the tradition of "suffering righteous" in Job.[231] Paul's desire to be *vindicated* by God hinges on a Christologically innovated Jewish tradition of the "suffering righteous," which primarily serves to address God's justification of a wrong verdict. In this work, I argue that this innovated tradition has been found embedded in Paul's creatively constructed story of Jesus Christ, comprised by His actions of suffering, death, resurrection, and *parousia*.[232] When Paul contests with his opponents that his suffering is ordained by God (level four), he is arguing that his story is a legitimate narrative representation of *the* ideal suffering righteous one (level three).[233]

With the enduring temporal thought from the story of Christ, the hope displayed by Paul takes on one fundamental advancement as compared to that of Job. As the dispute between Job and his "friends" remains unresolved within the immediate episode of

---

[229] For previous discussions of the concept of "narrative necessity" and its regulative capacity, see chapter 3.1.2.3.

[230] As will be explained later, this "state of righteousness" does not point to the status that believers receive from the salvation of Christ when they first put their faith in Him. Such status of righteousness highlights the benefit (sonship) that believers receive in a court scene with God acting as the Judge. This is not the issue at stake in the context of Philippians. Here, what concerns Paul is that he is proved right in the contestation of testimonies for the recognition of God's work in his suffering experiences. For more details on the meaning of δικαιοσύνη in Philippians as understood by this work, see chapter 5.3.2.

[231] According to Joachim Gnilka, terms like αἰσχύνω and μεγαλύνω in Phil. 1:20 actually belong to the field of early Judaism's tradition of the "suffering righteous." Here, such terminologies have been "transferred" to Christ, which renders God's specific ways of σωτηρία in Philippians as embodied in the prototypical (or ideal) "suffering righteous" figure—Christ Jesus. See Reumann, "The (Greek) Old Testament," 199, quoting Joachim Gnilka, *Der Philipperbrief* (Freiburg: Herder, 1976), 67n.24.

[232] Kleinknecht, *Der Leidende Gerechtfertigte*, 302–3, 10; Reumann, "The (Greek) Old Testament," 199.

[233] However, Paul's purpose of alluding to Job is not to make himself a direct prototype or antitype of Job. Paul does not identify himself with the "classical" tradition of the "suffering righteous" in Job *directly*. The fulfillment of the "suffering righteous" comes through Jesus Christ, which is then positively received by Paul. Cf. Hays, *Echoes of Scripture*, 22; Reumann, "The (Greek) Old Testament," 195.

Job 13:12-18 and the larger frame of Job chapters 4–27, Job occasionally shows signs of deep frustration: he suffers in innocence, without understanding the real cause of his suffering (Job 1:6-12). He also suffers due to the lack of an arbiter between him and God (Job 9:33-35, 16:19-21, 31:35-37).[234] What Job lacks is thus a mediator who intervenes as a judge to bring him out of the misery of fruitless contentions with his "friends" and *especially God*.[235] In contrast, Paul's confidence of vindication is arguably stronger because of the things God has done for him *in Christ*. In Christ, Paul has found a renewed paradigm of interpreting his hardship. In Christ, Paul has renewed his way of looking at his past, present, and future. While those wise men have failed to illuminate Job, Christ has become the ultimate source of wisdom to Paul.[236] And, as the following exegesis of the story of Christ will show, in Christ Paul has even found positive meanings for a contestation of testimonies within his own identity-formation process (cf. Phil. 1:18). In short, in Christ Paul has found his perfect arbiter—the ideal "suffering righteous" figure of Christ Jesus, who alone has personified the renewed "criteriology of the divine."

4.3.3.3 *"Ending": The Ultimate Vindication of the Suffering Righteous*

While the foundation of Paul's testimony lies ultimately in the story of Christ, the significance of creating an "alluded story" *from this particular episode* (Job 13:13-18) is characterized by the crisis of a "forked-path" in which Job's suffering episode can be perceived as *leading to different endings and ethical conclusions*. Within this episode, we are not told about the result of the ending of Job (and his friends). Similarly, notwithstanding Paul's multiple expressions of confidence in the exaltation of Christ *through the Philippian community* (Phil. 1:6, 20), his repeated exhortations actually reflect the exigency that such a positive response from the community can be threatened and altered. Considering this, *the inclusion of Job's experience at the ending of his whole story* becomes hugely important for Paul.[237]

According to Ricoeur, the ending of a story not only represents a stop-point or outcome of a story, but it also denotes the point of perspective from which the voice of the narrator can be heard (*totum simul*).[238] It provides the story flow with "an order of moral or ethical significance."[239] According to the reading experiences introduced in mimesis3, just as Job is finally vindicated through God's intervention in Job 38–42 (esp. 42:5), Paul *temporally orients the reading experiences* of the community so that the current episode of Paul's chains can be read *with a teleological drive* toward an ending similar to that of Job. In nesting his own story over that of Job, Paul constructs

---

[234] Tremper Longman III, "Disputation," in *DOTWPW*, ed. Tremper Longman III and Peter Enns (Nottingham: InterVarsity Press, 2008).
[235] Gert Kwakkel, "Righteousness," in *DOTWPW*, ed. Tremper Longman III and Peter Enns (Nottingham: InterVarsity Press, 2008).
[236] Cf. Longman, "Disputation."
[237] While Paul's allusion to Job is comprised of just five Greek words in one verse, the temporal and teleological sense of this phrase necessarily expands our attention to the ending of Job's story and incorporates it into our understanding of Paul. Cf. ibid.
[238] Dowling, *Ricoeur on Time and Narrative*, 6; Ricoeur, *T&N I*, 159–60.
[239] See chapter 3.1.3.

a rhetorical push or promotion of further movement toward his narrative closure.²⁴⁰ Whereas the opponents will read Paul's chains and the Philippian community's suffering as leading to an end of destruction (αὐτοῖς ἔνδειξις ἀπωλείας, Phil. 1:28), with Paul's *alternative paradigm of time* the community could read their own suffering as *leading* to the glorious endpoint of Paul's narrative (cf. 3:20-21).²⁴¹ Just as Job's accusers are exposed by God at the end of the story, those preachers who reject Paul's testimony will be unmasked.²⁴² Just as the sufferings of Job ultimately contribute to the configuration and progress of Job's story toward his σωτηρία, Paul's chains will turn into the path of σωτηρία (see Figure 5). This is the eager expectation and hope of Paul (τὴν ἀποκαραδοκίαν καὶ ἐλπίδα μου, Phil. 1:20).

However, Paul's hope cannot be imparted to the narrative of the Philippian community by himself alone. According to Phil. 1:19-20, apparently there seems to be a close link between the exaltation of Christ and the prayer (δέησις) participation of the Philippian community.

This is not to say that the Philippian community's participation *is* the exaltation of Christ. But based on Ricoeur's notion of the never-ending chain of interpretations within the transmission of testimony, the testimony from Paul the original witness has clearly become the object of interpretation to the other "Christian" hearers in Rome

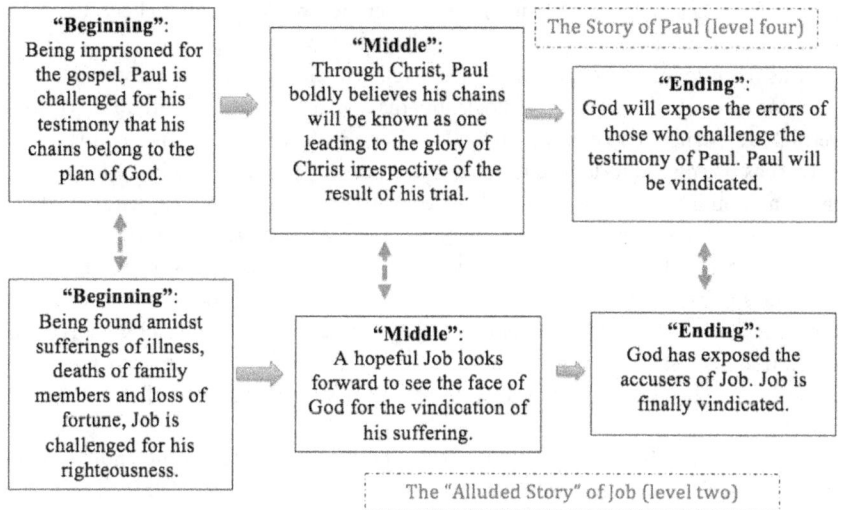

Figure 5 The story of Paul nested upon the "alluded story" of Job.

---

²⁴⁰ Ibid., 67; Hays, *Echoes of Scripture*, 20-3. While Hays and I share a lot in terms of our broad understanding of Paul's theological situation, we differ in terms of our way of articulating Paul's literary strategy. According to Dunn, Hays seems not to have paid enough attention to the logic of assumed narrative structure in his later works. See Dunn, "Whose Story?," 218.
²⁴¹ For previous discussions of this paradigm of time, see chapter 3.2.
²⁴² Hays, *Echoes of Scripture*, 23.

and Philippi.²⁴³ In this transmission stage of Paul's testimony, it can be argued that the exaltation of Christ, whose manifestation inevitably has something to do with the προκοπὴν τοῦ εὐαγγελίου (Phil. 1:12), is virtually tied to the reception and hence participation of the Christ-followers first in Rome, and followed by the Philippian community.²⁴⁴ Just as the "Christians" in Rome have to decide on the authenticity of the original witness ("Does the narration of Paul fit our understanding of God?"), the Philippian community also have to judge whether they should regard this narrative as a true revelation from God.²⁴⁵

The importance of this participative decision may explain why Paul sees the community's prayers as one of the means by which his σωτηρία will come, as he puts this ahead of the help of the Spirit of Jesus Christ (ἐπιχορηγίας τοῦ πνεύματος Ἰησοῦ Χριστοῦ, 1:19). While the "alluded story" of Job may help in the articulation of Paul's determination and hope, the Philippian community's reading and imaginative identification with Job or Paul do not amount to the formation of their ethical identity as proposed by that narrative.²⁴⁶ As Ricoeur has reminded us, the formation of ethical identity for the community cannot be assumed even though they have read, comprehended, and sympathized with the narrative identity of Job and Paul.²⁴⁷ To complete the identity-formation process, each member must make a decision to bind herself to the ethical dimension of Paul's narrative so that Paul (and God) can count on her. A whole-hearted prayer (δέησις) of each member would amount to her intentional participation in the form of promise to Paul and to God.

This intentional participation has been well modeled by Paul. In a contestation of testimonies in which diverse teleological paths and futures are drawn, no objectively verifiable evidence can be proposed by Paul. Thus, instead of understanding his appeal of trust as premised on "logical necessity," a better way to probe into Paul's theological thinking would be as a kind of "narrative necessity."²⁴⁸ In particular, I contend that Paul's experience of confidence is well articulated by a certitude and conviction, through which Paul, in self-engaged truthfulness, affirms his seeking of God's revelation and persuades the community to trust in him.²⁴⁹ It is toward the final tribunal of God at the time of what I call the *cosmological* upper limit of time, that Paul perseveres in reiterating his testimony of his whole life. An alternative historical trajectory of God's salvation has been proposed to cohere with Paul's current temporal experience in prison.

By "pegging" his own death (personal upper limit of time) to the ending of the stories of God and Christ, Paul has firmly shown his hope and conviction of receiving God's vindication. Together with the willingness to sacrifice his life for the gospel (cf.

---

[243] See p.101ff.
[244] Cf. Ricoeur, "HT," 133–4; Greisch, "Testimony and Attestation," 82.
[245] Cf. Ricoeur, "HT," 133–4.
[246] See chapter 3.2.6.
[247] Cf. Ricoeur, OAA, 114–15, 52–68. The best a reading of Paul's epistle (undergirded by Paul's narrative world) can serve is as an imaginative space in which each of the community members can experiment by substituting and recognizing herself with the narrative characters of Job and Paul.
[248] For previous discussions of the concept of narrative necessity, see chapter 3.1.2.3.
[249] For previous discussions of the concept of truthfulness within testimony, see chapter 3.3.3.

Phil. 1:21, 2:16-18), Paul has pushed his conviction to the utmost limit.[250] With this magnitude of conviction, he has identified himself with the humiliated prophets in the OT for their fidelity to the Lord and strengthened the truthfulness of his testimony. In truthfulness, Paul declares that his imprisonment will be remembered by the Philippian community as bringing glory to Christ (1:19). It is this *Christocentrically modified conviction of Job* that Paul finds useful in fostering an experience of self-engaged assurance within his own life and that of the Philippian community.[251]

4.3.4 Conclusion

In this section, I have articulated the σωτηρία for which Paul hopes with an analysis of the dialectical and temporal structure of a narrative. Through an "alluded story" of Job, I have explained how the larger context of Job can become a "theologically edifying context"[252] for Philippians along a tradition of "suffering righteous." Not only do Job and Paul share a similar context of being accused by their fellow "God-followers," but they also share a similar hope of being vindicated by God. While both suffer physical hardships, the core of their struggle belongs chiefly to the contestation of theological explanation regarding their suffering experiences. What is different is that in Christ, Paul has found the foundation for his assured *Aletheia* marked by hope and truthfulness. As the exegesis of the next section will show, the experience of this assurance hinges on believers' awareness of the inaugurated eschatological era of Christ, and a pertinent discernment of God's righteous act.

4.4 Christ's Eschatological Era Demands Believers' Discernment (1:3-11a)

In Phil. 1:3-11a, two things stand out as particularly relevant to the direction of this work. First, Paul's reflection of his own relationship with the community is always anchored by their participation in his gospel ministry. Second, in the reflection Paul repeatedly refers to a few *temporal markers*.[253] Why does Paul do this? How could these actions help strengthen Paul's case within his contestation of testimonies with his opponents? It is with these questions in mind that I start to investigate 1:3-11a.[254]

---

[250] For previous discussions of the function of sacrificing one's life in one's testimony, see chapter 3.3.3.4.
[251] Cf. the meaning of τῇ πίστει τοῦ εὐαγγελίου (Phil. 1:27) in chapter 4.1.3.
[252] Fowl, "Use of Scripture," 173.
[253] For example, in 1:5 Paul says that they have been participating in the gospel *from the first day till now* (ἀπὸ τῆς πρώτης ἡμέρας ἄχρι τοῦ νῦν). Then in 1:6, he mentions a conviction (πεποιθὼς) that the One (God the Father) who *began* a good work in the Philippian community (ὁ ἐναρξάμενος ἐν ὑμῖν ἔργον ἀγαθὸν) in the past, will perfect it until *the day of Christ Jesus* (ἐπιτελέσει ἄχρι ἡμέρας Χριστοῦ Ἰησοῦ). For an alternative understanding of ἄχρι as "at," see Fee, *Paul's Letter*, 86.
[254] 1:11bc will not be taken into account in this section because of the presence of a few variant readings. For a discussion of the significances of these variants, see note 143 in chapter 6.4.3.

After characterizing the past with the participation of the Philippian community in the gospel (1:5), Paul further identifies them as συγκοινωνούς μου τῆς χάριτος πάντας ὑμᾶς ὄντας (1:7). Most English Bibles translate the μου here as "with me," which basically renders the phrase as "all of you are partakers of grace with me."[255] The meaning of χάρις in this interpretation would likely be the "absolute grace of God,"[256] highlighting that both the community and Paul are receivers of God's blessing. However, such a reading has been doubted by multiple interpreters.[257] Both Brent Nongbri and Silva argue that it is probably better to understand μου as modifying τῆς χάριτος instead of συγκοινωνούς.[258] The translation would then be rendered as "You are all partakers of my grace," highlighting the community's specific participation in the *ministry* of Paul.[259] Facing a crisis of losing the Philippian community as his support, Paul is concerned not with a sharing of "divine grace in general," but specifically the community's continual identification with *his* gospel ministry. If in Phil. 1:29a Paul attributes the suffering of the community as *graciously* given by God (ὑμῖν ἐχαρίσθη), the χάρις here should reflect the community's past participation in the ministry of Paul as a kind of suffering on behalf of Christ.[260] The option proposed by Nongbri is preferred.[261]

4.4.1 Remembering the Community's Past Truthful Witnessing

However, such a testimony is not accepted without challenge. Just as Paul's testimony receives diverse receptions in Rome, a similar contestation of testimonies has also been found in Philippi. According to Ricoeur, testimony bears witness to "something that cannot be seen or fully articulated."[262] Those past events of the Philippian community's participation in

---

[255] NASB95, NET, ESV, HCSB, NRSV, NIV. Cf. Fee, *Paul's Letter*, 91n.88, in which Fee discusses the awkwardness of translating μου as "with me."
[256] Silva, *Philippians*, 47, quoting Vincent, *Philippians*.
[257] Silva, *Philippians*, 47–8; Brent Nongbri, "Two Neglected Textual Variants in Philippians 1," *JBL* 128, no. 4 (2009): 803–6. See also the translation of KJV. For a list of scholars who either support or reject such interpretation, see Nongbri, "Two Neglected Textual Variants," 804n.4.
[258] It is noteworthy that a few manuscripts of the type "Western witnesses" (Claromontanus (sixth century), Sangermanensis (ninth century), Boernerianus (ninth century), and Augiensis (ninth century)) provided the reading of "συγκοινωνούς τῆς χάριτος μου," which would have rendered my interpretation of connecting μου to τῆς χάριτος even more trustworthy. However, even if we stick to the current NA[28] reading as supported by the authoritative manuscript P[46], the phrase συγκοινωνούς μου τῆς χάριτος is still ambiguous enough to allow the interpretation of understanding μου as modifying τῆς χάριτος. One such support comes from Phil. 4:14, in which Paul clearly uses μου to modify the following noun. For details, see Nongbri, "Two Neglected Textual Variants," 804–6.
[259] It is beyond the scope of this book to review the way the Philippian community supports Paul. To know more about previous scholars' investigation on the financial aspect in Philippians, see David E. Briones, *Paul's Financial Policy: A Socio-Theological Approach* (London: Bloomsbury T&T Clark, 2015); Julien M. Ogereau, *Paul's Koinonia with the Philippians: A Socio-Historical Investigation of a Pauline Economic Partnership* (Tübingen: Mohr Siebeck, 2014).
[260] Cf. Fee, *Paul's Letter*, 91.
[261] This understanding of χάρις also fits better with Paul's habit of using χάρις to refer to his apostolic ministry. Additionally, a similar phrase (καλῶς ἐποιήσατε συγκοινωνήσαντές μου τῇ θλίψει) is found in Phil. 4:14, in which the personal pronoun μου clearly modifies the following noun phrase τῇ θλίψει instead of the preceding συγκοινωνήσαντές. See Silva, *Philippians*, 47; Nongbri, "Two Neglected Textual Variants," 806.
[262] Leichter, "The Dual Role of Testimony," 373–4.

Paul's ministry can be narrated and imparted with totally different meanings, giving rise to another version of memory.[263] Paul's remembrance of what the Philippian community had done is, in fact, a testimony with *his subjective meaning embedded*.[264] They are *remembered* events, not objective historical facts. Likewise, his opponents can also incorporate these same past occurrences into their narration with an interpretation totally different from that of Paul.[265] Given the co-inheritance of narration and confession in testimony, the logic of a testimony can never be extracted and independently verified.[266] With inevitable subjective meanings embedded, the testimonies of both Paul and the Jewish Christian leaders are not to be accepted uncritically. How then can Paul show the Philippian community that it is his testimony that bears the truthful witness to what really happened, and qualify his as the more trustworthy of the two?[267]

What Paul must do is to consolidate his truthfulness before the Philippian community. As Ricoeur points out, testimony is about trust or distrust between people. As the witness Paul appeals to himself; judgment from the Philippian community ultimately means authenticating him on the mode of truthfulness. In 1:3-8, Paul reaffirms his truthful relationship with the community in a loving manner. In the chiastic structure of 1:3-8,[268] Paul recalls his prayer (δέησις, 1:4) and affection (σπλάγχνον, 1:8) for the community in the A-A' pair of verses (1:3-4 and 1:8), and focuses on the active role of the community in supporting him in the B-B' pair of verses (1:5 and 1:7).[269]

What needs to be analyzed is the particular manner of the community that has supported Paul. In 1:7, while δεσμός clearly refers to Paul's current imprisonment, the meaning of ἀπολογία and βεβαίωσις has brought scholars into another perennial debate. Based on the repeated usage of ἀπολογία in this epistle, it should at least point to Paul's current defense of the gospel as one of the causes of imprisonment.[270] What confuses scholars the most is the meaning of βεβαίωσις. Do ἀπολογία and βεβαίωσις refer to different aspects of the same issue or do they point to issues of different times and places?[271]

Scholars have been alert to the technical or legal senses of ἀπολογία and βεβαίωσις.[272] Commonly used in the law court during the first century, one option is to treat both ἀπολογία and βεβαιώσει as the legal side of the activities corresponding to his δεσμός. However, it is doubtful that such a legal sense would have exhausted

---

[263] Cf. Pellauer, *Ricoeur: A Guide for the Perplexed*, 110.
[264] Cf. ibid., 116.
[265] Ibid., 110.
[266] Ricoeur, "HT," 133–4.
[267] It is possible that Paul's imprisonment can be seen as God's disapproval of his work. See Fee, *Paul's Letter*, 34–7; Melick, *Philippians*, 40; Bauckham, *Jesus and the Eyewitnesses*, 5.
[268] Fee, *Paul's Letter*, 76.
    A:1:3-4   Paul's affection and commitment to the community
    B:1:5   Philippian community's history of supporting Paul
    C:1:6   God's continuous working in the Philippian community
    B':1:7   Philippian community's history of supporting Paul
    A':1:8   Paul's affection and commitment to the community
[269] The meaning of διὰ τὸ ἔχειν με ἐν τῇ καρδίᾳ ὑμᾶς in 1:7 can be taken as Paul's remembering the community in his heart or the community's remembering of Paul. For details, see Melick, *Philippians*, 59–60; Sumney, *Philippians*, 11–12.
[270] Phil. 1:7, 16.
[271] Fee, *Paul's Letter*, 92.
[272] Hawthorne, *Philippians*, 28; Bockmuehl, *Philippians*, 64.

Paul's meaning. Generally speaking, βεβαίωσις refers to a "process of establishing or confirming something."²⁷³ Regarding its cognate adjective βέβαιος, with a symbolic meaning of "that on which one can walk," it is often employed to modify λόγος to denote its being well-founded and convincing.²⁷⁴ Taken in the context of God's word, it serves to guarantee the veracity of prophecy and promise.²⁷⁵ Finally, the primary biblical meaning of the cognate verb βεβαιόω is to "carry out," "fulfill," or "realize."²⁷⁶ Among these uses, a twofold sense of βεβαιόω is always found. First, certain gospel work has been accomplished by God's servants. Second, this accomplishment has subsequently brought a *guarantee* to those who receive the result of the work.²⁷⁷ Thus, βεβαιόω pertains not only to the sanction or confirmation of a truth in its completion, but also the consequence of a *confidence* received.²⁷⁸

It is in light of such usage and function of the βεβαιο- word-group that I understand and agree to Spicq's take on βεβαίωσις in Phil. 1:7: "you [the Philippian community] associate yourselves with my grace in the defense and the establishing (or realization) of the gospel."²⁷⁹ Within Paul's narrative world, it is *through the community's participation in the processual realization* (βεβαίωσις) *of Paul's ministry* that they are identified as his coworkers. While Paul may have employed ἀπολογία and βεβαίωσις to address his defense in the upcoming legal activities, the specific mentioning of their coparticipation in his gospel ministry in the immediate context strongly implies that it is *through the process of suffering for the gospel* that the mission or work of the gospel becomes accomplished.²⁸⁰ Thus, what ἀπολογία and βεβαίωσις mean is an enlarged vision of Paul and the community having joined forces in accomplishing (βεβαίωσις) the work of the gospel through suffering.

Another effect of Paul's remembrance points to the fostering of confidence (the experience of a guarantee) in the heart of the Philippian community. According to Ricoeur, every witness builds her case not on objectively verifiable logic but the mode of conviction—truthfulness. Based on its epistemological function in which a witness assures her of being guided by God, what Paul remembers is thus more than a factual report of the community's past, but a sustained period and lasting memory of the community's truthful witnessing of God's guidance in which the community's collective identity has been formed. While other "Christian" leaders might treat the community's previous suffering with Paul as unnecessary, within Paul's appreciation, the community has been encouraged to *stay truthful to this testimony, memory, and identity*. It is in the midst of this intertwining and mutually affirming relationship between himself and the community that Paul looks forward to building an intersubjective solidarity between him and community (what Ricoeur calls a "natural institution").²⁸¹

---

273 BDAG, s.v. "βεβαίωσις," 173.
274 *TLNT*, s.v. "βέβαιος, κτλ," 1:280–1.
275 See Rom. 4:16, 2 Pet. 1:19.
276 Examples can be found in Rom. 15:8, 1 Cor. 1:6, Phil. 1:7, Heb. 2:3. See *TLNT*, s.v. "βέβαιος, κτλ," 1:282–3; BDAG, s.v. "βεβαιόω," 172–3.
277 *TLNT*, 1:283.
278 *TLNT*, 1:283n.6. In 1 Corinthians, the recipients of the confidence are supposed to be the Corinthian community. In Romans, it should be the Jewish people.
279 *TLNT*, 1:283n.6.
280 Cf. Fee, *Paul's Letter*, 93.
281 See chapter 3.3.3.5 for previous discussions of this "natural institution."

4.4.2 The Foundation of Paul's Conviction: Inauguration of an Eschatological Era by God and Christ

At the central layer of the chiastic structure, Paul stresses God's active involvement in the testimony of the Philippian community. While the Philippian community has shown no serious sign of "betraying" Paul, with the recently escalated persecutions (discordance) happening to Paul and themselves (cf. Phil. 1:30) some chaos has arisen among the community with respect to their future suffering with Paul (cf. 1:27-28, 2:1-4, 4:3). While it seems that the community as a whole would tend to side with Paul's testimony and make themselves dependable to Paul, they cannot just rely on their previous narrative configuration and dispositions to cope with the new adversity. While their previous suffering experience can be marked as something stable and habitual, their recent temporal experience of these escalated persecutions has shifted them away from the "pole" of character toward the "pole" of self-constancy, where each community member *must intentionally construct her own resilience in keeping her fidelity to Paul*.[282] Without a renewed narrative configuration undergirding their upcoming responses to the new adversity, the kind of concordance and pertinent conviction previously enjoyed within their previous form of suffering with Paul (4:14-16) will continue to be weakened. As the following exegesis of the story of Paul shows, it is exactly at this moment other "Christian" leaders show up at Philippi and offer the community alternative testimonies regarding the suffering experiences of Paul and the community. It is amid contesting paradigms of orientating the lives of the Philippian community that Paul writes to the community with a renewed narrative configuration. Competing versions of the "little" history of the Philippian community have been offered.

In 1:6, the story of the community's ongoing commitment ἀπὸ τῆς πρώτης ἡμέρας ἄχρι τοῦ νῦν (1:5) is nested on top of a story in which God actively works in the lives of the community from the beginning (ἐνάρχομαι) until His perfecting (ἐπιτελέω) ἄχρι ἡμέρας Χριστοῦ Ἰησοῦ. Two key "players" are introduced along the trajectory of this narrative: God the Father (level one) and Christ Jesus (level three). On the one hand, without denying the need of the community's active decision, their participation in Paul's ministry originates *with* the work of God Himself (cf. ὁ ἐναρξάμενος ἐν ὑμῖν ἔργον ἀγαθὸν in Phil. 2:13).[283] On the other hand, such work will be perfected until the Day of Christ Jesus (ἐπιτελέσει ἄχρι ἡμέρας Χριστοῦ Ἰησοῦ).

4.4.2.1 Debate of Theological Overtones over Terms of Temporal Markers

While most scholars agree that Paul emphasizes the involvement of God to explain the ultimate origin of Paul's confidence (πεποιθὼς αὐτὸ τοῦτο, 1:6), among them there is a great debate concerning the presence of theological overtones in a particular group of words: ἔργον ἀγαθόν, ἐναρξάμενος followed by ἐπιτελέσει, and ἡμέρας Χριστοῦ

---

[282] Cf. Ricoeur, *OAA*, 118, 65.
[283] Melick, *Philippians*, 59.

Ἰησοῦ.²⁸⁴ In other words, besides meanings relevant to the Philippian community's immediate context, are there any other implicated connotations of God's actions beyond? One popular interpretation was developed by Martin, who argues that ἔργον ἀγαθόν has the sense of a new creation alluding to the tradition of God's creation as good work (Gen. 2:2).²⁸⁵ However, such an allusion has been seriously doubted by Fee (and other scholars), who argues that ἔργον ἀγαθόν, ἐνάρχομαι, and ἐπιτελέω should all be understood primarily in the context of the Philippian community's activity.²⁸⁶

While I agree with Fee on the rather weak sign of allusion to Gen. 2:2, a negation of allusion to this verse does not necessarily rule out the possibility of other theological overtones from the OT. In fact, according to the chiastic structure in 1:3-8, Paul seems to have deliberately pulled together heterogeneous stories of God the Father, Christ Jesus, the Philippian community, and himself into a cohesive whole. In the light of the meaning-making process as illuminated by the model of a nested structure of stories, the issue at stake could be looked upon as this: should we approach the interpretation of 1:6 as primarily showing the stories of the community and Paul in the foreground, with the stories of God and Christ appearing in the far distant (if not irrelevant and far-fetched) background? Or should we see the stories of God and Christ right at the core of the nesting of stories, playing key roles within the interpretation of this verse and the immediate context? While the former option would focus on God's unfailing character as Paul's foundation of confidence, the latter would add to this specific elements found within the stories of God and Christ, which might involve theological overtones from the OT. To answer this question, an investigation of this text concerning the stories of God and Christ will be needed. It is why we now turn our attention to the temporal marker: ἡμέρας Χριστοῦ Ἰησοῦ.

4.4.2.2 The Story of Christ: "Day of Christ" as the Cosmological Upper Limit of Time

Widely accepted as bearing its root of meaning from the OT prophetic theme "The Day of the Lord" (וִיהִי הַיּוֹם / ἡ ἡμέρα κυρίου), the temporal image of ἡμέρας Χριστοῦ Ἰησοῦ has been unceasingly discussed by scholars regarding its historical background and pertinent meaning.²⁸⁷ Even though no consensus has been reached, it is generally accepted that such temporal images signify "a time of Yahweh's unmistakable and powerful intervention . . . into the affairs of this world."²⁸⁸ On occasions with the role of a divine warrior, "The Day of the Lord" will bring "warning and hope" through cosmic

---

[284] While some scholars interpret the reference of ἔργον ἀγαθὸν as being about the financial support the community gave to Paul, it does not make too much sense that Paul would relate such giving to the eschatological Day of Christ. See Melick, *Philippians*, 57–8.
[285] Ralph P. Martin, *Philippians*, NCBC (Grand Rapids: Wm. B. Eerdmans, 1976), 65.
[286] Fee, *Paul's Letter*, 87; Melick, *Philippians*, 59; Silva, *Philippians*, 45–6.
[287] J. D. Barker, "Day of the Lord," in *DOTP*, ed. Mark J. Boda and Gordon J. McConville (Nottingham: InterVarsity Press, 2012); Mark D. Vander Hart, "The Transition of the Old Testament Day of the Lord into the New Testament," *Mid-America Journal of Theology* 9, no. 1 (1993): 5–25.
[288] Barker, "Day of the Lord"; Vander Hart, "Transition of the Old Testament," 3. This is also another demonstration that our analysis of Philippians cannot neglect its Jewish context.

upheaval, holy war, and destruction.²⁸⁹ While those who oppose the Lord will receive judgment and disaster, those who side with Him will receive salvation and rewards.²⁹⁰ In particular, it shows the Lord's "responsive relationship" to His people, stressing Yahweh's power *in shaping human affairs of this world toward His purpose.*

As A. Joseph Everson comments, prophets of different times would employ this temporal image to interpret "various momentous events—past, future or imminent" for their own specific agendas.²⁹¹ Instead of a static point in the future when Yahweh would intervene in this world, or a certain past historical event when ἡ ἡμέρα κυρίου had already happened, this "Day of the Lord" can represent diverse actions of the Lord based on what each prophet cares about.²⁹² For example, the post-exilic prophets, pressed by the need of giving encouragement and hope to the oppressed Israelites, reappropriated the temporal image from something having happened to something "international, global and universal" which points to the eschatological end.²⁹³ As the prophets' renewed story of God grinds with the stories of their own and the oppressed Israelites, those who truly desire the "Day of the Lord" will receive a modified experience and be given hope as seen from the perspective of an alternative future.

As analyzed by Larry J. Kreitzer, this kind of temporal image appears again in Philippians, but it has been redrafted into a unique expression—"Day of Christ (Jesus)" (ἡμέρα Χριστοῦ Ἰησοῦ). While Kreitzer's discovery of Paul's unique redrafting is valuable, his subsequent conclusion deviates from the direction of this work.²⁹⁴ This investigation argues that when Paul Christocentrically adopts and redraws the temporal image into the "Day of Christ Jesus," he is innovatively setting the temporal image with a new temporal frame of divine and human actions so as to show the active involvement of Christ in Paul's suffering for the gospel.²⁹⁵ While exegesis related to the temporal dimension of the story of Christ will be covered later, at this juncture it suffices to say that this "Day of Christ (Jesus)" will be a time of *Christ's* "unmistakable and powerful intervention into the affairs of this world" demanding the Philippian community's watchful attention.²⁹⁶ Specifically, based on Ricoeur's concept of the upper limit of time, with ἡμέρας Χριστοῦ Ἰησοῦ being set as the narrated *cosmological* upper limit for all levels of story within Paul's narrative world, the community's forthcoming reception and judgment of Paul's testimony (mimesis3) will be featured in light of a progression toward this temporal image as a teleological forward movement.²⁹⁷

---

²⁸⁹ G. Von Rad, "The Origin of the Concept of the Day of the Lord," *JSS* 4, no. 2 (1959): 108. Cf. M. Weiss, "The Origin of the 'Day of the Lord'— Reconsidered," *HUCA* 37 (1966): 29–41.

²⁹⁰ According to J. D. Barker, there are altogether fifteen verses in the OT with the exact phrase (מוֹיְהִיָה): Isaiah 13:6, 9; Ezekiel 13:5; Joel 1:15, 2:1, 11, 31, 3:14; Amos 5:18, 20; Obadiah 15; Zephaniah 1:7, 14 (2x); Malachi 4:5.

²⁹¹ A. Joseph Everson, "The Days of Yahweh," *JBL* 93, no. 3 (1974): 335; Barker, "Day of the Lord."

²⁹² Weiss, "Origin," 47.

²⁹³ Ladislav Cerny, *The Day of Yahweh and Some Relevant Problems* (Prague: Nakladem Filosoficke Fakulty University Karlovy, 1948), 79–80.

²⁹⁴ Upon a chronological analysis of the trajectory of Paul's redrafting, Kreitzer then concludes that the "Day of Christ" indicates an "emphasis away from the human appellative 'Jesus' to an ever-increasing titular assessment of his life and ministry." See Larry J. Kreitzer, *Jesus and God in Paul's Eschatology* (London: Bloomsbury Academic, 2015), 163.

²⁹⁵ Cf. Ricoeur, *T&N I*, 67; Ricoeur, "Life in Quest," 22.

²⁹⁶ Barker, "Day of the Lord."

²⁹⁷ Cf. Ricoeur, *T&N I*, 67.

With the image of a divine and military savior, this temporal image will be a point when Christ brings destruction, salvation, cosmic upheaval, and, most important of all, the transformation of His followers' humiliated bodies (Phil. 3:20).[298] As the closure of the story of Christ, this temporal image functions as the ultimate vantage point from which believers' suffering for the gospel will be evaluated.[299] It also signifies the exaltation and vindication of those whose identities have been articulated by a *present* lifetime of suffering for the gospel (3:20-21).[300] Thus, instead of recognizing this "Day of Christ" as a static and stand-alone future based on the representation of a *rectilinear* timeline, this Day actually "comes alive" within the narrative world of Paul as the shorthand reference to, and defining narrative event of, the story of Christ (level three). It is with respect to this cosmological upper limit of time or closure of history that Paul is competing against his multiple opponents. The community must watch out. The Day of Christ is drawing near, demanding to be incorporated into the emplotment of the Philippian community.[301]

4.4.2.3 *The Story of God: He Who Begins and Perfects Requires a Response from the Community*

Apart from the active involvement of Christ, what is equally important for the testimony reception of the Philippian community is the participation of God the Father (level one). In a subordinate clause of 1:6, Paul describes the identity of God the Father with this phrase: ὁ ἐναρξάμενος ἐν ὑμῖν ἔργον ἀγαθόν.[302] Behind the community's active participation in the gospel from the first day until now (Phil. 1:5), God is the one who began (ὁ ἐναρξάμενος, Phil. 1:6). While it is possible to understand the beginning point (ἐνάρχομαι) of God's good work at the time of the community's initial reception of the gospel, with the way Paul remembers the community as the only church participating in his ministry at the *beginning* of the gospel (ἐν ἀρχῇ τοῦ εὐαγγελίου, 4:15), this temporal point probably meant something personal to Paul.[303] In fact, when Paul singles out the community's support as the only one (εἰ μὴ ὑμεῖς μόνοι, 4:15) amid all other churches' refusals (4:14), he sees it as attesting to the community's participation in his suffering (συγκοινωνήσαντές μου τῇ θλίψει, 4:14). Without going into the details of the cause of other churches' refusal, what matters here is Paul's understanding that the Philippian community, since their beginning (ἀρχή) of participating in his ministry, have already been seen as suffering *amid differing*

---

[298] Barker, "Day of the Lord."
[299] Dowling, *Ricoeur on Time and Narrative*, 12, 49, 83-4.
[300] Larry J. Kreitzer, "Eschatology," in *DPL*, ed. Gerald F. Hawthorne and Ralph P. Martin (Leicester: InterVarsity Press, 1993). In other words, this "Day of Christ" has become the "eschatological goal of present life in Christ." See Fee, *Paul's Letter*, 86.
[301] Ricoeur, *T&N I*, 28, 84-5.
[302] Based on Phil. 2:13 (θεὸς γάρ ἐστιν ὁ ἐνεργῶν ἐν ὑμῖν), we can confirm the identity of this action of beginning and perfecting the good work (ὁ ἐναρξάμενος ἐν ὑμῖν ἔργον ἀγαθὸν ἐπιτελέσει, Phil. 1:6) should undoubtedly be God the Father.
[303] Heinz Giesen, "Eschatology in Philippians," in *Paul and His Theology*, ed. Stanley E. Porter (Leiden: Brill, 2006), 220n.17.

*responses among Christ-followers.*³⁰⁴ To Paul, this first day (τῆς πρώτης ἡμέρας) is a day filled with the community's love in the midst of rejection from other churches. Since that first day, amid contestation of testimonies among "Christians," God has begun the good work of guiding the Philippian community in suffering with Paul.

However, the connotations of ἐνάρχομαι here may not have been exhausted by the local story of the community. In a study focusing on theological overtones of ἐνάρχομαι and ἐπιτελέω within structures of embedded stories in LXX, J. Gerald Janzen insightfully highlights a linguistic and narrative pattern involving this word pair. According to Janzen, with the words playing the role of "nodal points of a narrative pattern," a local smaller narrative can be identified as embedded in another larger narrative of God's promise, which should then render the local story understood as an *epitome* of the larger narrative, sharing its "distinctive religious ethos."³⁰⁵ Janzen's work is certainly insightful, and his notion of the sharing of a "distinctive religious ethos" between narratives largely *resembles* Ricoeur's notion of the nesting and transposing of temporality among stories.³⁰⁶ However, in spite of his emphasis on the deep formative influence found within narrative patterns, his work is limited by a lack of elaboration on how one larger story could epitomize itself into a smaller story.

Based on the model of the nesting of stories, I contend that the local story of the community's active participation in suffering for the gospel, marked by God's ἐνάρχομαι and ἐπιτελέω of His good work, actually nests itself upon the narratives of God and Christ, which are framed by Christ's death/resurrection as the beginning, and Christ's transformation of believers' humiliated bodies as the ending. The word ἐνάρχομαι not only marks the time of the beginning of the Philippian community's participation in Paul's suffering ministry, but it also marks the beginning of the larger narrative in which God raises Jesus from death, which emphatically makes the local suffering story of the Philippian community possible.

While the Philippian community's "first-day" participation in the gospel and God's originating action (ἐνάρχομαι) constitute a significant part of Paul's narrative world, Paul's chief concern here lies in the *not yet decided future identity-making* of the

---

³⁰⁴ We are not told why all other churches (or perhaps only those in the province of Macedonia) did not support Paul at that moment, but Richard R. Melick is perhaps right to claim that while Paul's ministry in Macedonia has been troublesome, the biggest difficulty comes from the failure of churches' participation in his ministry. See Melick, *Philippians*, 156.

³⁰⁵ Janzen, "Creation and New Creation," 37, 42, 51n.10. Janzen writes, "[A] 'first day' in one's own life can receive its significance from its relation to a beginning or 'first day' in the historical past, that day, in turn, receiving its significance by its connection to a more ultimate beginning." Likewise, the ending (ἐπιτελέω) in one's personal story can receive an expansion of meaning when it is seen as bringing another promise of old to completion. "God's 'new things' are repeatedly characterized in relation to God's 'Former things'; . . . in Isa. 51:9-11, for example, the new act of salvation (51:11) which is already springing forth (see 43:1) is correlated with the old act of salvation in the Exodus (51:10) and, prior to that, with God's primordial act of world-creating (51:9)." See ibid., 32.

³⁰⁶ Janzen, "Creation and New Creation," 34–7. While Janzen does not reference Ricoeur in this article (he briefly references Heidegger and the concept of temporality in ibid., 49), a conceptual parallel with Ricoeur's idea is clearly seen in his proposal regarding the relation among narratives in one's meaning-making process, which is very similar to the model of nesting of stories as proposed by Ricoeur. In a recently published book, his indebtedness to Ricoeur on the "hermeneutics of resonance" has been made clearer. See Janzen, "Creation and New Creation," 37, 51n.10; Janzen, "Toward a Hermeneutics of Resonance," 242–4.

community. In 1:6, Paul singles out the core content of his conviction: until (ἄχρι) the Day of Christ Jesus, God the Father will accomplish the good work in the community (ἐπιτελέσει ἄχρι ἡμέρας Χριστοῦ Ἰησοῦ). While ἐνάρχομαι appears as an aorist participle in a subordinate clause, here ἐπιτελέσει (ἐπιτελέω) emerges as the main verb of God's (future) action.[307] Notwithstanding its future sense, the parallel effort between the community and God around ἐπιτελέω shows a continuous "sustaining activity" of God stretching from now until the final Day of Christ Jesus.[308] The function of ἐπιτελέω is thus *to reaffirm an ever-present nature of God's accomplishing act concealed beneath the decisions of the Philippian community* (cf. Phil. 2:13). As such, Paul unequivocally urges the need of a compliant and perpetual response from the community to an abundant promise from God.

Like ἐνάρχομαι, ἐπιτελέω refers not only to the continuous moments of perfecting the community's spiritual lives (their local story), but also connotes the ultimate moment that God accomplishes His global salvation in the larger narrative.[309] What God accomplishes on the "Day of Christ" will be a time of Christ's "unmistakable and powerful intervention into the affairs of this world," in which Christ will arrive with the image of a divine and military savior in transforming His followers' humiliated bodies (Phil. 3:20). Thus, within the larger stories of God and Christ, with ἐνάρχομαι marking the function of the "Beginning" and ἐπιτελέω marking that of the "Middle" and the "Ending," the eschatological era is flanked by Christ's death/resurrection as its inauguration, and Christ's transformation of the believers' humiliated bodies as the completion.

The inauguration of this temporal era is also accompanied by a renewed way of narrating God's act. At the dawn of this new era, during Paul's reflection on his suffering experiences, God has shown Paul that suffering for the gospel comes from Him, which then demands an innovated (renewed) narrative representation of the story of Christ. Janzen's notion of a shared "distinctive religious ethos" can be better explicated as a reappropriation of the life stories of Paul and the Philippian community in the light of the works of God and Christ. Instead of an abbreviated copy or an applied ethical principle, the temporalities of the local stories on levels four and five have been modified to build a coherent relation with that of the stories of God and Christ. The God who raises Jesus from death at the beginning is also the One who uses suffering to bring His work toward completion. It is this activity from God in initiating a new era of His salvation that Paul witnesses. It is through this renewed representation and hence updated configuration of his narrative world that Paul sets up suffering on

---

[307] Wallace, *Greek Grammar*, 571. The future tense of ἐπιτελέω is here identified as a kind of "Gnomic Future." Wallace writes, "The idea is not that a particular event is in view, but that such events are true to life. 'In the gnomic future the act is true of any time.'"

[308] Howard Marshall is perhaps right to point out that there is a simultaneous emphasis on God's actions and believers' initiative with respect to the growth (or work) of the Philippian community. See I. Howard Marshall and Karl P. Donfried, "The Theology of Philippians: The Shape of the Church," in *The Theology of the Shorter Pauline Letters* (Cambridge: Cambridge University Press, 1993), 159.

[309] In fact, unless we restrict Paul's understanding on this "Day of Christ Jesus" to the lifespan of the local Philippian community, such theological overtones of ἐπιτελέω are close to a certainty. Cf. Janzen, "Creation and New Creation," 34–7.

behalf of Christ as the core constitution of Christ's πολίτευμα and boundary marker for the Philippian community. Unfortunately, not all of the "Christ-followers" are equally convinced of the presence of such an era and this understanding of God ("criteriology of the divine").

4.4.3 Discernment of God's Act: Suffering for the Gospel as Essential (1:9-11)

It is certainly not surprising to see Paul pray for the "Christian" communities. What matters is that instead of a general prayer, his prayer in 1:9-11 focuses on the epistemological process and practical discernment of God's act amid a contestation of testimonies concerning his suffering experiences.[310] In 1:9, Paul prays (προσεύχομαι) that the community's love abounds further ἐν ἐπιγνώσει καὶ πάσῃ αἰσθήσει.[311] According to classical Greek usage, ἐπίγνωσις generally refers to "knowledge acquired in experiences" through verification and observation. It distinguishes itself (and its cognates) as denoting a kind of knowledge acquired from νοῦς as compared to αἴσθησις from sensual perception.[312] However, distinct from its classical Greek usage, ἐπίγνωσις in the LXX and NT does not denote knowledge comprised of purely objective verification, but a self-engaged acknowledgment of something related to the acts and will of God (or man).[313] Concerning αἴσθησις, according to its classical Greek and LXX usages, besides sensual perception αἴσθησις is often used to denote the acquiring of wisdom related to moral insight.[314] Thus its meaning here could refer to the community's discernment of God's ethical demand on them. Taking both ἐπίγνωσις and αἴσθησις into account, I argue that together they point to the epistemological mechanism of assuring a well-examined approval (δοκιμάζω) regarding "what is absolutely essential regarding life in Christ" (τὰ διαφέροντα).[315] In a context of contesting for the right to interpret the meaning of Paul's imprisonment, this epistemological mechanism would pertain to the discernment that suffering is beneficial to one's spiritual progress, culminating in being found sincere and blameless on the Day of Christ (1:10).

Considering Paul's uses of these categories of subjective knowledge acquisition, the epistemological dimension within *these discernment processes (1:9-11) should find its basis in Paul's renewed stories of God and Christ as told in 1:3-8*. Based on Ricoeur's dialectic of external narration and internal conviction within a chain of testimony

---

[310] Fee, *Paul's Letter*, 97.
[311] Ibid., 100-1.
[312] R. Bultmann, "γινώσκω, κτλ," *TDNT* 1:689-719.
[313] R. Bultmann, *TDNT* 1:689-719. Examples can be found in Heb. 10:26, 2 Pet. 1:3, 8, 2:20, 1 Tm. 2:4, Titus. 1:1, 2 Tim. 2:25, 3:7.
[314] It is often found in contexts where (spiritual) discernment is demanded. See Prov. 1:7, 17:10, Isa. 49:26, Wis. 11:13, 4 Macc. 8:4. See BDAG, s.v. "αἴσθησις," 29; G. Delling, "αἰσθάνομαι, κτλ," *TDNT* 1:187-9.
[315] Fee, *Paul's Letter*, 101; *TLNT*, s.v. "δοκιμάζω, κτλ," 1:353-61. Paul has used the same phrase δοκιμάζεις τὰ διαφέροντα in Rom. 2:18 to denote the Jews' approving of the vital things as according to the Law, though in a negative manner. Notwithstanding such negative connotation, there are still similarities between his usage in Romans and here, as both involve a self-initiated discernment of the vital things with respect to knowledge about God.

transmission, it is only after the Philippian community update the narrations of their suffering experiences through these stories of God and Christ that they can discern the renewed understanding of God and thereby approve God's act in their suffering. It is through the emplotment process of including the recent discordant suffering experiences in a renewed concordant narrative that the community reinforce the truthfulness of their testimony and thus affirm their discernment of God.

4.4.4 Conclusion

Being found in an eschatological era framed by Christ's death/resurrection and His *parousia*, a revelation has been disclosed to Paul in jail: the processual realization of the spread of the gospel necessarily involves a suffering process. Trapped in a contestation of testimonies, Paul resorts to a few theologically loaded temporal markers to help the Philippian community in discerning God's acts. In Philippians, suffering for the gospel does not come as an obstacle to the spread of the gospel nor a believer's spiritual growth. On the contrary, it is graciously essential to the *confirmation* (βεβαίωσις) process of God's salvation and to the spiritual growth of believers. With the "sustaining activity" of God the Father (level one) and the imminent temporal horizon of the "Day of Christ Jesus" (level three), the Philippian community has found themselves (level five) facing Paul's narrative world (level four) calling for their watchful attention and compliant response. If they persevere amid other ill-informed testimonies and stand firm to the promise of God, their identities will be firmly established and "filled with the fruit of righteousness which comes through Jesus Christ" (πεπληρωμένοι καρπὸν δικαιοσύνης τὸν διὰ Ἰησοῦ Χριστοῦ, 1:11a).

4.5 A Contrast of Ethical Dispositions among Contesting Testimonies (2:1-4)

With the formation of this "fruit of righteousness" being set as the life vision and aim of a "good life,"[316] suffering on behalf of Christ has become good not only to the progress of the gospel, but also to the inner lives of believers so that they can become εἰλικρινεῖς καὶ ἀπρόσκοποι (sincere and blameless) as they approach the Day of Christ (Phil. 1:10). In 2:1-4, apart from strengthening the internal unity of the community members, I contend that Paul highlights a polarizing contrast of ethical dispositions in order to encourage the community to support him.[317]

After affirming the community's past participation in the gospel and infusing the community's understanding of their past suffering with a list of honorable moral characteristics (2:1), Paul moves on to exhort the community to "complete my joy"

---

[316] Ricoeur, *OAA*, 172.
[317] Generally speaking, scholars agree that the function of this passage is for the benefit of the community's internal unity. But there are different nuances in scholars' interpretations. For details, see Silva, *Philippians*, 85–6.

(πληρώσατέ μου τὴν χαράν).³¹⁸ Following this, Paul substantiates his exhortation with the clause ἵνα τὸ αὐτὸ φρονῆτε. Appearing a total of ten times in Philippians, φρονέω occupies a pivotal role in the whole epistle.³¹⁹ In a manner that exceeds intellectual activities, and comprises moral attitude and conviction, φρονέω is used by Paul to denote the "fundamental human dispositions" (or mindset) of Christ (2:5), himself (1:7), the Philippian community (2:2, 3:15, 4:2, 10), and even those whose attitude is inappropriate (3:15, 19). Here, after complementing τὸ αὐτὸ φρονῆτε with two synonymous phrases, Paul substantiates the contrast between these diverse ethical dispositions.³²⁰

In a situation of contesting testimonies, it is difficult not to associate the negative moral characteristics of μηδὲν κατ' ἐριθείαν μηδὲ κατὰ κενοδοξίαν with the mindset of the Jewish Christian leaders. To understand the function of ἐριθεία, we have to pay attention to its use in 1:17 in which Paul uses it to taint those who proclaim Christ with intrigue to attain authoritative positions for their own.³²¹ With ἐριθεία personifying the character of his opponents, Paul has once again highlighted the lack of morality in their testimony. According to Ricoeur, one of the parameters for gauging the truthfulness of a testimony is to examine the witness's narrative unity of her life.³²² In this manner, what is strongly implied is the presence of other hidden stories as the real guiding narrative behind their claim: instead of being purely motivated by the gospel of Christ, the testimony of these Jewish Christian leaders has been driven by their own selfish agendas (cf. πρόφασις in 1:18).³²³ In other words, Paul has exposed the lack of truthfulness in the testimony of his rivals. Siding with their testimony would equate to walking a path of disguise and the selfish bidding for authoritative positions for themselves.

Such an exposure of his opponents' disguise is further intensified with the caution of κενοδοξία, which could point to their ambition for self-centered glory.³²⁴ While Silva is perhaps right to understand κενοδοξία as "involving a spirit of envy and provocation," such a reading of interpersonal strife neglects the close relation between the reception of glory from God and a faithful discernment of His action.³²⁵ In fact, on multiple occasions Paul has explicitly called for the right of his own praise and glory (cf. ἔπαινος in 1:11b and καύχημα in 2:16) on the Day of Christ.³²⁶ As Paul declares his imprisonment as coming from God, the source of his δόξα is firmly based on a rightful discerning of God's work in Christ. In the context of contesting for the right understanding of God's will, such rightful pursuance of glory is contrasted with a kind of baseless glory (κενοδοξία) exemplified by those who do not discern such work of God, and even desire to lead Paul into further troubles beyond his current

---

³¹⁸ BDAG, s.v. "πληρόω," 827–30.
³¹⁹ G. Bertram, "φρήν, κτλ," *TDNT* 9:220–35; BDAG, s.v. "φρονέω," 1065–6.
³²⁰ Phil. 2:1 τὴν αὐτὴν ἀγάπην ἔχοντες, σύμψυχοι.
³²¹ *TLNT*, s.v. "ἐρεθίζω, κτλ," 2:70; F. Büchsel, *TDNT* 2:660–1.
³²² Ricoeur, *OAA*, 157–63.
³²³ Cf. BDAG, s.v. "πρόφασις," 889; Fee, *Paul's Letter*, 124.
³²⁴ Cf. BDAG, s.v. "κενοδοξία," 538.
³²⁵ Cf. Silva, *Philippians*, 91; A. Oepke, "κενός, κτλ," *TDNT* 3:659–62.
³²⁶ For the discussion of a variant reading of Phil. 1:11bc in which Paul himself will receive praise, see note 143 in chapter 6.4.4.

imprisonment (θλῖψιν ἐγείρειν τοῖς δεσμοῖς μου, 1:17). In short, through the word pair ἐριθεία and κενοδοξία, Paul has underscored the incoherence between the stories of the desired Philippian community (level five) and the Jewish Christian leaders (level four), rendering their narrative configurations as utterly incompatible.

What is even more important is that these wicked dispositions are strictly incoherent with that of Christ as recorded in 2:5-11. With φρονέω marking the ethical disposition of Christ Jesus (2:5), a strong connection is created between the narrative and ethical identity of Christ Jesus and that of a desired community member.[327] Looking into the "earthly journey" (2:6-8) of Christ, one of His most defining ethical dispositions is ταπεινόω (2:8), which leads directly to His lifelong suffering to the point of death (exegetical details to be covered later). When Paul substantiates his exhortation to the community with ταπεινοφροσύνη (2:3), he is very likely referencing the meaning of the cognate verb ταπεινόω as exemplified by Christ's act of suffering and self-lowering.[328]

While humility is deemed to be morally inferior and despised by the dominant Greco-Roman culture (mimesis1),[329] *a whole new order of moral causality embodied by the story of Christ* steps into the horizon of the Philippian community.[330] Based on Ricoeur's notion of mimesis3, a narrative world comprised of another horizon of ethics and self-understanding has unfolded as the community read Philippians. As they step into this horizon, a drastically different perception of humility and even humiliation is felt. Thus, the comparison of ethical dispositions in Paul's exhortation (2:1-4) is actually undergirded by a contestation of horizons, memories, and narrative worlds. Suffering for the gospel, which necessarily involves both humility and humiliation, is attributed to ethical goodness and emotions.[331] Two radically different emotions, which belong to two narrative worlds with opposing temporalities, thus jockey with each other to win the identification of the community members. It is in the midst of these competing "perceptible" ἐνδείξεις (1:28) that Paul tries to shape the identity of the Philippian community.

In this manner, the formation of the community's ethical disposition is distinctively shaped along a narrative of volitional suffering. A coherence between the story of a suffering Christ Jesus (level three), and the story of a suffering Paul (level four) is then underscored, rendering their narrative configurations as at least compatible. The narrative, in which suffering on behalf of Christ marks the genuine representatives of Christ, becomes more easily accepted. In contrast, due to the wicked dispositions attributed to Paul's opponents, the temporally configured thought of their stories is seen as deviating from that of the story of Christ. This contestation of ethical dispositions leads to a clearer picture of the contestation of testimonies between Paul and the Jewish Christian leaders. While the Jewish Christian leaders build their testimony on selfish ambition and baseless glory, Paul's testimony is firmly built on the humiliation and

---

[327] Bockmuehl, *Philippians*, 109.
[328] Scholars are well aware of the great disparity between the meaning of humility in the Greco-Roman world and the OT. See W. Grundmann, "ταπεινός, κτλ," *TDNT* 8:1–6; Martin, *Philippians*, 101–2.
[329] The mimesis1 here refers to the supposed preunderstanding of humility as representative of the general public's perspective.
[330] Cf. Dowling, *Ricoeur on Time and Narrative*, 49.
[331] Cf. ibid., 12, 83–4.

humility of a suffering Christ. A sharp confrontation is developed between those who reject suffering for the gospel as coherent with the story of Christ, and those who accept it.

In a world where humility, humiliation, and suffering are firmly deemed to be inferior by the dominant Greco-Roman culture (mimesis1), what story of Christ can Paul construct so that his testimony is shown to be truthful? In the next chapter, I will start to analyze the story of Christ, in which I will find the guiding narrative of Paul's own narrative world.

4.6 Conclusion

Based on the foregoing five sections of Philippians (1:27-30, 1:12-18, 1:19-26, 1:3-11a, 2:1-4), I have demonstrated that the theme of a double contestation of narratives is at the core of Paul's challenge and concern in Philippians. Based on the theories of Ricoeur, I have delineated the nature of Paul's exigency as a contention of competing narratives and testimonies regarding the meaning of his suffering. While both the Roman authorities and the Jewish Christian leaders perceive suffering for the gospel of Christ as unnecessary, Paul sees it as the defining action of allegiance (πολιτεύομαι) to Christ. Having disclosed the temporal logic and self-engaged involvement within a testimony, it has become clear that the assurance (πίστις, 1:27) of the gospel on which the believers could depend is nothing close to a fact articulated by purely objective and verifiable logic. Considering the "alluded stories" of Job, Christ, God, and Paul's opponents, various narrative dynamics and epistemological aspects in Paul's theologizing process, including a contestation of truthfulness in reception of God's revelation (1:12-18), the temporal logic of Paul's hope of being vindicated by God (1:19-26), the "Day of Christ" as the cosmological upper limit of time (1:3-11), and a contestation of ethical dispositions (2:1-4), have been explicated. What remains to be shown is how Paul's unique version of the story of Christ guides his discourse in Phil. 2:5-11 and 3:17-21 and installs itself as the paradigmatic layer of thinking among all levels of story. This will be the focus of the next chapter.

5

Contestation of the Manifestation of God: The Paradigmatic Narrative of Christ (Phil. 2:5-11, 3:17-21)

The so-called "Christ-Hymn" (2:5-11) is one of the passages most investigated by biblical scholars. Driven by the sheer volume of diverse perspectives and assumptions, it has arguably brought many readers close to a kind of "intellectual paralysis."[1] Here, exegesis of this passage will be guided by a direction which sees 2:5-11 and 3:17-21 as the key texts undergirded by a recapitulation of a uniquely created story of Christ. According to Ricoeur, narrative is the supreme structure for providing a meaningful paradigm to the otherwise chaotic and discordant temporal experiences of humans.[2] Thus, the role of this uniquely constructed story of Christ (level three) is to provide the guiding "temporally configured thought" to which all other levels of story must conform. In the context of a contestation of testimonies, this story of Christ serves as the ultimate paradigm that justifies Paul's testimony to be truthful. It is with respect to this direction that I analyze this story.

Due to its often claimed hymnic nature, this "Christ-Hymn" has been approached by scholars for the "recovery" of the "original" structural layout to guide their interpretations.[3] For example, Lohmeyer, basing his work on an assumed symmetrical structure within an "original" *Sitz im Leben*, divides the passage into two strophes, each comprising three stanzas of three lines.[4] To do so, however, he has to unjustifiably cut the phrase θανάτου δὲ σταυροῦ as a "Pauline interpolation."[5] Charles Talbert explains

---

[1] A. B. Bruce, *The Humiliation of Christ in Its Physical Ethical and Official Aspects* (London: Macmillan, 1876), 8.
[2] Cf. Ricoeur, *T&N I*, 6; Paul Ricoeur, "The Human Experience of Time and Narrative," in *A Ricoeur Reader: Reflection and Imagination*, ed. Mario J. Valdes (Toronto: University of Toronto Press, 1991), 19, 21.
[3] This investigation takes the stand of Fowl on perceiving this passage as belonging to a batch of hymns found in the NT in the "general sense of poetic accounts of the nature and/or activity of a divine figure." See Fowl, *The Story of Christ*, 45.
[4] Ernst Lohmeyer, *Kyrios Jesus. Eine Untersuchung zu Phil. 2,5-11* (Heidelberg: Winter, 1928), 5–7, 65.
[5] Researchers (e.g., Joseph Fitzmyer) seeking for a perfect structure of the "Christ-Hymn" have tended to follow Lohmeyer and drop θανάτου δὲ σταυροῦ as a secondary "Pauline gloss." However, Hooker insists that a neatly balanced structure can be extracted from the hymn without any truncations. For details, see Joseph A. Fitzmyer, "The Aramaic Background of Philippians 2:6–11," *CBQ* 50, no. 3 (1988): 476–83; Morna D. Hooker, "Philippians 2:6-11," in *Jesus und Paulus: Festschrift für Werner Georg Kümmel zum 70*, ed. E. E. Ellis and E. Gräßer (Göttingen: Vandenhoeck & Ruprecht, 1975), 157–8.

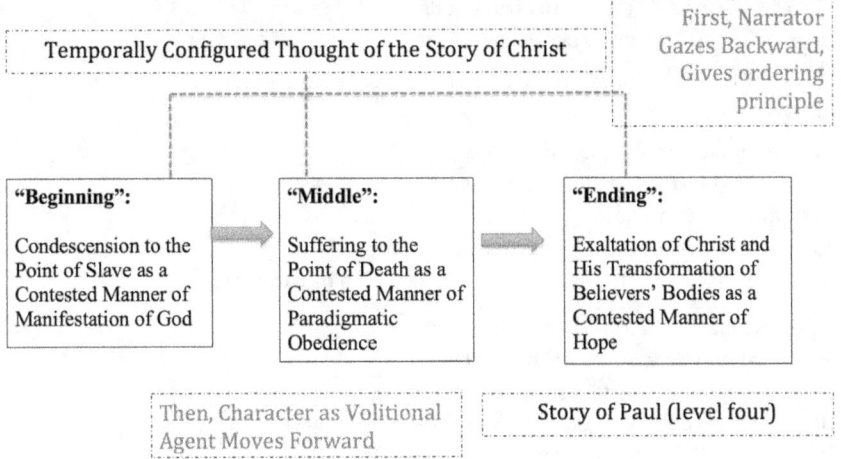

Figure 6 The temporal structure of the story of Christ.

the hymn on a strict pattern of inner parallelisms and repetition of key terms.[6] To fit this interpretation, the phrase "ἑαυτὸν ἐκένωσεν" has to be interpreted like "ἐταπείνωσεν ἑαυτὸν," describing the earthly Jesus. Any references to a preexistent state of Christ Jesus, widely found in 2:6 by scholars, is given up in a misguided manner.[7] Contrary to these efforts, I contend that the layout of this passage should first reflect exegetical considerations gauged within the immediate context of the epistle and Paul's own concepts.[8] Instead of deriving a layout from an isolated original (Lohmeyer), or an intratextual structure (Talbert), this work's proposed layout arises out of its function in providing Paul with an ultimate paradigm in giving meaning to his testimony. In particular, I argue that with this hymnic passage being itself in the form of a narrative, the hymn should be structured according to a temporal framework categorized into a "Beginning," a "Middle," and an "Ending" (see Figure 6).[9]

Layout of 2:5-11

5   Τοῦτο φρονεῖτε ἐν ὑμῖν ὃ καὶ ἐν Χριστῷ Ἰησοῦ,

Beginning:
6a   ὃς ἐν μορφῇ θεοῦ ὑπάρχων
6b   οὐχ ἁρπαγμὸν ἡγήσατο

---

[6] Charles H. Talbert, "The Problem of Pre-Existence in Philippians 2:6–11," *JBL* 86, no. 2 (1967): 141.
[7] Cf. Talbert, "Problem of Pre-Existence," 143–6, 53; Gregory P. Fewster, "The Philippian's 'Christ Hymn': Trends in Critical Scholarship," *CBR* 13, no. 2 (2015): 201. For opposing arguments, see R. G. Hamerton-Kelly, *Pre-Existence, Wisdom, and the Son of Man: A Study of the Idea of Pre-Existence in the New Testament* (1973), 157–8.
[8] Cf. Hooker, "Philippians 2:6–11," 152; Hawthorne, *Philippians*, 102.
[9] Cf. Lincoln D. Hurst, "Christ, Adam, and Preexistence Revisited," in *Where Christology Began: Essays on Philippians 2*, ed. Ralph P. Martin and Brian J. Dodd (Louisville: Westminster John Knox Press, 1998), 86, 94n.39; R. H. Fuller, *The Foundations of New Testament Christology* (London: Lutterworth, 1965), 207, in which Lincoln D. Hurst and R. H. Fuller, respectively, divide the hymn into three and five phases.

6c	τὸ εἶναι ἴσα θεῷ,
7a	ἀλλὰ ἑαυτὸν ἐκένωσεν
7b	μορφὴν δούλου λαβών,

Middle:

7c	ἐν ὁμοιώματι ἀνθρώπων γενόμενος·
7d	καὶ σχήματι εὑρεθεὶς ὡς ἄνθρωπος
8a	ἐταπείνωσεν ἑαυτὸν
8b	γενόμενος ὑπήκοος μέχρι θανάτου,
8c	θανάτου δὲ σταυροῦ.

Ending (Phil. 3:17-21 to be analyzed later):

9a	διὸ καὶ ὁ θεὸς αὐτὸν ὑπερύψωσεν
9b	καὶ ἐχαρίσατο αὐτῷ τὸ ὄνομα τὸ ὑπὲρ πᾶν ὄνομα,
10a	ἵνα ἐν τῷ ὀνόματι Ἰησοῦ
10b	πᾶν γόνυ κάμψῃ
10c	ἐπουρανίων καὶ ἐπιγείων καὶ καταχθονίων
11a	καὶ πᾶσα γλῶσσα ἐξομολογήσηται ὅτι
11b	κύριος Ἰησοῦς Χριστὸς
11c	εἰς δόξαν θεοῦ πατρός.

5.1 "Beginning": *Forma* of Slave in a Contestation of the Manifestation of God (2:6-7b)

The "Beginning" of this unit of the story of Christ comprises lines 6a-7b.[10] Right at the beginning, we are already surrounded by a few contentious and interrelated exegetical issues.[11] Because of the combination of its rare usage and prominent spot in 6b, the meaning of ἁρπαγμός has been one of, if not the most popular points of departure for the interpretation of the "Christ-Hymn."[12] Differentiated by senses of the noun as abstract or concrete, active action or passive object, and other considerations, ἁρπαγμός has been understood in a multitude of ways.[13] For example, Lightfoot sees ἁρπαγμός as a "prize/treasure" (a concrete and passive object), which then renders 2:6 with a meaning that Jesus does not see the "privilege of his equality with God" as something to be clung onto in a grasping manner (*res retinenda*).[14] Conversely, C. F. D.

---

[10] The grouping of lines 6a-7b into the unit of "Beginning" is supported by two considerations. First, the scope of their references lies in the preexistent (or pretemporal) stage of Christ and the beginning of His incarnation. Second, framed by the double use of μορφή in 6a and 7b as describing a certain aspect of Christ in His divine and incarnate state, lines in 6a-7b form a neatly chiastic structure.

[11] What do the phrases μορφῇ θεοῦ and τὸ εἶναι ἴσα θεῷ refer to? Do they mean the same? What is the meaning of ἁρπαγμός? How should we understand the phrase οὐχ ἁρπαγμὸν ἡγήσατο as a whole?

[12] BDAG, s.v. "ἁρπαγμός," 133.

[13] Cf. N. T. Wright, "Ἁρπαγμός and the Meaning of Philippians 2:5-11," *JTS* 37, no. 2 (1986): 342–3.

[14] Lightfoot, *Paul's Epistle*, 134. There have been different understandings on the use of various Latin phrases in differentiating the meaning of ἁρπαγμός. This work follows Wright's system of terminology. See Wright, "Ἁρπαγμός," 323–44.

Moule takes ἁρπαγμός as an abstract and active noun denoting an "act of snatching," which then gives the verse a meaning of Jesus not regarding "equality with God as consisting in *snatching*" (*res raptus*), but in a manner of giving oneself—even to death.[15] Numerous proposals can be cited here before we become victims of "intellectual paralysis."[16]

Based on the perspectives of Roy W. Hoover, I contend that ἁρπαγμός should bear the sense of "something to be taken advantage of."[17] With the identification of a double accusative construction featuring ἁρπαγμός and ἡγέομαι as belonging to an idiomatic expression, Hoover insightfully *shifts our exegetical priority from the meaning of the single term ἁρπαγμός to the whole expression in 2:6*: οὐχ ἁρπαγμὸν ἡγήσατο τὸ εἶναι ἴσα θεῷ.[18] In this idiomatic context, ἁρπαγμός no longer denotes the usual meaning of "robbery" or "violent seizure."[19] The overall meaning of 2:6 should then be that "Christ did not regard his equality with God as something to be used for His own advantage."[20] Moreover Hoover also discovers that τὸ εἶναι ἴσα θεῷ should refer to "something already present and at one's disposal" which *will remain*.[21] Thus, what concerns Paul here does not relate to Christ's keeping of "equality with God" (τὸ εἶναι ἴσα θεῷ) as seen by proponents of kenotic theology.[22] Paul's interest first and foremost lies in Christ's attitude toward the exploitation of such equality with God.[23]

Implied in this attitude of Christ in not using "equality with God" for His own advantage is the contrast and charge against attitudes that maximize advantages for oneself *in relation to one's own entitled position*.[24] Along with this direction, the issue at stake becomes one with serious consequential and future connotations: *what will Christ do* compared to the "norms" of other people who will act according to their own advantage?[25] Based on Ricoeur's understanding of narrative as fundamentally constituted with ethical judgment, the point of departure in the temporal structure of the "Christ-Hymn" should be accentuated with the function of polemically challenging the actions of certain people.[26] Some scholars have seen it as a challenge against efforts

---

[15] C. F. D. Moule, "Further Reflexions on Philippians 2:5-11," in *Apostolic History and the Gospel: Biblical and Historical Essays Presented to F. F. Bruce*, ed. W. Ward Gasque and Ralph P. Martin (Exeter: The Paternoster Press, 1970), 272.

[16] For an introduction of scholars' past researches on ἁρπαγμός, see Wright, "Ἁρπαγμός," 321–52.

[17] Roy W. Hoover, "The Harpagmos Enigma: A Philological Solution," *HTR* 64, no. 1 (1971): 102–6; Fowl, *The Story of Christ*, 56.

[18] Hoover, "The Harpagmos Enigma," 95. Hoover bases his work on Werner W. Jaeger but goes beyond Jaeger through rectifying some of his arguments. According to Hoover, ἅρπαγμα and ἁρπαγμός were not only used synonymously back then in the Hellenistic period but were, in particular, interchangeable within such idiomatic context. Based on this discovery, Hoover relies on idiomatic expressions of ἅρπαγμα for the meaning of ἁρπαγμός in Phil. 2:6, consolidating the claim of Jaeger. For details, see ibid., 107–9, 17–18.

[19] Ibid., 98.

[20] Ibid., 118.

[21] Ibid. As stressed by Hoover, you do have to own something before you can take advantage of it. See also Wright, "Ἁρπαγμός," 339, 44.

[22] Fewster, "The Philippian's 'Christ Hymn,'" 200.

[23] Hoover, "The Harpagmos Enigma," 118–19.

[24] Wright, "Ἁρπαγμός," 339.

[25] Ibid.

[26] Cf. Ricoeur, *T&N I*, 55–8; Ricoeur, *OAA*, 114–15, 152–68.

of human beings in general, alluding to a picture of Adam desiring to be like God.[27] Regarding this ethical function, I suggest two sets of ethical contrast found within this "Christ-Hymn."

5.1.1 Contestation of Allegiances: Christ versus Earthly Rulers

First, the hymn could be used as a challenge against the imperial worship in which the Roman emperors are *exalted* from their position to be like gods.[28] As proposed in the review section, the community's escalating suffering develops in part from their refusal to participate in the worship of the emperors. As the exegesis of Phil. 1:28 has shown, it is amid these hardships that there arises a contestation of interpreting the community's suffering experience between the political authorities and Paul. According to Samuel Vollenweider, using ἁρπαγμός Paul alludes to the antithetical relationship of imperial power and the dominion of Christ.[29] Situating 2:5-11 in the "traditions about the typical ruler who is violent and who presumes to take a divine role," Vollenweider discerns the overtone of a contestation of allegiance to the true "Lord."[30] Between the imperial household of Caesar's family (cf. Καίσαρος οἰκίας in 4:22) who exalt themselves to be like gods (6bc), and Christ Jesus who ἑαυτὸν ἐκένωσεν (7a), *who will be the community's true κύριος whom they will trust in giving meaning to their suffering?*[31] It is thus probable that Paul has the self-exalting Roman emperors in mind when he writes οὐχ ἁρπαγμὸν ἡγήσατο τὸ εἶναι ἴσα θεῷ.[32]

5.1.2 Contestation of God's Knowledge: The Manifestation of God through a Slave

The second ethical function concerns the dialectic between μορφῇ θεοῦ and μορφὴν δούλου. For a long period of time interpreters have tended to use 2:6-7 as a "*dictum probans*" to affirm the divinity of Jesus Christ against heresies like those of the Arians and Socinians.[33] Interpretations of such kind perceive μορφῇ θεοῦ as standing for the nature of God in the sense of a "concrete object" (οὐσία or φύσις).[34] The battle for orthodoxy then *revolves around the contention that taking on the nature of the human*

---

[27] L. W. Hurtado, *How on Earth Did Jesus Become a God? Historical Questions about Earliest Devotion to Jesus* (Grand Rapids: Wm. B. Eerdmans, 2005), 100; James D. G. Dunn, "Christ, Adam, and Preexistence," in *Where Christology Began: Essays on Philippians 2*, ed. Ralph P. Martin and Brian J. Dodd (Louisville: Westminster John Knox Press, 1998), 75-83. For arguments against the contrast between Christ and Adam, see Hurst, "Christ, Adam, and Preexistence Revisited," 84-95; Jean-François Collange, *The Epistle of Saint Paul to the Philippians*, trans. A. W. Heathcote (London: Epworth Press, 1979), 82-3.

[28] Samuel Vollenweider, "Der 'Raub' der Gottgleichheit: Ein Religionsgeschichtlicher Vorschlag zu Phil 2.6(-11)," *NTS* 45, no. 3 (1999): 431; Wright, "Ἁρπαγμός," 339, 45.

[29] Vollenweider, "Der 'Raub' der Gottgleichheit," 427; Wright, *Resurrection*, 228.

[30] Vollenweider, "Der 'Raub' der Gottgleichheit," 431.

[31] Hoover, "The Harpagmos Enigma," 118; Fowl, *The Story of Christ*, 56.

[32] Heen, "Phil 2:6-11," 128-36.

[33] Wright, "Ἁρπαγμός," 348; Richard C. Trench, *Synonyms of the New Testament* (London: Macmillan, 1880), s.v. "μορφή, κτλ," 261-7.

[34] Trench, *Synonyms*, s.v. "μορφή, κτλ," 261-7.

slave does not require any diminishing of the substance of God's nature. However, based on the foregoing analysis of ἁρπαγμός, which states that Christ's "equality with God" is always assumed to be there, affirmation of the divinity of Jesus does not appear to be the chief concern of Paul.[35] What is Paul's main concern when his description of Christ moves from μορφῇ θεοῦ to μορφὴν δούλου? What relation between μορφῇ θεοῦ and μορφὴν δούλου does Paul want to convey?

Based on Ricoeur's dialectic of innovation and sedimentation regarding a living tradition, and the dialectic of external narration and internal conviction for a testimony, I argue that Paul wants to highlight Christ's μορφὴν δούλου as the necessary means to discern the identity and work of God. In particular, *Paul intends to innovate a narrative character of Christ*, which would, in turn, enable the Philippian community to gain a renewed knowledge of God (internal "criteriology of the divine") and strengthen their trust toward his testimony on suffering.[36] In this book, instead of taking μορφή as representing either the internal (or metaphysical) substance or the external appearance of something,[37] μορφή should be understood as close to the Latin "*forma*," which "signifies the form as it is the utterance of the inner life."[38]

The meaning of μορφή then points to *a specific mode of being which reflects Jesus's unique identity, encapsulating His forma of God through the forma of an earthly slave*.[39] During His earthly slave journey, Jesus not only assumed μορφή δοῦλος with an abiding μορφή θεός, but also that His invisible μορφῇ θεοῦ has been, and could only be seen through this μορφὴν δούλου.

In this manner, any knowledge of the invisible God is *necessarily mediated* by the visible slave Christ Jesus.[40] In other words, *to assure one's understanding of the transcendent God, one must follow the story of this earthly slave Christ Jesus*. With this understanding, a critical issue at stake emerges: With the Greco-Roman people generally presuming God as always taking a glorious image, how could the gentile Philippian community accept Paul's innovated theology that God is manifested via the suffering process of a lowly slave? What Paul is asking does not pertain to the effectiveness of Jesus's salvation in bringing people an entry into God's Kingdom through death, but the value of the *suffering process as exhibited throughout His life*. How can a slave who has lost all his rights, subjected himself to another, and suffered humiliation from even the general public, still manifest the splendor and glory of God?[41] According to the general consensus of Paul's time (mimesis1),[42] perhaps we may say μορφῇ θεοῦ is everything but μορφὴν δούλου. In the narratives of most

---

[35] Ibid.
[36] Cf. Wright, "Ἁρπαγμός," 346.
[37] Cf. Hawthorne, *Philippians*, 111–14; J. Behm, "μορφή, κτλ," *TDNT* 4:742–59.
[38] Trench, *Synonyms*, s.v. "μορφή, σχῆμα, ἰδέα," 261–7. While μορφή generally means "form, outward appearance or shape," its specific connotation here has to be determined from the parallel structure of μορφῇ θεοῦ and μορφὴν δούλου in Phil. 2:6–7. See BDAG, s.v. "μορφή," 659; Melick, *Philippians*, 101.
[39] *TLNT*, s.v. "δοῦλος, κτλ," 1:380–6; Trench, *Synonyms*, s.v. "μορφή, σχῆμα, ἰδέα," 261–7.
[40] *TLNT*, s.v. "κενός, κενόω," 2:310.
[41] *TLNT*, s.v. "δοῦλος, κτλ," 1:380–6.
[42] The mimesis1 here stands for the commonly accepted rules of perceiving the presence of God and understanding the value of being a slave.

contemporary people, the figure of a slave is just too discordant with the manifestation of the glory of God.

It is this issue that prompts Paul's point of departure in the "Beginning" of this unique story of Christ: a manifestation of God through a story of Jesus as a *suffering slave*.[43] Trapped in a contestation of testimonies with other "Christ-followers" in Rome (and Philippi), Paul has been challenged by them in the same way: "How can you as a prisoner reflect the presence of God?" Facing a contestation concerning the meaning of his suffering, Paul cannot ascertain his knowledge of God by resorting to objective arguments.[44] What Paul can do is to ground his testimony in a unique story of Christ in which Christ is portrayed as a slave who "shares" his life situation of being challenged on legitimately manifesting the presence and working of God.

Taking into account the abased connotation of δοῦλος,[45] instead of taking κενόω in its literal sense of giving up something, I argue that the κενόω in ἑαυτὸν ἐκένωσεν (7a) serves to express two ideas *metaphorically*.[46] First, it is about the unfathomable condescension of Christ from divine transcendence to the lowly state of a slave.[47] In this manner, δοῦλος is read with a sense of inferiority, against a background of δουλεία and ἐλευθερία (slavery versus freedom).[48] Second, it points to the degree of His sacrifice within His voluntary submission to His master (God the Father) and faithful participation in His upcoming vocation. In this manner, δοῦλος is read with a sense of excellence, against a background of being God's faithful instrument in His work.

It is with these two paradoxical senses that we must ask: Can the seemingly humiliating process of Paul's imprisonment reflect the glorious working of God? In light of Christ's κενόω, the answer is an obvious yes. And has Paul's suffering for the gospel deviated too much from God's normative way of working? In light of Christ's κενόω, with Him as God's appointed δοῦλος in carrying out His salvation, the answer is an obvious no.

Based on Ricoeur's mimesis theory, I argue that it is the narrative causality and temporality implicit along the story of Christ with which Paul builds a coherent relationship.[49] Paul's suffering can thus become a more sensible and followable instrument of making God recognizable by His followers.[50] *What concerns Paul in*

---

[43] Cf. Wright, "Ἁρπαγμός," 346; F. F. Bruce, "St. Paul in Macedonia. 3. The Philippian Correspondence," *BJRL* 63 (19881): 270.

[44] Cf. Ricoeur, *MHF*, 162; Ricoeur, "HT," 136–47; Bauckham, *Jesus and the Eyewitnesses*, 505.

[45] I do not agree with the view of Joachim Jeremias, who argues that δοῦλος serves here *alone* as an honorable title of Jesus and has its allusive background coming from the fourth servant song of Isaiah (Isaiah 52–3). His view has been emphatically rejected by John S. Pobee and Fowl. See J. Jeremias, "παῖς θεοῦ," *TDNT* 5:654–717; Pobee, *Persecution and Martyrdom*, 52; Fowl, *The Story of Christ*, 73–4.

[46] Cf. Fee, *Paul's Letter*, 210; *TLNT*, s.v. "κενός, κενόω," 2:309; Hurst, "Christ, Adam, and Preexistence Revisited," 89. Spicq writes, "Its meaning is metaphorical; so it is not a 'theological' technical term, but a term of a religious soul contemplating the mystery of Christ and gaining the sense of divine transcendence and creaturely nothingness."

[47] *TLNT*, s.v. "δοῦλος, κτλ," 1:380–6; Moule, "Further Reflexions," 268. Moule writes, "slavery meant, in contemporary society, the extreme in respect of deprivation of rights. A slave, as property sold to another, scarcely belonged to himself."

[48] BDAG, s.v. "ἐλευθερία," 316; Pobee, *Persecution and Martyrdom*, 52.

[49] Cf. Ricoeur, *T&N I*, 53.

[50] Cf. ibid., 67.

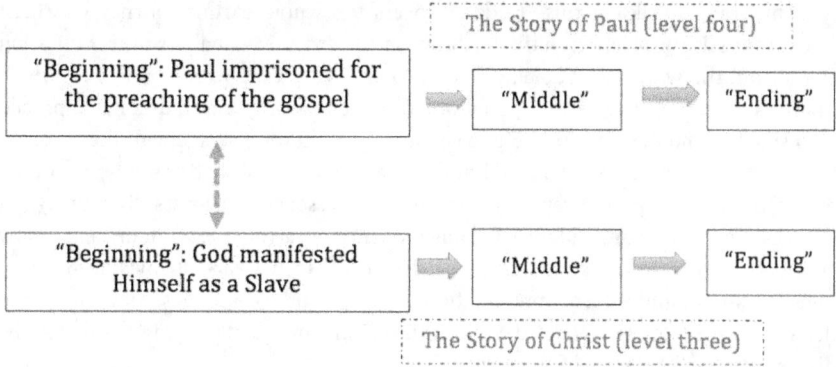

Figure 7 The story of Paul nested upon the story of Christ—The "Beginning."

the accusations from his opponents becomes something that also concerns (the narrative identity of) Christ Jesus. With this uniquely constructed "Beginning," Paul has started to build his case in supporting his testimony (see Figure 7).

5.2 "Middle": Suffering to the Point of Death in a Contestation of the Paradigmatic Obedience (2:7c-8)

7c ἐν ὁμοιώματι ἀνθρώπων γενόμενος·
7d καὶ σχήματι εὑρεθεὶς ὡς ἄνθρωπος
8a ἐταπείνωσεν ἑαυτὸν
8b γενόμενος ὑπήκοος μέχρι θανάτου,
8c θανάτου δὲ σταυροῦ.

After hooking the "Beginning" of Christ's story to that of his own as sharing the *same* concern, Paul provides further coherence between the "Middle" of Christ's story and that of his own so that his story (level four) can be seen as a legitimate narrative representation of the story of Christ. According to Ricoeur, the "Middle" of a story is marked by occurrences of contingent and discordant events that are often contrary to the expectation of readers.[51] In rhetorical terms, the *doxa* of the readers has started to be challenged by the self-engaged imaginative plot. Such unexpected elements that arise in the mind of the reader are tied to the manner and magnitude in which the originally glorious Christ suffers within His earthly journey. How does the glorious yet slavish character of Christ respond to the horrific and the discordant sufferings of His life? And how does this inform Paul's way of responding to his own sudden change of circumstances? It is in light of these two questions that we approach this section.

---

[51] Ricoeur, *T&N I*, 73; Currie, *The Unexpected*, 37.

Temporally speaking, this "Middle" covers the whole earthly journey of Christ Jesus from His incarnation until His death on the cross. My analysis of this duration starts from the word pair ὁμοίωμα (likeness) and σχῆμα (appearance) in 7cd, which again has received diverse interpretations from scholars.[52] One traditional approach is to situate σχῆμα as opposed to μορφή and approach the passage with the focus on the contrast between the divine and human nature of Christ. For example, according to Lightfoot, while μορφή represents the intrinsic essence of Christ's divinity, σχῆμα denotes the external attributes that change in Christ's earthly life without causing any changes to His internal divine essence.[53] However, such clear-cut division between internal essence and external presentation of μορφή and σχῆμα does not do justice to the text here. As I have explicated earlier, this reading mistakenly restricts μορφή as the divine nature in the sense of an essence.[54]

5.2.1 Christ's Identification with Humans: The Ultimate Paradigm for Paul

I argue that Paul's intended sense of ὁμοίωμα and σχῆμα actually lies in Christ's identification with the earthly lives of ordinary human beings.[55] Generally taken as referring to mere outward appearances (something static), σχῆμα is used here to dynamically describe Christ's being recognized (or found, εὑρίσκω) by His fellow people as an "ordinary" human being (σχήματι εὑρεθεὶς ὡς ἄνθρωπος) just like them.[56] Specifically, it points to the *earthly actions, capacities, limitation,s and lifestyles* as manifested by Christ publicly in lines 8abc.[57] Such emphasis on His *resemblance to humanity* is also supported by the preceding phrase ἐν ὁμοιώματι ἀνθρώπων γενόμενος in 7c. In comparison to Paul's other use of ὁμοίωμα in Romans, where he mentions Christ's likeness to the sinful flesh of a human being in order to qualify Him as a *contrast* to the law of sin and death (ἐν ὁμοιώματι σαρκὸς ἁμαρτίας, Rom. 8:2-3), the reference to Christ's likeness in Phil. 2:8abc embraces the general aspects of being human (ἐν ὁμοιώματι ἀνθρώπων) to highlight His *similarity* to the human race.[58] The sinfulness of humans, and Christ's lack of sin, is not mentioned.[59]

In this investigation, the identification of Christ with humanity through His actions is hardly accidental. Instead of positing Christ primarily as a contrast to Adam or to

---

[52] Fee, *Paul's Letter*, 198; BDAG, s.v. "σχῆμα," 981; BDAG, s.v. "ὁμοίωμα," 707.
[53] J. B. Lightfoot, F. J. A. Hort, and J. E. B. Mayor, "Recent Editions of St Paul's Epistles," *JCSP* 3, no. 7 (1857): 114; Trench, *Synonyms*, s.v. "μορφή, σχῆμα, ἰδέα," 265–6.
[54] Ibid., 261-7.
[55] Ralph P. Martin, *Carmen Christi: Philippians 2:5-11 in Recent Interpretations and in the Setting of Early Christian Worship* (Grand Rapids: Wm. B. Eerdmans, 1983), 206; Pobee, *Persecution and Martyrdom*, 52.
[56] Fee, *Paul's Letter*, 215; J. Schneider, "σχῆμα, μετασχηματίζω," *TDNT* 7:954-8; Fowl, *The Story of Christ*, 61.
[57] Trench, *Synonyms*, s.v. "μορφή, σχῆμα, ἰδέα," 261-7. Trench, quoting Johann Albrecht Bengel, comments, "He was by men found in fashion as a man, the σχῆμα here signifying his whole outward presentation, as Bengel puts it well: 'σχῆμα, *habitus, cultus, vestitus, victus, gestus, sermones et actiones*.'"
[58] Cf. BDAG, s.v. "ὁμοίωμα," 707.
[59] Gnilka, *Der Philipperbrief*, 121.

other sinful human beings "in" Adam, Christ's actions of identification with humanity in general revolve around *the meaning, origin, and value of suffering for God as a human being*. Without denying the preexistence of Christ before His incarnation nor His divine nature afterwards,[60] this interpretation does not show an ironic contrast between Christ and humans as proposed by Hooker, but a "forthright correspondence" that allows Paul and other Christ-followers to identify with the *human* Christ in suffering.[61] It serves to create a unique story of Christ and in particular its "Middle," in which we find the ultimate paradigm of responding to the seemingly discordant experience of suffering for the work of God. It is through this response of Christ that Paul and others could assure the working of God in their own earthly journeys of suffering.

What is in view then is not a "fallen world" which only an obedient and thus sinless Christ can save. Instead, within Paul's contestation of testimonies with other "Christ-followers," Paul's concern lies in the establishment of an earthly suffering story which, with a genuine human Christ in the *forma* of a δοῦλος, can manifest the *forma* of God and provide the paradigm in giving meaning to his suffering. If God is righteous in Christ's cruel suffering, He is also righteous in using the suffering of Paul (and others) in His plan of redemption.[62] And if God is "right," Paul is also "right."

5.2.2 Meaning of ἐταπείνωσεν ἑαυτὸν: A Voluntary Act in Lowering Himself

Another distinctive feature in Christ's response to His life of discordance emerges from the voluntary nature of His suffering, which relates specifically to the meaning of ἐταπείνωσεν ἑαυτὸν. Most English Bibles translate ἐταπείνωσεν ἑαυτὸν as "He humbled himself," which based on today's English usage might imply that Jesus lowered His level of "unhealthy pride" through embracing the virtue of humility.[63] But as Nancy V. Wiles points out, among those "authentic Pauline epistles" Paul has never used the ταπεινό- word-group as a virtue.[64] Instead, what this word-group connotes is always some "negative social circumstances or experiences."[65]

---

[60] O Michel, "Zur Exegese von Phil. 2,5–11," in *Theologie als Glaubenswägnis. Festschrift für K. Heim zum 80. Geburtstag* (Hamburg: 1954), 77–95, cited by Martin, *Carmen Christi*, 205.

[61] Hooker, "Philippians 2:6–11," 162. On the other hand, such "forthright correspondence" between Christ and humanity does not deny the presence of a difference between the nature of Christ and other human beings. For discussions that emphasize the humanity of Jesus here, see Fewster, "The Philippian's 'Christ Hymn,'" 200–1; John Harvey, "A New Look at the Christ Hymn in Philippians 2:6-11," *ExpTim* 76, no. 11 (1965): 337–8.

[62] Righteousness here means "God is right" over His choice and manner of working in His plan of redemption. For more details on the meaning of δικαιοσύνη in Philippians as understood by this work, see chapter 5.3.2.

[63] For example, NASB95, NET, ESV, NRSV, KJV, HCSB.

[64] Nancy V. Wiles, "From Apostolic Presence to Self-Government in Christ. Paul's Preparing of the Philippian Church for Life in His Absence" (PhD, University of Chicago, 1993), 50–70. According to Wiles, the word which Paul uses to expresses the concept of humility as a virtue is πραΰτης. See ibid., 57.

[65] Wiles, "Apostolic Presence," 51.

Likewise, Reumann translates ἐταπείνωσεν ἑαυτὸν as "he experienced humiliation for himself."⁶⁶ While this translation has the merit of anticipating the negative suffering experience of θανάτου δὲ σταυροῦ in 8c, on two grounds it may have deviated from what Paul really means.⁶⁷ First, with ἐταπείνωσεν ἑαυτὸν being structured as a conceptual parallel to ἑαυτὸν ἐκένωσεν in 7a, the emphasis of the reflexive pronouns is found *on Christ's initiative in His actions rather than Himself as the recipient of His acts*.⁶⁸ In both of these cases, it is Christ who *on His own initiative* (although prompted, He actively undertook an action rather than being acted upon passively) acts against His own advantage by stepping down from His "entitled privilege."⁶⁹ Such an understanding better fits Christ's distinctive attitude of not utilizing his equality with God for His own advantage but engaging in actions of incarnation and condescension for the benefit of others.⁷⁰ Second, while Christ did go through experiences of humiliation, translating ἐταπείνωσεν ἑαυτὸν as "he humiliated Himself" might imply that Christ deliberately hurt His own dignity and self-respect, which is not supported by the text.

The best translation for ἐταπείνωσεν ἑαυτὸν then, similar to our understanding of κενόω, is one with a more *metaphorical* sense: "He (on his own initiative) *lowered* Himself."⁷¹ Suffering and humiliation are crucial to the story of Christ, but, as Martin insightfully comments, "It is *the free act of* Christ which leads Him to humiliation."⁷² Thus, the "earthly journey" (2:6-8) of Christ is first and foremost defined by an act of voluntary choice in regard to His life of suffering. Not only did He make a *choice* not to use His status of equality with God for His own advantage with His incarnation, but He

---

⁶⁶ Reumann, *Philippians*, 351, 654; BDAG, s.v. "ταπεινόω," 990.
⁶⁷ H. Giesen, "ταπεινόω," *EDNT* 3:334–5.
⁶⁸ Scholars have come to different conclusions regarding the relationship between ἑαυτὸν ἐκένωσεν in 7a and ἐταπείνωσεν ἑαυτόν in 8a. For example, Käsemann believes that incarnation has become a concrete historical event in the ἐταπείνωσεν ἑαυτόν. However, here I tend to see ἑαυτὸν ἐκένωσεν as referring to the incarnation and ἐταπείνωσεν ἑαυτὸν to Christ's condescension. Thus, they should be understood as following a chronological order within the forward tracing of a story. See Ernst Käsemann, "Kritische Analyse von Phil. 2, 5-11," *ZThK* 47, no. 3 (1950): 341; Bruce N. Fisk, "The Odyssey of Christ: A Novel Context for Philippians 2:6-11," in *Exploring Kenotic Christology: The Self-Emptying of God*, ed. C. Stephen Evans (Vancouver: Regent College Publishing, 2009), 58n.28; Wright, "Ἁρπαγμός," 336. For arguments supporting an atemporal reading, see James D. G. Dunn, *Christology in the Making: A New Testament Inquiry into the Origins of the Doctrine of the Incarnation* (London: SCM, 1989), 120.
⁶⁹ Cf. Hellerman, *Reconstructing Honor*, 130.
⁷⁰ Here, it is very important for us to differentiate two kinds of suffering. What this work affirms is a kind of Godly ordained suffering that happens to a Christ-follower out of her care for others during evangelistic efforts. It is not to be confused with suffering for its own sake, nor deliberately setting up oneself to suffer.
⁷¹ Such lowering does not involve Christ's ontological state as a divine being. Instead, it impacts mainly His functional role with respect to God, and the recognition of Him from people as a divine Being equal to God.
⁷² Martin, *Carmen Christi*, 212; David P. Moessner, "Turning Status 'Upside Down' in Philippi: Christ Jesus' 'Emptying Himself' as Forfeiting Any Acknowledgment of His 'Equality with God' (Phil 2:6-11)," *Horizons in Biblical Theology* 31, no. 2 (2009): 140. One of the implications of this initiative of Christ is His ultimate sovereignty *during* His suffering. His suffering is not a defeat by others, but part of a divine plan.

also *continued to make choices* of committing to such a path of humiliation during His own life.[73] Christ was not lowered *by* others. He *chose* to lower Himself.[74]

One useful implication for Paul is that while his fate has seemingly come under the control of the Roman authorities, the decisive and significant factor of his suffering arises from his *voluntary and compliant response to God's master plan of salvation*. Just as Christ's suffering at the hands of the authorities has *turned out* to arise out of Christ's voluntary submission to God's will, in his contestation of testimonies with other "Christian" leaders Paul's chains will *turn out* (cf. Phil. 1:12-13) to be known as his voluntary obedience to the plan of God.

5.2.3 The Manifestation of God: Christ the Volitional Agent Narrates Death as Limit

While Christ's voluntary act takes center stage in our explication of Phil. 2:6-8, in Christ's lifelong suffering there is one specific historical event that *stands out* from others: His death on the cross. In Christ's earthly journey, such an act of voluntary abasement "reaches its sharpest climax" when He died in the "scandal of a cross."[75] Based on the contemporary writings from the first century, many scholars have noted the degree of cruelty and humiliation represented by the cross.[76] According to the practice of the Romans, it is the "folly" (μωρία, 1 Cor. 1:18),[77] torture, and obscenity that no words can describe.[78] It represents "the lowest rung of the ladder" to which a human being can descend.[79] As Martin Hengel describes, it is a "slave's death."[80] Such abhorrence rises to an ever higher level within the Jewish tradition. It represents a curse from God on the victim.[81] As Donald Green comments, "the stigma went beyond social disgrace to a declaration of God's spiritual judgment against the victim."[82] Crucifixion signals God's despisal and punishment.

---

[73] Hurtado, *How on Earth*, 97, 102; Hurst, "Christ, Adam, and Preexistence Revisited," 84–5.
[74] Fisk, "Odyssey of Christ," 65. Comparing the "Christ-Hymn" with Greco-Roman fiction, Bruce N. Fisk emphatically points out the unique occurrence of Christ's initiative to go into humiliation. He writes, "For Paul, it matters that Christ himself took the initiative and willingly stepped downward. At the centre of Paul's Jesus story, we find voluntary self-abasement . . . no hero in our secular corpus ever chooses to step down into humiliation. Setbacks and hardships in the novels are always imposed involuntarily, by some external force."
[75] W. Grundmann, *TDNT* 8:1–6. See also Fee, *Paul's Letter*, 217–8; Hellerman, *Reconstructing Honor*, 143.
[76] To name a few examples: Tacitus, *Annales* xv. 44; Cicero, *Verrine Orations*, 5.158; Seneca, *The Epistulae Morales ad Lucilium*, 14.5; Plutarch, *Life of Pericles*, 28.3. See Martin Hengel, *Crucifixion in the Ancient World and the Folly of the Message of the Cross* (London: SCM Press, 1977), 87; Lucius Annaeus Seneca, *Seneca's Letters from a Stoic*, ed. Richard Mott Gummere (New York: Dover Publications, 2016), 30.
[77] Hengel, *Crucifixion*, 1–3.
[78] Cicero, *Verr.*, 2.5.170; Hengel, *Crucifixion*, 87; Donald E. Green, "The Folly of the Cross," *TMSJ* 15, no. 1 (2004): 62–5.
[79] Martin, *Carmen Christi*, 221.
[80] Hengel, *Crucifixion*, 51–63. Cf. Hellerman, *Reconstructing Honor*, 129–56.
[81] Green, "Folly," 65. See Deut. 21:23.
[82] Ibid.

But there is a controversy regarding the exact function of θανάτου δὲ σταυροῦ. For example, Otfried Hofius argues that the phrase θανάτου δὲ σταυροῦ should represent the goal (*Zielangabe*) of Christ's incarnation instead of just a consequence of His obedience.[83] In other words, Christ came to be a man with the sole intention to die on the cross. While Hofius's perspective has the merit of marking the exceptional and even singular nature of Christ's shameful death from His lifelong suffering, his exegetical overemphasis on θανάτου δὲ σταυροῦ as the only incident that matters in leading to Christ's exaltation causes him to overlook the indispensable dimension of *Christ's willful and voluntary process* throughout His earthly journey of incarnation and condescension in 2:6-8. How can we appropriately mark the unparalleled event of θανάτου δὲ σταυροῦ without sacrificing the whole voluntary journey of Christ?

In response to this, the concept of death as an *earthly* upper limit of human time from Ricoeur can be of use. With Christ highlighted as a volitional agent and an obedient figure, *the function of θανάτου δὲ σταυροῦ should serve as the ultimate limit (both physically and temporally) against which Christ has kept his obedience to God*.[84] Instead of differentiating θανάτου δὲ σταυροῦ as a master goal or a consequence of obedience, it is better to *poetically* understand (not define propositionally) Christ's death on the cross as a narrative event which Christ the protagonist has incorporated into His own story. Like fellow human beings, Christ the protagonist moved forward in His earthly temporal journey and engaged in making ethical choices by His actions.[85] While narrating death as the Christocentric *earthly* upper limit of time for the story of Paul will be discussed later, what matters here is that in the forward movement of the protagonist Christ, even with imminent and unrivalled calamitous changes to His body, Christ has intentionally chosen to *see* such accepting of "destiny" as remaining obedient and thus faithful to His mission and to God.[86] In terms of Ricoeur's dialectic of external narration and internal conviction, not even the inclusion of a shameful death on the cross in His own narrative configuration could dissolve Christ's internal conviction that God manifests Himself through His (Christ's) suffering. It is in *such narration of the upcoming way of death* that Christ voluntarily shaped and manifested His own Godly identity.

Such a narration of Christ is further punctuated with another peculiarity—the seemingly lifelong invisibility of the presence of God. Referencing the contemporary Greco-Roman novels, Bruce N. Fisk insightfully highlights the eccentric phenomenon

---

[83] Hofius, *Der Christushymnus*, 60–4.
[84] Such an understanding does not contradict or deny the function of substitutionary atonement as brought about by the death of Christ. This substitutional or vicarious function is not the message Paul primarily wants to convey in Philippians. In this work, I contend that what concerns Paul here revolves around Christ's acting as a volitional agent throughout His lifelong abasement. At the end of this lifelong abasement is the ultimate upper limit. On the one hand, it denotes *the conclusive temporal point until which Christ has persevered* on the path of suffering. On the other hand, it stands for *the utmost limit of challenge which Christ has withstood along His journey of obedience* to God. For details of the concept of "volitional agent," see chapter 3.1.3.
[85] Overextending the anthropological dimension of Christ Jesus, without qualifications, to the extent that includes the human condition of partial knowledge, limited horizon, and a lack of omniscience could be beyond what Paul intends here.
[86] Cf. "Figure 2: Three concentric spheres of narrative consciousness" in chapter 3.1.3, in which Christ the protagonist can be seen as belonging to the level of character.

of God's absence during Christ's whole suffering journey in 2:6-8.[87] While gods of those novels are always actively seen as close to the protagonists, God the Father of Christ has been found nowhere on the earthly stage of Christ's journey. Such an absence becomes even more striking when we compare the active presence of God in Paul's other depictions of redemption (Rom. 3:25; 5:8; 2 Cor. 5: 18-21). Thus, while Christ's suffering remains publicly observable and commonly understood as signs of folly and curse (mimesis1),[88] evidence of God's presence continuously remains unobservable and thus almost impossible to believe. There is simply no (commonly observable) sign of God's help. If there is any, it is a sign of destruction (ἔνδειξις ἀπωλείας, Phil. 1:28). Just as the suffering journey of Christ appears to be unaccompanied by God and runs against the wisdom of His time, Paul's testimony to his current imprisonment as being God's plan contrasts against the wisdom of the political authorities and the Jewish Christian leaders. In short, it is in such *a widely received narrated absence* of God that Paul asks for the trust of a narration of God's *presence*.

Along the direction of the conclusion in the previous section ("Beginning," 2:6-7b), which arrives at the paradox of the *forma* of a slave manifesting the *forma* of God, I contend that it is within a sense of something close to absurdity that Paul highlights the degree of Christ's obedience to God through suffering. Just as Christ's humbling reaches the "lowest rung of the ladder,"[89] the *tension* between the recognition of Jesus in the *forma* of God and His sheer humbling as a slave *culminates*.[90] Just as θανάτου δὲ σταυροῦ forms what Fee describes as "the sharpest imaginable contrast" with μορφῇ θεοῦ in 6a, it paradoxically *sets up a horizon from which the Philippian community could see the most glorious self-manifestation of God in Christ's life journey*.[91] In other words, it is at this narrated upper limit, the place generally perceived as the most difficult to "see" the presence of God, that we encounter the most unbelievable impact of the *forma* of a suffering slave manifesting the *forma* of a glorious God.

Here I argue that *this narrative horizon serves as the most persuasive historical evidence in aligning and convincing the Philippian community to identify with Paul's testimony*. In Christ's identification with θανάτου δὲ σταυροῦ the Philippian community have been most persuaded to see the theophany and *forma* of God.[92] From the lowest point of the life of a *slave* Christ they are most enabled to see the protagonist Christ identifying Himself with Paul.[93] As Wright comments, Christ's incarnation and crucifixion have become the "*appropriate* vehicles for the dynamic self-revelation of God."[94] A "new understanding of God" has been revealed *through* Jesus's crucifixion.

---

[87] Fisk, "Odyssey of Christ," 70.
[88] The mimesis1 here stands for the common rules of interpreting the meaning of dying on the cross by the general public at the time of Paul.
[89] Martin, *Carmen Christi*, 221.
[90] Bockmuehl, *Philippians*, 6.
[91] Fee, *Paul's Letter*, 217.
[92] Eastman, "Incarnation as Mimetic Participation," 3-4, 18; Eduard Schweizer, "Discipleship and Belief in Jesus as Lord from Jesus to the Hellenistic Church," *NTS* 2, no. 2 (1955): 97.
[93] Based on Ricoeur's idea of emplotment, only those elements of Christ that are useful in constructing such an image of Christ would be included in Paul's narrative. For example, resurrection, which is often utilized by Paul as evidence of Christ's divine sonship, is not included.
[94] Wright, "Ἁρπαγμός," 346.

This new understanding is now manifested through the story of Paul in which the Philippian community are invited to identify with Paul, through which they could *see* the glory of the suffering God. As the following exegesis will show, it is with respect to this historical and earthly journey of Christ's suffering and death that Paul marks the *temporal point of beginning* of his testimony.

5.2.4 Resonance between Christ and Paul: The Contestation of Discernment of God's Righteousness in Suffering

If the issue at stake in the previous "Beginning" section is "how can a δοῦλος reflect the presence of God?," such controversy is here further sharpened to "how can a person who died in the manner of a slave reflect the presence or working of God?"[95] It is exactly with respect to this unconventional and derogatory view that Paul finds the death of Christ on the cross resonant and helpful to his present situation.[96] Just as the demeaning death of Christ has turned out to be arguably the most glorious manifestation of God, Paul has found his imprisonment μᾶλλον εἰς προκοπὴν τοῦ εὐαγγελίου ἐλήλυθεν (Phil. 1:12). If Christ has to follow a path of obedience (ὑπήκοος, 2:8b) to God that walks against mainstream wisdom and ethical values (mimesis1),[97] Paul also has to be obedient to God who has chosen the *unusual* way of imprisonment to manifest Himself amid other contesting "wisdom." If God can be *discerned* (αἴσθησις, 1:9) even through the magnitude of humiliation in the cross of Christ, then God can certainly be *discerned* in the suffering of Paul and the Philippian community members (see Figure 8).

In this work, I argue that when Christ saw that accepting his manner of death was obedience to God, he was accomplishing (βεβαίωσις, Phil. 1:7) the gospel by beginning (ἐνάρχομαι, Phil. 1:6) a temporal and eschatological era with a new paradigm of discerning the *forma* of God. The story of Christ has provided the paradigmatic foundation for Paul and the Philippian community in giving meaning to their suffering in their testimonies. The community members can then discern that suffering on behalf of Christ is indeed "absolutely essential regarding life in Christ" (cf. 1:10).[98]

---

[95] Cf. W. Grundmann, *TDNT* 8:1–6.
[96] The resonance does not, however, take the form of an exact parallel between the story of Christ and Paul. There are no direct counterparts to Christ's divine origin and His ultimate judgment in Paul's experience as depicted in 3:10-11. Even the self-emptying of Christ and Paul's rejecting of his previous credentials are not on equal terms! Besides certain resonances, their stories interact in the sense that Paul changes his own story to fit with that of Christ. Cf. Dorothea Bertschmann, "Is There a Kenosis in This Text? Rereading Philippians 3:2-11 in the Light of the Christ Hymn," *JBL* 137, no. 1 (2018): 242–3, in which Bertschmann provides a list of "weighty omissions" regarding the verbal links and echoes between the "Christ-Hymn" and Paul's own discourse in Phil 3:2-11. According to Bertschmann, a strictly parallel reading of these passages cannot be sustained. See ibid., 246–7.
[97] The mimesis1 here stands for the assumed way of understanding suffering and humiliation held by the general public of the Greco-Roman world at the time of Paul.
[98] Fee, *Paul's Letter*, 101; *TLNT*, s.v. "δοκιμάζω, κτλ," 1:353–61.

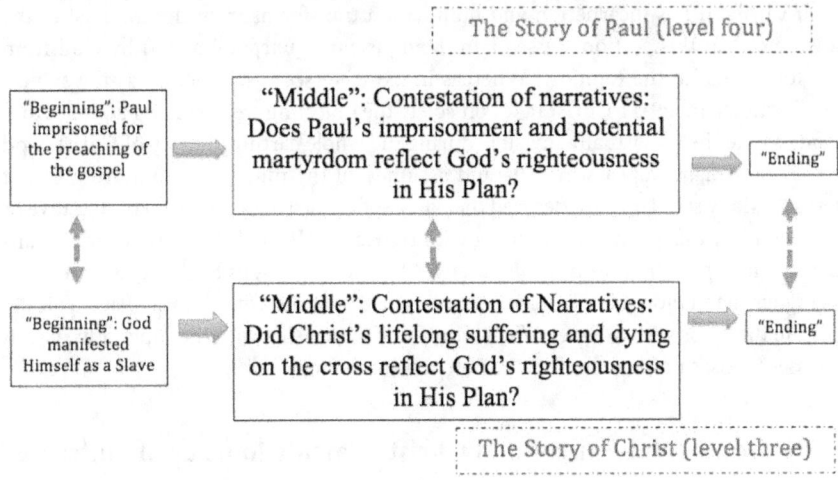

Figure 8 The story of Paul nested upon the story of Christ—The "Middle."

5.3 "Ending": Vindication of Christ and Believers in a Contestation of Hope (2:9-11, 3:17-21)

9a	διὸ καὶ ὁ θεὸς αὐτὸν ὑπερύψωσεν
9b	καὶ ἐχαρίσατο αὐτῷ τὸ ὄνομα τὸ ὑπὲρ πᾶν ὄνομα,
10a	ἵνα ἐν τῷ ὀνόματι Ἰησοῦ
10b	πᾶν γόνυ κάμψῃ
10c	ἐπουρανίων καὶ ἐπιγείων καὶ καταχθονίων
11a	καὶ πᾶσα γλῶσσα ἐξομολογήσηται ὅτι
11b	κύριος Ἰησοῦς Χριστὸς
11c	εἰς δόξαν θεοῦ πατρός.

As the suffering and death of Christ was seen by the political authorities and mainstream society as leading to destruction, another upper limit of time on a *cosmological* scale must be provided to aid the reception of the meaning of the *earthly* upper limit of Christ. To do so, the "Ending" unit of the story of Christ must provide a closure (a temporal point of ending) which allows Paul to see his own suffering as moving toward a Godly approved purpose. In other words, Paul must present an alternative closure of the "grand" historical trajectory in which the Philippian community, Paul, and his opponents are found. Based on Ricoeur's mimesis theory, when the Philippian community *follow* the story of Christ from the start to the end, their experience of their current sufferings could be refigured by this *cosmological* upper limit of narrative.[99] In this section, I will analyze this *telos*, which provides the ethical conclusion to the story of Christ.

---

[99] Cf. Ricoeur, *T&N I*, 67.

If Christ in His incarnation and humiliation transforms from the topmost to the lowermost, in this section we see Him being exalted (ὑπερυψόω, 2:9) by God from the lowermost to the topmost. Whereas in 2:6-8 we see Christ acting as the subject of all actions, in 2:9-11 Christ takes on solely the object figure, receiving actions from God.[100] After being virtually invisible during the whole earthly journey of Christ, God the Father finally appears in v. 9a and assumes all the initiative in honoring Christ Jesus.[101] Many scholars have debated the nature of ὑπερυψόω as either a comparative or a superlative. Christ gives up nothing with respect to His divine nature, which means that the interpretation of the "comparative" that sees Christ as having gained a status as higher than before does not make much sense. Instead, with the way Paul typically adds to the verbs with the prefix ὑπερ-, the force should side with the superlative which stresses Christ's uniqueness and absoluteness in the highest.[102]

5.3.1 God's Total Approval of Christ's Earthly Journey of Suffering

In this investigation, *the chief meaning of this highest point refers to God's vindicating response to Christ's earthly journey of obedience through suffering.* With the use of διὸ καί instead of contrastive conjunctions like ἀλλά or δέ, what Paul highlights in God's exaltation (ὑπερυψόω) here lies *not in the reversal of Christ's humiliating fortune,* as if that represents some defeat or misfortune which requires God to reverse.[103] This exaltation is also not something that Christ earns as a reward, which could be something implicated by the "suffering righteous" tradition.[104] Instead, διὸ καί points to God's *total approval* of Christ's earthly life of suffering and marks such a life of faithfulness as the necessary ground for His *vindication* of Christ. Along with a Christological centering of the "suffering righteous" tradition, the faithful Christ has ideally embodied the paradigmatic assurance of vindication at the end time. It is with this newly installed paradigm (cf. πίστεως Χριστοῦ in Phil. 3:9) that believers assure themselves in receiving vindication at the end time.

Here, it is with respect to this vindication that God shares His own name/title (τὸ ὄνομα τὸ ὑπὲρ πᾶν ὄνομα) with Christ in v. 9b. Based on the phrase κύριος Ἰησοῦς Χριστός in v. 11b and in particular the intertextual allusion to Isa. 45:23, Fee argues that this name is κύριος (the Lord), which is "none other than *the* name, Yahweh itself."[105] While Fee's explanation may have settled the debate concerning τὸ ὄνομα as referring to κύριος, his approach has neglected the specific connotation of ὄνομα as arising from the identity of κύριος in the context of Isa. 45:18-25. While τὸ ὄνομα correctly points to the personal appellation of κύριος (v. 11b), with ὄνομα often being used to

---

[100] Fee, *Paul's Letter*, 219; Fisk, "Odyssey of Christ," 69.
[101] Except in v. 6a where we read μορφῇ θεοῦ ὑπάρχων.
[102] Martin, *Carmen Christi*, 240–1, quoting Wilhelm Michaelis, *Zur Engelchristologie im Urchristentum. Abbau der Konstruktion Martin Werners*. (Zürich: Heinrich Majer, 1942), 41.
[103] Hurtado, *How on Earth*, 90.
[104] Cf. Moessner, "Turning Status 'Upside Down' in Philippi," 141.
[105] Fee, *Paul's Letter*, 221–2, especially 221n.20. See also Silva, *Philippians*, 110. For an alternative interpretation that sees the name here as referring to "Jesus," see Moule, "Further Reflexions," 270. For perspectives that regard ὄνομα as not directly referring to "κύριος," but the name/identity of YHWH, see George Howard, "Phil 2:6–11 and the Human Christ," *CBQ* 40, no. 3 (1978): 381–6.

denote a certain "spiritual reputation" of the name's bearer, Paul most probably conveys something more by the phrase τὸ ὄνομα τὸ ὑπὲρ πᾶν ὄνομα.[106] In particular, based on scholars' researches on the usage of ὄνομα in honor discourse, I argue that the meaning of τὸ ὄνομα should refer to a specific kind of *honor* arising from the narrative identity of the Lord in His actions within the context of Isaiah. Thus, in order to understand thoroughly the exaltation (ὑπερυψόω, 9a) and name (ὄνομα, 9b) conferred to Christ Jesus, we have to study the Isaiah context to which this whole passage alludes.

5.3.2 Context of Isaiah: Contestation of Testimonies on Cyrus as God's Instrument

In the LXX of Isa. 45:23, the Lord declares His solemn oath: ὅτι ἐμοὶ κάμψει πᾶν γόνυ καὶ ἐξομολογήσεται πᾶσα γλῶσσα τῷ θεῷ, which is widely supported by scholars as the target of allusion in Phil. 2:10-11.[107] Literally speaking, it suggests that each person from all nations will come to bow their knees (πᾶν γόνυ κάμψῃ) and that their tongue (γλῶσσα) will profess (ἐξομολογέω) allegiance to God. However, what confuses interpreters is the nature of such bowing and professing. One commonly accepted interpretation is that such actions denote a whole-hearted worship to Jesus.[108] What is highlighted then turns into a defense that such worship to Jesus would not violate the monotheistic belief in Jewish tradition.[109]

Without denying the contribution of this "Christ-Hymn" to the formation of Christology within the boundary of Jewish monotheistic tradition, based on the larger context of Isa. 45:23 and its correspondences with Phil. 3:20-21,[110] I argue that the connotations articulated in Phil. 2:9-11 extend beyond people's worship to Christ and encompass people's receiving judgment from Christ.[111] At Isa. 45:24-25 where the immediate literary unit draws to a close, we see a *future* picture juxtaposing contrasting results happening to two opposing groups. While those who act against the Lord will be put to shame (αἰσχυνθήσονται πάντες, LXX Isa. 45:24), those of the "offspring of the children of Israel" will be glorified (ἐνδοξασθήσονται πᾶν τὸ σπέρμα τῶν υἱῶν Ισραηλ).[112]

---

[106] Cf. H. Bietenhard, "ὄνομα, κτλ.," *TDNT* 5:242-83; Hellerman, "Vindicating God's Servants," 96; J. William Fuller, "'I Will Not Erase His Name from the Book of Life' (Revelation 3:5)," *JETS* 26, no. 3 (1983): 302-4. Regarding the four different uses of ὄνομα ("Name of a Person," name as a person's reputation, "Name for 'Person,'" and prepositional combinations) as suggested by Hans Bietenhard in the NT, J. William Fuller argues insightfully that there does *not* exist "hard and fast semantic boundaries" between these uses. For example, each instance of ὄνομα comes with a combination of different relative strengths of name and reputation. Such logic helps explain my understanding of the meaning of ὄνομα in Phil. 2:9-11, which on the one hand affirms (not newly gives) the personal appellation YHWH/The Lord as already owned by Jesus, and on the other hand stresses the reputation of the highest Lordship with respect to all people and the cosmos.

[107] Bauckham, "Worship of Jesus," 133; Beale and Carson, *Commentary*, 837-8.

[108] Melick, *Philippians*, 107; Hofius, *Der Christushymnus*, 37-40.

[109] Bauckham, "Worship of Jesus," 128-37; Silva, *Philippians*, 112.

[110] Ibid., 183. As observed by Silva, the correspondences include "δόξα, οὐρανός, ὑπάρχω, ταπεινόω, σχῆμα, μορφόω, κύριος."

[111] Cf. ibid., 111-2; Melick, *Philippians*, 117.

[112] J. A. Motyer, *Isaiah: An Introduction and Commentary* (Downers Grove: InterVarsity Press, 1999), 330; Klaus Baltzer, *Deutero-Isaiah: A Commentary on Isaiah 40-55*, ed. Peter Machinist, Hermeneia (Minneapolis: Fortress Press, 2001), 250.

With the continuity between 45:23 and 45:24-25, it is certainly probable that both groups of people will participate in the actions of κάμπτω and ἐξομολογέω. The actions of κάμπτω and ἐξομολογέω may then be characterized in one stroke in Isa. 45:23 as: submission followed by the judgment.[113] Bending of all knees (πᾶν γόνυ κάμψῃ) should be seen as an act of "homage to the ruler."[114] Thus, ἐξομολογέω does not mean "proclamation with thanksgiving" or "confession of faith," but the acknowledging of the Lord as the universal God "in a neutral sense."[115] However, while both of these people groups will admit that righteousness and strength are in the Lord (δικαιοσύνη καὶ δόξα πρὸς αὐτὸν ἥξουσιν, LXX Isa. 45:24), only those "offspring of Israel" who *gladly* do so will receive righteousness, vindication, and glory from the Lord (ἀπὸ κυρίου δικαιωθήσονται καὶ ἐν τῷ θεῷ ἐνδοξασθήσονται, 45:25).[116] In contrast, for that "to be shamed" group, they will do it only in a mode of "enforced submission."[117]

What becomes significant is the context in which actions of these two groups were seen as contrasting responses to the Lord. While a thorough analysis of the entire Book of Isaiah is obviously beyond the scope of this book, what matters here is that the immediate Isaiah literary context has been punctuated by a serious dispute between the Lord and the Israelites around one particularly thorny issue: the choosing of Cyrus as God's instrument (44:28–45:1) for His redemptive plan. Addressing the disheartened Israelites near the end of the Babylonian exile (Isa. 40:27, 49:14, 51:17-23, 54:11), throughout the literary context of 44:23–47:15 in which the passage of 45:18-25 is found, the prophet's primary concern lies in vindicating the Lord's *right and authority* in using Cyrus as His "Χριστός" (the anointed, 45:1).[118] What the prophet desires the people of God to believe is that "from the beginning of generations" (ἀπὸ γενεῶν ἀρχῆς) it is the Lord who raises Cyrus (41:4) so that Babylon will be destroyed (45:1-3, 46:11) and Jerusalem will be rebuilt (44:26-28, 45:13).[119] It is in this particular sense that the Lord should be recognized as *the master of history*. While Cyrus is by no means identified as the ideal and faithful servant in Isaiah 49-55, his rising and work is interpreted by the prophet as the *realization of God's righteous salvation* (Isa. 46:8-13) in his time.[120]

However, many of the Israelites have refused to accept Cyrus as God's instrument (45:9-10, 46:12).[121] Based on Ricoeur's HT, within their receptions of the prophet's testimony, the event of Cyrus being marked out as their "Messiah" is just too discordant to be incorporated with their previous understanding of God ("criteriology of the

---

[113] It would be more appropriate than a calling of worshipping the Lord. On the other hand, this is not to deny the element of God's calling the people of the nations to salvation as reflected in Isa. 45:22. This is just not the primary focus of the text.

[114] Baltzer, *Deutero-Isaiah*, 250.

[115] Martin, *Carmen Christi*, 263–4.

[116] Motyer, *Isaiah*, 330; BDAG, s.v. "δικαιόω," 249. One of the usual meanings in δικαιόω is: "to render a favorable verdict, vindicate."

[117] Motyer, *Isaiah*, 330.

[118] Carroll E. Simcox, "The Role of Cyrus in Deutero-Isaiah," *JAOS* 57, no. 2 (1937): 158–71.

[119] Rikki E. Watts, "Consolation or Confrontation: Isaiah 40–55 and the Delay of the New Exodus," *TynBul* 41, no. 1 (1990): 41.

[120] Watts, "Consolation or Confrontation," 31, 41; John N. Oswalt, *The Book of Isaiah, Chapters 40–66*, NICOT (Grand Rapids: Wm. B. Eerdmans, 1998), 232.

[121] Watts, "Consolation or Confrontation," 43–9, 54, 58; Oswalt, *Isaiah, 40–66*, 208.

divine"). The notion of employing a pagan king to be God's instrument in blessing His chosen people simply deviates too much from their sedimented theological tradition, which makes it especially difficult to be discerned as representing God's righteous act.

In fact, the theme of the Israelites' disbelief and God's subsequent frustration with their failure in discerning His plan are found throughout the chapters of Isa. 40-48 (40:27, 42:18-25, 43:22, 45:9-13, 46:8, 12, 48:1).[122] As J. W. Miller has insightfully observed, Deutero-Isaiah is marked by polemical language that discloses an "increasing opposition between the prophet and his audience."[123] To counter the Lord's lack of *ability* to help the Israelites (46:1-2), the prophet presents the Lord as the sole creator of the universe (40:12-26, 44:24, 45:12, 18).[124] To counter the Lord's lack of *willingness* to help the Israelites (40:27), the prophet presents Him as the sole master of history (41:25-26, 43:9-10, 44:6-8, 24, 45:7, 9, 11-12, 21, 46:1-5).[125] Even more emphatically, based on His status as the sole creator of the universe *and* the master of history, it is to counter the Lord's lack of *righteousness* in choosing Cyrus to save the Israelites that the prophet presents Him as *right*.[126] He is righteous in His calling of Cyrus (41:2, 45:13). He is righteous in His calling of Cyrus *for* His promise to the Israelites (41:8-10, 45:8). And above all, He is righteous in seeing such calling as leading to the ultimate universal Lordship of Himself (45:23). Such righteousness in view does not point to the sense of justice commonly understood in the court scene in which God acts as a fair judge.[127] Instead, it emphasizes that the Lord is right by His actions of salvation so that *He deserves a compliant discernment and response from His people* (45:19). Failure to discern such a righteous act of God is seen as moving away from righteousness (46:11-12).[128]

In light of the above, I argue that there exists *a theme of a contestation of testimonies* between the prophet (and God) and those unbelieving Israelites (44:24-28, 45:9-13, 46:5-11, 48:1-16) with respect to the rise and work of Cyrus.[129] While all the "offspring of Israel" (Isa. 45:25) discern and accept God's act in Cyrus as righteous, the "to be shamed" group have separated themselves (οἱ ἀφορίζοντες ἑαυτούς, LXX 45:24) from His righteous act in disbelief.[130] How can the rising and work of Cyrus be viewed as

---

[122] Watts, "Consolation or Confrontation," 35; Oswalt, *Isaiah, 40–66*, 208.
[123] Watts, "Consolation or Confrontation," 35; J. W. Miller, "Prophetic Conflict in Second Isaiah," in *Wort - Gebot - Glaube*, ed. Walther Eichrodt and H. J. Stoebe, Abhandlungen zur Theologie des Alten und Neuen Testaments (Zürich: Zwingli Verlag, 1970), 77–85.
[124] Watts, "Consolation or Confrontation," 37; John N. Oswalt, "Isaiah," in *NDBT*, ed. T. Desmond Alexander and Brian S. Rosner (Downers Grove: InterVarsity Press, 1993), 220.
[125] Walter Brueggemann, *Isaiah (Volume 2, Chapters 40–66)*, Westminster Bible Companion (Louisville: Westminster John Knox Press, 1998), 18; A. Schoors, *I Am God Your Saviour: A Form-Critical Study of the Main Genres in Is. 40–55*, SuppVT 24 (Leiden: Brill Archive, 1973), 294n.59, 298.
[126] John N. Oswalt, *Isaiah*, NIVAC (Grand Rapids: Zondervan, 2003), 52–3.
[127] BDAG, s.v. "δικαιοσύνη," 247–9.
[128] Cf. Jason M. Silverman, "Cyrus II," in *LBD*, ed. John D. Barry et al. (Bellingham: Lexham Press, 2016).
[129] Watts, "Consolation or Confrontation," 37; Miller, "Prophetic Conflict," 77–85. Walter Brueggemann comments, "The disputation speech is a dominant form of witness in Second Isaiah, precisely in the exile *when truth is in crisis and evidence is uncertain* [my emphasis]." See Walter Brueggemann, *Theology of the Old Testament: Testimony, Dispute, Advocacy* (Minneapolis: Augsburg Fortress, 1997), 120.
[130] Arvid S. Kapelrud, "The Main Concern of Second Isaiah," *VT* 32, no. 1 (1982): 57; Baltzer, *DeuteroIsaiah*, 220.

leading to ὅτι ἐμοὶ κάμψει πᾶν γόνυ καὶ ἐξομολογήσεται πᾶσα γλῶσσα τῷ θεῷ (LXX Isa. 45:23b)?[131] How can it be reasonable that God calls a pagan king who does not even know Him (45:4)? In fact, does not another phase of subjugation under another pagan empire serve as further proof of God's abandonment of His people? It is against such *contestation and rejection of the Lord's work in Cyrus as leading to His future universal exaltation* that the prophet Isaiah admonished the people of God.[132]

5.3.3 Nesting of Stories of Paul and Christ on That of Isaiah: New Phase of Eschatological Lordship

Based on the model of the nesting of stories as suggested by Ricoeur, I contend that when Paul alludes to the prophecy in Isaiah 45:23, he is actively engaging in a theologizing process which is best modeled by a structure in which the story of Paul (and Christ) in Philippians is nested upon an "alluded story" of Isaiah.[133] In this creative emplotment process, the "Beginning" of both their stories is marked by an offensive event to the Israelites being used by God; in Isaiah, it is the calling of Cyrus, in Philippians, it is the suffering of Paul (and Christ). In the "Middle" of both stories, there are unexpected discordances and unresolved controversies concerning the meaning of such events with respect to God's redemptive plan. In Isaiah, it is whether Cyrus's edict, which brings the Israelites' return to Zion and the temple's restoration, signifies God's sovereignty on earth.[134] In Philippians, it is whether Paul's suffering can be justified as coming from God and is representative of Christ's Lordship. Toward the "Ending" of the stories, both are marked by a scene of universal homage to the Lord in which the controversy is resolved. In Isaiah, all will acknowledge God's righteous act in Cyrus, which is followed by God's approval of those "children of Israel." In Philippians, all will recognize God's utmost approval of Christ's suffering as manifesting His *forma* (Phil. 2:9-11), followed by approval of those who also suffer for the gospel (Phil. 3:20-21).

Based on the above, what God grants Christ in τὸ ὄνομα τὸ ὑπὲρ πᾶν ὄνομα is not just a sharing of His personal appellation ("the Lord" or "YHWH"), but a *new phase of eschatological Lordship* to which all people must submit:[135] His earthly manner

---

[131] For an explanation of why the Israelites found it difficult to accept Cyrus as God's anointed, see Watts, "Consolation or Confrontation," 42.

[132] Cf. Kapelrud, "Main Concern," 57; Brueggemann, *Isaiah*, 78–9.

[133] As I have explained above, such nesting of stories does not mean that the meaning of the story of Christ or Paul here directly follows that "alluded story" of Isaiah. Instead, it is Paul's present concern that is driving his self-engaged hermeneutics in his creation of an "alluded story" of Isaiah. What I am doing is to make use of a temporal framework (beginning, middle, and ending) to model Paul's creative theologizing process so that we can discern how Paul, in his emplotment, *creates* meaning and identity for himself.

[134] John Goldingay, *The Message of Isaiah: A Literary-Theological Commentary* (London: MPG Books, 2005), 253–75.

[135] This Lordship does not refer to a regaining of divinity status, as if Christ has lost His divinity. It is also not a new title or name that He acquires after His death. Nor is it primarily about the hypostatic union of Jesus that does not violate Jewish monotheistic tradition. It is also not something Christ *earns* from God as a "reward," which is supported by Meyer. For details, see Silva, *Philippians*, 108–9; Martin, *Carmen Christi*, 232.

of suffering and view of death has become the new and essential paradigm for all *true* God-followers (Phil. 1:29). Instead of a new title or name or divine status, *this Lordship refers to a new functional office undertaken by Christ within an eschatological period framed by His death and parousia.*[136] Just as the Lord awaits His people (after the fall of Babylon) to trust in His commissioning of what Lisbeth S. Fried calls the "temporary office" of Cyrus, God the Father awaits His people to trust in Christ Jesus's eschatological Lordship from the time of His death until His *parousia*.[137] If God's act in "anointing" Cyrus (Isa. 45:1) deserves a compliant response, how much more should God's act in Christ Jesus deserve a faithful and whole-hearted acknowledgment?

What is intriguing is that within this eschatological era, such Lordship of Christ *does not correspond to a universally realized* state of sovereignty that everybody has witnessed.[138] While Christ's Lordship should have already started in light of His ascension to heaven and the Church's worship of Him, the present trials facing Paul and other true God-followers seem to deny (at least partially) the present reality of Christ's Lordship, and locate it in the ultimate future.[139] Indeed, Kreitzer and Collange are right to emphasize the future orientation in Isa. 45:23 and Phil. 2:10-11 as contrary to a complete realization of Christ's Lordship in the present.[140] However, instead of differentiating the paradox of Christ's Lordship as either present or future, I argue that Paul's core concern lies in setting up an ultimate cosmological upper limit of time as the day of judgment (cf. Day of Christ in Phil. 1:6, 10, and the *parousia* of Christ in 3:20-21) with which the Philippian community members must reckon *now*.

The cause for this concern is that *within this eschatological era, there are bound to be different ways of incorporating Christ's universally acknowledged Lordship in the future and the manner of His Lordship in the present.* In other words, there is a dialectical relationship between Christ's universally *acknowledged Lordship* in the future, and His *veiled and contested Lordship* in the present.[141] The issue at stake is not whether the Lordship of Christ is complete or not, but the temporal process of realization (hence the incomplete sense) of Christ's *triumphant* (hence the complete sense) Lordship. In particular, it is about the contentious manner of this process of realization, which reflects the way in which the Philippian community understands and integrates their "little" narrative and God's "grand" historical trajectory of His salvation. It is in

---

[136] Cf. Martin, *Carmen Christi*, 236; Kreitzer, *Jesus and God*, 116.

[137] Lisbeth S. Fried comments on the important yet limited role of Cyrus in Deutero-Isaiah: "Cyrus, although anointed, is not the king of Judah, since the royal title מלך is not used. YHWH takes Cyrus by the hand but does not seat him at his right hand, as he does the Davidic king in Psalm 110." See Lisbeth S. Fried, "Cyrus the Messiah? The Historical Background to Isaiah 45:1," *HTR* 95, no. 4 (2002): 349.

[138] Contra Hellerman, "Vindicating God's Servants," 97, in which Hellerman focuses on the future reality (after *parousia* of Christ) of "the public recognition and acknowledgement of Christ's divine status." The reality of Christ's Lordship is not only "veiled during the incarnation," but also *contested* during the eschatological era.

[139] Martin, *Carmen Christi*, 266–70; Schweizer, "Discipleship and Belief in Jesus," 95–6.

[140] Kreitzer, *Jesus and God*, 117; Collange, *Philippians*, 106.

[141] Evidence of Christ's present Lordship is found throughout the epistle. In 1:27 and 3:20, we see it is Christ's πολίτευμα, not that of the Roman Empire, which is *already* dictating his followers' citizenship and earthly hope. In 1:12-14 and 4:22, we see the imprisonment of Paul not only has not hindered the spread of the gospel but has in fact brought about at least an increase of Christ's sovereignty in "the whole imperial guard and everyone else" (1:13).

compliance with this manner that the contestation of testimonies between Paul and the Jewish Christ-followers comes in to play. In Paul's narrative world, God's past act in choosing Cyrus to kick off His restoration of Israel has become another *teleological drive* which gives a strong rhetorical push toward his narrative closure.[142]

Based on the way Paul exhorts the Philippian community (1:27-30, 3:17-21), the best way to describe Paul's primary interest is that the community's fate on that *future* day hinges on their responses *now*.[143] Contrary to most interpreters who try to resolve the paradox of Christ's Lordship in the churches of now and the cosmos of the future,[144] Phil. 2:10-11 and 3:20-21 actually serve as *the horizon from which the community sees Christ coming as the judge of the world*. As the foregoing analysis on the "Day of Christ Jesus" has disclosed, it will be a future time of Christ's "unmistakable and powerful intervention into the affairs of this world" demanding the Philippian community's watchful attention *now*.[145] Those opposing the righteous acts of the Lord will receive judgment and disaster. Those siding with His righteous acts will receive salvation and rewards.[146]

5.3.4 Contrasting Fates Following Contesting Narratives on the Role of the Body (3:17-21)

This solemn picture of judgment at the end of the story of Christ is further attested in Phil. 3:17-21.[147] Just as there are two groups of people receiving contrasting fates in Isa. 45:24-25, in Phil. 3:17-21 we see Paul articulate two contrasting destinies happening to two groups of people when Christ returns. One distinctive difference between them seems to be their contesting attitudes toward the role of their bodies with respect to suffering. On the one hand, there are those enemies of the cross of Christ (τοὺς ἐχθροὺς τοῦ σταυροῦ τοῦ Χριστοῦ, 3:18) characterized by an end of destruction (τὸ τέλος ἀπώλεια, 3:19),[148] bodily desire as god,[149] a perverse understanding of glory and shame, and a mindset of earthly thinking. We are not told clearly the identity of these enemies.[150] But judging from the polemical language and strong emotion in the immediate context, it is safe to conjecture that they walk with an opposite mindset and

---

[142] See Ricoeur, *T&N I*, 67; Hays, *Echoes of Scripture*, 20–3.

[143] Cf. Hellerman, "Vindicating God's Servants," 97.

[144] Hofius, *Der Christushymnus*, 48–51; Schweizer, "Discipleship and Belief in Jesus," 95–6; Martin, *Carmen Christi*, 269.

[145] Barker, "Day of the Lord."

[146] According to J. D. Barker, there are altogether fifteen verses in the OT with the exact phrase (יְהִי יוֹם): Isaiah 13:6, 9; Ezekiel 13:5; Joel 1:15; 2:1, 11, 31; 3:14; Amos 5:18, 20; Obadiah 15; Zephaniah 1:7, 14 (2x); Malachi 3:13.

[147] On the conceptual parallel between the passages of Phil. 2:6-11 and 3:17-21, see Morna D. Hooker, "Interchange in Christ and Ethics," *JSNT* 8, no. 25 (1985): 3–17.

[148] Here (3:19) ἀπώλεια, which appears in 1:28, is used again. Besides this, σωτήρ in 3:20 is also a cognate of σωτηρία in 1:28. The meaning of suffering for the gospel of Christ, which is contested in 1:28 between Paul and his opponents, will finally be resolved in Christ's *parousia* depicted in 3:19-20.

[149] Loh and Nida, *Translator's Handbook*, 117.

[150] Based on the extraordinarily severe emotions (κλαίω, 3:18) exhibited by Paul in his charge against them, I tend to see them as ex-members of the Philippian community. For scholars who hold such views, see Hansen, *Philippians*, 30; Vincent, *Philippians*, 116–17; Karl O. Sandnes, *Belly and Body in the Pauline Epistles* (Cambridge: Cambridge University Press, 2002), 144.

lifestyle with respect to that of Christ (2:6-8), Paul (3:17), and those "citizens of heaven" (ἡμῶν γὰρ τὸ πολίτευμα ἐν οὐρανοῖς ὑπάρχει, 3:20).

In particular, contrary to Christ's self-lowering life journey, in which He did not use His equality with God as the grounds to avoid an earthly path of bodily suffering, these people take their bodily pleasure as their god and live a life completely converse to that of Christ Jesus.[151] As Karl O. Sandnes insightfully argues, Paul's concern over the use of bodies is primarily a theological issue, instead of a moral one. While Paul's "belly-dictum takes lifestyle as its point of departure,"[152] his ultimate concern "develops from the idea of the body's participation in Christ's suffering as well as his glorious body."[153] Sandnes writes,

> Paul's concern to present a holy and blameless congregation has a bearing upon bodily practices. The body is either an instrument for glorifying Christ or a means of worshipping oneself. Thus belly-devotion appears as a contrast with the true worship of Christ. This is so since worshipping Christ involves the body; Christ's bodily sufferings as well as his glorious body form two aspects with which believers identify.[154]

If the category of idolatry is somehow applicable to describe those who reject the Lord's anointing of Cyrus but submit to the idols of the nations,[155] here in Philippians a selfish use of one's body is understood also as belonging to this category.[156] In other words, refusal to participate in suffering for the gospel is identified not only as immoral, but idolatrous.

On the other hand, there are those who are marked by a hope of their *humiliated bodies* being transfigured into conformity with the body of Christ's glory (ὃς μετασχηματίσει τὸ σῶμα τῆς ταπεινώσεως ἡμῶν σύμμορφον τῷ σώματι τῆς δόξης αὐτοῦ, 3:21). Instead of seeing the accent of such bodily transfiguration as upgrading from an inferior (humble) state to a superior (glorious) state, such change of form (μετασχηματίζω) is actually highlighted as a future vindication of those Christ-followers who have identified themselves with Christ's Lordship through a *bodily* suffering for the gospel now (Phil. 1:5-7, 27-30, 4:14).[157] This meaning is supported by three observations.

First, on multiple occasions in Philippians we have seen those God-followers' suffering marked by the sacrifice of their bodies, including Christ (2:9), Paul (1:20-22, 2:16-18), and Epaphroditus (2:25-30). With the prominent themes of suffering

---

[151] Cf. ibid., 164.
[152] Ibid., 145.
[153] Ibid., 164.
[154] Ibid.
[155] According to the way the prophet solemnly argues against those idol makers (Isa. 42:17-19, 44:9-20, 46:2-7), it is probable that some of the Israelites may have already opted for trusting idols from Babylon or other nations (cf. Jer. 44:15-19; Ezekiel 8:7-18). See Brueggemann, *Isaiah*, 1-7.
[156] Ibid., 148-9.
[157] Doble Peter, "'Vile Bodies' or Transformed Persons? Philippians 3.21 in Context," *JSNT* 24, no. 4 (2002): 4-5, 25-6; Orr, "Christ Absent and Present," 82n.257. For scholars who approach the meaning of this transformation as comparing inherent states of human body and that of a heavenly Christ, see Melick, *Philippians*, 144; Fee, *Paul's Letter*, 381-2.

and death recurring among their stories, it is reasonable to suggest that some of the community's experiences of suffering included bodily suffering.

Second, while it is not the only time Paul speaks of a physical resurrection or transformation at the end of time (cf. 1 Cor. 15:35-54), nowhere else do we find Paul explicitly make such a transformation *a direct action of Christ Himself as a human figure*.[158] With the issue at stake beyond a clarification on the doctrine of the physical resurrection of the body, I contend that the best starting point in interpreting such action would be the contextual metaphor implicated in 3:20-21 as suggested by Rossow.[159] Based on the scene in which Roman citizens are being threatened by foreign people, Christ is depicted as the political and military leader of a πολίτευμα intervening to rescue His citizens and bring about a victory.[160] As I have explained earlier, besides the Greco-Roman symbolic contexts of allegiance and military battle, what should not be neglected is the Jewish tradition of using the πολιτεύ- word-group within the Israelites' theological reflection of their collective identities amid oppression. Taking all these into account, the physical transfiguration here in 3:20-21 would mean Christ's ultimate vindication of the Philippian community who, amid a contestation of narratives with both the political authorities and the Jewish Christian leaders, have identified themselves with Christ's mindset on the use of the body in suffering.

Third, the target of conformity in view, that is, the body of Christ's glory (τῷ σώματι τῆς δόξης αὐτοῦ), originates from the "same" body with which Christ had suffered during His earthly lifetime. Just as the glory that Christ finally manifests in His body originated from the ultimate humiliation of the same body (Phil. 1:9-11, 2:9-11), the transfiguration of the Philippian community members' bodies and hence their glorification will result from the "site" where they have been humiliated: their earthly bodies.[161] As Sarah Harding comments, "it is one and the same σῶμα that accompanies humans in the overlap of aeons and the new aeon (minus what is jettisoned at death)."[162] If σχῆμα in 2:7 refers to Christ's earthly suffering actions as recognized by fellow human beings in 2:8, I suggest that the cognate μετασχηματίζω (cognate of σχῆμα) would specifically refer to the *physical* transfiguration of the *humiliated* bodies (ὃς μετασχηματίσει τὸ σῶμα τῆς ταπεινώσεως ἡμῶν, 3:21), which have endured for Christ. If μορφή in 2:6 refers to an identity encapsulating Jesus's unique identity of His *forma* of God *and* an earthly slave, the phrase σύμμορφον (cognate of μορφή) τῷ

---

[158] For an opposing viewpoint, see Robert H. Gundry, *Sōma in Biblical Theology: With Emphasis on Pauline Anthropology* (Cambridge: Cambridge University Press, 1976), 177–80.

[159] Cf. Rossow, "Preaching," 76–82, 272–7; Wright, *Resurrection*, 230. For details of discussion on the perspective of Rossow, see p.122ff.

[160] This is the only time among Paul's "undisputed letters" that Jesus Christ is addressed by the title σωτήρ (savior). In the context of Philippi, such a title would be most readily perceived as belonging to Caesar and Augustus, who are called "the Savior of the World" and "the Savior of Humankind," respectively.

[161] Cf. J. Schneider, *TDNT* 7:954–8; Gundry, *Sōma in Biblical Theology*, 182. Johannes Schneider alerts us to an interesting fact that the only occurrence of μετασχηματίζω in the entire LXX (4 Macc. 9:22) serves to describe a "transforming of the martyrs into incorruptibility at death." There is thus a strong resemblance of the themes of bodily suffering, loyalty to God, and future vindication between there and the usage here at Phil. 3:21.

[162] Sarah Harding, *Paul's Eschatological Anthropology: The Dynamics of Human Transformation* (Minneapolis: Augsburg Fortress, 2015), 309.

σώματι τῆς δόξης αὐτοῦ would distinctively mean a *sharing* of the approval Christ received from God for His faithfulness during the earthly journey.

Thus, a strong *link* of continuity is seen not only between one's present body before death and future body after, but the present use of the body and one's ultimate destiny before Christ.[163] Instead of being viewed as representing a more external and fleeting dimension of human existence, the *earthly* σῶμα to be transfigured is here *the "vehicle"* that attests to the believers' coming conformity (σύμμορφος) with the identity of the highest. The use of body has been given great importance in Philippians.[164] In this manner, we may say that the body has become the "site of contestation," and the "site of hope" for the Philippian community.[165]

To conclude, with respect to Christ's eschatological Lordship in which suffering for the gospel has become *the* paradigm for all true God-followers, what we see here is again a contestation of narratives that relates specifically to the use of their bodies.[166] To those enemies of the cross, bodily suffering for Christ simply does not fit their earthly mindset (οἱ τὰ ἐπίγεια φρονοῦντες) of "belly-worship." The end of their stories is simply destruction (ὧν τὸ τέλος ἀπώλεια, 3:19). On the contrary, for those who see their suffering for the gospel as coming from God, even though they do suffer and perhaps have their bodies humiliated, their present experience will be dominated by a hope (ἀπεκδέχομαι) of their future vindication in Christ's *parousia*, which will be achieved through a transfiguration of their bodies. Not only will they be proved right, that their suffering for the gospel indeed comes from the Lord, but also, they will come to share the glory of Christ, which is distinctively marked by a body once humiliated.

Through a narrative comprised of Christ's voluntary actions of incarnation and suffering on the cross, followed by God the Father's (level one) consequential recognition of Christ Jesus's Lordship as the teleological ending of the narrative, Paul has created a foundation for the justification of his suffering. Just as God will vindicate His "contested" appointment of Cyrus and Christ Jesus, He will vindicate Paul, who has found himself trapped in a contestation of testimonies regarding an "unconventional" act of God. If those "offspring of the children of Israel" (Isa. 45:25) have discerned God's act in Cyrus rightfully, how much more should the Philippian community discern and understand God's act of ordained suffering in Jesus and Paul (see Figure 9)?

---

[163] Cf. Harding, *Paul's Eschatological Anthropology*, 407–20.

[164] Melick comments that the redemption talked about here in Philippians "culminated in a change of the body itself." See Melick, *Philippians*, 144.

[165] It is easy to follow the recent trend among scholars in saying that the σῶμα represents the whole human person instead of just one distinct anthropological part. Without denying this view, in this work, it is the use of the body, which is highlighted as the symbolic "medium of expression," that attests Paul's contestation of narratives with his opponents. See Harding, *Paul's Eschatological Anthropology*, 305–6; Thomas Deidun, "Beyond Dualisms: Paul on Sex, Sarx and Sōma," *The Way: Contemporary Christian Spirituality* 28 (1998): 201.

[166] Cf. Melick, *Philippians*, 61. If the defense and confirmation of the gospel (Phil. 1:7) are the arenas where the grace of God operates, and this grace is specifically referred as believers' suffering for the gospel, then perhaps we can safely say that the body of believers has become the *site* where God's grace operates.

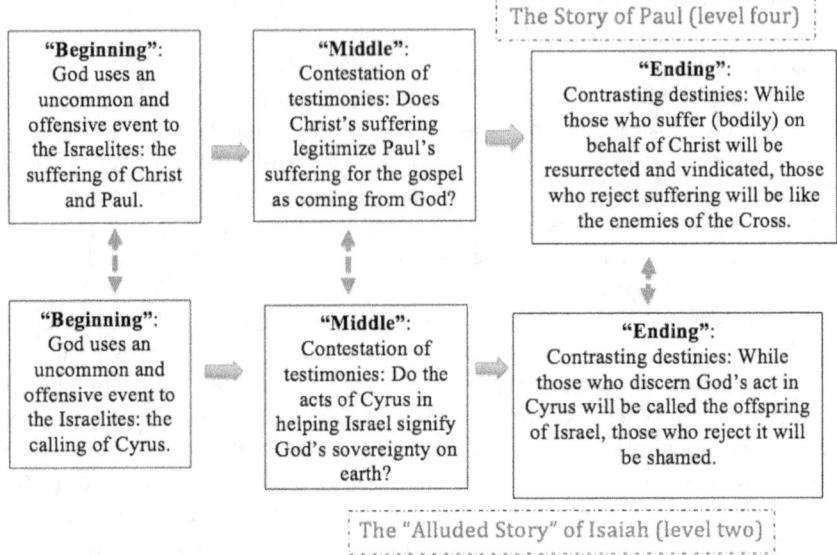

Figure 9 The story of Paul nested upon the "alluded story" of Isaiah.

5.4 Conclusion

This story of Christ has displayed how Jesus's suffering is acceptable, faithful, and instrumental within God's righteous plan of salvation. Just as what God has done through Cyrus corresponds to the surprising beginning (ἐνάρχομαι, 1:6) of a renewed temporal era within God's continuous mastery over the history of the world, His work in Christ Jesus has inaugurated the final eschatological era in which suffering on behalf of Christ has become the definitive act of His followers (1:29, 2:13). Between Christ's death and future *parousia*, all believers (1:29) are invited to participate in suffering for Christ, corresponding to the *teleological process* towards God's vindication of Christ. Christ's *universally acknowledged Lordship* will be manifested by His vindication of His followers through transfiguring their humiliated bodies during suffering for the gospel (2:9-11, 3:20-21).

It is with respect to this unique story of Christ that Paul shapes the Philippian community's identity. While Paul's story is the exemplary one for the community, it is upon *this inimitable and singular story* of the humanlike yet divine Christ that Paul and the community could found their own identities.[167] What is important to note is that it is not only what Christ has done in the past, but also *what He alone will be doing at the upper limit of this eschatological era in which all levels of other stories find their meaning*. With His promise of transfiguring believers' bodies as an act of vindication of their

---

[167] While the Philippian community imitate Paul, they shape their identity "in Christ." Part of the precedence of the story of Christ can be explained by the terminal nature of the story of Christ. See note 108 in chapter 3.2.1.

suffering (3:20-21), the closure of Christ's story has been connected to and coincides with the closures of all other stories. It is thus this paradigmatic story of Christ that sets the ultimate temporal limit of the stories of Paul and the community, and thus provides the vantage point from which to regulate their contingent life experiences with the Christ-story's temporality. In other words, it is by means of this story of Christ that God's "grand" history of salvation becomes the ultimate paradigm with which the "little" story of the Philippian community must fit. It is through this coherence that Paul updates the *doxa* of the Philippian community and competes against the *endoxa* of his opponents.

As a *modified* parallel to the thoughts of Meyer and Barclay,[168] I argue that *a radical structure of time, marked by its capacity of setting the ultimate temporal upper limit for all other stories*, has been being installed into the backbone of the identity-formation processes of Paul and the community. Such identities will always be marked *as "derivatives" created out of the radical "matrix"*—the story of Christ.[169] However, such radical supremacy of Christ's story would not exclude its interconnections with other human narratives to be counted as part of the essential identity-formation processes of believers. In fact, as Dunn and Silva have argued, Paul has clearly given prominence to believers' initiative and dedicated efforts in Philippians (1:4-8, 9-11, 27-30, 2:12-15, 3:12-14, 4:4-6, 12-13). Instead of positing the stories of God or Christ as bearing a nature incompatible or independent with the stories of Paul or the Philippian community,[170] in multiple scenarios Paul depicts pictures of joint collaboration between the agencies of God and humanity.[171] As inspired by Ricoeur's dialectic of time as sequence and configuration, *the story of Christ will be anchored into the lives of believers only when their lives are undergirded by a chronological sequence of their life episodes which reflects a configuration coherent with the temporality of the story of Christ*. Agencies of God, Christ, and believers are all involved within the making of the identity of the Philippian community.

However, Paul is not the only one claiming to have grasped God's viewpoint regarding the story of Christ. While both Paul and the Jewish Christian leaders "believe" in Christ, their respective story of Christ (level three) would differ due to their disparate understandings of suffering on behalf of Christ. Thus, not only are there two competing narrations regarding the suffering experience of Paul (level four), but there are two competing narrations regarding the meaning of Christ's suffering (level three). *An element of a contestation of narratives has been introduced into the formation of this radical structure of time.* As the analysis that follows will show,[172] two competing versions of the "Christian temporal era" (cf. Phil. 1:4-7), from which diverse manners of extending the paradigmatic character of Jesus's suffering into the lives of believers, seem to come to the fore. It is at the dawn of this contestation of temporal eras that the

---

[168] See chapter 1.3.4.
[169] This radical nature of Christ's story is also comprised by the transcendental identity of Christ with whom nobodies could parallel: only He exists both in the *forma* of God (ἐν μορφῇ θεοῦ ὑπάρχων, Phil. 2:6) and in the *forma* of a slave (μορφὴν δούλου).
[170] Cf. Barclay, "Paul's Story," 139.
[171] Silva, *Philippians*, 120–1; Dunn, "Philippians 3.2–14," 489. See also note 155 in chapter 1.3.5.
[172] See the section "Contestation over the Demarcation of Time" in chapter 6.4.

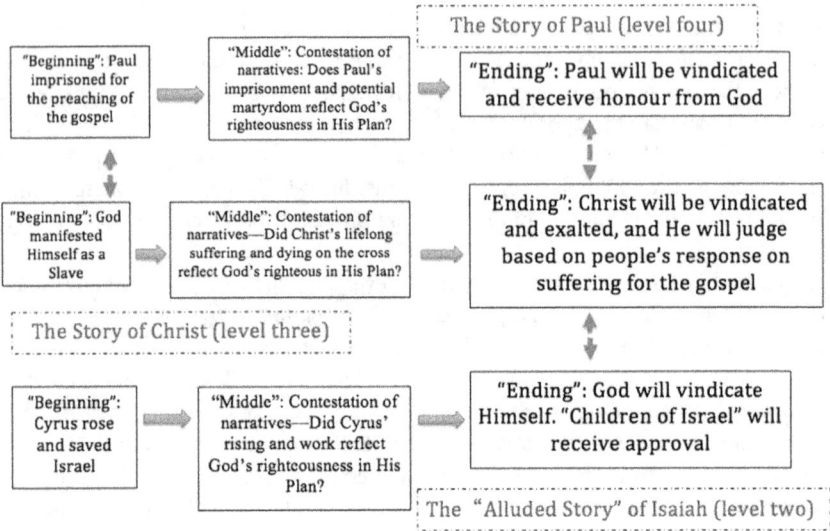

Figure 10 The story of Paul nested upon the story of Christ and the "alluded story" of Isaiah—The "Ending."

meaning of believers' suffering becomes the center of controversy between Paul and his opponents (see Figure 10).

With God's upcoming vindication of Christ being set as the event occurring at the narrated upper limit of time, Paul has provided the temporal logic with which the earthly suffering of both Christ and His followers should be viewed.[173] Should the Philippian community believe in Paul's testimony? Should they commit themselves in "retracing forward" what *Paul's* God has already "traced backward," so that the narrative closure of their personal story of suffering is shifted away from the present point of humiliation, and forward to the future day of glory when Christ returns?[174] It is with these questions in mind that we begin the next chapter, in which we will find the story of Paul acting as the exemplar of the Philippian community.

---

[173] Cf. Ricoeur, *T&N I*, 67.
[174] Cf. ibid., 157–60; Currie, *The Unexpected*, 44–5.

6

Contestation of Temporalities: The Exemplary Narrative of Paul (Phil. 3:1-21)

After constructing a particular story of Christ as the ultimate paradigm for his theology of suffering, Paul moves on to articulate the effect of such a paradigm on his own story.[1] As I have explained earlier, what matters to Paul is not limited to the meaning of his own sufferings for the gospel, but also to the meaning of sufferings in the lives of the Philippian community. In a situation where some Jewish Christian leaders (Phil. 3:2) offer another testimony against that of Paul, these two meanings are seriously contested. To persuade the community to imitate him (3:17), Paul must show the truthfulness of his testimony and how such a story of Christ has impacted his own life. In particular, he must show that the way he narrates his life represents the core constitution of Christ's πολίτευμα and a boundary marker for the Philippian community.

This story of Paul in 3:1-21 can be divided into five sections organized in a chiastic structure:

A: Contestation of Authority in Interpreting the Past (3:1-6)
    B: Discarding Past Jewish Way of Thinking (3:7-9)
        C: Contestation of the Present Experience (3:10-11)
    B': Focusing on the Eschatological Ending (3:12-16)
A': Contestation of Demarcation of Time (3:17-21)

In 'A' (3:1-6) Paul *looks back* at his once treasured Jewish background within a polemical context of confronting those Jewish Christian opponents. In 'B' (3:7-9) Paul dismisses such Jewish privileges as something *past*.[2] In 'C' (3:10-12) Paul reflects on his *present* spiritual journey of knowing Christ through concepts of suffering and resurrection. In 'B'' (3:12-16) Paul affirms the importance of a processual journey toward a *future*

---

[1] The meaning of this "paradigm" does not refer to a strict imitation or copying of Christ's actions as narrated in the story of Christ (2:5-11, 3:17-21). Without denying elements of imitation, it refers primarily to the way of thinking and relating to God with which Paul must adjust his own in light of the story of Christ.
[2] Something he cannot rely on regarding his current situation.

goal in Christ. Lastly, in 'A'' (3:17-21) Paul *looks forward* to the future transformation of believers' bodies.[3]

6.1 A: Contestation of Authority in Interpreting the Past Story of Israel (3:1-6)

Traditionally, scholars tend to interpret 3:1-6 as a passage closely parallel to Paul's discourse of a "law-free gospel" in Galatians and Romans, in which Paul has seemingly abandoned his Jewish credentials as "garbage" (σκύβαλον, 3:8) in light of the grace found in the salvation of Jesus Christ.[4] The issue becomes the understanding of a "Christian gospel" as "God's free, undeserved grace and not of human achievement."[5] However, this interpretive direction is open to serious doubt. As I have explained earlier, the contestation between Paul and the Jewish Christian leaders recorded here does not revolve around the necessary criteria of being accepted as a "Christian." Instead, the controversy is the necessity and meaning of suffering for the gospel as displayed by Paul. With this overarching theme across the whole epistle, our understanding of 3:1-6 will look for connections and hence continuity between this passage and previous chapters of the epistle. Finding such connections will help confirm the viewpoint of this project, which is about the contestation of narratives concerning the meaning of Paul's suffering.

Such a connection can be found in Phil. 3:1. After encouraging the community to rejoice in the Lord, Paul writes τὰ αὐτὰ γράφειν ὑμῖν ἐμοὶ μὲν οὐκ ὀκνηρόν, ὑμῖν δὲ ἀσφαλές (3:1). While some interpreters treat "the same things" (τὰ αὐτὰ) as referring to Paul's previous exhortation to rejoice (2:18),[6] this understanding has been emphatically rejected by Lightfoot and Fee.[7] Here I argue that such "same things" refer to Paul's repeated admonitions around the topic of suffering for the gospel of Christ throughout the epistle. In other words, what follows in 3:2-16 matters to Paul not only as his own background story but also as part of his argument in his contestation with his opponents. In fact, besides the widely accepted meaning of "being safe" (ἀσφαλής, 3:1), Victor Furnish has insightfully suggested another more probable meaning for ἀσφαλής: a kind of specific, concrete, and dependable knowledge which provides *assurance*.[8] Trapped within a contestation of testimonies in which competing projections of the future are presented, Paul would not hesitate (οὐκ ὀκνηρός, 3:1) in giving them further reiterations of his testimonies recorded in chapters one and two.[9]

---

[3] While Phil. 3:17-21 has already been covered earlier as part of the story of Christ, the significant connections of this passage with Phil. 3:1-16 contribute to its inclusion as part of the story of Paul.
[4] Dunn, "Philippians 3.2-14," 470; Fee, *Paul's Letter*, 296.
[5] G. B. Caird, *Paul's Letters from Prison*, NCBC (Oxford: Oxford University Press, 1976), 134.
[6] For a list of interpreters who take such a view, see Fee, *Paul's Letter*, 292n.13.
[7] Fee, *Paul's Letter*, 292-3; Lightfoot, *Paul's Epistle*, 125.
[8] Victor P. Furnish, "The Place and Purpose of Philippians III," *NTS* 10 (1963): 83-6; *TLNT*, s.v. "ἀσφάλεια, κτλ," 1:212-19; Christoph Heilig, *Hidden Criticism? The Methodology and Plausibility of the Search for a Counter-Imperial Subtext in Paul* (Tübingen: Mohr Siebeck, 2015), 141.
[9] Cf. *TLNT*, s.v. "ὀκνέω, ὀκνηρός," 2:577.

6.1.1 The Identity of Opponents and Their Influence on the Philippian Community

Such reiterations are headed by a series of warnings using three βλέπω and three κ-pejorative yet somewhat cryptic word-groups, which have received numerous proposals on their exact referents.[10] Taking into account Paul's subsequent references to the Jewish identity marker of circumcision (περιτομή, 3:3) and a list of Jewish privileges (3:5-6), the most probable identity behind these κ- word-groups are a group of Jewish people.[11] More uncertainties are involved over their "religious" background. While some scholars choose to see them as non-"Christians,"[12] evidence of their "Christian" affiliation, as Mikael Tellbe has neatly summarized from multiple scholars, is relatively more justifiable.[13] This work will accordingly take this position.

What is more important is the way these pejorative words function within Paul's contestation with these Jewish Christian opponents. First, if "dogs" (κύων) bear any allusion to a group of inauthentic and untrustworthy religious leaders found in Isa. 56:10-12,[14] "evil workers" (κακοὺς ἐργάτας) probably refers specifically to their "missionary" nature similar to that of Paul, as they engage in the work of the gospel toward the Philippian community with an evil intent.[15] What is even more derogatory is κατατομή. With κατατομή not being found in the whole of the NT, LXX, and all the works of Philo and Josephus, its meaning has to be derived from the usage of its cognate verb κατατέμνω in the LXX and the particular context here.

According to Helmut Koester, in the LXX κατατέμνω is reserved to denote "the forbidden rite of slitting the skin" in the form of "cultic incisions."[16] Thus, when Paul immediately follows the κατατομή with the wordplay of περιτομή in ἡμεῖς γάρ ἐσμεν ἡ περιτομή (Phil. 3:3), we can safely assume two things. First, the contest here between Paul and his opponents probably centers on the practice and meaning of applying circumcision (περιτομή) to the Philippian community.[17] Second, when Paul

---

[10] Βλέπω generally means to be ready to learn about something that is hazardous or beware of something. See BDAG, s.v. "βλέπω," 178. For a list of different proposals for the identities of these opponents, see Reumann, *Philippians*, 278–9; Nanos, "Paul's Reversal," 475–9.

[11] Silva, *Philippians*, 147; Tellbe, "Sociological Factors," 98–100. For proposals that see the list as referring to pagan people groups, see K. Grayston, "The Opponents in Philippians 3," *ExpTim* 97 (1986): 170–2; Nanos, "Paul's Reversal," 448–82. For a critique of Nanos's viewpoint, see de Vos, *Church and Community Conflicts*, 268n.124.

[12] A. F. J. Klijn, "Paul's Opponents in Philippians 3," *NovT* 7 (1965): 278–84; Hawthorne, *Philippians*, xlvi.

[13] Tellbe, *Paul between Synagogue and State*, 260–1; Tellbe, "Sociological Factors," 99.

[14] Peter-Ben Smit, "In Search of Real Circumcision: Ritual Failure and Circumcision in Paul," *JSNT* 40, no. 1 (2017): 95. While it is difficult to ascertain the exact background of thought when Paul uses the word κύων, its general derogatory force is clear here.

[15] Cf. Bockmuehl, *Philippians*, 187; John B. Polhill, "Twin Obstacles in the Christian Path: Philippians 3," *RevExp* 77, no. 3 (1980): 361; Smit, "In Search of Real Circumcision," 84. This is one of only two occurrences of the word ἐργάτης used by Paul in the "undisputed Pauline epistles." The other usage is found in 2 Cor. 11:13, where he employs "ἐργάται δόλιοι" (deceitful workers) to describe those false apostles in Corinth, who probably could also be Jewish Christians.

[16] Helmut Koester, "κατατομή," *TDNT* 8:109–11; Helmut Koester, "The Purpose of the Polemic of a Pauline Fragment," *NTS* 8, no. 4 (1962): 320. To know more about the origin of the prohibition of cutting one's body in the OT (LXX), see Lev. 21:5, 1 Kings 18:28, Hosea 7:14.

[17] Koester, "Purpose of the Polemic," 320; Fee, *Paul's Letter*, 296; Tellbe, *Paul between Synagogue and State*, 262.

applies the pejorative marker κατατομή to his Jewish opponents, but gives the highly honored marker περιτομή to the gentile Philippian community (and himself), he is emphatically declaring that it is the Philippian community and himself, rather than the Jewish Christian leaders, who stand under God's promises as the true people of His covenant (a *pars pro toto* argument).[18] A contestation of the identity of the people of God is in view here.[19]

Because of this controversy over the identity of the people of God around the practice of circumcision, many scholars view the theological dispute at stake here as largely identical to the debate concerning justification by faith (πίστεως δικαιοῖ, Gal. 3:8) versus works of the law (ἔργων νόμου, Gal. 3:10) as found in Gal. 3:1-14.[20] However, if the issue here revolves around such a contention, why do we see no charge against or defense of Paul's apostleship?[21] If the issue concerns entry into salvation, it is unimaginable for the Jewish Christian leaders not to have undermined Paul's apostolic authority, which would almost certainly cause Paul to respond by affirming his apostleship.[22] What kind of a dispute would involve Paul, a group of Jewish Christian leaders, and a group of gentile believers over the practice of circumcision and the debate of suffering for Christ?

Inspired by Mikael Tellbe, I argue for a sociological context in which the community is advised by some Jewish Christian leaders to receive physical circumcision, which could help avoid suffering due to a citywide obligation to participate in the imperial cult. Receiving circumcision could grant them the religious and social identity of a Jewish sect, and thus give them recognition from the local communities and authorities, and even exemption from participating in the imperial cult.[23] Quoting Barclay, Tellbe comments,

> J. M. G. Barclay suggests that the major sociological reason why a gentile church in the middle of the first century CE would have been attracted by the Judaizers' message was the precarious social identity of gentile Christians. Newly converted Christians could no longer participate any longer in their ancestral religious practices, nor 'were they members (or even attenders) of the Jewish synagogues although they had the same Scriptures and much the same theology as those synagogues.' . . . gentile Christians believers, who understood themselves as true

---

[18] Cf. Koester, "Purpose of the Polemic," 320; Smit, "In Search of Real Circumcision," 85.

[19] The analysis of the meaning of περιτομή here is in accordance with my previous explanation on the connotation of πολιτεύομαι in 1:27. Both of these keywords have been used by Paul to convey the contestation of the right to be called the people of God along the tradition of the Israelites.

[20] Koester, "Purpose of the Polemic," 320; Fee, *Paul's Letter*, 296, 301-2. According to this approach, the debate concerning circumcision again springs from the controversy as to whether circumcision is a pre-requisite for salvation. Paul was then one promoting the belief of justification by faith.

[21] Cf. Gal. 1:13-2:10.

[22] L. L. Belleville, "Authority," in *DPL*, ed. Gerald F. Hawthorne and Ralph P. Martin (Leicester: InterVarsity Press, 1993). L. L. Belleville writes "There are very few of Paul's letters where his authority is not highlighted. It may be observed in the opening section of his letters where he commonly identifies himself as 'Paul, an apostle of Christ Jesus' (Rom., 1 Cor., 2 Cor., Gal., Eph., Col., 1 Tim., 2 Tim., Tit.)." However, nowhere do we find any mentioning of Paul's apostleship here in Philippians, including the beginning of the epistle.

[23] Tellbe, *Paul between Synagogue and State*, 263.

Jews... had a precarious social identity. At the same time as they were rejected by the Jews as *not* belonging to the Jewish tradition, they were being held responsible by the civic community for withdrawing from the traditional and civic cults and disturbing the *pax deorum*. In such a situation gentile converts would quite understandably have been impressed by the Judaizers' message: by accepting the act of circumcision and identifying with the local Jewish community—a community with deep roots and traditions, unlike the upstart Christian movement—they would have held a more recognizable and acknowledged place in Roman society.[24]

In light of such social situation, Tellbe offers his insight:

> I would suggest *that the most likely reason why the Judaizers' teaching appealed to the Philippians had to do with the achievement of social and political protection*. In order to escape from opposition and suffering, circumcised Christians may have claimed Jewish identity to be reckoned as belonging to a community that in the past had been granted special status by Rome, and consequently claim the rights and privileges of the Jewish Diaspora communities.[25]

While those Jewish Christian leaders have presented the trusting of a Jewish identity as compatible to having one's trust in Christ, Paul sees such a move as totally incoherent with their quest for an "in Christ" identity.[26] Thus, the dispute between Paul and the Jewish Christian leaders does not lie in the role of circumcision (and the law) in the community's entry to a rightful standing before God the Judge.[27] Instead, the dispute lies in a contestation of discerning God's righteous act concerning Paul's chains and the Philippian community's suffering experiences. In Ricoeur's terms, it is a contestation of the external narration of God's work as well as a contestation of an internal "criteriology of the divine." According to Paul's renewed understanding of God, it is He who has used his chains to spread the gospel and has allowed present and future suffering experiences to shape the identities of the Philippian community.

6.1.2 The Marker of Manipulating or Representing God (Κατατομή and Περιτομή)

Although Paul has not systematically explicated his current polemic, we can still discern a significant difference between his explication here and his two other similar arguments in Galatians and Romans. Without disregarding the differences among the

---

[24] Tellbe, *Paul between Synagogue and State*, 263–4. See also Tellbe, "Sociological Factors," 103n.29; John M. G. Barclay, *Obeying the Truth: Paul's Ethics in Galatians* (Edinburgh: T&T Clark, 1993), 58–9. However, this desire to get circumcised does not deny the fact that generally speaking, receiving of circumcision for a non-Jew is something despised by the Roman culture. See Karin B. Neutel and Matthew R. Anderson, "The First Cut is the Deepest: Masculinity and Circumcision in the First Century," in *Biblical Masculinities Foregrounded*, ed. Ovidiu Creanga and Peter-Ben Smit (Sheffield: Sheffield Phoenix, 2014), 228–44.
[25] Tellbe, *Paul between Synagogue and State*, 264.
[26] Ibid., 264.
[27] Cf. "ἐναρξάμενοι πνεύματι" in Gal. 3:3.

discourses in his letters to the communities in Galatia and Rome, what is common between them is that the significance of physical circumcision, in terms of its being an identity boundary marker between the Jews and the gentiles within God's salvation plan, *has become diminished*.[28] In contrast, the role of circumcision in the discourse of Philippians is different and intricate: while there is the unsurprising rejection of circumcision as Paul dismisses a list of credentials (3:5-8), he paradoxically applies this Jewish identity marker *affirmatively* onto the Philippian community (note the emphatic "we" in ἡμεῖς γάρ ἐσμεν ἡ περιτομή). If circumcision has lost its fundamental value in God's plan, why did Paul confuse his friends in Philippi with such a metaphor?

This question can be answered if we understand two contesting traditions found within the Hebrew Bible. First, on multiple occasions (Gen. 34, Jos. 5, Exo. 4:24-26) the act of circumcision really seems to have protected the Israelites.[29] Kelly A. Whitcomb writes,

> Circumcision was ultimately a sign of God's covenant and the blessing it brings. . . . The Mosaic law further specifies that males must be circumcised in order to participate in the Passover [an event to commemorate God's protection of the Israelites], and male slaves and resident aliens could participate in the Passover only after they had been circumcised (Exo. 12:43–49). . . . In Joshua 5, the Israelites were circumcised just before their battle with Jericho, which they won; in Gen 34, they were victorious by circumcising the Shechemites.[30]

After God installed physical circumcision as *the* covenant with Abraham and all his future descendants (Gen 17), *physical circumcision has arguably become the chief sign for His people in assuring God's covenantal promise, presence, and protection*. Since the time of the "Maccabean Revolt," the significance of keeping this "Abrahamic tradition" had, in fact, surged to the point of a national "make or break issue."[31] Thus, it is reasonable to assume that at the time of Paul, the tradition of seeing physical circumcision as a sign of ensuring God's covenantal protection was still well received and trusted.

However, there is *another contesting tradition* as embodied by the word κατατομή. While scholars have been aware of its particular reference to the forbidden pagan practices of cultic self-mutilation,[32] its affiliation to the cultic priests' intention to *coercively* gain blessing or protection from their deities has not been sufficiently

---

[28] See Rom. 2:25-29, Gal. 2-3.
[29] Kelly A. Whitcomb and Getachew Kiros, "Circumcision," in *LBD*, ed. John D. Barry et al. (Bellingham: Lexham Press, 2016).
[30] Whitcomb and Kiros, "Circumcision."
[31] James D. G. Dunn, *The Partings of the Ways: Between Christianity and Judaism and Their Significance for the Character of Christianity* (London: SCM Press, 1991), 29. Talking about the "common core" of Second Temple Judaism during the time of the first century before 70 C.E., Dunn addresses the supreme significance of circumcision: "Here again the importance of circumcision as marking out identity and defining boundary was massively reinforced by the Maccabean crisis. Hellenistic antipathy to such bodily mutilation caused many Jews to abandon this key covenant marker. In the words of 1 Maccabees, 'They built a gymnasium in Jerusalem, according to Gentile custom, and removed the marks of circumcision, and abandoned the holy covenant' (1 Macc. 1:14-15). In the consequent revolt and suppression, circumcision was clearly for many the 'make or break' issue."
[32] Fee, *Paul's Letter*, 300; Reumann, *Philippians*, 462.

addressed.³³ Just as the prophets of Baal were cutting themselves to *manipulate* the actions of Baal (1 Kings 18:28), the Israelites (Hosea 7:14) were cutting themselves to *manipulate* the actions of YHWH or Baal. Thus, within Paul's narrative world, contrary to the tradition that circumcision could be trusted as a sign and assurance of God's covenantal protection,³⁴ exploiting circumcision for safety to avoid suffering for the gospel is despised as similar to using self-cutting to *manipulate* God. What these false teachers or workers propose to the Philippian community amounts to an illegitimate way of understanding the act of God. What they have suggested to the community does not come from God.

6.1.3 The Contestation on the Definition of Circumcision: The True Marker of God's Covenantal People

According to Paul, it is amid these contesting traditions that he and the Jewish Christian leaders strive for the right to reappropriate the definition of circumcision as the identity boundary marker for the Philippian community. Given that the contemporary ritual norm for circumcision would lead one to enter "Judaism," both the Jewish Christian leaders and Paul could be viewed as offering certain kinds of "deviations from a prescribed ritual procedure."³⁵ Based on Ricoeur's dialectic of innovation and sedimentation, both of their testimonies could be identified as "coming from" the living tradition of the Jews.³⁶ What is common to the Jewish Christian leaders and Paul is that the assumed conventions (and hence temporality) within the prefigured Jewish interpretation of circumcision have been altered respectively within their testimonies. In other words, the causal relationships among the stories of God, Israel, Christ, and these "theologians" (levels one to four) have been rewritten.

According to the Jewish Christian leaders' "criteriology of the divine," receiving circumcision is probably narrated as continuous with God's previous protection of His people in the OT. Instead of taking physical circumcision as a ritual of transforming the Philippian community into proselytes of Judaism, it is now seen as a Godly assured way of gaining His protection while remaining as "Christians." Suffering like Paul is rendered as unnecessary. In contrast, according to Paul's understanding of God, receiving circumcision to avoid suffering equates only to an entry to the "membership" of those who manipulate God. The Jewish Christians leaders' reappropriation of circumcision thus leads to a deviation from complying with God's eschatological righteous acts. Only suffering for the gospel could lead them to become the true People

---

[33] According to the *ESV Study Bible*, the prophets' "attempt to manipulate Baal into action involves self-mutilation." See *The ESV Study Bible* (Wheaton: Crossway Bibles, 2008), 1 Kings 18:28-29.

[34] Whitcomb and Kiros, "Circumcision." While the precise means of protection from God and the involvement of the Israelites could vary a lot across cases, what is shared across the Israelites' various experiences is that they were able to perceive the marker of circumcision as bringing them the initial assurance and the subsequent protection from God.

[35] Ute Hüsken, "Ritual Dynamics and Ritual Failure," in *When Rituals Go Wrong: Mistakes, Failure, and the Dynamics of Ritual*, ed. Ute Hüsken, Numen Book Series (Leiden: Brill, 2007), 361–2. See also Smit, "In Search of Real Circumcision," 77.

[36] Cf. Ricoeur, "Text," 181–2.

of the Lord. It is within this contestation of the meaning of κατατομή and περιτομή that circumcision takes on the function and significance of a *membership ritual*.

Due to these two competing emplotment processes, contesting meanings and identities have been created out of the "same" *membership procedure*. Which ritual will the Philippian neophytes choose?

This contestation over the mediating role of guiding believers to understand God's righteous act is further supported by three participial phrases, which all serve to substantiate the circumcision ritual (ἡ περιτομή) with more *innovative definitions*. Just as Paul uses three epithets to describe his opponents, he uses another three to identify the Philippian community and himself as the true people of God. The first is οἱ πνεύματι θεοῦ λατρεύοντες. With the use of λατρεύω, Paul further qualifies such a people group as one *chosen* by God to serve Him.[37] Rather than taking Paul as abolishing circumcision altogether (and breaking abruptly with God's past actions in the story of Israel), the instrumental dative phrase οἱ πνεύματι θεοῦ stresses that such community (ἡ περιτομή) has been "engendered by the Spirit of God."[38] Instead of favoring an *internal* attitude over an *external* ritual,[39] or *inner* morality over *outer* legality,[40] Paul is *adapting* the old Jewish marker of God's covenant with His recent "eschatological working": the indwelling of the Spirit of God.[41] As Fee has argued, besides the resurrection of Christ, it is the giving of the Spirit which "would mark the beginning of God's final wrapup."[42] In other words, the accent of πνεύματι θεοῦ lies on the *beginning* (cf. ἐνάρχομαι in Phil. 1:6) of a new temporal era inaugurated by the death and resurrection of Christ Jesus.

Such compliance with God's righteous act is further illustrated by another participial phrase: καυχώμενοι ἐν Χριστῷ Ἰησοῦ. Generally speaking, scholars agree that καυχάομαι refers to believers' taking pride or boasting in Christ Jesus.[43] Such "boasting" is then taken as evidence of believers' true reconciliation with God through faith in Christ.[44] However, I argue that this interpretation has read Paul's concern from elsewhere into Philippians, and has not paid enough attention to the polemical dimension implied in καυχάομαι. Though scholars have been aware of the usages of καυχάομαι in the LXX as involving polemical disputes between the honor of God and the vainglory of humans (Judg. 7:2; Ps. 27:1, 48:7, 52:1; Jer. 9:22-23),[45] its relation to the

---

[37] BDAG, s.v. "λατρεύω," 587; Hawthorne, *Philippians*, 175; H. Strathmann, "λατρεύω, λατρεία," *TDNT* 4:58-65.
[38] Fee, *Paul's Letter*, 301. For the discussion of a variety of perspectives on the understanding of the πνεύματι here, see Reumann, *Philippians*, 464-5.
[39] K. Hess, "Serve, Deacon, Worship," in *NIDNTT*, ed. Colin Brown (Grand Rapids: Zondervan, 1986), 3:544-9.
[40] Hawthorne, *Philippians*, 176.
[41] Smit, "In Search of Real Circumcision," 93n.73; Everett Ferguson, "Spiritual Circumcision in Early Christianity," *SJTh* 41, no. 4 (1988): 496. According to Everett Ferguson, the Spirit has been taken by the apostle Paul as "the seal of the new covenant on the analogy of circumcision as the seal of the Mosaic covenant." For details of his argument, see ibid., 485-97.
[42] Fee, *Paul's Letter*, 329.
[43] BDAG, s.v. "καυχάομαι," 536.
[44] Fee, *Paul's Letter*, 155, 298-9.
[45] BDAG, s.v. "καυχάομαι," 536; F. B. Huey, *Jeremiah, Lamentations: An Exegetical and Theological Exposition of Holy Scripture* (Nashville: Holman Reference, 1993), 121-2.

polemical dispute among God's believers over the knowledge of God has largely been neglected.

Despite its highly abbreviated manner, Paul's use of καυχάομαι here has been recognized by scholars as springing from Jer. 9:23-24, in which the larger context comprises a dispute between false anthropocentric boasting and true theocentric boasting.[46] While Fee has alerted us to the theme of circumcision in the literary context of Jer. 9:25-26, his subsequent analysis does not offer much insight beyond the traditional understanding of a dispute between salvation by faith and by works.[47] While there have been multiple times in which Paul has coalesced the topics of circumcision and boasting,[48] what makes the one here special is that unlike the cases in Romans and Galatians, Paul's discourse does not revolve around the dispensable nature of circumcision in believers' entry to salvation.[49] What scholars have failed to notice is that both the literary contexts of Phil. 3:2-3 and Jer. 9:23-26 are composed of contentions concerning "true circumcision," and affiliation to the knowledge of assurance of God's blessing and protection.[50]

In light of this similarity, I argue that Paul's theologizing process here can be best modeled by a nesting of stories in which certain dimensions of the story of Paul (and Christ) are nested upon a certain "alluded story" of Jeremiah. In this emplotment process, both the "Beginning" of their stories are marked by the people of God being threatened by a pagan nation. In Jeremiah it is the nation Babylon who are on their way to conquer Jerusalem, threatening the security and self-understanding of the Jewish people: if we are the People of the Lord, how would God lead us to face such an imminent threat? In Philippians, it is the Roman authorities who are persecuting the Philippian community because of their reluctance to participate in the imperial worship. How should the Philippian community, as a newly formed gentile religious community, understand the guidance of God to face such an imminent threat?

In the "Middle," both stories are marked by a contestation of "defense strategies" with respect to such imminent threat. In both stories there are some Jewish leaders, who are *supposed* to play the role of God's servants (cf. τοὺς κύνας and τοὺς κακοὺς ἐργάτας in 3:2), giving testimonies that the marker of physical circumcision could lead to God's guidance and protection. In both cases, rather than rejecting altogether the value of circumcision, proper circumcision is separated from improper circumcision.[51] In the "alluded story" of Jeremiah, the Israelites were developing a procircumcision "anti-Babylonian coalition" with Egypt, Edom, Ammon, Moab, and certain Arab groups to fight against the uncircumcised Babylon.[52] Sadly, according to Jeremiah, without true

---

[46] Fee, *Paul's Letter*, 154–5; Gail R. O'Day, "Jeremiah 9:22-23 and 1 Corinthians 1:26-31: A Study in Intertextuality," *JBL* 109, no. 2 (1990): 261–2.
[47] Fee, *Paul's Letter*, 154–5, 298–9, 301, in particular, 299n.58, 301n.65.
[48] Rom. 2:23-25; Gal. 6:13-15, Phil. 3:3-5.
[49] In both of the other two discourses, we see Paul clearly lean on dismissing the value of circumcision.
[50] See the discussion on the understanding of πίστις as an assurance in the phrase τῇ πίστει τοῦ εὐαγγελίου of Phil. 1:27 in chapter 4.1.3.
[51] Smit, "In Search of Real Circumcision," 93; James D. G. Dunn, *Romans 1-8*, WBC 38A (Dallas: Thomas Nelson, 1988), 125.
[52] Richard C. Steiner, "Incomplete Circumcision in Egypt and Edom: Jeremiah (9:24-25) in the Light of Josephus and Jonckheere," *JBL* 118, no. 3 (1999): 505; Huey, *Jeremiah*, 122; J. M. Sasson, "Circumcision in the Ancient Near East," *JBL* 85 (1966): 473–6. With Judah being put second

obedience to the Lord, such a "circumcision coalition" guarantees nothing from the Lord.[53] It is against such a false and deceptive strategy of assuring God's protection that the prophet Jeremiah rebukes the Israelites as simultaneously having received circumcision physically, yet remaining uncircumcised figuratively.[54]

Likewise in Philippians, there are some Jewish Christian leaders who resort to the strategy of applying physical circumcision to the Philippian community so that they will be saved from *unnecessary* suffering. Within their narrative world, believing in Jesus probably does not necessarily involve suffering on behalf of Jesus (cf. Phil. 1:29). Thus, the Philippian community should follow their tradition of receiving God's blessing and protection through circumcision. Against this, Paul rebukes these evil servants of God as τὴν κατατομήν, whose self-cutting has alienated them from God's true covenantal community (ἡ περιτομή). According to Paul, God's true covenantal community belongs only to those who are willing to suffer on behalf of Christ (Phil. 1:27-30).

According to Ricoeur, what God has done in both cases involves a dialectic of external narration and internal conviction. Just as Jer. 9:23-26 narrates God's working in accordance with the beginning of a refreshed era with an innovated manner of understanding Him, what God has done in Christ Jesus marks the beginning of an eschatological era in which knowledge of God has been mediated by the innovative actions of a suffering Christ. For many Israelites in the days of Jeremiah, the defeat of Judah by Babylon had been unacceptable. Thus, what had been cast into doubt is the narration that despite Judah's defeat, YHWH should still be honored as the Lord who keeps exercising mercy, and judgment, and *righteousness* upon the earth.[55]

Similarly, for certain Philippian community members, suffering for the gospel of Christ has probably reached a degree that seemingly cannot cohere with their understanding of God. What is being contested is whether their sufferings should be seen as the ἔνδειξις (Phil. 1:28) of the active fulfillment of YHWH's Lordship within a period of Christ's "eschatological Lordship," in which knowledge and assurance of God's *righteous* acts are now mediated *through* the *processual* suffering story of Christ.[56] Καυχώμενοι ἐν Χριστῷ Ἰησοῦ then means putting one's confidence in, and orientating one's life story around, this story of Christ.

Toward the "Ending" of the stories, both are marked by a juxtaposition of hope and judgement. In Jeremiah, while the prophet encourages the Israelites to put their confidence in the uninterrupted sovereignty of God, those who have not circumcised their heart will be punished. Likewise in Philippians, though not explicitly articulated, those who mutilate themselves (κατατομή) will receive their judgment just as those pagan prophets would do at the end time. All three stages of contestation are shown in Figure 11.

---

instead of first or last in the list of nations, she is removed from any special divine favor from the Lord. She is just the same as other pagan neighbor nations, which all deserve to be punished.

[53] J. A. Thompson, *The Book of Jeremiah*, NICOT (Grand Rapids: Wm. B. Eerdmans, 1980), 321–2. The "men of Judah and inhabitants of Jerusalem" still need "circumcision of the heart" (Jer. 4:4).

[54] Steiner, "Incomplete Circumcision," 504; Thompson, *Jeremiah*, 271–339.

[55] In the eyes of many of the Israelites at the time of Jeremiah, the narration in Jer. 9.23-26 is just too incoherent with their "criteriology of the divine."

[56] Cf. the meaning of τῇ πίστει τοῦ εὐαγγελίου in 1:27 in chapter 4.1.3.

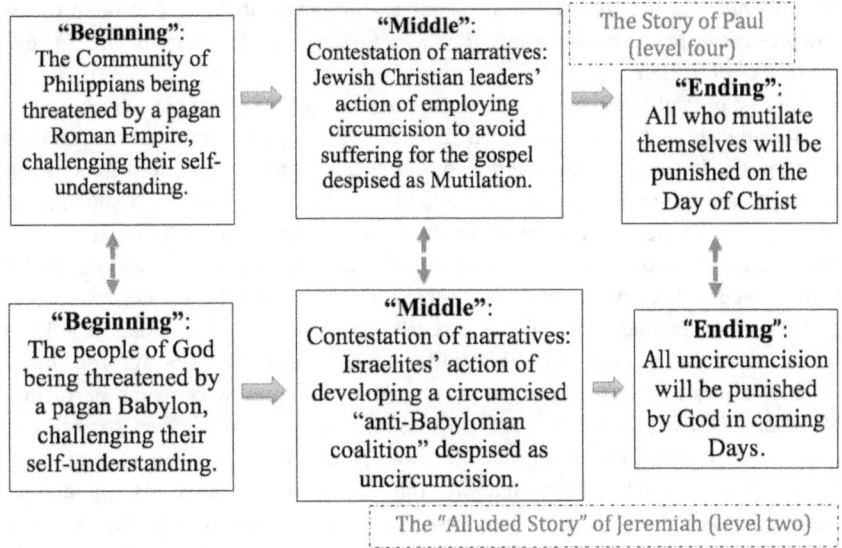

Figure 11 The story of Paul nested upon the "alluded story" of Jeremiah.

It is within this polemical context between Paul and a group of Jewish Christian leaders that the following list of Paul's credentials should be understood. Rather than seeing this list as something of "Judaism" rejected by Paul in the wake of his conversion to "Christianity," these seven items should be viewed as a demonstration of how Paul, in the time before he knows Christ, *perfectly* qualified himself as the best representative of God as an Israelite and, in particular, a member of the Pharisee group. Within his contestation with the Jewish Christian leaders, who may well come from the sect of the Pharisees, such perfect credentials serve primarily to show that he outrivals (ἐγὼ μᾶλλον, 3:4) his opponents in terms of his excellence in discerning the relation between God's *past* work among the Israelites and His *new* work through the death and resurrection of Christ.[57]

Such outrivalling is mediated through a list filled with seven extremely enviable religious identity markers among the Jews. With circumcision being at the center of the controversy, it is not surprising to see Paul head up his items of confidence in the flesh (πεποίθησιν καὶ ἐν σαρκί, 3:4) with περιτομῇ ὀκταήμερος. Symbolically speaking, having received circumcision on the eighth day not only signifies the *earliest* moment a person can gain (though rather passively) his identification with the "Abrahamic covenant" (Gen. 17:3-14), but also entails the *beginning* of his full commitment and lifelong faithfulness to God's covenant with Israel.

Such "religious origin" is followed by three other inherited privileges of ἐκ γένους Ἰσραήλ (of the nation of Israel), φυλῆς Βενιαμίν (of the tribe of Benjamin), and Ἑβραῖος ἐξ Ἑβραίων (a Hebrew of Hebrews), which culminates to form a picture of a

---

[57] Cf. Todd D. Still, "(Im)Perfection: Reading Philippians 3.5-6 in Light of the Number Seven," *NTS* 60, no. 1 (2014): 139–45; Andrew S. Jacobs, "A Jew's Jew: Paul and the Early Christian Problem of Jewish Origins," *The Journal of Religion* 86, no. 2 (2006): 262.

perfectly *pure* origin of Jewish identity. Paul has thus given himself the most entrusted and prestigious Jewish background suitable for further considerations to participate in the service of the Lord.

This list of Paul's passively inherited privileges is followed by three actively sought out accomplishments in 3:5b-6, which all relate to Paul's past devotion to the standard found in the Israelites' mainstream tradition.[58] Besides the Gospels and Acts, this is the only reference to Φαρισαῖος in the whole NT. What is probably highlighted is the "thinking" dimension of the Pharisee Paul as he had devoted himself to the study of the law. Coupled with this Pharisaic background is the "emotional" dimension in which Paul persecuted the Church according to his zeal (κατὰ ζῆλος) for the Lord.[59]

Heretofore, Fee has been able to categorize Paul's previous credentials as a list of *human achievements*. However, this understanding becomes seriously problematic when it comes to Paul's zeal in persecuting the Church: how can such pernicious bloodshed of his past be counted now as achievement? While Fee struggles to accommodate such persecuting into the concept of achievement (something about which one can boast) and thus relegates this into an irony against his opponents,[60] I contend that the reference to this persecution serves to emphasize Paul's superior commitment and thus higher authority over his Jewish opponents regarding the right to interpret those Jewish traditions shared between him and them. What concerns Paul is not the morally wrong aspect of this bloodshed, but *his unparalleled zeal for the Mosaic Law and the Lord as demonstrated by the persecution*. In this manner, it is still something worth boasting about among the circle of the Israelites (though ultimately proved wrong).

Last but certainly not least, Paul's development of himself as the supreme expert of the Jewish Law culminates at the phrase κατὰ δικαιοσύνην τὴν ἐν νόμῳ γενόμενος ἄμεμπτος. Rather than seeing the phrase as denoting sinlessness and representing a general attitude of relying on human works to gain salvation among the Israelites, the phrase should be rendered as "I have shown myself blameless with respect to the standard of righteousness as found in the Mosaic Law."[61] Its primary function is *to laud Paul's attitude in serving God* as "first-class" among his compatriots.[62] Thus, to further understand the meaning of δικαιοσύνη and νόμος in Philippians, we have to be aware that *within such a master narrative framework (the story of Paul as seen from his current self) there exists a subframe (a story of Paul as seen from his past self) in which judgments*

---

[58] Still, "(Im)Perfection," 139–40.
[59] H.-C. Hahn, "Zeal," in *NIDNTT*, ed. Colin Brown (Grand Rapids: Zondervan, 1986); Pobee, *Persecution and Martyrdom*, 24.
[60] Fee, *Paul's Letter*, 303–10; Pobee, *Persecution and Martyrdom*, 117. There are two basic observations that make the possibility of an irony slim. First, there is no transition of words and tone between this credential and the previous ones. If the previous ones are all truly enviable marks among the Israelites, it is strange to expect Paul to suddenly reverse to something ironic. Second, if this is ironic, how could Paul in 3:7 comment that he saw it as gain (κέρδος)?
[61] Cf. Sumney, *Philippians*, 76; Reumann, *Philippians*, 487.
[62] It attests not to Paul's past "getting into" the covenant, nor his "staying in." Cf. Reumann, *Philippians*, 486; E. P. Sanders, *Paul and Palestinian Judaism: A Comparison of Patterns of Religion* (Minneapolis: Fortress Press, 1977), 544–5. It is also not his subjective self-evaluation, which is read by Krister Stendahl. See Krister Stendahl, "The Apostle Paul and the Introspective Conscience of the West," *HTR* 56 (1963): 200–1.

*were made using an old system of values.*⁶³ It is only after we realize the roles played by δικαιοσύνη and νόμος in the *old* subframe that we can understand their meanings within the *current* master story of Paul.

In short, these last three credentials all join together to endow Paul with the image of the most admirable Jewish religious expert one can imagine. Together with the previous four inherited "spiritual origins," they function to affirm Paul as the "archetypal Jew" for his assured excellence in relation to both God and His people.⁶⁴ In other words, his understanding of the Jewish God YHWH is the most authoritative one, which other Jews and gentile believers should look up to. In recounting his *past*, Paul offers the renewal of a narrative trajectory in which his "little" story nests upon and coheres with God's "grand" story from the time of Jeremiah.

With the resonance between these stories, another *teleological drive* toward his narrative closure has been created.⁶⁵

However, paradoxically, as the following subsection will show, it is only *after* such boasting and affirming of Paul as an "archetypal Jew" that God's *past way of dealing with the Israelites* can be reconfigured and even refuted in light of God's *new* act in Christ Jesus.

6.2 B: Contestation of Assurance of God's Righteousness (3:7-9)

6.2.1 The Dialectic of Boundaries between "Old Judaism" and "New Christianity"

In Phil. 3:7, all previous credentials that have been highly valued as gain (κέρδος) suddenly plummet and become loss (ζημία). With the use of a perfect tense ἥγημαι, the lasting significance of a deliberate change of attitude from Paul is clearly in view. While certain traditional interpretations take this verse and the current discourse of comparison (3:7-9) as evidence of Paul totally renouncing his Jewish background and religion in light of his "conversion" to the new "Christianity,"⁶⁶ such understanding does not do justice to the essentially *dialectical* nature of Paul's transformation, and the intra-Jewish polemical context as explained earlier.⁶⁷ Inspired by the work of Andrew Jacobs, the debate between Paul and the Jewish Christian leaders should be seen as a contest in which both parties try to take control of what Jacobs calls "the boundaries of Judaism and Christianity."⁶⁸ While a thorough analysis of such

---

[63] Cf. Fee, *Paul's Letter*, 309n.20; Reumann, *Philippians*, 487.
[64] Jacobs, "A Jew's Jew," 258–70. In the field of Biblical Studies the term "archetypal Jew" was probably coined by Andrew S. Jacobs.
[65] See Ricoeur, *T&N I*, 67; Hays, *Echoes of Scripture*, 20–3.
[66] Cf. Thomas R. Schreiner, *Romans*, BECNT (Grand Rapids: Baker Books, 1998), 553; Zetterholm, *Approaches*, 82–3.
[67] Cf. Silva, *Philippians*, 157–8; Punt, "Paul's Jewish Identity," 255.
[68] Jacobs, "A Jew's Jew," 269–70; Dunn, "Paul's Theology," 332.

boundaries is beyond the scope of this book,[69] Jacobs's proposal is illuminating to the current investigation. During Paul's construction of an early exemplary "Christian identity," there is an indispensable "appropriation of a Jewish voice" within a seemingly paradoxical Christian framework.[70] In other words, which parts of the *old* Jewish heritage and ideology should be kept by the *new* "Christian" community, and which parts should be changed? In terms of Ricoeur's theory, it is within this dialectic of innovation and sedimentation that Paul and the Jewish Christian leaders battle for the right to answer these questions of *theological appropriation*. And it is within this appropriation that questions concerning the gentile Philippian community are asked:[71] What are the relations between the practice of a bodily circumcision, and its pertinent metaphorical meaning in light of God's recent righteous act in Christ?[72] How should the community *think* (φρονέω) in the face of upcoming oppression from the Roman political authorities, and the defense strategy from the Jewish Christian leaders, both of which have immense consequences for their bodies? Thus, we may say that the contestation between Paul and his Jewish opponents revolves around the way that certain elements of "*old* Jewish" and "*new* non-Jewish" are fused together in light of a particular situation.[73]

Understanding of such *dialectical appropriation* can only be obtained if we can successfully disclose the narrative dynamics within Paul's narrative world beneath his arguments. From Ricoeur's perspective, both of the narrative worlds of Paul and his Jewish Christian opponents are actually constituted by how various heterogeneous and discordant elements are joined together into a single and concordant narrative. Taking into account Paul's way of articulating his personal story, these elements at least include the "who,"[74] the "what,"[75] and, most important of all, the elements of "when." While Paul and the Jewish Christians leaders are creating different narratives regarding the value of suffering for the gospel, both of their narratives are constituted by more or less these same elements.

Despite sharing the same elements, what is seriously disparate are their dialectics of discordance and concordance involved in integrating Paul's chains. Being the

---

[69] For relevant discussions, see Karin B. Neutel, *A Cosmopolitan Ideal: Paul's Declaration 'Neither Jew Nor Greek, Neither Slave Nor Free, Nor Male and Female' in the Context of First-Century Thought* (London: T&T Clark, 2015), 72–143; Matthew Thiessen, *Contesting Conversion: Genealogy, Circumcision, and Identity in Ancient Judaism and Christianity* (Oxford: Oxford University Press, 2011), 111–41, 46–8; Skarsaune, *Shadow of the Temple*, 277–422.

[70] Jacobs, "A Jew's Jew," 286; Dunn, "Paul's Theology," 332–7.

[71] It is important not to confuse the current dialectic with a direct contention between "Judaism" and "Christianity." While the latter contention highlights "Christianity" as a rival religious sect and ideology to "Judaism," the current dialectic sees the "*old* Judaism" as the matrix from which a "*new* Christianity" is born.

[72] Neutel, *A Cosmopolitan Ideal*, 12. For a discussion on the various perspectives as proposed by Paul's contemporaries, which center on the relation between the need of practicing physical circumcision and its allegorical meaning, see Neutel, *A Cosmopolitan Ideal*, 102–3; John M. G. Barclay, "Paul and Philo on Circumcision: Romans 2.25-9 in Social and Cultural Context," *NTS* 44, no. 4 (1998): 536–56.

[73] Jacobs, "A Jew's Jew," 286.

[74] Such elements include at least: God, Christ, Paul, Israelites, Philippians, the political authorities, etc.

[75] Such elements include at least: circumcision, self-laceration, Jewish privileges, bodily suffering, imprisonment, the Cross, the advancement of the gospel, resurrection, etc.

most primitive feature of narrative temporality,⁷⁶ such a dialectic governs the logic of answers to a few critical questions pertinent to the *temporal boundaries* of various actions:⁷⁷ First, does God's "Abrahamic covenant" of bodily circumcision and its related provisions of blessing and protection belong strictly to the *past*? In other words, should the tradition of identifying God's protection as coming from bodily circumcision be seen as discordant with discerning God's righteous acts of now? Second, how does God's δικαιοσύνη manifested through Christ's *lifelong* suffering and death relate to believers' *present* situation of suffering? In other words, should believers' suffering be considered concordant with God's righteous acts of now? Third, how does Christ's *future* transformation of believers' bodies relate to believers' *present lack of vindication*? In other words, should the meaning of believers' *present* suffering follow a logic of hope toward the *eschatological parousia* of Christ?

Instead of answering these questions in propositional form, the key to these questions is found in the *teleological* principle of an emplotment process that drives various discordant events into an anticipated and concordant closure.⁷⁸ While we do not possess a copy of the forms of persuasion presented by the Jewish Christian leaders, based on Paul's writing and the social context proposed above, we may safely infer three things. First, seeing Paul's imprisonment as God's work is simply too discordant with the anticipated closure and hence temporality of their own story. Facing a zealous Paul who keeps promoting the thinking of suffering on behalf of Christ, these Jewish Christian leaders, who are suggesting circumcision to avoid suffering and could probably see such actions as bringing themselves glory when Christ returns, virtually have no choice but to speak against Paul.

Second, seeing circumcision as a sign of protection from God is *concordant* with the temporality of their own story. If God has been granting them and other gentile neophytes exemption from participating in the imperial worship through the practice of physical circumcision,⁷⁹ why should the Philippian community not use it for the advancement of the gospel of Christ and even to the benefit of their spiritual journey? Thus, their version of the story of Christ, which would also consist of His death and resurrection, does not need to alter the well-accepted "Jewish norms" of applying the rite of bodily circumcision to gentile neophytes.

Last, while the testimony of these Jewish Christian leaders exhibits a similar interplay of innovation and sedimentation to that of Paul, with their continual acceptance and even encouragement of physical circumcision, the proportion of innovation within their testimony is less than Paul's, whose testimony practically points to a total rejection of physical circumcision for the gentile believers. With less deviation from

---

⁷⁶ Ricoeur, *T&N II*, 4–5.
⁷⁷ As a reflective discourse, the logic of Paul's letters is in fact governed by an "underneath" story. See Hays, *The Faith of Jesus Christ*, 22.
⁷⁸ Cf. Ricoeur, *OAA*, 147; Dowling, *Ricoeur on Time and Narrative*, 6.
⁷⁹ Cf. Punt, "Paul's Jewish Identity," 252. On this proposed phenomenon of gentile God-fearers sharing the privileges of the Israelites, Jeremy Punt writes, "various ancient sources indicate that Jews were given concessions that allowed them to largely maintain their customs and beliefs, so that they, notwithstanding occasional outbreaks of violence against them, were relatively settled during imperial times. The early followers of Jesus who were Jewish or associated with Jews shared in these privileges."

the traditional practice and ideology of "Judaism," the temporality of the testimony of these Jewish Christian leaders will be more similar to that of the prevailing "Judaism" than that of Paul.[80] A stronger sense of continuity with God's previous work, which "naturally" represents some trustworthy principles of interpretation (mimesis1), has been offered by the testimony of Paul's Jewish opponents. With this intra-Jewish debate happening amid a gentile community who probably desire to see themselves as "true Jews" bearing a relation of continuity with the ancient people of God,[81] the trustworthiness of their testimony would then be "naturally" higher than that of Paul. Less evidence would be required from them to persuade the Philippian community.

6.2.2 Updating God's Old Act in Israel with His New Act in Christ

Entangled in this contestation of testimonies, in which there exists no objective logic to prove his religious claim, Paul the "underdog" cannot resort to propositional reasoning against these "dogs" (κύων, Phil. 3:2). To win this battle, Paul must construct himself as a superlative Jewish religious expert so that he can "out-Jew the Jewish threat."[82] In this intra-Jewish polemic, *Paul is not rejecting but innovating his Jewishness* so that he can invalidate the narrative claims of his Jewish opponents and alone claim the right to interpret those previous works of God.[83] In light of the recently introduced discordant chains, how can Paul strengthen the trustworthiness of his testimony? Based on Ricoeur's HT, *Paul must increase the truthfulness of his testimony by refreshing his own story with renewed stories of God, Israel, and Christ.*

Specifically, the otherwise discordant "little narratives" of himself and the Philippian community (levels four and five) must be fitted into renewed "grand narratives" of God, Israel, and Christ (levels one to three),[84] so that God's new way of showing Himself through believers' suffering can be presented in a concordant narrative.[85] It is through

---

[80] This comparison of temporality is taken in regard to the meaning of physical circumcision, which is given affirmative meanings within both narratives of "Judaism" and the Jewish Christian leaders. For the discussion of the theory behind this, see chapter 3.2.

[81] Cf. Tellbe, "Sociological Factors," 103n.31. Cf. 1 Cor. 10:1-5, where Paul uses οἱ πατέρες ἡμῶν (our fathers) to relate the gentile Corinthian community members to the Israelites in the time of Moses. Both Barclay and Tellbe argue that the early gentile Christ-followers, as taught by Paul (and even the Jewish Christian leaders), could probably see themselves as "true Jews," which bear a relationship of continuity with the ancient people of God. See also ibid., 103n.29; Tellbe, *Paul between Synagogue and State*, 263–4; Barclay, *Obeying the Truth*, 58–9.

[82] Jacobs, "A Jew's Jew," 275.

[83] Cf. W. D. Davies, *Paul and Rabbinic Judaism: Some Rabbinic Elements in Pauline Theology*, 2nd ed. (London: SPCK, 1955), 323. Davies writes, "It appears that for the Apostle the Christian Faith was the full flowering of Judaism, the outcome of the latter and its fulfilment; in being obedient to the Gospel he was merely being obedient to the true form of Judaism. The gospel for Paul was not the annulling of Judaism but its completion, and as such, it took up into itself the essential genius of Judaism."

[84] In light of the cosmological significance of the stories of God and Christ, their "grandness" should not be difficult to understand. The "grandness" of the story of Israel arises from the nature of the current contestation as an intra-Jewish debate, in which certain parts of the collective memory and history of Israel are being modified and contested. The identity-making processes of Paul and the Philippian community are essentially connected to this contestation of the stories of Israel.

[85] See chapter 3.3.3.2.

this renewal that Paul experiences the truthfulness of his testimony, and becomes a trustworthy witness to the Philippian community.

Instead of expressing a fuller dependence on God's grace in Christ against human achievements in general, the metaphorical language of gain and loss (κέρδος, ζημία) reflects Paul's present desire for his future glory on the Day of Christ.[86] Consistent with his repeated focus on the ultimate "upper limit of time" (Phil. 1:6, 10, 2:16),[87] such gaining consists of a *present* hope toward the *eschatological* disclosure (verdict) of his being *right* regarding the current contestation. It is with the hope of constructing a theologically coherent narrative representation of the story of Christ (level three) within his own story (level four) that Paul wants to gain Christ (Χριστὸν κερδήσω, 3:8) and be shown to be in Him (εὑρεθῶ ἐν αὐτῷ, 3:9).[88]

In contrast, trusting in the narrative constructed by the Jewish Christian leaders would deviate from experiencing the grace of God, which would be a huge loss (ζημία). It is in this polemical contestation of narratives that the gaining of Christ "requires the loss of all former things" treasured by Paul. Any continual reliance on these *formerly* accepted Jewish markers of God's blessing will inevitably hinder one's knowing of Christ, which presumably would be a goal shared also by the Jewish Christian leaders. It is in light of such seeking of Christ that these things (πάντα)[89] should be discarded (a sense of discontinuity with the past)[90] and even treated as "dung" (σκύβαλον, 3:8).[91] With one perfect and two present tense forms of ἡγέομαι in 3:7-8, "*a continuous temporal process* of considering all this as loss" is highlighted.[92]

While both of the narratives of Paul and his opponents involve a certain past, present, and future, *Paul's narrative hinges more on the hope of a currently contested future.* This is in contrast to the narrative of his opponents, which features a shape close to a "past-oriented form" of the Israelite ethnic identity. As Lola Romanucci-Ross and George De Vos write, "Ethnicity is a past sense of allegiance. . . . On its deepest level, ethnicity provides a quasi-religious sense of group belonging affording continuity and purpose."[93] Thus, the Jewish Christian leaders could rely on *the continual fulfilling of Israel's "well-established" chronicle* as their source of confidence. In contrast, Paul's narrative hinges on *the fresh beginning of Christ's eschatological era with "less historical*

---

[86] Sumney, *Philippians*, 77; *TLNT*, s.v. "ζημία, κτλ," 2:157–60. According to Spicq, the terms κέρδος and ζημία, which belong to the language of business, have also been "used for all sorts of advantages and acquisitions" including the religious dimension.

[87] Such glory or boasting is clearly seen in Phil. 2:16: "εἰς καύχημα ἐμοί."

[88] BDAG, s.v. "εὑρίσκω," 411–12; H. Preisker, "εὑρίσκω," *TDNT* 2:769–70.

[89] For a discussion on the exact meaning of "all things," see Silva, *Philippians*, 156–7.

[90] While both Paul and his Jewish opponents construct their "Christian" identities in relation to God's past work in Israel, the narrative of the Jewish Christians actually presents a greater continuity with the past, which is epitomized in the continual practice of *bodily circumcision*. In comparison, the narrative of Paul, without severing its relationship with the past, has allowed a new future to break in which will be marked by *bodily suffering* vindicated by Christ.

[91] *TLNT*, s.v. "σκύβαλον," 3:263–5.

[92] Tannehill, *Dying and Rising*, 117. Bracketed by these ἡγέομαι is the word ζημιόω, which probably refers to Paul's voluntary renunciation as inspired by Christ's initiative in His obedience, and not to him being punished or deprived by others.

[93] L. Romanucci-Ross and G. A. De Vos, "Ethnic Identity: A Psychocultural Perspective," in *Ethnic Identity: Creation, Conflict, and Accommodation*, ed. L. Romanucci-Ross and G. A. De Vos (London: AltaMira Press, 1995), 350.

support." It is in this particular polemic of temporality that the story of Christ from Paul, and the story of Israel from the Jewish Christian leaders, become antitheses.

Such a contention between disparate temporal frameworks of the future and the past finds its expression again in 3:9, where "μὴ ἔχων ἐμὴν δικαιοσύνην τὴν ἐκ νόμου" does not refer to Paul's previous false reliance to gain "one's (right) relationship with God" by human achievement or Torah observance,[94] but the renunciation of his formerly assumed paradigm (3:4-6) in assessing one's assurance of rightfully acting and speaking for God. It is worth noting that among Paul's multiple phrasal constructions involving νόμος and δικαιοσύνη (Rom. 3:21, 9:31, 10:4-5; Gal. 2:21, 3:21; Phil. 3:6, 9), only here in Phil. 3:9 does he refer to it with a possessive pronoun (ἐμός), which could be seen as evidence that he is not talking about a general (false) reliance on the Mosaic Law to attain rightful relationship with God, but *his former way* of discerning God's presence and hence assuring his being in God. The paradigm Paul *now* relies on comes totally from Christ's faithfulness (διὰ πίστεως Χριστοῦ, 3:9) articulated by His obedience to God through suffering to the point of death (2:5-8).

An immense amount of literature has been produced on the type of genitive implied in πίστεως Χριστοῦ, which makes a complete review on the alternatives of subjective and objective impossible.[95] In light of my analysis of the story of Christ, which highlights Christ as One who faithfully keeps His obedience to God through persevering to the point of death, the subjective genitive (Christ's faithfulness) is preferred. In particular, because of its capacity to accentuate the contrast between Christ's *newly* installed paradigm of faithfulness, first with "my righteousness" attained by Paul through his own *faithfulness* to the "old" Jewish paradigm, and second with those Jewish Christian leaders who are still boasting with these "old" Jewish credentials, the interpretation offered by the subjective genitive fits nicely with the immediate context.[96]

Specifically, the primary function of this "Christological reading" (subjective genitive) is to install itself as the *new* and foundational way of theological thinking that *transcends* the *old* Jewish way regarding believers' suffering. In terms of Ricoeur's dialectic of external narration and internal conviction, this "Christological reading" revolves around how the narration of Christ's faithfulness (πίστεως Χριστοῦ, Phil. 3:9) exhibited in His story of *suffering* overrides certain Jewish traditions within Paul's old way of understanding God's work (not the whole "Judaism," nor his Jewish ethnic identity), and instructs the *present* life of Paul and the Philippian community. It is with this goal of thought that Paul hopes to be found in Him (εὑρεθῶ ἐν αὐτῷ, 3:9).

---

[94] Fee, *Paul's Letter*, 323–5; Silva, *Philippians*, 159–60. While Fee denies the understanding of δικαιοσύνη as "justification," his subsequent explanations sound very much like it.

[95] There is no reason to assume that Paul must have applied the same type of genitive construction among all the seven occurrences of πιστις Χριστου (Rom. 3:22, 26; Gal. 2:16 (2x), 20, 3:22; Phil. 3:9). The discussion of πιστις Χριστου or πίστεως Ἰησοῦ with respect to the overall Pauline theological framework is beyond the scope of this book. For a review of the general perspectives from the camps of subjective and objective genitive, see Matthew C. Easter, "The Pistis Christou Debate: Main Arguments and Responses in Summary," *CBR* 9, no. 1 (2010): 33–47; Chris Kugler, "ΠΙΣΤΙΣ ΧΡΙΣΤΟΥ: The Current State of Play and the Key Arguments," *CBR* 14, no. 2 (2016): 244–55; Paul J. Achtemeier, "Apropos the Faith of/in Christ. A Response to Hays and Dunn," in *Pauline Theology, Volume IV: Looking Back, Pressing On*, ed. David M. Hay and E. Elizabeth Johnson (Minneapolis: SBL, 1997), 82–92.

[96] Cf. Sumney, *Philippians*, 80; Foster, "Πίστις Χριστοῦ Terminology," 94.

Contrary to what Paul Foster observes as a "virtually uniform agreement among all commentators" that the phrase ἐπὶ τῇ πίστει (3:9) denotes a human response,[97] I contend that the phrase is better translated as "on the basis of the assurance" that has been brought by the story of Christ.[98] While Foster and most other scholars tend to interpret Paul as discussing the way through which entry to salvation is gained,[99] Paul's agenda actually lies in derailing the *sense of security provided from the testimony of the Jewish Christian leaders* (through receiving physical circumcision), and affirming the sense of God's guidance within suffering. The πίστις in 3:9 then refers to the self-engaged guarantee as described in 1:27,[100] in which Paul exhorts the Philippian community to fight through the assurance resulting from *believers' trust in a positive future promised by the story of Christ*. In fact, if we recall our previous analysis on the nesting of Paul's story on that of Job,[101] the gravity of such future (hence temporal) dimension of hope and trust in God becomes huge. It is within this lifelong journey of suffering, which is essentially marked by a continuous emplotment process constituted by uncertain futures, that Paul builds his assurance around the ultimate future of Christ. Based on this assurance (ἐπὶ τῇ πίστει), no matter what upcoming sufferings spring up, Paul and the community can still incorporate these discordant events into a concordant whole, guided by the story of Christ.[102]

Likewise, within Paul's nesting of his own story with those of Isaiah, Jeremiah, and even Christ Jesus, the one common denominator between them is a kind of assurance based on believers' *hope in God's promised future irrespective of opposing evaluations*. No matter what seemingly hopeless and humiliating events (discordant events happening in their respective "Middle") happen to the people of God in the time of Isaiah and Jeremiah, Paul and Jesus, God's righteous actions (τὴν ἐκ θεοῦ δικαιοσύνην, Phil. 3:9) will be experienced by those who put their hope in His *accomplishing Lordship* and His future vindication.[103] In this manner, τὴν ἐκ θεοῦ δικαιοσύνην (3:9) is perhaps best understood as Ernst Käsemann argues, as an *action* of "God's sovereignty over the world revealing itself eschatologically in Jesus,"[104] which points to God's covenantal

---

[97] Foster, "Πίστις Χριστοῦ Terminology," 97. Most English Bibles translate the phrase as "on the basis of faith" (NASB95, NIV) or "based/depending on faith" (ESV, NRSV, HCSB).

[98] The phrase ἐπὶ τῇ πίστει is not found elsewhere in the whole NT.

[99] Foster, "Πίστις Χριστοῦ Terminology," 100. Such understanding sees the righteousness as concerning a forensic rightful standing before God the Judge.

[100] It is perhaps not a coincidence that both occurrences of πίστις in 1:27 (τῇ πίστει) and 3:9 (ἐπὶ τῇ πίστει) are constructed in the form of a dative.

[101] See chapter 4.3.2.

[102] Cf. Ricoeur, "Life in Quest," 21–2.

[103] This direction of interpreting the θεοῦ δικαιοσύνην in Phil. 3:9 emphasizes God's saving activity and sovereignty disclosed through the eschatological events of Christ's death, resurrection, and transformation of believers' bodies. For details, see Ernst Käsemann, "Gottesgerechtigkeit bei Paulus," *ZThK* 58 (1961): 367–78; Ernst Käsemann, "The Righteousness of God in Paul," in *New Testament Questions for Today* (London: SCM, 1969), 172; Jonathan A. Linebaugh, "Righteousness Revealed: The Death of Christ as the Definition of the Righteousness of God in Romans 3:21-26," in *Paul and the Apocalyptic Imagination*, ed. Ben C. Blackwell, John K. Goodrich, and Jason Maston (Minneapolis: Fortress Press, 2016), 223–5, referencing Ernst Käsemann, *Exegetische Versuche und Besinnungen II* (Vandenhoeck & Ruprecht, 1970), 183–5.

[104] Käsemann, "Righteousness of God," 180; Linebaugh, "Righteousness Revealed," 223.

faithfulness and saving *activity* toward His own people.[105] Just as Job waits confidently for the divine deliverance and judgment that will prove him right, likewise Paul awaits God's *saving activities* from his present moment until the final Day of Christ.[106] It is within such "rightful" deliverance of God, first for Jesus Christ (2:9-11) and then for himself, that Paul assures the community that they will be *vindicated* in Christ. A newly established Christocentric historical trajectory has been found by Paul.

In short, in 3:1-6 and 3:7-9 we witness Paul undermine the circumcision strategy from the Jewish Christian leaders by rendering it obsolete. According to Paul, reliance on this "outdated" Jewish paradigm in discerning God's righteous acts is simply incoherent with the way God works through His saving activities. In contrast with his future-oriented assurance, Paul has exposed the deceitful allurement of protection found from the past-oriented narrative of the Jewish Christian leaders.

In order to follow the antithetic parallelism within Paul's logic, before we investigate the central unit (3:10-12) of the chiastic structure I will examine the passages in 3:12-16 and 3:17-21 to see how Paul counters these past attractions with the hope of a particular future.

6.3 B': Contestation of the Mature Way of Thinking (3:12-16)

In this section I approach 3:12-16 as a "temporal counterpoint" to 3:7-9: if the Jewish Christian leaders count on God's old work in assuring God's righteous acts, my analysis of 3:12-16 will show how the future-oriented manner of thinking originating from the story of Christ will function in Paul's life. After anchoring his present story within the unfinished chapter of the story of Christ through the metaphor of running in a race (3:12-14), Paul exhorts the community to follow this disclosure (ἀποκαλύπτω, 3:15) with a prudent attitude (3:15-16).

6.3.1 The Finishing of an Unfinished Yet Assured Future (3:12-14)

With the noticeable similarities between 3:12 and 3:13-14, my interpretation of Paul's autobiographical journey in 3:12 will be guided mainly by the running metaphor in 3:13-14. Within the narrative world that undergirds these two units, Paul has nested his own story onto that of Christ such that at the "Ending" of these nested stories, Paul's future has been divinely ordained by Christ Jesus and God.

---

[105] Käsemann, "Righteousness of God," 172; Linebaugh, "Righteousness Revealed," 224, 36; Douglas A. Campbell, "An Echo of Scripture in Paul, and Its Implications," in *The Word Leaps the Gap: Essays on Scripture and Theology in Honor of Richard B. Hays*, ed. J. Ross Wagner (Grand Rapids: Wm. B. Eerdmans, 2008), 388.

[106] Cf. Reumann, "The (Greek) Old Testament," 197. See also Linebaugh, "Righteousness Revealed," 236, in which Linebaugh reflects on the way Paul derives his meaning of δικαιοσύνη θεοῦ and comments that it is "in the enactment of eschatological judgment that both judges unrighteousness and justifies the righteous" that Paul hopes for the future.

One of the traditional understandings of the clause ἐφ' ᾧ καὶ κατελήμφθην ὑπὸ Χριστοῦ ['Ιησοῦ] in 3:12 is to see it as the cause of Paul's striving.¹⁰⁷ With the prepositional phrase ἐφ' ᾧ understood as "because" (causal function),¹⁰⁸ the usual perceived reference behind this "seizing" (or laying hold, καταλαμβάνω) of Paul would be the "Damascus road" event in which Paul was "seized" by the risen Jesus.¹⁰⁹ However, while this interpretation of recalling Christ's past gracious act is grammatically possible, such understanding deviates from the future accent of Paul's current discourse.

Instead, the phrase ἐφ' ᾧ should be translated as "for which," which effectively makes the clause ἐφ' ᾧ . . . ['Ιησοῦ] the object of the main verb διώκω in 3:12. Such a purposeful reading of 3:12 is further strengthened if we take the aorist in κατελήμφθην (the second occurrence of καταλαμβάνω in 3:12) as a "proleptic aorist," which according to Buist M. Fanning "involves a rhetorical transfer of viewpoint, envisaging an event yet future as though it had already occurred."¹¹⁰ According to Ricoeur's understanding in mimesis3, we may say that Paul actualizes this "transfer of viewpoint" when he first nests his own story (level four) on that of Christ (level three), and then follows the flow of the combined story to the closure, and from *there* gazes backward at his current situation and himself.¹¹¹ It is through such temporal "retracing forward" of what God the Lord of history has already "traced backward," that Paul experiences the "not-yet" as "already" in his self-understanding.¹¹² It is such an *alternative schema of time* that enables him to "see" the ending of his own story from now, and sees now from the "ending."¹¹³ The whole sentence of διώκω δὲ εἰ καὶ καταλάβω, ἐφ' ᾧ καὶ κατελήμφθην ὑπὸ Χριστοῦ ['Ιησοῦ] in 3:12 could then be translated as "but I strive to lay hold of that for which Christ Jesus will have laid hold of me."

While traditional interpretations understand the aorist of κατελήμφθην in 3:12 as denoting a past action, the proleptic aorist allows us to accommodate a temporal dynamic focusing on the unfinished future, yet allowing Christ's owning of Paul as "prior to" Paul's seeking of Christ.¹¹⁴ While Christ's laying hold of Paul has *already* started to become a present experience for Paul, it is the *not-yet* and complete "owning" (κατελήμφθην) of Paul by Christ on the eschatological Day of Christ¹¹⁵ that Paul sees as an *assured* target as he presses on to lay out of Christ (διώκω δὲ εἰ καὶ καταλάβω, 3:12).¹¹⁶ Even though chronologically speaking this complete "owning of Paul" by Christ has not occurred yet, by sharing the viewpoint of God *the Lord of history*, each

---

¹⁰⁷ Silva, *Philippians*, 176.
¹⁰⁸ Wallace, *Greek Grammar*, 342.
¹⁰⁹ BDAG, s.v. "καταλαμβανω," 519–20; Fee, *Paul's Letter*, 346n.32; Hawthorne, *Philippians*, 208.
¹¹⁰ Buist M. Fanning, *Verbal Aspect in New Testament Greek* (Oxford: Oxford University Press, 1994), 269. See also Wallace, *Greek Grammar*, 563.
¹¹¹ Cf. Ricoeur, *T&N I*, 157–61; Dowling, *Ricoeur on Time and Narrative*, 6, 51.
¹¹² Cf. Ricoeur, *T&N I*, 157.
¹¹³ Cf. Currie, *The Unexpected*, 44–5.
¹¹⁴ With Ricoeur's narrative theory and the nesting of stories between that of Christ and Paul, the temporal dynamic and the future force of the "proleptic aorist" is made more understandable. Cf. Ricoeur, *T&N I*, 67; Ricoeur, "Life," 431; Fee, *Paul's Letter*, 346.
¹¹⁵ Cf. Pfitzner, *Paul and the Agon*, 140–1; Reumann, *Philippians*, 536.
¹¹⁶ Due to this proleptic aorist, a particular temporal accent of the kind of "already but not yet" is brought to the fore: not even the articulation of the present dynamics involved in the suffering journey (3:10-11) should displace such a future aspiration and hope in the narrative world of believers. See Dunn, "Philippians 3.2-14," 488; Sumney, *Philippians*, 84.

episode of Paul's current suffering can now be read in light of its teleological forward movement toward a definite closure, which is as if it had already happened.

This experience of assurance is crucial to the identity formation of both Paul himself and the Philippian community. Trapped in a double contestation of narratives with the political authorities and the Jewish Christian leaders, the community's temporal perception of their own sufferings fundamentally hinges on which future they have chosen as the ending of their own stories. Their perception of "now" depends on the particular "ending" they choose to see now. If the community align themselves with the destructive ending (ἀπώλεια) as proposed by the authorities (1:28), or the ending from the Jewish Christian leaders, imitating Paul's suffering would be very unwise. It is with respect to this contestation of the meaning of suffering that Paul articulates such an *assured future picture of being owned by Christ*, in hope.[117]

Based on the metaphor of running a race, this heavenly call of God in Christ Jesus (τῆς ἄνω κλήσεως τοῦ θεοῦ ἐν Χριστῷ Ἰησοῦ, 3:14) can be visualized as situated at the "finishing line" of a race. While Paul elsewhere uses κλῆσις in referring to God's calling of His people with respect to the beginning of their spiritual journeys, only here does he employ κλῆσις for the point of finishing.[118] Using the metaphorical "finishing line" to underscore the supreme significance of fixating on the *eschatological* Day of Christ as his final goal (σκοπός, 3:14) and prize (βραβεῖον, 3:14), Paul has further accentuated the futility of the *past-oriented* paradigm in 3:7-9.[119] Concerning the precise accent of this metaphor, Victor Pfitzner is thus right to say:

> The τελειότης which is the goal of the Apostle's striving dare not be reduced to moral perfection, but must rather be understood as the culminating point of his apostolic ministry and his life "in Christ" . . . What the Apostle wishes to stress is not how far he has already run, or how far he still has to go, but rather the fact that he has *not yet* reached the goal of his endeavour.[120]

It is with respect to this unfinished *temporal and experiential* journey that Paul has not attained (Οὐχ ὅτι ἤδη ἔλαβον, 3:12) or finished (ἤδη τετελείωμαι, 3:12).[121] While Fee may have exaggerated in his comment that "perfectionism is hardly an issue,"[122] he is probably correct to pinpoint Paul's concern as "perseverance with regard to Christ and

---

[117] Cf. Ricoeur's philosophical analysis on the intrinsic nature of hope within humans' delayed fulfillment of desire in Rebecca K. Huskey, *Paul Ricoeur on Hope: Expecting the Good* (New York: Peter Lang Publishing Inc., 2009), 31–2.

[118] Among those "undisputed letters" of Paul, κλῆσις has been used by Paul in 1 Cor. 1:26, 7:20; Rom. 11:29. For relevant discussions, see Fee, *Paul's Letter*, 349n.49; J. Eckert, "κλῆσις," *EDNT* 2:240–4; BDAG, s.v. "κλῆσις," 549.

[119] Although Paul does not state explicitly the nature of this prize, from the immediate context it would be to fully know Christ and be completely owned by Him, which will happen on the Day of Christ. Taking into account the current polemical discourse, and Paul's repeated desire of vindication and glory (Phil. 1:6, 11, 2:16-18, 3:20-21), such knowledge would be closely affiliated to the wisdom God accomplishes in His salvation through Christ and His followers. See Fee, *Paul's Letter*, 348–9.

[120] Pfitzner, *Paul and the Agon*, 139, 41.

[121] Ibid., 139. For an analysis of taking the aspect of incompleteness as referring to an experiential process instead of a mental knowledge, see Melick, *Philippians*, 137–8.

[122] Cf. Fee, *Paul's Letter*, 347. As my explanation in chapter eight will show, we cannot completely rule out the connotation of "imperfection" within this metaphor.

the gospel."[123] To complete his mission from God and help realize Christ's Lordship, Paul must run with utmost perseverance toward the finishing line just like a race runner.[124]

In this intra-Jewish theological polemic, the Jewish Christian leaders have found an assurance for their testimony from a *narrated continuity* with God's past work in Israel (physical circumcision). What form of permanence can Paul develop to foster his own kind of assurance? As suggested by Ricoeur's HT, the chief logic within Paul's affirmation of God's revelation comes in the form of a sustained truthfulness.[125] What matters then is that Paul has both truthfully narrated the original testimony,[126] and subsequently remained faithful to it.[127] Thus, Paul's perseverance to the finishing line can be understood as *the reiteration of his testimony over his whole life journey*, that no matter what suffering experiences lies ahead, he will narrate his life according to the faithful suffering story of Christ (πίστεως Χριστοῦ, 3:9).

It is through this mode of conviction and participation that Paul presents his case against the Jewish Christian leaders. While the Jewish Christian leaders perceive nothing meaningful regarding the Philippian community's suffering, Paul sees it as pointing to the *finishing* of God's righteous act in Christ. While the Jewish Christian leaders see Paul's suffering as meaningless or a sign of God's abandonment, Paul sees it as an essential pathway to the *final* goal of being laid hold of by Christ and the fulfillment of God's salvation plan. Thus, it is this irreplaceable *eschatological future* of the stories of God, Christ, and himself that Paul finds indispensable to the identity formation of the Philippian community. Disregard of this not-yet future closure equates to not only cutting the latter half of the story of Christ (2:9-11, 3:17-21), but also nullifying the intended "Theologic" (temporally configured thought) within Paul's narrative world.[128] The teleological forward movement would cease to work.[129] The Philippian community members would fail to share the viewpoint of God the Lord of history. The community will be left only with the narratives of the political authorities and the Jewish Christian leaders. The alternative schema of time, which has enabled Paul to see the ending of his own story, and sees the present from the "ending," would have no influence on the Philippian community. In other words, it is specifically with respect to this imaginative and alternative schema of temporal closure that Paul intends to update the *doxa* of the Philippian community and compete against the *endoxa* of his opponents.

---

[123] Ibid., 347. This is not to deny that Paul and the Philippian community are yet to reach the perfect state. It is just not the focus of Paul here in 3:12-14. For a list of scholars' perspectives on the meaning of the thing Paul is thinking to attain, see Reumann, *Philippians*, 562.

[124] Scholars have failed to reach a consensus on the meaning of the running metaphor, and in particular the reference to what Paul deliberately neglects or pays no attention to (τὰ μὲν ὀπίσω ἐπιλανθανόμενος). For details, see Fee, *Paul's Letter*, 348–50, 348n.42; Reumann, *Philippians*, 539. For an analysis of the function of athletic imagery in Philippians 3:12-14 from a Greco-Roman perspective, see Arnold, *Christ as the Telos*, 43–52, 197–202.

[125] With his testimony revolving around a yet to be known future, this is how Paul assures his knowledge and conviction of God's guidance, and convinces the Philippian community in accepting his testimony as truthful. Cf. Ricoeur, "HT," 130.

[126] Paul must ask himself: "Did he receive God's testimony with an intention to glorify God? Did he share the testimony to the Philippian community with an intention to bless their lives? . . . etc."

[127] For pertinent discussions of the concept of truthfulness, see chapter 3.3.3.

[128] Cf. Ricoeur, *T&N I*, 30.

[129] Cf. ibid., 137–42; Ricoeur, "Life," 431.

6.3.2 Paul's Story: "Golden Rule" and "Golden Example" (3:15-16)

It is in regard to the importance of the future-oriented mindset that Paul in Phil. 3:15ff. explicitly discusses the community's various behaviors. To show the function of these pragmatic instructions within Paul's exigency, we have to first deal with the meaning of the word τέλειος in 3:15. Some scholars have embraced the view that τέλειος bears an ironic meaning.[130] Such an understanding would provide the τετελείωμαι (τελειόω) in 3:12 with a meaning of "have attained perfection."[131] Viewing Paul's discourse as primarily concerned with the attainment of spiritual or moral perfection with the juxtaposition of not having been made perfect (ἢ ἤδη τετελείωμαι, 3:12) and Paul's subsequent inclusion of himself as among the "perfect" (τέλειος, 3:15) can only then be explained if Paul is being ironic. Paul is then expressing a reproach toward those Philippian community members who think of themselves as having reached the state of perfection.

While the above explanation is semantically possible,[132] multiple opposing views have been proposed by other scholars. In particular, when we understand the τελειόω in 3:12 as bearing the sense of *not having finished a course of life's journey* (hence temporal), another coherent explanation can be proposed with no irony needed: The τέλειος in 3:15 should reflect Paul's reminder that all those (Ὅσοι οὖν, 3:15) *mature* Philippian community members should have their mindset (τοῦτο φρονῶμεν, 3:15) oriented after the manner stated in 3:12-14.[133] Regardless of the unexpected circumstances (discordances) ahead of the community, the future-oriented and persevering mindset within Paul's spiritual journey as presented in 3:12-14 is already perfect in providing guidance, a model of mature thinking and behavior in front of God. Paul's own story, constituted by an emplotment process involving stories of God, Israel, Christ, and himself (levels one to four), has been constructed as *the exemplary story* for the Philippian community through demonstrating a hope toward the eschatological endpoint (3:12-14). The practical instructions in 3:12-14 have become the "golden rule" and "golden example" for the Philippian community when navigating their daily lives.

Adoption of Paul's future-oriented thinking would not only shape the testimony of the community in coherence to the temporality of the story of Paul, but more importantly, to the temporality of the story of Christ, bringing them to be "in Christ." Thus, regardless of the levels of maturity that the community members have attained in terms of embracing such thinking, each member should continue to "behave in conformity" (στοιχέω, 3:16)[134] to this "golden rule" as her foundation of thinking.

---

[130] Hawthorne, *Philippians*, 211-12; Lightfoot, *Paul's Epistle*, 153; Still, "(Im)Perfection," 147.
[131] Koester, "Purpose of the Polemic," 322; Vincent, *Philippians*, 107; Loh and Nida, *Translator's Handbook*, 109-10.
[132] BDAG, s.v. "τελειόω," 996.
[133] As both Caird and Fee agree, the typical Pauline use of ὅσος brings a connotation of inclusion rather than partition (Rom. 6:3, Gal. 3:27). In other words, instead of bringing out a partitive sense (some do and some do not), Paul most likely uses this pronoun to convey the meaning as "As many as we all do." This also better explains the inclusion of himself through the subjunctive clause τοῦτο φρονῶμεν. See Fee, *Paul's Letter*, 355-6; Caird, *Paul's Letters from Prison*, 144-5. For Paul's other use of τέλειος as denoting mature in the "undisputed letters," see Rom. 12:2, 1 Cor. 2:6, 14:20.
[134] BDAG, s.v. "στοιχέω," 946.

Perhaps as a general and supplementary follow-up to this "golden rule," we can see Paul in 3:15-16 add: if anyone in any matter does their thinking according to a narrative different from the one stated in 3:12-14, God will disclose (future tense of ἀποκαλύψει) also this (τοῦτο) mindset to them. "Only, with respect to what we have attained, let us keep on in the same course."[135]

6.4 A′: Contestation over the Demarcation of Time (3:17-21)

As inspired by Ricoeur, each instance of one's identity formation may be seen to rest upon a narrative structure with a certain beginning and ending. One issue at stake in this work is with which temporal event should the "Beginning" and "Ending" of the Philippian community be aligned? While previous analyses of nested stories in Phil. 1:19, 2:10-11, 3:3 looked for the temporal and analogical resonances between Paul's story and those of Job, Isaiah, and Jeremiah and indirectly compared the testimonies of Paul and the Jewish Christian leaders, here we look directly at the divergent demarcations of time found within their testimonies. Based on the polemic highlighted by the meaning of physical circumcision in 3:1-6, I argue that the Jewish Christian leaders have inappropriately anchored the "Beginning" of their narrative to God's earlier act within His covenant with Israel (Gen. 17:12). In contrast, Paul has rightfully aligned the "Ending" of his narrative with Christ's ultimate judgment in His *parousia* (the cosmological upper limit of time). In what follows, I am going to demonstrate that the discourse of Paul (and the Jewish Christian leaders) could be guided by a narrative world whose temporal "Beginning" and "Ending" have been marked by the "milestone events" within God's master plan of salvation ("Bracket A" of Figure 12). It is in this polarized demarcation of time that I approach 3:17-21 as a "temporal counterpoint" to 3:1-6.

While I have analyzed the narrative substructure of Paul's discourse according to the form of upper and lower levels as depicted in "Bracket B," here it is "Bracket A" that receives attention. Even with this presentation of chronologically lining up key milestone events within God's masterplan of salvation, the correct way of looking at the "transition" of eras mentioned above pertains *not to a linear and chronological transit, but a renewed dialectic of combining previous and new events.*[136] In other words, the best way to model this transition *does not lie in an incisive shift of chronological time, but a renewal of the way of narrating God's past actions with His new ones in Christ.* Such covenantal renewal from God, however, has been diversely received among His followers, which pertains to *two divergent demarcations of time* from Paul and the Jewish Christian leaders.

---

[135] Reumann's translation of 3:16. See Reumann, *Philippians*, 561–2.

[136] According to Ricoeur, when a previous story is incorporated into a present narration, something "new" is produced. The newly formed narrative "takes the place of" the previous story referred to. However, paradoxically, the previous story is also the "same" story that is talked about before and after the new narration. Ricoeur refers to this paradoxical phenomenon as a dialectic of discontinuity and continuity.

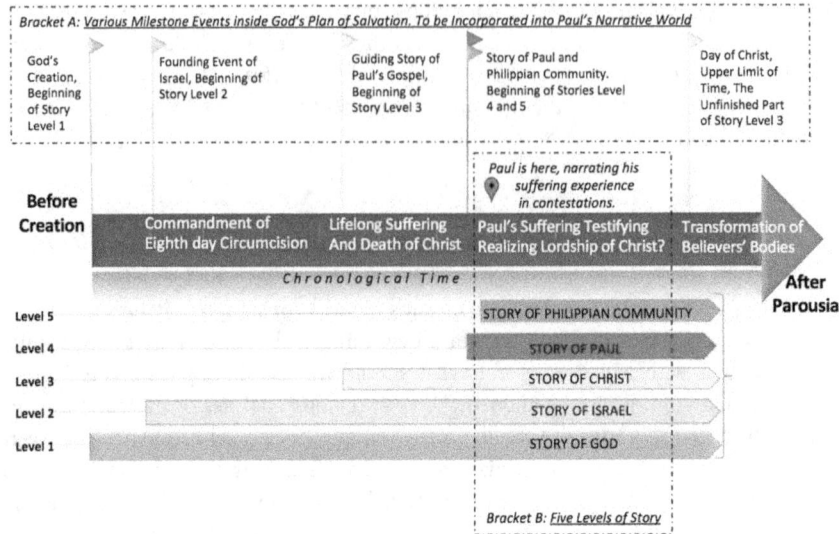

Figure 12 "Milestone events" as divergent demarcations of time within competing testimonies for God's master plan of salvation.

In Figure 12, each of the milestone events corresponds to the beginning of a certain level of story in "Bracket B." Situated in his own time, the contention between Paul and the Jewish Christian leaders centers on the way these various levels of story are synthesized together into a unified whole. In particular, regarding their disparate responses to the meaning of believers' suffering, the temporal markers used in framing the "Beginning" and "Ending" of their narratives will result *from the selection and exclusion of these milestone events.*[137] These moments, which attest to God's multiple phases of beginning (ἐνάρχομαι, Phil. 1:6) and finishing (ἐπιτελέω, Phil. 1:6) of His good work, are bestowed with different degrees of significance among the narratives of Paul and the Jewish Christian leaders.

6.4.1 The Redefining of Circumcision: God's Renewed Covenantal Act in Christ Jesus

The redefining of circumcision (3:1-6) matters not only to the stories of Paul and the Philippian community. It also signifies *a cosmological renewal of the way God deals with His people through His righteous act in Christ*. Illuminated by Ricoeur's dialectic of external narration and internal conviction, we may say that one "tiny" discrepancy of the narration of a set of events (the suffering of Paul and the Philippian community) through a reworked term actually reflects an enormous breach between the "criteriology of the divine" of Paul and the Jewish Christian leaders. How could the redefining of the social marker of circumcision bring out such an immense implication?

---

[137] Cf. Ricoeur, *T&N II*, 23; Ricoeur, *OAA*, 141–2.

While circumcision had long been practiced among many other peoples besides Jews,[138] scholars have been aware that during the time of Paul it was still widely considered by "typical Jews" as one of, if not the most significant "emblem[s] of difference between Jews and the rest of the world."[139] Notwithstanding the *synchronic dynamics* between contemporary "Jews looking out 'From inside' and Graeco-Romans looking in 'From outside,'"[140] the issue at stake here does not pertain to the handling of social interactions between the Jews and gentiles within the community of God's followers.

Instead, this redefining of circumcision in "Christian terms" (3:3) serves primarily to show *the diachronic tension regarding God's renewed covenantal act in Christ Jesus and His old covenant with the Israelites* (Gen. 17:12). Circumcision not only emerges as the "primary issue" between Paul and his opponents,[141] but also as one theological marker of the "transition" of God's salvation plan from an old era to a new one. Circumcision is not only the milestone event found at the beginning of the story of Paul (level four), but also the one at the beginning of Israel's covenantal story with God (level two). Thus, while the redefining of circumcision certainly registers its meaning in Paul's personal story (level four), its theological overtone cannot be neglected. It is with respect to the ignorance and awareness of God's renewed covenantal act in Christ Jesus that we examine the demarcations of time within the testimonies of the Jewish Christian leaders and Paul.

6.4.2 The Demarcation of Time within the Jewish Christian Leaders' Testimony

While both Paul and the Jewish Christian leaders claim to be followers of God and Christ, their emplotment processes have been marked with drastically different temporal logics. In particular, the "same" milestone moments in "Bracket A" of Figure 12 have been synthesized into two *competing versions* of testifying to God's various actions within the history of humankind. For the Jewish Christian leaders, when they offer circumcision as a "survival strategy" to the Philippian community, the corresponding demarcation of time, with the chronological temporal markers, would be as shown in Figure 13.

According to Figure 13, at the "Beginning" of this story Israel receives the covenantal blessing and protection from God (Gen. 17:12). Since then, people who receive circumcision and consent to such a narrative would be eligible in claiming the assurance of God's covenantal guidance in light of the God-ordained marker: physical circumcision. While Christ has come and died for the Jews and the gentile nations, in the eyes of these Jewish Christian leaders, as depicted by Paul, the connection or

---

[138] Tet-Lim N. Yee, *Jews, Gentiles and Ethnic Reconciliation: Paul's Jewish Identity and Ephesians* (Cambridge: Cambridge University Press, 2005), 78.
[139] Yee, *Jews, Gentiles and Ethnic Reconciliation*, 78; Tellbe, "Sociological Factors," 103; Barclay, *Obeying the Truth*, 56–7, 57n.59.
[140] Cf. Dunn, *Partings of the Ways*, 28.
[141] Koester, "Purpose of the Polemic," 320; Fee, *Paul's Letter*, 296; Tellbe, *Paul between Synagogue and State*, 262.

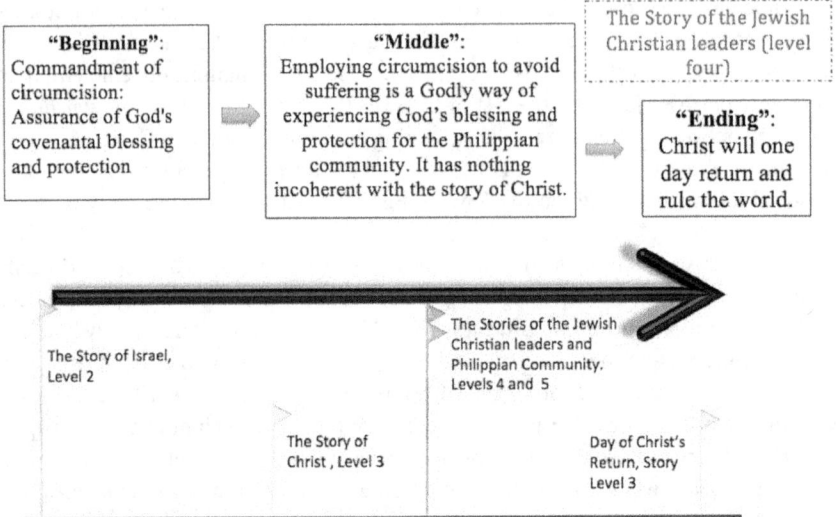

Figure 13 The demarcation of time within Jewish Christian leaders' testimony.

relevance between the story of Christ and the suffering experiences of the Philippian community is not particularly prominent.

What is more prominent is that there should be a strong sense of continuity between God's past act of installing circumcision and His continuous blessing and protection to the Philippian community.[142] If God has protected the Israelites through the practice of physical circumcision in ancient times, the recent past, and the present, there is no reason why the God-followers in Philippi should not believe that He will continue to use such a method to bless them.

Thus, it is by means of such continuity with the past working of God in Israel (level two), and the irrelevance of the story of Christ (level three), that the Jewish Christian leaders build the coherence of their narrative logic, and suggest circumcision to the Philippian community.

6.4.3 The Demarcation of Time within Paul's Testimony

However, such a demarcation of time has been seriously opposed by Paul (see Figure 14). There are at least three temporal features within the narrative of Paul that are fundamentally different from those of the Jewish Christian leaders. First, instead of aligning the "Beginning" of his story with the "Beginning" of the story of Israel (level two), it has now been replaced by the story of Christ, which features His suffering, death, and resurrection.

Second, while the Jewish Christian leaders boast that physical circumcision is a marker of God's blessing through the avoidance of suffering, in the "Middle," Paul

---

[142] Tellbe, "Sociological Factors," 103n.29, 31; Tellbe, *Paul between Synagogue and State*, 263–4; Barclay, *Obeying the Truth*, 58–9.

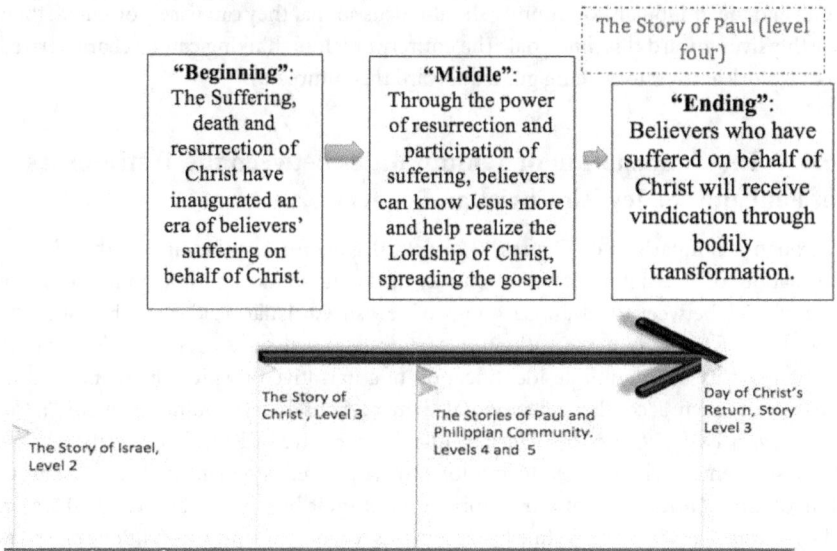

Figure 14 The demarcation of time within Paul's testimony.

firmly puts his confidence in a story of Christ who has inaugurated a new era of experiencing God's grace: suffering on behalf of Him (τὸ ὑπὲρ αὐτοῦ πάσχειν, 1:29). While the Jewish Christian leaders see little correspondence between the story of Christ and believers' suffering, Paul not only sees plenty between them but values them (3:10-11, to be explicated below).

Finally, while suffering and even bodily humiliation is not something the Jewish Christian leaders would appreciate or even think of as they prepare for the Day of Christ, at the "Ending" of Paul's narrative Paul's current sufferings for Christ will be vindicated, rewarded, and praised (1:11, 2:16).[143] The humiliated bodies of His followers will be transformed into the likeness of Christ. It is thus the day on which

---

[143] Philippians is permeated with Paul's personal concern for *himself* (1:7, 1:11, 2:2, 16, 4:14). There is the presence of a seemingly selfish desire in 1:11. Based on the reading of εἰς δόξαν καὶ ἔπαινον θεοῦ at the end of 1:11 (NA[28]), it is commonly understood that the fruit of righteousness coming from Jesus Christ will lead to the glory and praise of God. However, scholars have been alerted by a peculiar textual variant from arguably the oldest manuscript of Paul's letters P[46] and many others, which reads εἰς δόξαν θεοῦ καὶ ἔπαινον ἐμοί (to the glory of God and praise for me [Paul]). Because of its seemingly self-centered remark, the evidence of originality of this reading is not easily dismissed. In fact, based on a highly parallel pattern of thought found in 2:15-16, which talks of the making of the blameless Philippian community as the basis of Paul's future boasting, it is understandable that the community's wellbeing could lead to Paul's receiving praise. It is not about Paul taking glory away from God or Christ, but Paul sharing God's glory and receiving God's praise (ἔπαινος) after enlightening the community in discerning God's will as against the opponents. It denotes God's approval for Paul's faithful service. If the community could shine in radiance like the righteous servant found in the tradition of Jewish apocalypticism (an allusion to Dan. 12:3 in Phil. 2:15), it is probable that in Phil. 1:11 Paul has himself sharing the shining of God's glory. For discussions of the above textual variants, see Bruce M. Metzger, *A Textual Commentary on the Greek New Testament*, 2nd ed. (New York: United Bible Societies, 1994), 544; Nongbri, "Two Neglected Textual Variants," 807, 808n.23.

Paul and the Philippian community should focus so that they can wisely orientate their earthly lives toward this *final* goal. The entirety of Paul's thinking can be characterized as a historical trajectory being guided toward this future day.

6.4.4 The Contestation of Temporalities between the Testimonies of Paul and the Jewish Christian Leaders

Through a comparison of Figures 13 and 14, I have further shown that the identity formation of the Philippian community is being made amid a contestation of testimonies between Paul and a group of Jewish Christian leaders with respect to *a conflict of temporal demarcations of narratives*. Based on Ricoeur's understanding of temporality as the unique identification of a narrative of which the demarcations are a part, such a conflict of temporal demarcations indeed points to *a conflict of temporality and historical trajectory*. While the narrative of Paul's opponents features a "past-oriented" shape close to the form of Israel's ethnic identity, Paul's narrative hinges more on the *hope* of a transformation of their humiliated bodies (3:20-21) in the *eschatological future*.[144] While his opponents rely on the *continual fulfilling of Israel's past tradition*, Paul's narrative hinges on *the beginning of the accomplishing of Christ's Lordship*. It is in this particular conflict of temporality and historical trajectory that *the story of Christ from Paul, and the story of Israel from the Jewish Christian leaders, become antitheses*.[145]

In particular, it is with respect to the *degree of continuity between the story of Israel and the story of Christ* that the contestation arises. While the Jewish Christian leaders see nothing discordant between their past reliance on circumcision (level two) and God's new act in Christ (level three), Paul is a witness to it and adapts his previous understanding of the story of Israel and applies the story of Christ (level three) as the *new* guiding story. This change of temporality is accompanied by the change of allegiance from Israel's past tradition to Christ's new πολίτευμα, His eschatological era. Christ-followers of Philippi have been found at the dawn of such a new temporal era. It is regarding this *present experience* of true Christ-followers that we approach Phil. 3:10-11.

6.5 C: Contestation of the Value of Present Experience (3:10-11)

We have observed how Paul contrasts the *past* within his understanding of the story of Israel (3:1-9) with his *future* aspiration of the closure of the story of Christ (3:12-21). Here in the middle, I will approach 3:10-11 with a heuristic lens concerning the *present* experience of Paul, which has been founded on the arrival of an updated

---

[144] Cf. Romanucci-Ross and De Vos, "Ethnic Identity," 350; Yee, *Jews, Gentiles and Ethnic Reconciliation*, 71.
[145] Tellbe, *Paul between Synagogue and State*, 264. Tellbe writes, "'Christidentity' means suffering, in contrast to Jewish identity which in this context implies social safety and security."

paradigm found in the story of Christ Jesus. While the Jewish Christian leaders articulate his suffering as unnecessary and self-inflicted, Paul interprets his experience from a different "criteriology of the divine" found within the faithfulness of Christ (πίστεως Χριστοῦ, 3:9). Trapped in a contestation of narratives with those Jewish Christian leaders and the authorities, Paul has to address his *present* experience so that the Philippian community could anticipate what they should "feel about" their own suffering. Only through this could they better identify their own present experiences with what Paul has articulated as something gracious from God (ὑμῖν ἐχαρίσθη, 1:29) and an opportunity of seeing the glory of God (2:8). It is within this contestation of testimonies that we approach 3:10-11, which is syntactically located within a long and complex sentence structure from 3:8 to 3:11.[146]

6.5.1 Not Subjugation but the Power of Christ's Resurrection

Rather than framing his suffering as a subjugation experience due to the *power* of the imperial authorities, Paul sees such experience as a journey which *empowers* him to know Christ *personally* (τοῦ γνῶναι αὐτὸν κτλ).[147] Following the explanatory καί,[148] Paul substantiates this knowing with something called "the *power* of His resurrection" (τὴν δύναμιν τῆς ἀναστάσεως αὐτοῦ). Instead of seeing ἀνάστασις as just a single and completed event of Jesus,[149] Grant Macaskill is right to comment that behind the reference of "the *power* of His resurrection" is something that can be *experienced*.[150] It is not just the power that raised Jesus from death, but one that, since His resurrection, has been *made available to be experienced* by Christ-followers in the midst of the accomplishing Lordship of Christ. It is the power of the resurrection of Christ through which God the Lord of history has inaugurated the eschatological era.[151] It is the power that the resurrected Christ *now* exercises as Lord.[152]

6.5.1.1 *The Empowering of Paul amid a Contestation of Testimonies*

What remains to be told is the dimension from which this force is experienced by Paul. I argue that this experience would relate to God's *continuous empowering* of Paul in withstanding the sufferings and keeping his faithful service to the Lord amid a contestation of testimonies (Phil. 1:6, 19, 2:13, 4:7, 13, 19). Taking into account Paul's inclusion of the active role of God through τὴν ἐκ θεοῦ δικαιοσύνην in 3:9

---

[146] Albert L. Lukaszewski and Mark Dubis, *The Lexham Syntactic Greek New Testament: Sentence Analysis* (Logos Bible Software, 2009), Phil. 3:8-11.

[147] In this work, 3:10-11 is taken as one unit connected to the prepositional phrase διὰ πίστεως Χριστοῦ, τὴν ἐκ θεοῦ δικαιοσύνην ἐπὶ τῇ πίστει in 3:9. See Lukaszewski and Dubis, *Lexham Syntactic Greek New Testament*, Phil. 3:10-11. For a list of scholars' perspectives, see Fee, *Paul's Letter*, 327n.49.

[148] Wallace, *Greek Grammar*, 673; Greenlee, *Exegetical Summary*, 173.

[149] Concerning the tendency of understanding the resurrection here as only denoting a past event, see Huskey, *Paul Ricoeur on Hope*, 37–8.

[150] Grant Macaskill, *Union with Christ in the New Testament* (Oxford: Oxford University Press, 2014), 246.

[151] This emphasis of God as the Lord of history is also attested by Paul's previous "alluded stories" of Isaiah and Jeremiah.

[152] For the specific meaning of the Lordship of Christ in Philippians, see chapter 5.3.3.

(right after πίστεως Χριστοῦ), *this continuous empowering would be a specific case of God's covenantal faithfulness toward His own people* (cf. 2:13).[153] In other words, it is something that God the Father has done throughout His whole history of salvation. Such is the nature of the *driving force* behind Paul's perseverance amid his contestation with the authorities and the Jewish Christian leaders. Just as God's sovereignty has been revealed within contestations of testimonies in the cases of Job, Isaiah, and Jeremiah, Paul is confident that God's covenantal faithfulness and saving activity will continue to be revealed in his case.[154] While participating in the sufferings of Christ, Paul firmly believes that he is experiencing the power of His resurrection.[155] Where could Paul gain such assurance (ἐπὶ τῇ πίστει, 3:9)? The answer would be the active force of τὴν δύναμιν τῆς ἀναστάσεως αὐτοῦ.

6.5.1.2 Symbolic Trajectory Awaiting Believers' Active Engagement

While this power has been experienced by Paul, this active force is not something universally experienced or recognized. This lack of recognition is made evident by the suffering inflicted on the Christ-followers by the political authorities in Philippi (1:28). What is even more controversial is the trait in which this Lordship could be recognized among the Christ-followers. As I have explained above, there is a dialectical relationship between Christ's *universally acknowledged Lordship* in the future and His *contested Lordship* in the present.[156] There are bound to be different ways of narrating Christ's universally acknowledged Lordship in the future and the manner of His Lordship in the present. I argue that within Paul's testimony, resurrection symbolizes the *beginning* of Christ's eschatological Lordship and the realization of *believers' victory* during Christ's upcoming rescue of His citizens (3:20-21).[157] "The power of His resurrection" thus points to *a kind of symbolic trajectory that awaits believers' active engagement in a lifelong manner*.[158] While the end of this trajectory will be Christ's universally acknowledged Lordship and power manifested in His transforming of believers' bodies, the present "traveling along" of this symbolic trajectory arises from believers' holding out their hope toward the aforementioned victory.[159] It is along this symbolic journey of contestation of narratives that Paul aims to know Christ, and narrates his adversity as an experience of suffering on behalf of Christ. Historical development in Christ's eschatological era is thus punctuated by chains of testimony of His earthly representatives.

---

[153] Käsemann, "Righteousness of God," 172; Linebaugh, "Righteousness Revealed," 223–4, 36.

[154] Thus, the contestation at stake is not whether the power of God has been manifested in His resurrection of Christ, but whether such power has really been manifested to those who suffer for the gospel, which in turn serves to accomplish the work of the gospel (βεβαιώσει τοῦ εὐαγγελίου, Phil. 1:7) and brings about the processual realization of Christ's Lordship.

[155] Cf. Macaskill, *Union with Christ*, 245–7.

[156] For details of this dialectic, see chapter 5.3.3. Within the narration of the authorities, their narration of Christ's Lordship is equal to the story of folly.

[157] For discussions of this metaphor in 3:20-21, see chapter 4.1.1.1.

[158] Cf. Frederick S. Tappenden, *Resurrection in Paul: Cognition, Metaphor, and Transformation* (Atlanta: SBL, 2016), 3ff., in which Tappenden argues that "resurrection functions as a metaphor that Paul and his communities live by."

[159] For an opposing view that sees the resurrection mentioned here as strictly referring to the future resurrection, see Koester, "Purpose of the Polemic," 323n.4.

6.5.2 The Modification of the Temporal Structure of Jewish Apocalyptic Tradition

This experience of suffering on behalf of Christ is further described by the following phrase καὶ [τὴν] κοινωνίαν [τῶν] παθημάτων αὐτοῦ, which is understood here as denoting the numerous eschatological persecutions to be experienced by all Christ-followers.[160] Regarding the matrix behind Paul's theology of suffering as the pathway to the knowledge of and even union with Christ,[161] interpreters have proposed various prevailing Jewish traditions of the Second Temple period including "Messianic Woes,"[162] "Suffering Martyrs,"[163] and "Jewish Apocalypticism."[164] While a thorough analysis of this issue is beyond the scope of this book, I argue that Paul's Christological adaptation of what I call the "suffering righteous" tradition in the above, has probably *emerged through a modification of the temporal structure of the Jewish apocalyptic tradition*, which thereby significantly increases the value of the present process of suffering. This temporal structure is commonly known as the "Two Ages."[165]

According to this Jewish apocalyptic tradition of viewing time as a scheme of dualistic ages,[166] the current age of evil and oppression is insignificant in comparison to the future age of the Lordship of the Messiah after His *parousia*.[167] As Loren Stuckenbruck comments, "The former is a time marked by evil manifested through suffering and wrongdoing within the created order; the latter envisions the establishment of divine rule that will wipe out evil and put to right all wrongs and injustices in line with God's purposes for the created order."[168] With this view of suffering dominated by the manifestation of evil,[169] the anticipation or hope for the future (latter) Age in "Judaism" would be accompanied by a (relative) disregard over the present Age. Hope toward the future Age coincides with an attitude of vanity toward the present. Based on the similarity among the Jewish Christian leaders and

---

[160] Stanley E. Porter, "Tribulation, Messianic Woes," in *DLNTD*, ed. Ralph P. Martin and Peter H. Davids (Downers Grove: InterVarsity Press, 1997). For the perspective that sees παθημάτων αὐτοῦ as referring to redemptive death of Christ, see Schweitzer, *Mysticism*, 141–59.
[161] Cf. Loren T. Stuckenbruck, "Posturing 'Apocalyptic' in Pauline Theology: How Much Contrast to Jewish Tradition?," in *The Myth of Rebellious Angels*, WUNT 335 (Grand Rapids: Wm. B. Eerdmans, 2017), 255.
[162] For perspectives that support the framework of "Messianic Woes," see Jewett, "Epistolary Thanksgiving," 50–1; Wright, *People of God*, 277–9.
[163] It is arguable that Paul's theology of believers' suffering for the gospel as the true mark of God's people has some conceptual affinities to the tradition of the "suffering martyrs" in Jewish apocalyptic literature. For details, see Pobee, *Persecution and Martyrdom*, 49–72; Stephen A. Cummins, *Paul and the Crucified Christ in Antioch: Maccabean Martyrdom and Galatians 1 and 2* (Cambridge: Cambridge University Press, 2001), 54–90.
[164] John J. Collins, *The Apocalyptic Imagination: An Introduction to Jewish Apocalyptic Literature* (Grand Rapids: Wm. B. Eerdmans, 1998), 268.
[165] For a critique of the oversimplification with this "Two Ages" scheme, see John J. Collins, "Apocalyptic Eschatology as the Transcendence of Death," *CBQ* 36, no. 1 (1974): 21–43. For a defense of its usefulness, see Stuckenbruck, "Posturing 'Apocalyptic,'" 244.
[166] Tappenden, *Resurrection in Paul*, 19; Stuckenbruck, "Posturing 'Apocalyptic,'" 247.
[167] Cf. Andrew T. Lincoln, *Paradise Now and Not Yet: Studies in the Role of the Heavenly Dimension in Paul's Thought with Special Reference to His Eschatology* (Cambridge: Cambridge University Press, 2004), 179.
[168] Stuckenbruck, "Posturing 'Apocalyptic,'" 243–4.
[169] Cf. Gal. 1:4.

the traditional "Judaism" over the use of circumcision in avoiding suffering, I suggest that the *inherent value of suffering* as seen by the Jewish Christian leaders in this present Age is at best of the logical order of a "Despite."[170] In other words, their hope is marked by the attitude that *despite* being triumphed over and subjugated by some evil powers, believers of God will, *in the future Age*, be saved by God. Salvation from God, in a sense, lies *only* in the future.

This is where Paul's testimony deviates hugely from the temporality of the Jewish Christian leaders. In light of the "breaking in" of a *heavenly* Christ Jesus into the history of mankind, which marks the beginning of an eschatological era characterized by the "power of the resurrection," this dualistic frame of time, and the pertinent way of narrating the reality and hence God's actions, have been fundamentally altered. Specifically, it is *this particular aspect of Jewish apocalyptic tradition* that tends to *"minimize the significance of present history"* that has been altered by Paul.[171] Within Paul's "Christian Apocalyptic," a unique temporal dynamic of the present and the future has been created. Instead of being treated as something insignificant or unnecessary, *suffering on behalf of Christ now represents the working out of "the life of the age to come" on earth*. Against the narration of the Jewish Christian leaders, his earthly suffering experiences have become the necessary means for *disclosing* the knowledge of God's righteous acts and *experiencing* the power of Christ's resurrection. Just as Paul's insistence to cast physical circumcision (Phil. 3:3) as something past has stirred up a point of contention with the Jewish Christian leaders, this understanding of suffering has become something discordant to the Jewish Christian leaders.[172]

6.5.3 "Death of Christ" as the Christocentric Earthly Upper Limit of Time

To strengthen the trustworthiness of his testimony, Paul instills a sense of narrative causality and hence continuity between his present suffering experiences and the glory Christ received from God in light of His death. While σύμμορφος articulates the final form of believers' bodily resurrection to the likeness of the body of Christ's glory (3:21), the cognate verb συμμορφίζω in the phrase συμμορφιζόμενος τῷ θανάτῳ αὐτοῦ (3:10) describes a process of ever closer *conformity process* to Christ's death.[173] Regarding Paul's thought on suffering in Phil. 3:10, Macaskill writes,

---

[170] Cf. my discussions in chapter 4.2.1.
[171] Cf. Lincoln, *Paradise*, 179; Stuckenbruck, "Posturing 'Apocalyptic,'" 243.
[172] Cf. Acts 14:22, 1 Thess. 3:3, Rom. 8:17, Col. 1:24. The difficulty of grasping the temporality of Paul's thoughts as related to resurrection has been covered by Tappenden and Lincoln. According to Tappenden, the reception of the teaching of Paul on resurrection ideals in the first century "evince[s] (real or potential) misunderstanding with regard to temporality (1 Cor. 4:8; 15:12; Phil. 3:12; 1 Thess. 4:13–15:11)." What troubles the audiences of Paul is the understanding of the right balance "between the already and the not yet," which has alerted scholars on the potential discrepancies between the temporality of thoughts in Paul's undisputed lettersand those "deutero-Pauline" letters. For details, see Tappenden, *Resurrection in Paul*, 235; Lincoln, *Paradise*, 182–3.
[173] In contrast, the Jewish Christian leaders' ignorance of God's empowering results in little continuity between believers' suffering in the present Age and their fate in the future.

while Paul understands himself to have already participated in the death and resurrection of Jesus and to have been physically affected by that participation, a further level of co-experience is still possible. In fact, quite specifically, Paul's own bodily death is seen as a key transition into a new experience of 'Christ and the power of his resurrection', one that may not be different in nature from that which he experiences already, but is different in level. Hence, 'to live is Christ and to die is gain' (1:21). But even this has a further eschatological horizon for Paul ... (3:20-1).[174]

Macaskill's emphasis of the experiential dimension of "the power of His resurrection" is shared by the writer of this work. What I want to add to his understanding is a proleptic tone or temporality of Paul's current suffering experience as found *already in being conformed* (συμμορφίζω, 3:10) toward that eschatological state of the body of Christ's glory (3:21). Instead of a single past event, the "death of Christ" now plays the role of a *Christocentric earthly upper limit of time* toward which Paul's exemplary testimony is directed.[175] On the one hand, situated at the end of Christ's earthly journey, this "death of Christ" has served as the ultimate upper limit against which Christ the volitional agent has kept his *lifelong* obedience to God. On the other hand, metaphorically speaking, this "death of Christ" is also situated at the end of the narrative trajectory of "the power of His resurrection," which allows Paul (and other believers) to set it *continuously* as the teleological aim of his life narrative. Just as God acknowledges Christ's lifelong suffering as *the proper forma* (μορφή, 2:6-7) of His self-manifestation, He will vindicate Paul's earthly suffering experiences as originating from His righteous acts.

With Christ's death epitomizing both his earthly human journey (2:7-8) and God's ultimate approval for believers, Paul can *look past the limit* of his upcoming death and thus, with *assurance*, experience his present sufferings as leading to his glory (1:11, 2:16-18, 3:17-21).

Paul's present narration of his being conformed to the "death of Christ" is thus a self-engaged, yet Godly powered process in which all his current sufferings progress toward this temporal closure as a teleological movement.[176] At the teleological ending of his earthly journey is the expectation of a physical resurrection from among the dead (εἴ πως καταντήσω εἰς τὴν ἐξανάστασιν τὴν ἐκ νεκρῶν, 3:11).[177] Instead of seeing εἴ πως as denoting doubt, it expresses Paul's positive expectation of his resurrection and highlights the value of suffering during Paul's earthly time as preceding this physical resurrection.[178] In short, Paul has greatly highlighted the value of his earthly journey of suffering in 3:10-11.

---

[174] Macaskill, *Union with Christ*, 246.
[175] For a discussion on Ricoeur's concept of upper limit of time, see chapter 3.2.4.
[176] Cf. Ricoeur, *T&N I*, 67.
[177] Tannehill, *Dying and Rising*, 121n.16; Gnilka, *Der Philipperbrief*, 197.
[178] J. Alec Motyer, *The Message of Philippians* (Downers Grove: IVP Academic, 1984), 170. Regarding the element of uncertainty in εἴ πως, Motyer is perhaps right to comment that "The resurrection is certain; the intervening events are uncertain." Instead of labeling this as doubt, it is better to understand it as belonging to the dialectic of an uncertain deliverance from imminent trouble and a convinced ultimate deliverance found in the "alluded story" of Job in Phil. 1:19-26 (cf. Phil. 2:16-

6.6 Conclusion

In this chapter, I have analyzed the story of Paul through the chiastic structure of 3:1-21. In 3:1-6 (A), we have seen how Paul establishes himself to be the "archetypal Jew" in order to win in the contestation of authority in interpreting the *old* story of Israel. Such contention of the past continues in 3:7-9 (B), in which we find a contestation of assurance of aligning oneself with God's righteous acts due to the clash of paradigms from Christ's faithfulness and the *past* Jewish way of thinking. Such contestation of the *past* finds its counterpart in 3:12-16 (B') and 3:17-21 (A'), where a *future-oriented* way of thinking is put into focus. While Paul in 3:12-16 highlights the *future* eschatological ending as an argument within a contestation of the mature way of thinking, in 3:17-21 he accentuates the *future parousia* of Christ as the Day in which his narrated testimony, comprised by a unique demarcation of time, will be approved by Christ's transformation of believers' humiliated bodies. Finally, at the center of the chiastic structure (3:10-11), Paul asserts his *present* suffering experiences as the essential means to know Christ. Through these methods, Paul has framed his own story to be the exemplary model in order that the Philippian community members can follow after it. While the story of Christ is taken by this work as the paradigmatic story for the community, it is the fully human story of Paul that the Philippian community should imitate.

While Paul's "Christian identity" necessarily hinges on the actions of Christ, his exemplary identity formation also fundamentally occurs within his own existing Jewish identity and linear historical time.[179] As inspired by Ricoeur's dialectic of time as sequence and configuration, Paul's "Christian identity" is formed *only* when he continuously synthesizes heterogeneous episodes *of his own timeline* (e.g., existing cultural contexts and ethnic identities) into a sequence that accords not with the temporality of the political authorities nor the Jewish Christian leaders, but with that of his uniquely constructed story of Christ. In particular, regarding the contestation of testimonies that concerns Paul the most, it is through the "relativization" of his previous boasting as "dung" (3:4-8) that the radical structure of time found inside the story of Christ comes into effect. The "Christian identity" formation of Paul (and the Philippian community) will always be constructed within the transformation of his existing life contexts.

However, as a *modified* parallel to the thoughts of Brawley and Campbell, such transformation of his existing life contexts would not exclude a *critical dependency* on the uniquely transcendental story of Christ. Believers of different times and cultures would perhaps face different degrees of challenge and different ways of contestation regarding their allegiances to Christ (cf. Phil. 1:28), which necessarily render their sequences of life stories as seemingly disparate. However, their "Christian identities" formation can still be marked by *the same configured temporality* found inside the story of Christ. Through these stories all "Christians" have located themselves within the same eschatological era and above all, the same upper limit of time to which they

18). In this manner, πὼς is better translated as "somehow" as "a marker of undesignated means or manner." See BDAG, s.v. "πὼς," 901.

[179] Cf. the thoughts of Brawley and Campbell in chapter 1.3.3.

look forward. In this manner, they share the same suffering (cf. 1:30), the same grace of God (cf. 1:29), and the same journey of knowing Christ (cf. 3:10). It is through this dependency on the radical story of Christ that their lives transform. The notion of a common transcendental foundation for the formation of a universal communal "Christian identity" is preserved.

In Philippians, it is within this transformation of Paul that we find the theme of a contestation of testimonies. Not only are Paul and the Philippian community both suffering for the gospel (1:30), but they both also have been trapped within a contestation of testimonies. Paul has shown the Philippian community how he responds to such a contestation of testimonies. How should the Philippian community respond to Paul? This will be explicated in the next chapter.

7

The Intended Narrative of the Philippians

Voluntary Retelling of Paul's Testimony (Phil. 2:12-16A)

In the previous chapters, I have discussed the stories of Christ and Paul in detail. While the former acts as the paradigmatic story (level three) to which all other stories must conform, the latter serves as the exemplary story (level four) that the Philippian community members (level five) must follow. However, according to Ricoeur, the identity formation of the Philippian community will not be completed until they themselves tell their own stories and commit to them. Thus, Paul expects them to respond on their own initiative in the making of their own narratives (level five). It is regarding this dimension of the community members' identity formation that I select Phil. 2:12-16a to illuminate this intended participation of the community. There are three reasons for this choice. First, situated immediately after the main presentation of the story of Christ (2:5-11), this is the first passage in which we find Paul exhorting the community to act with a clear view of the paradigmatic story of Christ.[1] Second, this passage is situated before 2:16b-18, in which Paul implies the possibility of his upcoming martyrdom. 2:12-16a thus effectively acts as his "final words" before his death. Last, while theoretically the whole epistle relates to the response of the community, in the limited space of this book I have to be selective. It is for these reasons that I believe this passage would serve best for my goal. Based on the direction of this investigation, the three OT "alluded stories" in this passage will be analyzed again using the model of the nesting of stories.

7.1 With Fear and Trembling amid the Contestation of Allegiance with Political Authorities (2:12-13)

The first nesting of stories is found in 2:12-13. The importance for the community members in taking the initiative is demonstrated by Paul's use of the imperative phrase

---

[1] Cf. David McAuley, *Paul's Covert Use of Scripture: Intertextuality and Rhetorical Situation in Philippians 2:10–16* (Eugene: Pickwick Publications, 2015), 7. McAuley writes, "The ὥστε of Phil 2: 12 introduces an hortatory section of the discourse that *prompts a response* [my emphasis] to the climactic death and exaltation of Christ and actions of God described in Phil. 2:5–11."

τὴν ἑαυτῶν σωτηρίαν κατεργάζεσθε in 2:12. In working out (κατεργάζομαι) their salvation,[2] Paul reminds them that they have to do it μετὰ φόβου καὶ τρόμου. Scholars have proposed different understandings of this phrase, including "psychological weakness," rhetorical strategies that encourage either obedience or guilt, theology of fear, "Pharisaic piety," and humility toward one another.[3] Such divergent views originate from Paul's multiple uses of phrases involving both φόβος and τρόμος.[4] Coupled with similar combinations of φόβος and τρόμος in numerous passages of the LXX,[5] it is not surprising to find scholars satisfied with viewing the phrase in 2:12 as some general attitude of reverence toward God.[6] However, as David McAuley has emphatically argued, despite not being a verbatim quotation, it is highly probable that there exists a thematic allusion between Paul's use of this phrase in Phil. 2:12 and the LXX Ps. 2:11.[7] According to McAuley, both literary contexts of the two verses (Ps. 2 and Phil. 2:9-13) can be identified with the theme of the enthronement of God's anointed one.[8] In both contexts φόβος and τρόμος together call for allegiance to the newly enthroned Messiah.[9]

What remains to be shown is the specific theme that Paul wants to draw from Psalm 2 to facilitate his exhortation to the Philippian community. At the "Beginning" of the "alluded story" of Psalm 2, the lordship of a Davidic Messiah has just been installed (Ps. 2:6-7) amid rebellious devising by some earthly pagan kings and their people (2:1-3).[10] In the "Middle," even with YHWH's overwhelming superiority regarding His power over earthly matters (2:4-6), instead of seeing YHWH's immediate punishment or inhibition toward these earthly kings, we see the *newly* enthroned king, the son of YHWH, command an obedient attitude of reverence and fear (2:10-11) from these earthly kings.[11] In the "Ending" (2:11-12), even though there exists a *definite* closure of contrasting consequences (either ἀπόλλυμι or μακάριος), we are not told how those earthly kings and their people would respond to the newly enthroned Messiah.[12] Will they continue to devise rebellious plots against the Messiah and perish from the

---

[2] BDAG, s.v. "κατεργάζομαι," 531.
[3] Cf. Reumann, *Philippians*, 385-6.
[4] See 1 Cor. 2:3, 2 Cor. 7:15, Eph. 6:5.
[5] See Gen. 9:2, Ex. 15:16, Deut. 2:25, 11:25, Judith 2:28, 15:2, 1 Macc. 7:18, 2 Macc. 15:18, 23, 4 Macc. 4:10, Ps. 54:6, Ode. 1:16, Is. 19:16.
[6] Cf. Fee, *Paul's Letter*, 237; Hawthorne, *Philippians*, 141-2.
[7] McAuley, *Paul's Covert Use of Scripture*, 178-98; Reumann, *Philippians*, 385-6.
[8] McAuley, *Paul's Covert Use of Scripture*, 191-3, quoting Hans-Joachim Kraus, *Theology of the Psalms*, trans. K. Crim (Minneapolis: Augsburg, 1986), 112-13; John H. Eaton, *Kingship and the Psalms* (London: SCM, 1976), 111-12. According to McAuley, there are two ceremonial acts within the enthronement procedure of an ANE tradition. First, "the new king was given a ruling mandate or decree from the deity, along with the bestowal of a throne name, the purpose being to legitimate the new king's rule." Second, "the king ascended his throne to proclaim the commencement of his rule and to give an ultimatum to the nations—from the outset his speech was intended to issue a warning." Based on Ben-Porat's model of literary allusion, McAuley argues for the presence of such acts in both the literary contexts of Ps. 2 and Phil. 2:9-13, and concludes that both include concepts of anointing, installation, legitimating, and empowering God's Messiah.
[9] McAuley, *Paul's Covert Use of Scripture*, 194.
[10] Cf. Gerald H. Wilson, *Psalms 1*, NIVAC (Grand Rapids: Zondervan, 2002), 109.
[11] LXX Ps. 2:10-11: δουλεύσατε τῷ κυρίῳ ἐν φόβῳ καὶ ἀγαλλιᾶσθε αὐτῷ ἐν τρόμῳ. Cf. Wilson, *Psalms*, 111.
[12] McAuley, *Paul's Covert Use of Scripture*, 196.

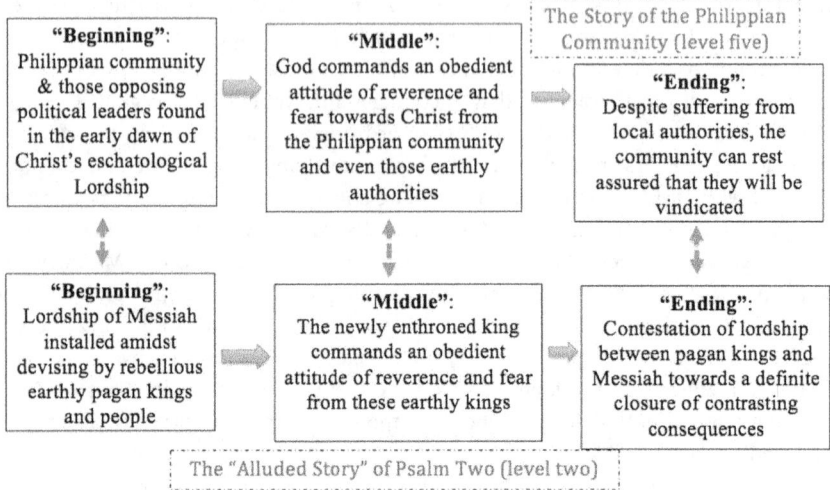

Figure 15 The story of the Philippian community nested upon the "alluded story" of Psalm 2.

righteous way (ἀπολεῖσθε ἐξ ὁδοῦ δικαίας, 2:12)? Or will they finally discern (συνίημι, 2:10), repent, and serve the Lord with fear, and rejoice in Him with trembling (LXX Ps. 2:11)? We are thus left with *the theme of a lasting and processual contestation of power and lordship* between the pagan kings and the Messiah toward the end of the story, where a definite closure of contrasting consequences is there awaiting.[13] While those who trust in Him will be blessed (μακάριοι πάντες οἱ πεποιθότες ἐπ᾽ αὐτῷ, Ps. 2:12), those who do not accept His commands will perish.

It is upon the narrative trajectory of this "alluded story" from Psalm 2 that the story of the Philippian community must be nested (Figure 15). In the "Beginning" of the community's story, they have found themselves, together with those opposing political leaders, in the early dawn of Christ's eschatological lordship. In the "Middle," despite the implied overwhelming power of resurrection from Christ, the earthly authorities are not punished immediately. Through His own working (θεὸς γάρ ἐστιν ὁ ἐνεργῶν ἐν ὑμῖν, Phil. 2:13) God commands the obedience of the Philippian community toward Christ with a proper attitude of reverence and fear (μετὰ φόβου καὶ τρόμου, 2:12-13).[14] During the process of hoping for the ultimate "Ending" of Christ's eschatological era (3:21), even though the community has to suffer amid the contestation of lordship between the Roman Empire and Christ (1:28-29),[15] they can rest assured that their

---

[13] While McAuley tends to see the Philippian community themselves as bearing tendencies to reject suffering for the gospel, and thus highlights those earthly leaders' decision as a direct warning to the Philippian community, I tend to shift the blame to the political authorities and the Jewish Christian leaders as those who are trying to weaken the Philippian community's commitment to Paul's version of the gospel. To know more about the stand of McAuley, see ibid., 175–7.

[14] Arguably, though only implicitly, even those earthly authorities have been commanded to be obedient toward Christ. Cf. Phil. 1:13, 4:22.

[15] On the one hand, it is a real contestation in the sense of a contention of the allegiance of the believers. On the other hand, it is really *not* a "genuine" contestation in the sense that God is always

suffering will be vindicated and all the pagan nations will be subjugated by Christ. All they need to do is to *take the initiative* in discerning (δοκιμάζω, 1:10) this way of God's righteousness (3:9), which has been revealed by the suffering story of Christ.[16] Will the Philippian community respond μετὰ φόβου καὶ τρόμου?

7.2 Without Grumbling and Dispute amid the Contestation of Testimonies with Other "God-Followers" (2:14-15b)

14 Πάντα ποιεῖτε χωρὶς γογγυσμῶν καὶ διαλογισμῶν,
15a ἵνα γένησθε ἄμεμπτοι καὶ ἀκέραιοι,
15b τέκνα θεοῦ ἄμωμα μέσον γενεᾶς σκολιᾶς καὶ διεστραμμένης,

After strengthening the community to withstand the contestation of power and lordship between the political authorities and Christ, Paul in 2:14-15 moves on to encourage them concerning the more complicated and fundamental contestation: the contestation of testimonies between himself and the Jewish Christian leaders. Here, Paul blends two sets of closely related OT stories into his narrative world. First in 2:14, we have allusions to the Israelites' recurrent grumbling (γογγυσμός) against Moses and God in Ex. 15:22-17:7 and Num. chapters 14-17.[17] Second, based on the phrase γενεᾶς σκολιᾶς καὶ διεστραμμένης in Phil. 2:15, an allusion to the wider story in Deut. 32:5 is generally supported.[18] However, while such allusions have caught the attention of many, ascertaining their specific contributions to Paul's concern in Philippians is still a puzzle.[19]

In what follows, I argue that it is with respect to an integrated "alluded story" of Israel composed of the themes of grumbling Israelites and the "crooked and perverse generation," upon which Paul intends to nest the story of the Philippian community (level five). What Paul desires to show is that the Jewish Christian leaders' rejection of his testimony is actually counted as an act of disobedience to God just like the Israelites in the OT. The Philippian community should thus distance themselves from their theological thinking and reject their testimony.

---

the sovereign Lord of human history and Christ has already assumed His "eschatological office" of Lordship. Cf. my discussion of the meaning of Christ's Lordship in chapter 5.3.3.

[16] One of the conceptual parallels between Ps. 2 and Phil. 2:9-13 is the importance of correctly orientating one's walk of life according to the righteous acts of God. In Ps. 2, before the pagan kings could serve the Lord with fear and rejoice in Him with trembling, they need to discern (συνίημι, Ps. 2:10) or they would perish from the righteous way (ἀπολεῖσθε ἐξ ὁδοῦ δικαίας, Ps. 2:12). In Philippians, the community need to orientate their mindset (φρονέω, Phil. 2:2, 5, 3:15, 4:2, 10) in a way according to the way of Christ.

[17] Bockmuehl, *Philippians*, 155; Fowl, "Use of Scripture," 174–6; BDAG, s.v. "γογγυσμός," 204; "διαγογγύζω," 227. For occurrences of such grumbling, see Exo. 15:24, 16:2, 7-12, 17:3; Num. 14:2, 27-29, 16:41, 17:5, 10.

[18] Fee, *Paul's Letter*, 242; Silva, *Philippians*, 124.

[19] For a list of different perspectives that see the phrase as denoting "the whole unbelieving world," the "pagan Philippi," the "non-Christian contemporaries," "the adversaries of Phil 3: 2ff.," or the "harsh masters of slave," see McAuley, *Paul's Covert Use of Scripture*, 200–1. See also Fowl, "Use of Scripture," 174–5; Reumann, *Philippians*, 391–2.

What cannot be missed at the "Beginning" of this integrated "alluded story" is God's mighty deliverance of the Israelites from the hands of the Pharaoh. Since the beginning of this exodus, God's covenantal faithfulness (πιστός, LXX Deut. 32:4) and unceasing righteousness (δίκαιος, 32:4) have been miraculously demonstrated to the Israelites not only throughout the plagues, but also in three specific occasions (Ex. 15:22-27 at Marah, Ex. 16:1-36 in the wilderness, Ex. 17:1-7 at Rephidim).[20] In the "Middle," however, even after experiencing God's mighty presence in so many ways, instead of displaying trust and gratitude the Israelites persist in grumbling to Moses and God (Ex. 15:24, 16:2, 7-12; 17:3) over matters of water and food, during the rebellion in entering the promised land (Num. 14:2), and the revolt of Korah (Num. 16:41, 17:5, 10).[21] All of these essentially represent actions of rejecting God's commands (Ex. 16:20, 28) and tempting God (Ex. 17:2, 7, Num. 14.22).

According to Douglas Stuart, such testing of the Lord and questioning of His presence (Ex. 17:7) is in fact tantamount to a manipulation of God, refusing to wait for God's provision, challenging that God should have done better with respect to the Israelites' circumstances.[22] As Stephen Fowl has said, "Israel has failed to perceive God's economy of salvation; they have failed to attend to God's saving deeds and their implications."[23] Specifically, I contend that it is *over their course of multiple adverse circumstances that their rejection of YHWH's Lordship emerges* in the form of challenging the God-ordained leadership of Moses (and Aaron).[24] The adverse nature of those situations is obvious in the three stories of Ex. 15:22- 27, 16:1-36, and 17:1-7, in which the Israelites grumble about the lack of water and food.

During their rebellion in entering the promised land, it is the projected hardship in their upcoming battle with the sons of Anak that causes them to grumble against Moses and Aaron (Num. 14:2, 27-29). Seemingly, even after witnessing God's mighty acts in relation to the plagues, pillars of cloud and fire, parting of the Red Sea, and provision of food and water, they are still not satisfied with Him as their God (cf. Num. 14:11), and would not trust in His provision and guidance.

As inspired by Ricoeur's dialectic of external narration and internal conviction, we may say that these Israelites' internal understanding of God ("criteriology of the divine") allows only an external narration of events in which the god brings them no suffering at all. The god which these grumbling Israelites would accept is thus one who would grant them nothing related to hardship and further suffering. To them, if any such hardship occurs, this deity must have left them (Ex. 17:7). Suffering for the Lord is just too discordant to be incorporated into their narrative. At the "Ending" of this integrated "alluded story," God finally judges these grumbling Israelites (Num. 14:27-29, Deut. 32:5).[25] In contrast to their faithful, righteous, and holy God (θεὸς πιστός

---

[20] McAuley, *Paul's Covert Use of Scripture*, 204–5; Peter E. Enns, "Grumbling," in *NDBT*, ed. T. Desmond Alexander and Brian S. Rosner (Leicester: InterVarsity Press, 2000).

[21] Cf. Enns, "Grumbling."

[22] Douglas K. Stuart, *Exodus: An Exegetical and Theological Exposition of Holy Scripture*, NAC 2 (Nashville: Holman Reference, 2006), 389, 92; Peter E. Enns, *Exodus*, NIVAC (Grand Rapids: Zondervan, 2000), 328–9.

[23] Fowl, "Use of Scripture," 176.

[24] Cf. Enns, *Exodus*, 328.

[25] Ibid., 328; Stuart, *Exodus*, 392.

... δίκαιος καὶ ὅσιος κύριος, LXX Deut. 32:4), they can only be rightfully called the children to be blamed (τέκνα μωμητά, 32:5),[26] and the crooked and perverse generation (γενεὰ σκολιὰ καὶ διεστραμμένη, 32:5).[27] What they deserve is to die in the wilderness and be shut out from the promised land.

With the above story, how should the Philippian community react to the testimony of Paul? Just as the Israelites in Exodus and Numbers have found themselves amid God's manifestations of His mighty power and covenantal faithfulness, the Philippian community must discern God's mighty presence and align the "Beginning" of their own stories with the inauguration of Christ's eschatological Lordship (Phil. 2:9-11). During the "Middle," the Philippians should distance themselves from the negative behaviors of those grumbling Israelites by avoiding the grumblings of the contemporary Jewish Christian leaders, whose contestation with Paul is perceived as challenging YHWH's Lordship and denying God's righteous acts in the sufferings of Christ and Paul.

It is amid these rebellious Jewish leaders who have declined to see God's work in Paul that the Philippian community must respond to God.[28] With the Jewish Christian leaders being associated with the grumbling Israelites, the Philippian community are

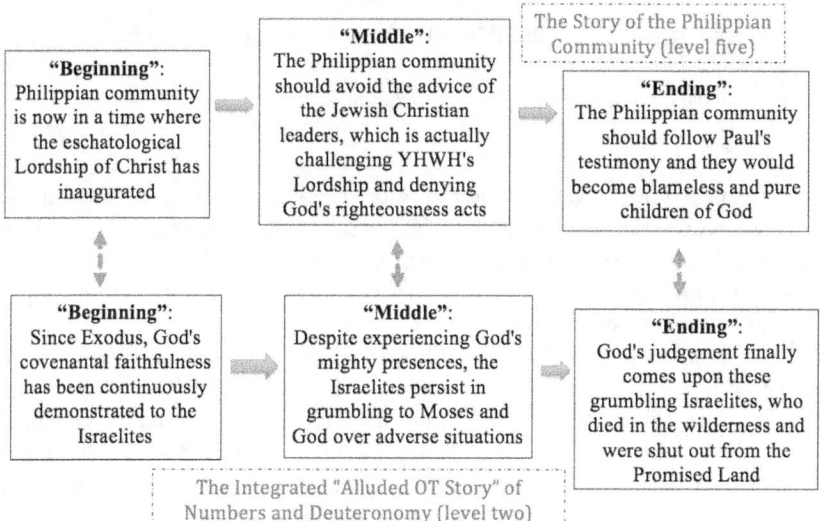

Figure 16 The story of the Philippian community nested upon the integrated "alluded story" of Numbers and Deuteronomy.

---

[26] LEH, s.v. "μωμητός."
[27] Cf. Peter C. Craigie, *The Book of Deuteronomy* (Grand Rapids: Wm. B. Eerdmans, 1976), 378-9; J. A. Thompson, *Deuteronomy: An Introduction and Commentary*, TOTC 5 (Downers Grove: InterVarsity Press, 1974), 325.
[28] Cf. McAuley, *Paul's Covert Use of Scripture*, 208. McAuley seems to place more stress on the phenomenon that "some Philippians were in danger of emulating the capitulation of Israel." In contrast, I shift the source of degeneration more away from the Philippian community and toward the Jewish Christian leaders.

urged not to trust the testimony of the Jewish Christian leaders and disregard God's saving actions again. Only by following the footsteps of Paul can they avoid being shut out from the "promised land" of God, which has been actualized and become accessible through the process of suffering on behalf of Christ. Only through this would they be found as "blameless and pure children of God without blemish" (ἄμεμπτοι καὶ ἀκέραιοι, τέκνα θεοῦ ἄμωμα, 2:15) at the "Ending" of their stories (cf. 1:10-11).

Through this nesting of the stories of the Israelites and the Philippian community, Paul has further strengthened his case against the Jewish Christian leaders. With those grumbling Israelites being judged by God as a crooked and perverse generation, an extremely negative tone is sounded in the minds of the community members. As they read the stories of these negative examples, the Philippian community are invited by Paul to see those Jewish Christian leaders as the ones who act against God's Lordship. If the Philippian community side with Paul's testimony, they would imitate Paul (Phil. 3:17) in suffering on behalf of Christ (see Figure 16). Will the Philippian community tell their testimony with the same temporality as that of Paul?

7.3 Suffering to the Point of Death amid the Double Contestation of Narratives (2:15c-16a)

15c   ἐν οἷς φαίνεσθε ὡς φωστῆρες ἐν κόσμῳ,
16a   λόγον ζωῆς ἐπέχοντες,

After recalling these *negative* experiences of the Israelites, another allusion that stimulates more *positive* hope toward the future is introduced by Paul in 2:15c-16a: ἐν οἷς φαίνεσθε ὡς φωστῆρες ἐν κόσμῳ, λόγον ζωῆς ἐπέχοντες. If the previous allusion points to the negative people group (Jewish Christian leaders) by which the Philippian community are now surrounded, the current allusion points to the *positive taking of their own initiative* amid such negative companions. Based on the phrase φαίνεσθε ὡς φωστῆρες, an allusion to the textual tradition of the "Old Greek" (OG) version of the LXX of Daniel 12:3 has been observed by a few scholars.[29] However, its function in relation to the rhetorical situation of Philippians has been understood in a number of ways.[30] I argue that this allusion to Daniel 12 (LXX^OG) *serves to provide an assurance of bodily resurrection* for the Philippian community, whose recent suffering might have escalated to the degree of not only bodily suffering but also death. Such a provision of hope can be explicated through a nesting of the stories of the insightful people (οἱ συνιέντες, LXX^OG 12:3) in Daniel and the community as intended in Phil. 2:15c-16a.[31]

---

[29] Fee, *Paul's Letter*, 246–7; McAuley, *Paul's Covert Use of Scripture*, 212–25. The "LXX" of the Book of Daniel is known for having two versions. To know more about the background of these two versions, see Amanda M. Davis Bledsoe, "The Relationship of the Different Editions of Daniel: A History of Scholarship," *CBR* 13, no. 2 (2015): 175–90.

[30] Fee, *Paul's Letter*, 246–8; McAuley, *Paul's Covert Use of Scripture*, 212–25.

[31] The LXX^OG quoted in the exegesis that follows comes from the Greek Septuagint edition of the LXX edited by Alfred Rahlfs (version 5.4) published by *Deutsche Bibelgesellschaft*, available via the Accordance Bible software version 12.2.7.

In his work which analyzes Paul's use of scripture in Philippians, McAuley explores various scholars' past efforts in understanding 2:15c-16a and tackles Fee's handling of allusion in the phrase φαίνεσθε ὡς φωστῆρες.[32] Although Fee has distinguished himself from other scholars in his awareness of the allusive relationship between Dan. 12:3 and Phil. 2:15c, his interpretation is seriously disputed by McAuley.[33] The issue at stake is that there are at least three witnesses representing the "original" Dan. 12:3 to which Paul can allude: the Hebrew MT, LXXTH, and LXX^{OG}.[34] In accord with scholars' general agreement that Paul prefers the LXX over the Hebrew OT as his source of allusion, the phrase φαίνεσθε ὡς φωστῆρες in Phil. 2:15c clearly follows LXX^{OG} Dan. 12:3 (φανοῦσιν ὡς φωστῆρες) but differs from the MT and LXXTH. Thus, the proper textual base of allusion within Paul's logic should be given primarily and even strictly to the LXX^{OG}. Because of this, Fee's assumed reliability of the words from MT as the source of meaning in Paul's allusion is rightly challenged by McAuley.[35] The base of allusion should instead come from the textual witness of LXX^{OG} Dan. 12:3 and its immediate literary context.[36] It is with respect to this scope of Daniel from LXX^{OG} that I start my analysis of the nesting of stories between Daniel and Philippians. First, let us analyze the "alluded story" of Daniel within Paul's narrative world.

7.3.1 The "Alluded Story" of Daniel

At the "Beginning" of the "alluded story" of Daniel, the Israelites have been experiencing severe political persecution (Dan. 11:21-45). Widely understood by scholars as referring to the time of Antiochus IV Epiphanes from 175–164 BC,[37] the Israelites have been suffering heavily in "a day of affliction"[38] (ἐκείνη ἡ ἡμέρα θλίψεως, 12:1). In the "Middle," instead of focusing on the demise of Antiochus, *the antithetical responses of*

---

[32] McAuley, *Paul's Covert Use of Scripture*, 212–5. Cf. Fee, *Paul's Letter*, 246–8.
[33] McAuley, *Paul's Covert Use of Scripture*, 214n.205. According to McAuley, Fee has committed the problem of relying heavily on the reading of MT as the source of their explanations on Paul's allusion to another text: LXX^{OG}.
[34] The majority of scholars agree that Paul displays a preference for the Greek OT over the Hebrew OT as his source of allusion: see Christopher D. Stanley, *Paul and the Language of Scripture: Citation Technique in the Pauline Epistles and Contemporary Literature* (Cambridge: Cambridge University Press, 1992), 254–5, 340; Florian Wilk, "The Letters of Paul as Witnesses to and for the Septuagint Text," in *Septuagint Research: Issues and Challenges in the Study of the Greek Jewish Scriptures*, ed. Wolfgang Kraus and R. Glenn Wooden (Atlanta: SBL, 2006), 254–68. For an opposing perspective, see Timothy H. Lim, *Holy Scripture in the Qumran Commentaries and Pauline Letters* (Oxford: Clarendon Press, 1997), 28, 140–60. For a critique of Lim's interpretation, see David Lincicum, *Paul and the Early Jewish Encounter with Deuteronomy* (Grand Rapids: Baker Academic, 2013), 53n.128; J. Ross Wagner, Review of *Holy Scripture in the Qumran Commentaries and Pauline Letters*, by Timothy H. Lim, *JBL* 120 (2001): 175–8.
[35] McAuley, *Paul's Covert Use of Scripture*, 214.
[36] Ibid., 17.
[37] Matthias Henze, "The Use of Scripture in the Book of Daniel," in *A Companion to Biblical Interpretation in Early Judaism*, ed. Matthias Henze (Grand Rapids: Wm. B. Eerdmans, 2012), 291; Steven Weitzman, "Plotting Antiochus's Persecution," *JBL* 123, no. 2 (2004): 233–4.
[38] The English translations of the current passage from LXX^{OG}, unless stated otherwise, all come from the *New English Translation of the Septuagint* (NETS), available online at http://ccat.sas.upenn.edu/nets/edition.

two groups of Israelites who are facing oppression are highlighted.[39] The first group are those who understand their sufferings as the cleansing and purifying of themselves (εἰς τὸ καθαρίσαι ἑαυτοὺς … καὶ εἰς τὸ καθαρισθῆναι, 11:35), attesting to their identity as the chosen people (καὶ εἰς τὸ ἐκλεγῆναι, 11:35) of God.[40] Facing sufferings and even martyrdoms, not only do they persevere to the point of death (11:32-33),[41] but they also help others to see such suffering as an act of submission to the Lord.[42] In the immediate context of the "shining like stars" (φανοῦσιν ὡς φωστῆρες) metaphor in 12:3, these "insightful people" (οἱ συνιέντες)[43] are those who hold fast to the words of God (οἱ κατισχύοντες τοὺς λόγους μου) through which they strengthen themselves.[44]

In contrast, there is another group identified as those who "abandoned the covenant of the holy one" (ἐγκατέλιπον τὴν διαθήκην τοῦ ἁγίου, 11:30). Facing what is called by Spence a "systematic attempt to put down Judaism,"[45] in which the people of God are persecuted literally even to the point of death, some Israelite leaders have *elected not to undergo hardship but abandon the holy covenant* and side with Antiochus' Hellenizing campaign (11:30).[46] As McAuley comments, they are "those who capitulated to *escape suffering and death*," and renounce their covenant with the Lord.[47] The metaphorical clause ἀπομανῶσιν οἱ πολλοὶ in 12:4,[48] whose rhetoric could be seen as a direct contrast to the "shining like stars" metaphor in 12:3, would signify what Redditt calls the "vacillating back and forth between their traditional faith and Hellenism,"[49] and

---

[39] McAuley, *Paul's Covert Use of Scripture*, 221.

[40] *LEH*, s.v. "ἐκλέγω." Cf. Joyce G. Baldwin, *Daniel: An Introduction and Commentary*, TOTC 23 (Downers Grove: IVP Academic, 2009), 216–17; John J. Collins, *Daniel: A Commentary on the Book of Daniel*, Hermeneia (Minneapolis: Fortress Press, 1994), 393.

[41] McAuley, *Paul's Covert Use of Scripture*, 221.

[42] John E. Goldingay, *Daniel*, WBC 30 (Waco: Thomas Nelson Inc., 1986), 303; Donald E. Gowan, *Abingdon Old Testament Commentaries: Daniel* (Nashville: Abingdon Press, 2001), 152.

[43] The "insightful" people have also been variously named as the "thoughtful ones of the nation" (ἐν νοούμενοι τοῦ ἔθνους, 11:33), "some of the insightful" (ἐκ τῶν συνιέντων, 11:35), and "those who understand" (οἱ διανοούμενοι, 12:10). They are also "the wise among many people" (συνήσουσιν εἰς πολλούς, NRSV 11:33), who stand firm and take action (κατισχύσουσι καὶ ποιήσουσι, 11:32), but ultimately "fall by sword" (προσκόψουσι ῥομφαίᾳ, 11:33). It is noteworthy that all these above groups are represented by the same Hebrew מַשְׂכִּילֵי in MT.

[44] *LEH*, s.v. "κατισχύω." What LXXTH has here (καὶ ἀπὸ τῶν δικαίων τῶν πολλῶν) is pretty close to the words (וְלִקְדֹּצְמוּ סִיבְרָה) in MT, but is completely different from that of LXX^OG (οἱ κατισχύοντες τοὺς λόγους μου).

[45] Henry D. M. Spence, *The Pulpit Commentary*, vol. 13, *Daniel* (London: Funk & Wagnalls, 1909), 317.

[46] Cf. Collins, *Daniel*, 384; Spence, *Daniel*, 317.

[47] McAuley, *Paul's Covert Use of Scripture*, 221. Cf. Paul L. Redditt, *Daniel*, NCBC (Sheffield: Sheffield Academic, 1999), 192, in which Redditt argues that the "many will go back and forth" in MT Dan. 12:4 may refer to the phenomenon that "many members of the larger Judean community would be vacillating back and forth between their traditional faith and Hellenism."

[48] To know more about the discrepancy among the readings of Dan. 12:4 from LXX^OG, LXXTH, and MT, see Davis Bledsoe, "Different Editions of Daniel," 175–90; Anthony A. Bevan, *A Short Commentary on the Book of Daniel: For the Use of Students* (Cambridge: Cambridge University Press, 2013), 202–4; Collins, *Daniel*, 399.

[49] Redditt, *Daniel*, 192; Louis Francis Hartman and Alexander A. Di Lella, *The Book of Daniel* (New York: Anchor Bible, 1978), 311. For an opposing view, see Silva A. Linington, "Covenant (תיר בּ.) in Daniel and the Dead Sea Scrolls: An Exposition of Daniel 9–12 and Selected Sections of the Damascus Document (CD), Community Rule (1QS), Hymns Scroll (1QHA) and War Scroll (1QM)" (ThD, University of South Africa, 2014), 163.

the apostatizing of many Israelites,[50] causing the land to be filled with unrighteousness (12:4).[51]

Using these contrasting responses to the call of suffering, the author of the book of Daniel exhorts the Israelites to willingly suffer for the Lord. While the Israelites have been trapped in a polemic of political allegiance between the Seleucid empire and their own "ethnic nation," I contend that *what really concerns the author of Daniel is the contestation of accepting the suffering testimony from the insightful people group*. As suggested by Ricoeur, two contesting testimonies have been presented to the minds of the Israelites. Like a "vast laboratory for thought experiments" two diverse narrations of suffering at the hands of Antiochus have been presented as options that may or may not match the Israelites' internal understanding of the Lord.[52] As Israel clearly cannot match the "earthly power" of the Seleucids, they must decide if they should build their hope on the political campaign of Antiochus to avoid suffering, or trust the testimony of the insightful (οἱ συνιέντες) in accepting the fate of suffering for the Lord.[53] It is *within this double contestation* that those insightful people are challenged to hold fast (κατισχύω, 12:3) to the words of God and persevere through suffering for God's holy covenant.

At the "Ending" of this "alluded story" there is again a metaphorical and eschatological picture of *contrasting outcomes for two people groups*. At the *hour* near the end of Antiochus's reign (ὥρα τῆς συντελείας αὐτοῦ, 11:45), an assurance through the coming rescue of the great angelic fighter Μιχαήλ is announced.[54] In a picture of "a vindication of the righteous," the insightful people (οἱ συνιέντες, 12:3) who have aligned their life with the righteous acts of the Lord through suffering even to death, will "light up like the luminaries of heaven" (φανοῦσιν ὡς φωστῆρες τοῦ οὐρανοῦ, 12:3). They will be like the stars of heaven forever and ever (12:3) and arise to everlasting life (12:2).[55] In contrast, those who have abandoned the holy covenant

---

[50] This is conveyed through the metaphorical image of people's frantic raging. See Hartman and Lella, *Daniel*, 261, 74, 310–11; NETS (Daniel); *LSJ*, s.v. "ἀπομαίνομαι," 209. Cf. the paradoxical yet reciprocal images of going mad and recovering from madness as suggested by lexicons of *LEH* and *LALS*. See *LEH*, s.v. "ἀπομαίνομαι"; *LALS*, s.v. "ἀπομαίνομαι."

[51] Cf. McAuley, *Paul's Covert Use of Scripture*, 221, in which McAuley identifies the ἀδικία as the persecution that eventually makes the Israelites panic and flee. However, such a reading would be inconsistent with the immediate literary context of Dan. 11:30–12:4, in which some unfaithful Israelites abandon the covenant *by their own initiative and thus are counted as responsible for their wrongdoings*. While the surrounding injustice certainly plays a role in the abandonment of the covenant, this is not the message highlighted.

[52] For discussions of the concept of narratives as experiments in a laboratory, see note 128 in chapter 3.2.6.

[53] While the readings of LXXTH and MT of Dan. 12:4 present a vision of increased knowledge, probably in the light of the seeking of the sealed wisdom of Daniel, LXX[OG] presents a picture in which people go mad and injustice increases. Cf. Gowan, *Daniel*, 154, in which the allusion to the futility of seeking the Lord in Amos 8:11-12 is taken into account.

[54] T. J. Meadowcroft, *Aramaic Daniel and Greek Daniel: A Literary Comparison* (Sheffield: Sheffield Academic, 1995), 250; Baldwin, *Daniel*, 224–5. Cf. Rev. 12:7.

[55] This interpretation is further supported by a literary *inclusio* of 12:1-4 and 12:13 in which all those who suffer for the Lord will be resurrected and vindicated. See Frederic Raurell, "The Doxa of the Seer in Dan-LXX 12,13," in *The Book of Daniel in the Light of New Findings*, ed. A. S. Van Der Woude (Leuven: Peeters Publishers, 1993), 524–8.

will have a drastically opposite fate characterized by shame, dispersion, and everlasting contempt (οἱ δὲ εἰς ὀνειδισμόν, οἱ δὲ εἰς διασπορὰν καὶ αἰσχύνην αἰώνιον, 12:2).[56]

7.3.2 The Story of the Philippian Community

The role of these insightful Israelites finds a strong resonance with the intended role of the Philippian community within Paul's narrative world. In the "Beginning," just like Paul, the Philippian community has been found amid severe political persecution (Phil. 1:12-18, 27-30). In the "Middle," just as there are two contrasting attitudes toward Antiochus's persecution and the necessity of suffering for the holy covenant, in Philippi the community has received two opposing testimonies from two Jewish authorities concerning the interpretation of the Scripture. Just as the concern of those insightful people in Daniel lies not in some general teaching (something which LXXTH and MT imply),[57] but the wisdom of properly interpreting God's words and discerning God's righteous acts for the seriously suffering community,[58] here in Philippians Paul is specifically exhorting the Philippian community to *discern the necessity of suffering on behalf of Christ* as a legitimate narrative representation of the story of Christ. If φανοῦσιν ὡς φωστῆρες τοῦ οὐρανοῦ (LXX[OG] Dan. 12:3) can contribute to the hope of resurrection and everlasting life in a seemingly hopeless context of the Seleucid empire,[59] φαίνεσθε ὡς φωστῆρες ἐν κόσμῳ in Phil. 2:15c would inspire an even more convincing hope in the light of the resurrected Christ.

What is noteworthy is that, comparing φανοῦσιν ὡς φωστῆρες τοῦ οὐρανοῦ in Dan. 12:3 and φαίνεσθε ὡς φωστῆρες ἐν κόσμῳ in Phil. 2:15, it is probable that Paul deliberately created two variations within his "alluded story" of Daniel. First, there is the change of tense from future to present in φαίνω. Second, there is the change of the "location" of the lights from heaven (οὐρανός) to the world (κόσμος). As a reflection of Paul's theological development, these two changes seem to imply that the process of "resurrection" has already begun during the earthly suffering of the Philippian community members (cf. Phil. 3:10-11).[60] In other words, *as they suffer on behalf of Christ, they are already shining like stars in the present earthly world*. Thus, there is not only a sense of continuity being built between believers' earthly suffering and their fate in the future but also a "pulling" of the future Age into the Present.[61] The Philippian community is already starting to live the life of "resurrection" (though this is not yet complete). When the community sees their current sufferings as a journey of

---

[56] McAuley, *Paul's Covert Use of Scripture*, 221. For a perspective that minimizes the theological intent presented by this distinctive reading of LXX[OG] as compared to that of the MT, see S. P. Jeansonne, *The Old Greek Translation of Daniel 7–12* (Catholic Biblical Quarterly Monograph Series) (Washington, DC: Catholic Biblical Association of America, 1988), 78. For a refutation of her arguments, see Raurell, "Doxa of the Seer," 530–2.
[57] Collins, *Daniel*, 393; Spence, *Daniel*, 336.
[58] Goldingay, *Daniel*, 303; Paul L. Redditt, "Daniel 11 and the Sociohistorical Setting of the Book of Daniel," *CBQ* 60, no. 3 (1998): 464.
[59] McAuley, *Paul's Covert Use of Scripture*, 225; Raurell, "Doxa of the Seer," 528.
[60] Cf. Fee, *Paul's Letter*, 246n.29.
[61] Cf. my discussion on Paul's innovation concerning the "Two Age" time structure in chapter 6.5.2.

"resurrection actualization" toward the future bodily resurrection, the temporality of their stories will be conformed to that of Paul (3:10-11). They will successfully imitate Paul (3:17). In short, the Philippian community shines on account of its testimony of suffering amid the dark generation in which the Roman Empire and the Jewish Christian leaders are opposed against Paul and God.

Just as those insightful ones are not teaching something general about resurrection,[62] Paul is not reminding his readers of something general about evangelism.[63] What Paul highlights instead is the double theme of the vindication of the shining sufferers, and the judgment of those evil people who either persecute God's people directly or persuade God's people to shun suffering.[64] In other words, it is the consequences of the contestation of narratives/testimonies *toward suffering and even martyrdom* that receive prominence. Just as we have seen a blending of the issues of ascertaining the righteousness of God and the contestation of testimonies among God's people within the "alluded stories" in Job (Phil. 1:19), Isaiah (2:10-11), and Jeremiah (Phil. 3:3), here within the "alluded story" of Daniel we encounter the controversy of properly discerning the understanding of God's righteous acts amid unconventional and adverse circumstances: *the martyrdom of many*.[65] If the events of the suffering of Job, the calling of Cyrus as God's anointed, and the falling of Jerusalem are all examples of the discerning of God's righteous acts amid contestations of testimonies, here in Daniel we see two groups of Israelites react to the call of suffering and even martyrdom in divergent ways.

If there is a *doubt* of God's role and hence His righteousness regarding the sufferings of the insightful people in Daniel, here in Philippians Paul is demonstrating his *assurance and joy* from God amid his probable upcoming martyrdom.

In a contestation of light and darkness, and "in the tradition of the Danielic martyrs," the Philippian community are shown by the insightful people and Paul a "steadfast refusal to capitulate under pressure."[66] Just as the insightful ones have to hold firm to the words of God amid those Israelites who abandon the holy covenant, Paul is exhorting the Philippian community that they have to "shine" (φαίνω, 2:15) amid those crooked and perverse Jewish Christian leaders. While the persecution arises primarily from the political authorities, the chief challenge for Paul and the Philippian community comes from those "Christ-followers" who contest Paul's testimony.

At the "Ending" of the story of the Philippian community, just as those insightful Israelites are told to hope for the coming of the great angel Michael, the Philippian community are told to hope for Christ the "military warrior" (Phil. 3:20-21).[67] If they

---

[62] Goldingay, *Daniel*, 306–7; Collins, *Daniel*, 392.
[63] This is a view proposed by Fee. See Fee, *Paul's Letter*, 247–8.
[64] Collins, *Daniel*, 392; Goldingay, *Daniel*, 307–8.
[65] Cf. Gowan, *Daniel*, 152, in which Gowan comments, "The deaths of the martyrs raised serious questions concerning the sovereignty and justice of God. The insistence of every chapter from 7 through 11 on the certainty that the rule of the tyrant would end soon was an answer to the sovereignty question, but the justice question remained in the air when too many of the righteous died before the tyrant. So the claim is now made for God's sovereignty even over death, that justice may be made manifest."
[66] McAuley, *Paul's Covert Use of Scripture*, 225.
[67] Not even death and martyrdom can limit the sovereignty and plan of God. See Linington, "Covenant (בְּ‏תיר.) in Daniel," 162; Gowan, *Daniel*, 152.

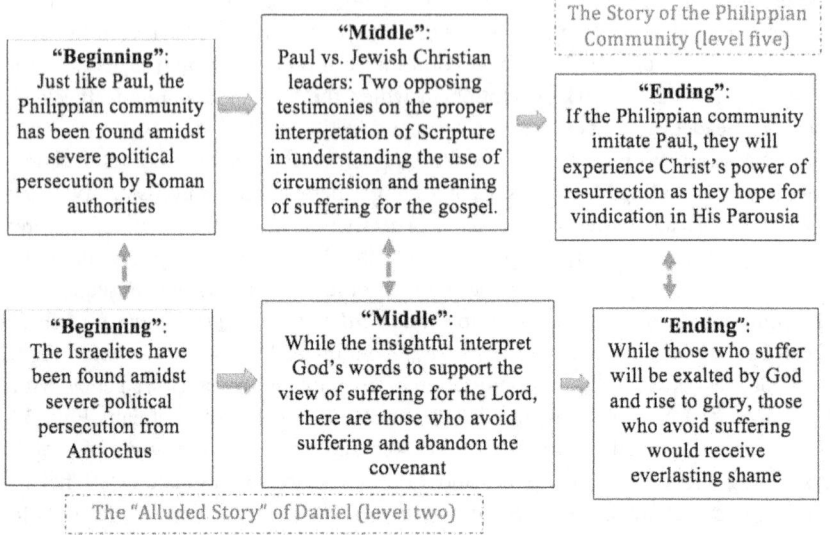

Figure 17 The story of the Philippian community nested upon the "alluded story" of Daniel.

follow Paul's testimony and comply with the Lord's righteous acts, they will be like those insightful ones who understand the righteousness of the Lord (Dan. 9:13) and strengthen themselves (12:3) by the words of God. As they suffer at the hands of the Roman authorities, their hope of God's sovereignty extends beyond the upper limit of their personal lives—death (Dan. 11:32-33, Phil. 1:9-26, 2:9-11, 16b-18, 25-30, 3:20-21) into the eschatological ending of human history marked by God's apocalyptic intervention (Dan. 11:45–12:1, Phil. 2:9-11, 3:20-21). Suffering by the authorities means destruction in the eyes of both the Seleucid and Roman Empires. Experiencing suffering for upholding God's covenant seems foolish in the eyes of the Jewish apostates at Antiochus's time and the Jewish Christian leaders at Paul's time. But with a similar viewpoint to the insightful ones in Daniel, the Philippian community will be able to see such sufferings and even martyrdom as part of God's righteous acts as He accomplishes His Kingdom.[68] At Christ's *parousia* (Phil. 3:20-21) they will be vindicated by Christ and their bodies will be transfigured (μετασχηματίζω, 3:21) into conformity with the glory of Christ's body (see Figure 17). Will the Philippian community participate in suffering on behalf of God?

7.4 Conclusion

In this chapter, I have analyzed the intended story of the Philippian community as hoped for by Paul. Through these three allusions to the stories of the Israelites, Paul has firmly

---

[68] For previous discussions on the relation between truthfulness and conviction, see p.103f.

marked the current situation of the Philippian community as one in which they have to take the initiative in aligning themselves with God's salvific plan amid contestation of narratives and testimonies. As informed by the allusions to the rebellious earthly pagan kings; the grumbling, crooked, and perverse Israelites; and the "insightful people," hardships springing from contestations with political authorities and other so-called "God-followers" are bound to arise. Discordances will continuously spring up to thwart the community's narrative configuration and hence commitment to God. Nevertheless, if each community member commits herself to the example of Paul, she will be able to orientate herself to the two opposite senses of time from within Paul's story. As she moves through contingencies with the *forward*-moving character of Paul, she will experience how each of Paul's suffering incidents progresses along a journey in which God, the ultimate master of human history, looks *back* from the vantage point of the end time and guides Paul (Phil. 1:6, 1:19, 2:10-11, 12-15, 3:3) toward its ultimate fulfillment: the vindication of believers' suffering on the Day of Christ (1:6, 2:9-11, 16, 3:20-21).

With the proposed coherence between the community's "little narratives" and God's "grand history" of salvation found at the times of Psalms, Exodus, Numbers, Deuteronomy, and Daniel, Paul invites the Philippians to imitate him (3:17). If they commit themselves to Paul's way of narrating, their temporal experiences of these contingent and uncontrollable future challenges are *all* going to be transformed into channels of God's grace (Phil. 1:29) and the means of knowing Christ (3:10-11). "The assurance of the gospel" (1:27) as brought about by the story of Christ will allow each of the Philippian community members, in truthfulness, to tell a testimony of her practical life after the temporality of Paul. Each community member who suffers for the gospel will, like Paul, receive God's covenantal faithfulness and continuous empowering in withstanding their sufferings amid contestations of narratives. Like Paul, she will experience the power of Christ's resurrection (3:10-11). She will strengthen her conviction toward her own testimony as a truthful one.[69] She will successfully imitate Paul (3:17). She will be "in Christ."

Previous scholarship has opted to endorse one side over the other regarding the phenomena of discontinuity and continuity and the pertinent temporal dynamic behind the early "Christian" identity formation. Based on Ricoeur's dialectic of time as sequence and configuration, I argue that the temporal experience of each Philippian community member necessarily consists of a dialectic of the member's own timeline in which episodes of her existing cultural contexts and ethnic identities are being creatively combined, and the temporally configured thought from the radical story of Christ from which she draws her ultimate meaning. As evident from the conclusions of the last three chapters (five to seven), the element of the contestation of testimonies has been found in each of these parts. According to chapter five, behind the uniquely constructed story of Christ (level three) in Paul's testimony actually lies *competing narrative configurations* regarding the discernment of God in the suffering of Christ. According to chapters six and seven, behind the reconstruction of the contextual stories of Paul and the Philippian community actually lies competing manners of extending the paradigmatic character of Jesus's suffering into the lives of believers. Consequently, it is reasonable to confirm that the community's "Christian identity" is being shaped amid a contestation of testimonies.

8

The Stages of the Philippian Community's Collective Identity Formation

Having analyzed the stories of Christ, Paul, and the Philippian community on levels three to five, I integrate certain exegetical results from the foregoing and capture more nuanced snapshots of the community's "Christian identity" formation process within the reconstructed experiences of the community members. The initial state of the Philippian community is one in which their identity has been recognized as belonging to a "pole" of character marked with a *stable narrative configuration and lasting ethical disposition of supporting Paul financially*. It corresponds to the time before they face the heightened persecution from the local authorities in Philippi and the imprisonment of Paul. Each instance of a community member's narrative identity, which will be shown as composed of different dialectics of her preacquired traditions and her intentional resilience, *evolves within the contestation of testimonies between Paul and the Jewish Christian leaders*.

Concerning the reconstruction of the community's historical context just before receiving Paul's letter, it is not difficult to observe two common interpretative strands which belong to two extremes of postulating the degree of the danger facing the Philippian community. At one end, some interpreters argue that the community faces no real dangers and no real opponents.[1] The various military and political metaphors used by Paul in the text are just rhetorical and preventive strategies to encourage the always supportive community to further support Paul and maintain their unity.[2] The letter is by and large a letter of friendship.[3] In a certain sense, their identity formation in Christ is already quite mature, if not complete. No major improvements are needed.

At another end, there are interpreters (e.g., McAuley) who are more aware of the implicit dangers throughout the letter. After paying attention to Paul's stern allusions, strong words, and emotional attitude, these interpreters expose the Philippian community members as bearing some previously unnoticed problematic attitudes that cause the problem of division, complaints about suffering, and even the questioning of their current leadership.[4] According to these interpreters, the Philippian community,

---

[1] Cf. deSilva, "No Confidence," 31–2; Peterlin, *Paul's Letter to the Philippians*, 90–2.
[2] Cf. Bloomquist, *Function of Suffering*, 49, 138, 52, 94–6.
[3] William Hendriksen, *Exposition of Philippians* (Grand Rapids: Baker Book House, 1962), 37–8.
[4] Hawthorne, *Philippians*, lxxiii; Martin, *Philippians*, 46; McAuley, *Paul's Covert Use of Scripture*, 35, 100–1, 176, 209.

just like the Galatian community members, have deviated away from some proper "Christian" ideas or behaviors. Serious identity reshaping toward Christ is needed.

While each of these two perspectives could explain certain phenomena in Philippians, neither could fully explain the copresence of these paradoxical phenomena. If the former strand focuses more on the joy and confidence that Paul has toward the community, the latter highlights the serious exhortations and potential dangers found throughout the epistle. In what follows, based on Ricoeur's threefold mimesis theory and the two modes of narrative identity (character and self-constancy),[5] I propose another interpretation that could potentially address both of these strands, and unveil the intricate dynamics in the identity formation of the Philippian community.

8.1 Mimesis1: The Community Is Forced to Live a Life beyond Previous Narrative Configuration

While the Philippian community are the ones who receive exhortations, they should *not* be seen as the ones who have primarily caused the exigency. While there are certain serious exhortations throughout the letter,[6] nowhere in the epistle does Paul directly reprimand the community, nor express his frustration toward them as he does explicitly in other epistles.[7] Rather than assuming the cause of Paul's concern as *originally* arising from their internal quarrels or complaints to Paul, I argue that the real "culprits" belong among those visiting Jewish Christian leaders, who act in line with those selfishly ambitious "Christ-followers" challenging Paul in the *praetorium* of Rome (1:12-18). The issue at stake could be better delineated with a reconstructed storyline.[8]

Since the time of their believing in Christ Jesus, the Philippian community has been participating in the work of Paul (2:12, 4:14-16). Despite their poverty (2 Cor. 8:1-5) they have been contributing financially to Paul and have committed themselves to the founder of their community (Acts 16:11-40). Through a long period of supporting Paul, they have gradually sedimented a lasting disposition and ethical value system articulated *by a stable narrative configuration*: whenever they know the financial needs of Paul, they will try their best to support him and narrate it as an act of serving God

---

[5] Cf. Mallett and Wapshott, "Challenges of Identity Work," 279. I am indebted to Mallett and Wapshott for their in-depth applications of the dialectic of *idem* and *ipse* in analyzing human resources problems in organization. For references, see ibid., 271–88; Oliver Mallett and Robert Wapshott, "Mediating Ambiguity: Narrative Identity and Knowledge Workers," *SJM* 28, no. 1 (2012): 16–26.

[6] Phil. 1:5-7, 9-11, 27-30, 2:12-18, 3:2-3, 15-21, 4:2-3.

[7] Cf. Rom. 6:17-18; Gal. 1:6-9, 3:1, 4:8-11, 4:19-20; 1 Cor. 3:1-3, 5:1-2, 6:1-11; 2 Cor. 6:11-12, 10:6-8, 11:1-3, 12:11; 2 Tim. 2:17-18, 3:8, 4:10; Tit. 1:10-13.

[8] This reconstructed storyline assumes a by-and-large unified relationship within the Philippian community. Contra Peterlin, *Paul's Letter to the Philippians*, 102, 224, in which Peterlin argues that there is serious dissension within the congregation arising from a "pro-Paul" and an "anti-Paul" group. For an introduction of scholars' hypotheses about the states of the Philippian community and their relation with Paul, see David E. Briones, Review of *Paul's Koinonia with the Philippians: A Socio-Historical Investigation of a Pauline Economic Partnership*, by Julien M. Ogereau, *RBL* (10.2016): 69–79.

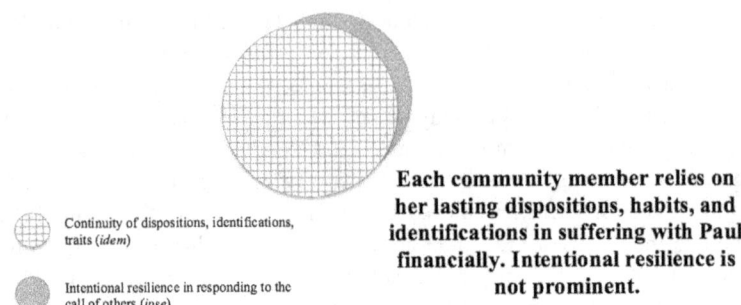

Figure 18 When each community member is steadily supporting Paul in a financial manner.

and suffering with Paul. With this shared story, they have identified Paul as embodying their "values, norms, ideals, models, and heroes,"[9] and in turn, built an ethical identity on which Paul can count. There are virtually no unexpected or discordant events happening in their lives that would threaten their commitment to this stable and concordant narrative configuration.[10] Not much intentional resilience then is required to keep this tradition and habit of supporting Paul. Through the provision of support from the lasting disposition, they recognize themselves as the *same* collective group toward their professed life goal.[11] The identity of each of the Philippian community members is characterized as belonging to the "pole" of character marked with a *stable narrative configuration and lasting ethical disposition* (Figure 18).[12] The temporal experiences of each member's narrated past, present, and future *have all been transformed nearly perfectly* according to her professed narrative configuration. The "little narratives" of the community fit perfectly with their perceived "grand history" of God.

Suddenly, Paul has been imprisoned in Rome. As he awaits trial, he faces the possibility of martyrdom for his gospel undertaking. According to Paul's rhetorically loaded descriptions, it is at this moment that certain selfishly ambitious "Christians" in Rome ridicule Paul and criticize his gospel strategy as being not from God (Phil. 1:12-18). At about the same time, due to the promotion of imperial worship in Philippi and the community's refusal to participate, the community has found themselves under ever-increasing oppression. Amid mounting concerns over the future of Paul and themselves, the Philippian community receive some visiting Jewish Christian leaders, who offer circumcision as a way to avoid suffering.

It is probably at this point that some of the Philippian community members start to reconsider their relationship with Paul, which causes quarrels among them (Phil. 2:1-4, 4:2-3). While the community has suffered with Paul, their previous suffering

---

[9] Cf. Ricoeur, *OAA*, 121.
[10] Cf. ibid., 142.
[11] Cf. ibid., 147–8; Cf. Mallett and Wapshott, "Mediating Ambiguity," 23.
[12] Her *ipse* has been "hidden behind" *her* idem.

experiences have largely been limited to economic suffering.[13] In light of Paul's possible martyrdom, not only would their expected forms of suffering expand, but their expected level of suffering would also escalate. The testimony of those Jewish Christian leaders, as an alternative "theological" perspective on the suffering of Paul, has perhaps exposed the partial nature of Paul's testimony. Two different ways of discerning God's actions have been embedded among the contesting testimonies. The once established and relatively stable ethical disposition in supporting Paul has started to weaken. It is conceivable that in the mingling of intimate memory with Paul (abundant yet old) and emerging doubt from the Jewish Christian leaders (small yet fresh), the Philippian community sends Epaphroditus to visit Paul, who after listening to Epaphroditus writes this epistle back to the community. With respect to his dear partners, how could Paul encourage them so that they would reject the testimony of the Jewish Christian leaders, and continue in following him?

Even though we are not told how the Philippian community responded to the Jewish Christian leaders before they received Paul's letter, their good track record (cf. πάντοτε ὑπηκούσατε in 2:12) and the not-yet realized martyrdom of Paul mean they probably have kept their loyalty to Paul without undergoing circumcision. However, the contingent discordances introduced by the imprisonment of Paul (1:12-18), his possible martyrdom (1:20-26),the expected rising level of persecution, the expanding ways of oppression, and, in particular, *an alternative way of witnessing the acts of God*, makes it highly probable that the conviction resulting from the concordance found in their previous narrative has begun to waver. The once persevering certitude toward the truthful interpreted narrative from their past has been weakened. Budding dispositions of doubt and fear, which may not have yet completely sedimented, have been introduced into the minds of the community members. The whole-hearted narrating of their suffering with Paul as matching their internal "criteriology of the divine" starts to fade.

In light of the escalating persecution, the community has no choice but to incorporate all those new and unfavorable elements (discordances) into their temporal experience. As they persevere in supporting Paul, *they have been forced to suffer beyond the manner undergirded by the previous narrative configuration.* They are *forced to live with a new life whose temporality has shifted from their previous one.*[14] The once perfect coherence between their "little narratives" and their perceived God's "grand history" has been weakened. While they wholeheartedly suffered with Paul economically in the *past*, they have *now* been trapped in an "unfamiliar territory" without a proper narrative to undergird their course. Questions like "how much suffering should we endure with Paul?," "how could we be sure that suffering with Paul amounts to something pleasing to God?," "is the advice from those Jewish Christian leaders worth at least considering?" will arise. Due to these concerns, doubts, and even contesting narratives, they can no longer *simply* rely on their previous stable habits, acquired identifications, heroes, and, in particular, *the previous narrative configuration* (*idem*).

---

[13] Cf. Oakes, "Re-Mapping," 312–14, 19.
[14] For previous theoretical discussions of this phenomenon of self-constancy, see chapter 3.2.6.2.

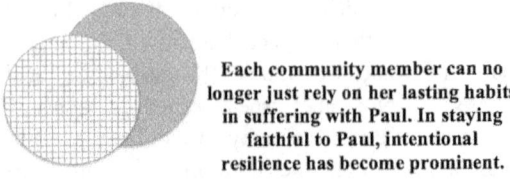

Figure 19 When Paul has been imprisoned, and the community has received escalating persecutions.

Instead, they must *persevere consciously and make an intentional resilience (ipse)* in keeping their fidelity toward Paul (Figure 19).[15]

However, even with such assumed loyalty from each of the Philippian community members, in the light of the escalating intensity of contingent discordances it would become increasingly difficult for each to keep her promise to Paul *when no solid narrative configuration can be created to undergird her thinking in coping with the new situation.*[16] Without a satisfactory explanation for her heightened suffering, the discrepancy between the temporality of her previously embraced tradition and the one forced into her life continues to grow. Consequently, the required level of intentional resilience (*ipse*) in maintaining her fidelity to Paul will continue to rise.[17] As the tension involved in holding together these sufferings within her promise to Paul escalates, her sense of her own identity will begin to lose plausibility and soundness. The narrative she holds on to in guiding her life actions will start to *lose real concordance*.[18]

The degree of truthfulness in her witness will drop. Without a renewed narrative from Paul to which she can reorientate her own stories, the influence of emerging doubt and contesting narratives will increasingly hurt her conviction to support Paul. Internal unity among members will start to degenerate. Following this line of thought, the community will likely reach the threshold of breaking their fidelity to Paul.

8.2 Mimesis2: Aligning with the Tradition of Dispute within God's People Regarding Suffering

The situation has come to the point where Paul must send the community a letter undergirded with an updated narrative (Figure 20). To consolidate the "Christian identity" of the Philippian community and help them understand the meaning of suffering for the gospel, Paul must provide the community with renewed stories that demonstrate the value of suffering and even, theoretically, martyrdom.[19] Thus, *Paul*

---

[15] Cf. Kunneman, "Ethical Complexity," 142. Metaphorically speaking, her *ipse* has "emerged" out of the shadow of her *idem*.
[16] For pertinent discussions of the dynamics involved in this situation, see chapter 3.2.6.2.
[17] Cf. Ricoeur, *OAA*, 118.
[18] Cf. Mallett and Wapshott, "Mediating Ambiguity," 22–23.
[19] While it may be wrong to perceive Paul as encouraging martyrdom (cf. LXX Dan. 12:3), the doubt arising from questions regarding the necessity of suffering to the point of death had probably become too significant for Paul to ignore. What is handled by Paul here is the management of the

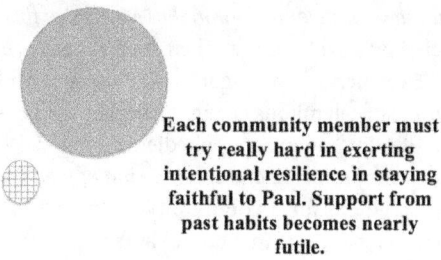

Each community member must try really hard in exerting intentional resilience in staying faithful to Paul. Support from past habits becomes nearly futile.

Figure 20 When emerging concerns have weakened the community's conviction, Paul writes.

writes with the theme of a contestation of testimonies in which believers' suffering and death, as well as the righteousness of God, are always included as the core issues. Multiple scenarios of contestation among God's people over the legitimacy of believers' suffering due to faithfully following God's way have been the common and critical issues among Paul's "alluded stories."[20] Rather than engaging in the intellectual question of clarifying the cause of believers' suffering and pinpointing God as the ultimate origin, Paul's interest lies in persuading the Philippian community to trust in the theological and practical necessity of believers' perseverance in suffering for the gospel amid contestation of testimonies.

Another prominent theme is one in which two groups of Israelites or pagans with opposing views on God's effective Lordship over the guidance of human history would end up with drastically divergent consequences.[21] With all these "alluded stories" being nested onto the suffering story of the Philippian community (and Paul), the identity formation out of their suffering experiences has been intrinsically blended with the theme of a contestation of testimonies amid the suffering of God's people, and the contestation concerning the righteousness of God.[22] One similarity between these events and the Philippian community's current situation is that these contestations of testimonies can only be "solved" by God's eschatological vindication.[23] The identity formation of the Philippian community is thus *infused and illuminated with the eschatological significance of these contentious events.* The *prototypical* dispute among God's people has found its expression in the story of the Philippian community.

Nevertheless, even with these many *human* examples (level two) attached to the story of the Philippian community, what stands out as *the paradigm* for the community is the unique story of Christ (level three). What is pivotal for Paul and the Philippian

---

expectation of suffering to the point of death, rather than teaching that conforming to the death of Christ and becoming martyrs are alike. Contra, Lohmeyer, *Die Briefe an die Philipper, an die Kolosser und an Philemon*, 5–6, in which Lohmeyer divides Philippians into five parts with the theme of martyrdom.

[20] Job 13:16, Jer. 9:23-24, Dan. 12:3.
[21] Isa. 45:23, Ex. 15–17, Num. 14–17, Deut. 32:5, Ps. 2:2.
[22] The issue of the righteousness of God here in Philippians means "God is right" over His choice and manner of working within His plan of redemption. For the understanding of righteousness of God in this work, see chapter 5.3.2.
[23] Isa. 45:23, Ex. 15–17, Num. 14–17, Deut. 32:5, Ps. 2:2, Phil. 1:11, 19, 2:16, 3:20-21.

community is that *they have been found within the "Middle" of this eschatological story*.[24] They are thus instructed by God to narrate their own experiences in compliance with this story of Christ,[25] in which the protagonist Christ, even with such an imminent and unrivaled magnitude of calamitous changes happening to His body, has chosen to see this acceptance of "destiny" as an act of obedience to God. With this paradigmatic story of Christ, *the ultimate prototype of a specific kind of God's righteous guidance has been established*. The paradigm for a community member in overcoming suffering, and even the challenge of death, is firmly built. Paul's rhetorical effectiveness revolves around a narrative world in which not only do those "little narratives" of himself and the Philippian community fit best with the "grand history" of God's salvation, but also the most glorious self-manifestation of God through Christ's manner of facing death (Phil. 2:6-8) becomes the historical fulcrum that points most decisively to Christ's identification with Paul's testimony. With this narration of the "death of Christ," concern and fear of death can be *turned into* anticipation of the sharing of Christ's glory (3:20-21). The community member can then view her contention with those Jewish Christians *as "part of the package" of following God*, and with assurance look forward to Christ's vindication (1:18, 2:9-11, 3:17-21). It is with respect to this renewed temporality that the Philippian community are invited to update their *doxa*.

8.3 Mimesis3: The Community's Retelling of Paul's Testimony

While the oppression from the authorities is certainly disturbing, what troubles the Philippian community the most is the "intra-Christian" debate between two well-respected Jewish authorities on the Scriptures. Within the "imaginative laboratory" of the community, as they walk along the trajectory of the Jewish Christian leaders' testimony, what they taste will be a kind of past-oriented temporal dynamic.[26] Doing so they would identify themselves with the old story of Israel, in which circumcision will be the definite mark of God's blessing. As each member rejects Paul's testimony, the tension of her intentional fidelity to Paul will reduce.

In contrast, if the Philippian community walk along the trajectory of Paul's testimony, what they taste will be a kind of future-oriented temporal dynamic.[27] The old story of Israel's circumcision will be transcended, and those Jewish Christian leaders will be seen as belonging to those "grumbling Israelites" in the Hebrew Bible. As each community member discerns and rereads the "alluded stories" and identifies herself with those characters, she will situate herself within the *limited horizon* of the various volitional beings,[28] and simultaneously share the *"totum simul"* perspective of

---

[24] While at its "Beginning" we have the earthly human episode of the divine Christ who died and rose (Phil. 2:6-8), at its "Ending" we have His coming *parousia* in which those who have suffered for Him will be vindicated and transformed bodily (3:20-21).

[25] See chapter 3.1.2.2 for an explanation of the kind of resonance and fitness assumed by this work.

[26] See Figure 13 in chapter 6.4.2.

[27] See Figure 14 in chapter 6.4.3.

[28] For previous discussions of the reading process which places the reader within the horizon of the volitional agent within the story, see chapter 3.1.3.

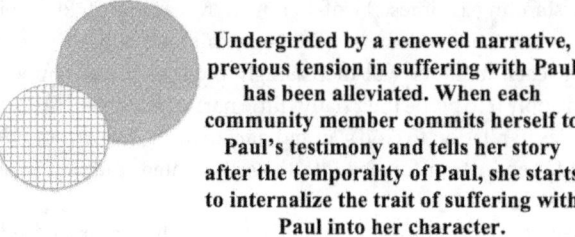

Figure 21 When the Philippian community starts to retell Paul's testimony.

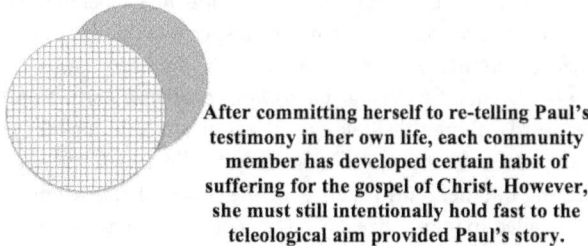

Figure 22 Even after the Philippian community has internalized Paul's testimony.

the narrator, Paul. Having found resonances between the "Beginning" of these stories and their own, in the reading of the "Middle" toward those "Endings," emotions of doubt (Phil. 4:6), hesitation (2:30, 3:1), injustice (1:17), fear (1:28), disunity (4:2), and destruction (1:28), which to different extents could have been shared between those volitional agents and the Philippian community reader, are swallowed up by the emotions of courage (3:12-14), hope (1:9-11, 19-20, 2:9-11, 3:20-21), reverence (2:12-15), love (1:4-8, 2:27-28), assurance (1:27, 4:12-13, 19), joy (1:18, 25-26, 2:2, 4:4, 10), and the most important of all, confidence of vindication (1:11b, 2:9-11, 3:20-21). As each member's doubt regarding suffering with Paul fades, suffering with Paul begins to become the "good life" that each member aims for. Previous tension in her intentional fidelity to Paul will lessen. Suffering for the gospel becomes the defining mark of God's blessing. The trait of suffering with Paul begins to be sedimented into each member's character (disposition) (Figures 21 and 22).

This will happen only if each community member intentionally refreshes her commitment to Paul and to God.[29] She can be thought of as saying to Paul (and to God): "Despite the availability of other narratives to look at suffering for the gospel, here is where I stand! You can count on me that I will suffer with you, even to the point of death!"[30] As each member compliantly reads and engages herself with the text of Philippians (mimesis3), her conviction of suffering for the gospel of Christ will begin to grow. In a much connected community in which members affect each other's outlook on life, such budding change will then not only be brought

---

[29] Cf. Ricoeur, *OAA*, 168; Ricoeur, *MHF*, 94.
[30] For pertinent discussions of this ethical commitment, see p.64ff. of this book.

into preunderstanding (mimesis1) of her next rereading of Philippians, but also that of other community members.[31] Through this intersubjective cycle of reading and refiguring, each member will increasingly internalize the temporality of Paul's testimony and apply it to guide their daily "little narratives" (4:4-13) and, in particular, their testimonies in relation to God's "grand narrative."[32] The constant threat of bodily suffering could then be transformed into the sedimented tradition of assurance even in the face of death.[33]

While I see the community as more able to fully embrace and practice the narrative of suffering with Paul on financial terms, what Paul exhorts now involves a much higher level of commitment and conviction, which would likely make the full acquiring of the habits and values of suffering for the gospel much more difficult. Subsequently, along her whole life journey of responding to the call of suffering for the gospel, *each community member would likely be found in a state of relying partly on her sedimented habits of suffering (idem), and partly on her intentional resilience (ipse)*. In other words, along this lifelong process of "discipleship" (cf. Phil. 3:12-14), instead of finding herself at the "pole" of a character in which she has *perfectly* built the call of suffering into her daily practice, or the "pole" of an extreme self-constancy in which she has failed to internalize any pattern of suffering from Paul into her traits, I argue that each member would probably find herself located at the "in-between" of these two "poles."

While she experiences support through her sedimented disposition and tradition (from her *past* efforts of intentional acquiring), due to the Jewish Christian leaders' opposing (and highly attractive) testimony, and the escalating political persecution they were facing, her temporal experiences of the past, present, and future *would not be perfectly transformed* according to her professed narrative configuration. A continuous intentional resilience oriented toward the upper limit of time at the end of Paul's story will always be needed. In other words, she must *focus on the teleological aim* provided by Paul's testimony in orientating her hope and guiding her daily choices *within a lifelong contestation of narratives/testimonies from Paul and his opponents*.[34]

Instead of seeing such imperfect state as failure, I argue that it is amid this lifelong journey of narrative contestation that the community members persevere toward the "finishing line" (Phil. 3:12-14) of their lives. As more and more community members tell their testimonies after this mature thinking (3:15-16) and particular temporality of Paul, there will be a circulation of testimonies in which God's multiple empowerments are seen and remembered. There will be a shared assurance toward the testimony of suffering for the gospel as *the* essential manner of being God's earthly representatives. The text of Philippians will become their shared "sacred text" from which they can identify their constitution.[35] With a shared "criteriology of the divine," there will be increasing numbers of *shared memories* of God's acts within their efforts

---

[31] See note 208 in chapter 3.3.3 for the discussion of this intersubjective dimension of reading in a community.
[32] See chapter 3.3.4 for relevant discussions of these "little narratives" and "grand narrative."
[33] Cf. Ricoeur, *OAA*, 166.
[34] Cf. ibid., 172.
[35] Cf. Ricoeur, "Sacred Text," 68–72.

of accomplishing (βεβαίωσις, 1:7) the work of the gospel. *A shared historical chronicle of the community will be formed.* In what Ricoeur calls the formation of a "natural institution," as each member commits truthfully to this shared chronicle, a shared intersubjective social bond among the members will be formed.[36] Their narratives will converge into one, forming their collective identity.

---

[36] See chapter 3.3.3.5 for previous discussions of the development of this shared memory and history, and this "natural institution."

9

Conclusion

This investigation has argued that the "Christian identity" of the Philippian community is being shaped amid a double contestation of narratives with divergent temporalities. Trapped in an intra-Jewish contestation of testimonies regarding the meaning of his suffering, Paul's success in shaping the community's "Christian identity" would hinge on their compliant reading and retelling of Paul's testimony distinguished by a Christologically adapted temporality.

Ever since Richard Hays's "discovery" of a narrative substructure beneath Paul's discourse, understanding of Paul's theological thinking has been renewed and enriched with various narrative components. Despite such development, no specialized narrative study has been devoted to the identity-formation processes in Philippians. And in scholarship on Philippians where the narrative method is given attention, a number of issues have seriously limited the depth of that work.

First, the applications of the narrative method are often relegated to forms of representing social identity theories. All of the various dimensions of narrative, including its underlying temporal structure, epistemological consideration, mode of ethical thinking, and the human agency as the source of meaning and center of experience, are not sufficiently addressed. Second, the unique contingent situation of the Philippian community is often ignored. The contexts discussed in the epistles of Galatians or Romans are often read into Paul's exigency in Philippians. In terms of Dunn's five levels of story substructure model, there has been a serious lack of attention to the narrative dynamics involving stories on levels four and five. Dynamics peculiar to the interactions between levels four and five, and the interactions between these two levels and levels one to three, are thus totally neglected.

Third, narrative analysis of the community's identity formation suffers from an inadequate explication of logic related to time. While scholars like Brawley and Campbell focus on the linear historical time and hence the continuity between previous stories of Israel and the new stories of "Christians," others like Meyer and Barclay engage primarily in the radical punctuation of time from the story of Christ and hence the discontinuity between this Christ story and other human stories. No special study has been devoted to "solve" these paradoxical phenomena of time. Narrative analysis of identity remains one partially covered project.

Fourth, as Horrell has stated, "every mode of thought is essentially a narrative" that shapes people's "conviction about the world." However, while narrative has been recognized as the chief mode of thinking through which we should analyze competing convictions regarding ethical issues, the dynamic of the contestation of narratives has not been employed by scholars in interpreting Philippians. The presence of any competing dynamics within the identity formation of the Philippian community has been altogether neglected by scholars. Without taking these dynamics into account, the application of a deep narrative analysis into the identity formation of the Philippians virtually becomes something ignored.

It is within these intellectual contours that I began the current research of applying narrative theory to the identity formation of the Philippian community, using Ricoeur's narrative theory as the backbone of my methodology. In particular, the referenced aspects include the threefold mimesis theory, notions of narrative identity and ethical identity, the hermeneutics of testimony, and the concept of temporality that runs through all these narrative expressions. With these theories, I have tried to answer the following research questions: What temporal logics can we employ in further understanding the identity formation of the Philippian community? What specific functions does the story of Christ play within Paul's contestation? And in what temporal dimensions does Paul compete with his opponents for the identity-making of the Philippian community? With what attitudes should the Philippian community respond to this contestation? It is through answering these questions that I reconstructed a nuanced identity-formation process of the community and affirmed that their "Christian identity" is indeed being shaped amid a contestation of narratives with divergent temporalities.

In chapter four, I analyzed Phil. 1:3–2:4 and demonstrated that Paul is facing a contestation of narratives with the Roman imperial authorities, and a contestation of testimonies with some Jewish Christian leaders. In 1:27-30, having investigated the proper symbolic framework for interpreting πολιτεύομαι, I showed that what Paul and the community can rely on does not come from objectively verifiable truth, but an assurance (πίστις, 1:27) of the gospel in which the believers must self-engage. I then showed evidence of the temporal dimension and narrative logic, which has found its expression through a contestation of truthfulness in the reception of Paul's testimony (1:12-18), Paul's hope of being vindicated by God amid accusations from other "God-followers" (1:19-26), Paul's call of watchful attention in light of the imminent temporal horizon of the "Day of Christ Jesus" (1:3-11), and a contestation of ethical dispositions between the true "Christ-followers" and those Jewish Christian leaders (2:1-4). In particular, I analyzed how Paul nests his story upon an "alluded story" of Job (Job 13:12-18) and delineates his hope and confidence of being vindicated by God regarding his suffering. I concluded that a Ricoeurian narrative analysis has enhanced our understanding of Philippians as an exigency worth approaching as a contestation of narratives.

In chapter five, I analyzed Phil. 2:5-11 and 3:17-21 and showed that Christ's seemingly humiliating suffering and death are, in fact, not only coherent with God's glorious identity, but essential to God's vindication at what I call the cosmological upper limit of time. Just as God surprisingly used Cyrus to inaugurate the beginning (ἐνάρχομαι, 1:6) of an era of His salvation, His use of a suffering Christ has surprisingly inaugurated the final eschatological era in which suffering for the gospel has become the definitive act of His followers. Seeing such universally acknowledged Lordship in hope, believers can then with assurance look forward to the transfiguration of their humiliated bodies during their earthly suffering and reject the narrative of the authorities and, more importantly, the testimony of the Jewish Christian leaders. With this radical story of Christ, Paul has provided the temporality with which the earthly suffering of both himself and His followers should be viewed. Believers should then construct the narrative sequences of their own stories in coherence with this temporality.

In chapter six, within the chiastically structured Phil. 3:1-21, I argued that Paul presents his own historical story to exhibit a temporality in direct opposition to that of the Jewish Christian leaders. Whereas the Jewish Christian leaders' testimony is marked by a past-oriented temporal dynamic and strong continuity to the old story of Israel, Paul's testimony is characterized by a future-oriented temporal dynamic, in which the assurance of God's blessing through physical circumcision has been transcended by the faithful suffering story of Christ. In particular, I analyzed how Paul nests his story upon an "alluded story" of Jeremiah (Jer. 9:23-26) and exposes the Jewish Christian leaders' deceptive theology and strategy in using physical circumcision to assure God's blessing and avoid suffering for the gospel. Instead of seeing suffering as futile, present suffering for the gospel has become the essential means of knowing Christ. Paul has thus presented his own story as a coherent narrative representation of the radical and paradigmatic story of Christ. It is with respect to this exemplary story of Paul that the Philippian community members should follow suit.

In chapter seven, I analyzed Phil. 2:12-16a and demonstrated that Paul has firmly nested the story of the Philippian community upon a historical trajectory composed of those intra-Jewish contentious occurrences within God's salvation timeline. In particular, I analyzed how Paul nests his story upon the "alluded stories" of Ps. 2, Ex. 15:22-17:7, Num. 14-17, and Dan. 12:3, and exhorts the Philippian community to obey God's call to suffering amid contesting responses from the political authorities and the Jewish Christian leaders. An important consequence of these "narrative necessities" is that while hardships springing from contestations with political authorities and other so-called "God-followers" are bound to arise, these contingent and uncontrollable challenges are *all* going to be transformed into the source of God's grace and the means of knowing Christ. While there exists no objective logic in obtaining certitude of God's guidance within their suffering, if each community member truthfully and voluntarily tells her own testimony with the same temporality of Paul's, she will strengthen her conviction toward her own testimony as a truthful one. Her "Christian identity" will be shaped in the same manner as Paul's.

Finally, in chapter eight, I integrated the findings from my research and mapped them onto three mimesis moments through which the collective identity formation of the Philippian community is shaped. I showed that along each community member's identity-formation stages, each instance of the community member's narrative identity, which consists of unique dialectics of her preacquired traditions and intentional resilience, evolves within the contestation of testimonies between Paul and the Jewish Christian leaders. Along these stages, I have shown that the "Christian identity" of the Philippian community is shaped amid a contestation of testimonies with divergent temporalities.

A successful shaping of the community's "Christian identity" would ultimately hinge on their awareness of the coherence between their "little stories" and the "grand history" of God's salvation, supported by Christ's suffering journey as the narrative beginning, and Christ's *parousia* as the narrative ending. With repeated and compliant reading of the letter and voluntary retelling of Paul's testimony, community members would start to participate in following the narrative trajectory of Paul's world, and engage in interpreting their practical experience. While the promotion of the community members' collective movement toward Paul's narrative closure is bound to be challenged by competing narratives and testimonies, Paul's rhetorical effectiveness is boosted by the "undeniable" historical evidence of God's *most glorious* self-manifestation through Christ's *most humiliating* suffering journey. With this being set as the narrative beginning, Paul has truthfully constructed a trajectory toward a narrative ending in which Christ will be exalted by God to the *highest*, and he and the Philippian community will be *personally* vindicated by Christ. As they persevere through adversity, they will together develop a commonly shared manner of understanding stories of themselves, Paul, Christ, Israel, and God. A collective identity, marked by a conviction of suffering on behalf of Christ in light of oppression from the political authorities, will be recognized by themselves and other people groups. They will then imitate Paul. They will be in Christ.

Theoretical Implications and Possibilities for Future Research

Building on the foregoing research, I will now provide a few possibilities for future research. First, instead of positing narrative research as just one of the subsidiaries of social identity theory or group theory, researchers should deepen their understanding of narrative theory. In particular, various dimensions of narrative, including its underlying temporal structure, epistemological considerations, modes of ethical thinking, and human agency as the source of meaning and center of experience, should all be given more attention.

Second, the dynamic of contestation among narratives should receive more prominence in scholars' future research. When "logical necessity" alone cannot thoroughly explain Paul's theologizing process, the quarrels and problems behind Paul's exhortation to the early "Christian" communities become best articulated by the theme of a contestation of narratives. Contestation, which is essential to the identity formation of the Philippian community, would likely also be essential to the identity formation of the Corinthians, Romans, and Galatians.

Third, based on Dunn's five levels of story model, the stories on levels four and five and their tension with the stories on levels one to three, deserve more attention from scholars. While the stories of various "Christian communities" are sometimes relatively obscure, a holistic discernment of Paul's theologizing requires an acute awareness of the narrative dynamics on this uppermost level. Without it, the contingent situation of each Pauline epistle will most likely be neglected. An understanding of various communities' identity-formation process would thus be incomplete.

Fourth, various theories of Ricoeur could be better employed. The model of the nesting of stories could become a heuristic device in explaining Paul's theology within his allusions to the OT. The model that includes the demarcations of a "Beginning," a "Middle," and an "Ending" could serve as a useful lens in disclosing the relationship between a self-engaged "alluded story" from the OT and the agenda of writers of the NT. While scholars have proposed many different theories in discerning and explaining the allusions between the OT and the NT, this model of nested stories could be one that takes narrative theory into better account.

Fifth, the concept of truthfulness as a mode of conviction could build an important bridge between the understanding of God and the understanding of oneself. Conviction within one's relationship with God should no longer be treated as just some psychological state, but the assurance from the concordance built within one's narration. The dialectic of narrating God's action and understanding oneself should no longer be separated. The degree of assurance or confidence one possesses can be analyzed through the various forms of truthfulness proposed in this investigation.

Bibliography

Abbott, H. Porter. "Story, Plot, and Narration." In *The Cambridge Companion to Narrative*, edited by David Herman, 39–51. Cambridge: Cambridge University Press, 2007.

Achtemeier, Paul J. "Apropos the Faith of/in Christ. A Response to Hays and Dunn." In *Pauline Theology, Volume IV: Looking Back, Pressing On*, edited by David M. Hay, and E. Elizabeth Johnson, 82–92. Minneapolis: SBL, 1997.

Aho, Kevin. *Existentialism: An Introduction*. Malden: Polity Press, 2014.

Alden, Robert. *Job: An Exegetical and Theological Exposition of Holy Scripture*. NAC 11. Nashville: Holman Reference, 1994.

Alexander, Loveday. "Hellenistic Letter-Forms and the Structure of Philippians." *JSNT* 37 (1989): 87–101.

Alkier, Stefan. "Intertextuality and the Semiotics of Biblical Texts." In *Reading the Bible Intertextually*, edited by Richard B. Hays et al., 3–22. Waco: Baylor University Press, 2015.

Andersen, Francis I. *Job: An Introduction and Commentary*. London: Intervarsity Pr, 1976.

Aristotle. *Aristotle in 23 Volumes*. Edited by W. D. Ross. Translated by H. Rackham. Vol. 21. Medford: Harvard University Press, 1944.

Aristotle. *Aristotle's Politics* (Greek). Edited by W. D. Ross. Medford: Clarendon Press, 1957.

Arnold, Bradley. *Christ as the Telos of Life: Moral Philosophy, Athletic Imagery, and the Aim of Philippians*. Tübingen: Mohr Siebeck, 2014.

Aune, David E. "Galatians 3:28 and the Problem of Equality in the Church and Society." In *Jesus, Gospel Tradition and Paul in the Context of Jewish and Greco-Roman Antiquity: Collected Essays II*, edited by David E. Aune, 524–49. Tübingen: Mohr Siebeck, 2013.

Baan, Ariaan W. *The Necessity of Witness: Stanley Hauerwas's Contribution to Systematic Theology*. Eugene: Pickwick Publications, 2015.

Baldwin, Joyce G. *Daniel: An Introduction and Commentary*. TOTC 23. Downers Grove: IVP Academic, 2009.

Ballantyne, Glenda. *Creativity and Critique: Subjectivity and Agency in Touraine and Ricoeur*. Leiden: Brill, 2007.

Baltzer, Klaus. *Deutero-Isaiah: A Commentary on Isaiah 40–55*. Edited by Peter Machinist. Hermeneia. Minneapolis: Fortress Press, 2001.

Barclay, John M. G. *Jews in the Mediterranean Diaspora: From Alexander to Trajan*. Berkeley: University of California Press, 1996.

Barclay, John M. G. *Obeying the Truth: Paul's Ethics in Galatians*. Edinburgh: T&T Clark, 1993.

Barclay, John M. G. "Paul and Philo on Circumcision: Romans 2.25–9 in Social and Cultural Context." *NTS* 44, no. 4 (1998): 536–56.

Barclay, John M. G. "Paul's Story: Theology as Testimony." In *Narrative Dynamics in Paul. A Critical Assessment*, edited by Bruce W. Longenecker, 133–56. Louisville: Westminster John Knox Press, 2002.

Barker, J. D. "Day of the Lord." In *DOTP*, edited by Mark J. Boda, and Gordon J. McConville, 132–43. Nottingham: InterVarsity Press, 2012.

Bauckham, Richard. *Jesus and the Eyewitnesses: The Gospels as Eyewitness Testimony*. Grand Rapids: Wm. B. Eerdmans, 2008.

Bauckham, Richard. "The Worship of Jesus in Philippians 2:9–11." In *Where Christology Began: Essays on Philippians 2*, edited by Ralph P. Martin, and Brian J. Dodd, 128–39. Louisville: Westminster John Knox Press, 1998.

Beale, G. K., and D. A. Carson. *Commentary on the New Testament Use of the Old Testament*. Grand Rapids: Baker Academic, 2007.

Belleville, L. L. "Authority." In *DPL*, edited by Gerald F. Hawthorne and Ralph P. Martin, 54–9. Leicester: InterVarsity Press, 1993.

Bennett, Alice. *Afterlife and Narrative in Contemporary Fiction*. Hampshire: Palgrave Macmillan, 2012.

Bertschmann, Dorothea. "Is There a Kenosis in This Text? Rereading Philippians 3:2–11 in the Light of the Christ Hymn." *JBL* 137, no. 1 (2018): 235–54.

Bevan, Anthony A. *A Short Commentary on the Book of Daniel: For the Use of Students*. Cambridge: Cambridge University Press, 2013.

Blasi, Anthony J. "Symbolic Interactionism as Theory." *Sociology and Social Research* 56, no. 4 (1972): 453–65.

Bleicher, Josef. *Contemporary Hermeneutics: Hermeneutics as Method, Philosophy and Critique*. London: Routledge, 1980.

Blevins, James L. "Introduction to Philippians." *RevExp* 77, no. 3 (1980): 311–25.

Bloomquist, L. Gregory. *The Function of Suffering in Philippians*. JSNTSup 78. Sheffield: Sheffield Academic, 1993.

Bloomquist, L. Gregory. "Subverted by Joy: Suffering and Joy in Paul's Letter to the Philippians." *Interpretation* 61 (2007): 270–82.

Blundell, Boyd. *Paul Ricoeur between Theology and Philosophy: Detour and Return*. Indiana: Indiana University Press, 2010.

Bockmuehl, Markus. *The Epistle to the Philippians*. London: A & C Black, 1997.

Bormann, Lukas. *Philippi: Stadt und Christengemeinde zur Zeit des Paulus*. NovTSup 78. Leiden: Brill, 1995.

Botha, Pieter J. J. "Assessing Representations of the Imperial Cult in New Testament Studies." *Verbum et Ecclesia* 25 (2004): 14–45.

Brändl, Martin. *Der Agon bei Paulus: Herkunft und Profil Paulinischer Agonmetaphorik*. Tübingen: Mohr Siebeck, 2006.

Brant, Jo-Ann A. "The Place of Mimēsis in Paul's Thought." *Studies in Religion* 22, no. 3 (1993): 285–300.

Brawley, Robert L. "From Reflex to Reflection? Identity in Philippians 2.6–11 and Its Context." In *Reading Paul in Context: Explorations in Identity Formation: Essays in Honour of William S. Campbell*, edited by Kathy Ehrensperger and J. Brian Tucker, 128–46. New York: T & T Clark International, 2010.

Brewer, Raymond Rush. "The Meaning of Politeuesthe in Philippians 1:27." *JBL* 73, no. 2 (1954): 76–83.

Briones, David E. *Paul's Financial Policy: A Socio-Theological Approach*. London: Bloomsbury T & T Clark, 2015.

Briones, David E. Review of *Paul's Koinonia with the Philippians: A Socio-Historical Investigation of a Pauline Economic Partnership*, by Julien M. Ogereau. *RBL* 10 (2016). https://www.bookreviews.org/.

Bruce, A. B. *The Humiliation of Christ in Its Physical Ethical and Official Aspects*. London: Macmillian, 1876.

Bruce, F. F. *1 & 2 Thessalonians*. WBC 45. Waco: Word, 1982.

Bruce, F. F. "St. Paul in Macedonia. 3. The Philippian Correspondence." *BJRL* 63 (1981): 260–84.
Brueggemann, Walter. *Isaiah (Volume 2, Chapters 40–66)*. Westminster Bible Companion. Kentucky: Westminster John Knox Press, 1998.
Brueggemann, Walter. *Theology of the Old Testament: Testimony, Dispute, Advocacy*. Minneapolis: Augsburg Fortress, 1997.
Bryan, Christopher. *Render to Caesar: Jesus, the Early Church, and the Roman Superpower*. Oxford: Oxford University Press, 2005.
Burk, Denny. "Is Paul's Gospel Counterimperial? Evaluating the Prospects of the "Fresh Perspective" for Evangelical Theology." *JETS* 51 (2008): 309–37.
Caird, G. B. *Paul's Letters from Prison*. NCBC. Oxford: 1976.
Calvin, John. *The Epistles of Paul the Apostle to the Romans and to the Thessalonians*. Edited by David W. Torrance, and Thomas F. Torrance. Translated by Ross Mackenzie. Grand Rapids: William B. Eerdmans, 1960.
Campbell, Douglas A. "An Echo of Scripture in Paul, and Its Implications." In *The Word Leaps the Gap: Essays on Scripture and Theology in Honor of Richard B. Hays*, edited by J. Ross Wagner, 367–91. Grand Rapids: Wm. B. Eerdmans, 2008.
Campbell, William S. *Paul and the Creation of Christian Identity*. London: T & T Clark, 2008.
Carter, James. *Ricoeur on Moral Religion: A Hermeneutics of Ethical Life*. Oxford University Press, 2014.
Cerny, Ladislav. *The Day of Yahweh and Some Relevant Problems*. Prague: Nakladem Filosoficke Fakulty University Karlovy, 1948.
Charles, R. H. *The Apocrypha and Pseudepigrapha of the Old Testament*. Oxford: Clarendon Press, 1913.
Chatman, Seymour Benjamin. *Story and Discourse: Narrative Structure in Fiction and Film*. New York: Cornell University Press, 1978.
Clines, David J. A. *Job 1–20*. WBC 17. Waco: Thomas Nelson, 1989.
Cohen, Shaye J. D. "Crossing the Boundary and Becoming a Jew." *HTR* 82, no. 1 (1989): 13–33.
Collange, Jean-François. *The Epistle of Saint Paul to the Philippians*. Translated by A. W. Heathcote. London: Epworth Press, 1979.
Collins, John J. "Apocalyptic Eschatology as the Transcendence of Death." *CBQ* 36, no. 1 (1974): 21–43.
Collins, John J. *The Apocalyptic Imagination: An Introduction to Jewish Apocalyptic Literature*. Grand Rapids: Eerdmans, 1998.
Collins, John J. *Daniel: A Commentary on the Book of Daniel*. Hermeneia. Minneapolis: Fortress Press, 1994.
Collins, Raymond F. *The Power of Images in Paul*. Collegeville: Liturgical Press, 2008.
Comstock, Gary L. "Two Types of Narrative Theology." *Journal of the American Academy of Religion* 55, no. 4 (1987): 687–717.
Craigie, Peter C. *The Book of Deuteronomy*. Grand Rapids: Eerdmans, 1976.
Crawford, Barry S. Review of *Paul and the Hermeneutics of Faith*, by Francis Watson. *CBQ* 68 (2006): 559–60.
Crites, Stephen. "The Narrative Quality of Experience." *Journal of the American Academy of Religion* 39, no. 3 (1971): 291–311.
Cummins, Stephen A. *Paul and the Crucified Christ in Antioch: Maccabean Martyrdom and Galatians 1 and 2*. Cambridge: Cambridge University Press, 2001.
Currie, Mark. *The Unexpected: Narrative Temporality and the Philosophy of Surprise*. Edinburgh: Edinburgh University Press, 2013.

Davies, W. D. *Paul and Rabbinic Judaism: Some Rabbinic Elements in Pauline Theology*. 2nd ed. London: S.P.C.K, 1955.
Davis Bledsoe, Amanda M. "The Relationship of the Different Editions of Daniel: A History of Scholarship." *CBR* 13, no. 2 (2015): 175–90.
de Vos, Craig S. *Church and Community Conflicts: The Relationships of the Thessalonian, Corinthian, and Philippian Churches with their Wider Civic Communities*. Atlanta: SBL, 1999.
Deidun, Thomas. "Beyond Dualisms: Paul on Sex, Sarx and Sōma." *The Way: Contemporary Christian Spirituality* 28 (1998): 195–205.
deSilva, David A. "No Confidence in the Flesh: The Meaning and Function of Philippians 3:2–21." *Trinity Journal* 15 (1994): 27–54.
DiMattei, Steven. "Biblical Narratives." In *As It is Written: Studying Paul's Use of Scripture*, edited by Stanley E. Porter, and Christopher D. Stanley, 59–93. Atlanta: SBL, 2008.
Dinkler, Michal Beth. "New Testament Rhetorical Narratology: An Invitation Toward Integration." *BibInt* 24, no. 2 (2016): 203–28.
Docherty, Susan. "'Do You Understand What You Are Reading?' (Acts 8.30): Current Trends and Future Perspectives in the Study of the Use of the Old Testament in the New." *JSNT* 38, no. 1 (2015): 112–25.
Donfried, Karl P. *Paul, Thessalonica and Early Christianity*. London: A&C Black, 2003.
Dowling, William C. *Ricoeur on Time and Narrative: An Introduction to Temps et Récit*. Notre Dame: University of Notre Dame Press, 2011.
D'Souza, Keith. "Ricoeur's Narrative Development of Gadamer's Hermeneutics: Continuity and Discontinuity." Ph.D., Marquette University, 2003.
Dunn, James D. G. "Christ, Adam, and Preexistence." In *Where Christology Began: Essays on Philippians 2*, edited by Ralph P. Martin, and Brian J. Dodd, 75–83. Louisville: Westminster John Knox Press, 1998.
Dunn, James D. G. *Christology in the Making: A New Testament Inquiry into the Origins of the Doctrine of the Incarnation*. London: SCM, 1989.
Dunn, James D. G. "The Narrative Approach to Paul. Whose Story?" In *Narrative Dynamics in Paul. A Critical Assessment*, edited by Bruce W. Longenecker, 217–30. Louisville: Westminster John Knox Press, 2002.
Dunn, James D. G. *The Partings of the Ways: Between Christianity and Judaism and their Significance for the Character of Christianity*. London: SCM Press, 1991.
Dunn, James D. G. "Paul's Theology." In *The Face of New Testament Studies: A Survey of Recent Research*, edited by Scot McKnight, and Grant R. Osborne, 326–48. Grand Rapids: Baker, 2004.
Dunn, James D. G. "Philippians 3.2–14 and the New Perspective on Paul." In *The New Perspective on Paul*, edited by 469–90. Grand Rapids: Eerdmans, 2007.
Dunn, James D. G. *Romans 1–8*. WBC 38A. Dallas: Thomas Nelson, 1988.
Dunn, James D. G. *The Theology of Paul the Apostle*. Edinburgh: T&T Clark, 1998.
Easter, Matthew C. "The Pistis Christou Debate: Main Arguments and Responses in Summary." *CBR* 9, no. 1 (2010): 33–47.
Eastman, Susan G. "Philippians 2:6–11: Incarnation as Mimetic Participation." *JSPL* 1, no. 1 (2011): 1–22.
Eaton, John H. *Kingship and the Psalms*. London: SCM, 1976.
Engberg-Pedersen, Troels. "Introduction: Paul Beyond the Judaism/Hellenism Divide." In *Paul Beyond the Judaism/Hellenism Divide*, edited by Troels Engberg-Pedersen, 1–16. Louisville: Westminster John Knox Press, 2001.
Enns, Peter E. *Exodus*. NIVAC. Grand Rapids: Zondervan, 2000.

Enns, Peter E. "Grumbling." In *NDBT*, edited by T. Desmond Alexander and Brian S. Rosner, 527–9. Downers Grove: InterVarsity Press, 2000.

Estelle, Bryan D. *Echoes of Exodus: Tracing a Biblical Motif*. Downers Grove: InterVarsity Press, 2018.

Evans, Craig A. "Jewish Exegesis." In *DTIB*, edited by Kevin Vanhoozer, 380–4. Grand Rapids: Baker Academic, 2005.

Everson, A. Joseph. "The Days of Yahweh." *JBL* 93, no. 3 (1974): 329–37.

Fanning, Buist M. *Verbal Aspect in New Testament Greek*. Oxford: Oxford University Press, 1994.

Fee, Gordon. *Paul's Letter to the Philippians*. NICNT. Grand Rapids: Eerdmans, 1995.

Ferguson, Everett. "Spiritual Circumcision in Early Christianity." *SJTh* 41, no. 4 (1988): 485–97.

Fewster, Gregory P. "The Philippian's "Christ Hymn": Trends in Critical Scholarship." *CBR* 13, no. 2 (2015): 191–206.

Fisk, Bruce N. "The Odyssey of Christ: A Novel Context for Philippians 2:6–11." In *Exploring Kenotic Christology: The Self-Emptying of God*, edited by C. Stephen Evans, 45–73. Vancouver: Regent College Publishing, 2009.

Fitzgerald, John T. *Cracks in an Earthen Vessel: An Examination of the Catalogues of Hardships in the Corinthian Correspondence*. SBLDS 99. Atlanta: SBL, 1988.

Fitzmyer, Joseph A. "The Aramaic Background of Philippians 2:6–11." *CBQ* 50, no. 3 (1988): 470–83.

Fodor, James. *Christian Hermeneutics: Paul Ricoeur and the Refiguring of Theology*. Oxford: Oxford University Press, 1995.

Ford, David F. "System, Story, Performance: A Proposal About the Role of Narrative in Christian Systematic Theology." In *Why Narrative? Readings in Narrative Theology*, edited by Stanley Hauerwas, 191–215. Eugene: Wipf & Stock Pub, 1997.

Foster, Paul. "Echoes Without Resonance: Critiquing Certain Aspects of Recent Scholarly Trends in the Study of the Jewish Scriptures in the New Testament." *JSNT* 38, no. 1 (2015): 96–111.

Foster, Paul. "Πίστις Χριστοῦ Terminology in Philippians and Ephesians." In *The Faith of Jesus Christ: Exegetical, Biblical, and Theological Studies*, edited by Michael F. Bird, and Preston M. Sprinkle, 91–109. Peabody: Non Basic Stock Line, 2010.

Fowl, Stephen E. "Philippians 1:28b, One More Time." In *New Testament Greek and Exegesis: Essays in Honor of Gerald F. Hawthorne*, edited by Amy M. Donaldson, and Timothy B. Sailors, 167–79. Grand Rapids: Eerdmans, 2003.

Fowl, Stephen E. *The Story of Christ in the Ethics of Paul: An Analysis of the Function of the Hymnic Material in the Pauline Corpus*. Sheffield: JSOT Press, 1990.

Fowl, Stephen E. "The Use of Scripture in Philippians." In *Paul and Scripture: Extending the Conversation*, edited by Christopher D. Stanley, 163–84. Atlanta: SBL, 2012.

Fredriksen, Paula. "Christians in the Roman Empire in the First Three Centuries CE." In *Companion to the Roman Empire*, edited by David Porter, 587–606. Oxford: Blackwell, 2006.

Fried, Lisbeth S. "Cyrus the Messiah? The Historical Background to Isaiah 45:1." *HTR* 95, no. 4 (2002): 373–93.

Friedman, Susan Stanford. "Spatialization: A Strategy for Reading Narrative." *Narrative* 1, no. 1 (1993): 12–23.

Friesen, Steven J. *Twice Neokoros: Ephesus, Asia, and the Cult of the Flavian Imperial Family*. RGRW 116. Leiden: Brill, 1993.

Fuller, J. William. "'I Will Not Erase His Name from the Book of Life' (Revelation 3:5)." *JETS* 26, no. 3 (1983): 297–306.

Fuller, R. H. *The Foundations of New Testament Christology*. London: Lutterworth, 1965.
Furnish, Victor P. "The Place and Purpose of Philippians III." *NTS* 10 (1963): 80–8.
Gadamer, Hans-Georg. *Truth and Method*. London: Sheed and Ward, 1975.
Gamble, Harry Y. *Books and Readers in the Early Church: A History of Early Christian Texts*. New Haven: Yale University Press, 1997.
Garland, D. E. "The Composition and Unity of Philippians: Some Neglected Literary Factors." *Novum Testamentum* 27 (1985): 141–73.
Garnsey, Peter, and Richard Saller. *The Roman Empire: Economy, Society and Culture*. Berkeley: University of California Press, 1987.
Garrett, Susan R. "The God of This World and the Affliction of Paul: 2 Cor 4:1–12." In *Greeks, Romans, and Christians: Essays in Honor of Abraham J. Malherbe*, edited by David L. Balch, and Everett Ferguson, 99–117. Minneapolis: Fortress, 1991.
Genette, Gerard. *Narrative Discourse: An Essay in Method*. New York: Cornell University Press, 1980.
Geoffrion, Timothy C. *The Rhetorical Purpose and the Political and Military Character of Philippians: A Call to Stand Firm*. Lewiston: Mellen Biblical Press, 1993.
Giesen, Heinz. "Eschatology in Philippians." In *Paul and his Theology*, edited by Stanley E. Porter, 217–81. Leiden: Brill, 2006.
Gnilka, Joachim. *Der Philipperbrief*. Freiburg: Herder, 1976.
Goldingay, John E. *Daniel*. WBC 30. Waco: Thomas Nelson Inc, 1986.
Goldingay, John E.. *The Message of Isaiah: A Literary-Theological Commentary*. London: MPG Books, 2005.
Gorman, Michael J. *Cruciformity: Paul's Narrative Spirituality of the Cross*. Grand Rapids: Eerdmans, 2001.
Gorman, Michael J. *Inhabiting the Cruciform God: Kenosis, Justification, and Theosis in Paul's Narrative Soteriology*. Grand Rapids: Wm. B. Eerdmans, 2009.
Gorringe, Tim. "Political Readings of Scripture." In *The Cambridge Companion to Biblical Interpretation*, edited by John Barton, 67–80. Cambridge: Cambridge University Press, 1998.
Gowan, Donald E. *Abingdon Old Testament Commentaries: Daniel*. Nashville: Abingdon Press, 2001.
Grayston, K. "The Opponents in Philippians 3." *ExpTim* 97 (1986): 170–2.
Green, Donald E. "The Folly of the Cross." *TMSJ* 15, no. 1 (2004): 59–69.
Greenlee, J. Harold. *An Exegetical Summary of Philippians*. 2nd ed. Dallas: SIL International, 2008.
Greisch, Jean. "Testimony and Attestation." In *Paul Ricoeur: The Hermeneutics of Action*, edited by Richard M. Kearney, 81–98. New Delhi: Sage Publications, 1996.
Gundry, Robert H. *Sōma in Biblical Theology: With Emphasis on Pauline Anthropology*. Cambridge: Cambridge University Press, 1976.
Gunther, John J. *St. Paul's Opponents and their Background: A Study of Apocalyptic and Jewish Sectarian Teachings*. Leiden: Brill, 1973.
Hafemann, S. J. "Paul and His Interpreters." In *DPL*, edited by Gerald F. Hawthorne, and Ralph P. Martin, 666–79. Leicester: InterVarsity Press, 1993.
Hafemann, Scott. "Suffering." In *DPL*, edited by Gerald F. Hawthorne, and Ralph P. Martin, 919–21. Leicester: InterVarsity Press, 1993.
Hahn, H.-C. "Zeal." In *NIDNTT*, edited by Colin Brown, vol. 3, 1166–8. Grand Rapids: Zondervan, 1986.
Hall, W. David. *Paul Ricoeur and the Poetic Imperative: The Creative Tension between Love and Justice*. New York: State University of New York Press, 2008.

Hamerton-Kelly, R. G. *Pre-Existence, Wisdom, and the Son of Man: A Study of the Idea of Pre-Existence in the New Testament*. Eugene: Wipf and Stock, 1973.

Hansen, G. Walter. *The Letter to the Philippians*. Grand Rapids: Eerdmans, 2009.

Harding, Sarah. *Paul's Eschatological Anthropology: The Dynamics of Human Transformation*. Minneapolis: Augsburg Fortress, 2015.

Harink, Douglas. "Paul and Israel: An Apocalyptic Reading." *Pro Ecclesia* 16, no. 4 (2007): 359–80.

Hartley, John E. *The Book of Job*. NICOT. Grand Rapids: Eerdmans, 1988.

Hartman, L. "Scriptural Exegesis in the Gospel of St. Matthew and the Problem of Communication." In *L'Évangile selon Matthieu: Rédaction et théologie*, edited by M. Didier, 131–52. Gembloux: Duculot, 1972.

Hartman, Louis Francis, and Alexander A. Di Lella. *The Book of Daniel*. New York: Anchor Bible, 1978.

Harvey, John. "A New Look at the Christ Hymn in Philippians 2:6–11." *ExpTim* 76, no. 11 (1965): 337–9.

Hawthorn, T. "Phil 1:12–19 with Special Reference to vv. 15, 16, 17." *ExpTim* 62 (1950): 316–17.

Hawthorne, Gerald F. *Philippians*. Edited by Ralph P. Martin. rev ed. WBC 43. Waco: Thomas Nelson, 2004.

Hays, Richard B. *The Conversion of the Imagination: Paul as Interpreter of Israel's Scripture*. Grand Rapids: Wm. B. Eerdmans, 2005.

Hays, Richard B. *Echoes of Scripture in the Letters of Paul*. New Haven: Yale University Press, 1989.

Hays, Richard B. *The Faith of Jesus Christ: The Narrative Substructure of Galatians 3:1–4:11*. Cambridge: Wm. B. Eerdmans, 2002.

Hays, Richard B. "Is Paul's Gospel Narratable?" *JSNT* 27, no. 2 (2004): 217–39.

Hays, Richard B., and Joel B. Green. "The Use of the Old Testament by New Testament Writers." In *Hearing the New Testament : Strategies for Interpretation*, edited by Joel B. Green, 222–38. Grand Rapids: William B. Eerdmans, 1995.

Heen, Erik M. "Phil 2:6–11 and Resistance to Local Timocratic Rule: Isa Thed and the Cult of the Emperor in the East." In *Paul and the Roman Imperial Order*, edited by Richard A. Horsley, 125–54. New York: Trinity Press, 2004.

Heidegger, Martin. *Being and Time*. Translated by John Macquarrie. Oxford: Basil Blackwell, 1978.

Heidegger, Martin. "The Origin of the Work of Art." In *Poetry, Language, Thought*, translated by Albert Hofstadter, 15–86. New York: Harper Perennial Modern Classics, 2013.

Heilig, Christoph. *Hidden Criticism?: The Methodology and Plausibility of the Search for a Counter-Imperial Subtext in Paul*. Tübingen: Mohr Siebeck, 2015.

Hellerman, Joseph H. "The Humiliation of Christ in the Social World of Roman Philippi, Part I." *BibSac* 160 (2003): 321–36.

Hellerman, Joseph H. "The Humiliation of Christ in the Social World of Roman Philippi, Part II." *BibSac* 160 (2003): 421–33.

Hellerman, Joseph H. *Reconstructing Honor in Roman Philippi: Carmen Christi as Cursus Pudorum*. New York: Cambridge University Press, 2005.

Hellerman, Joseph H. "Vindicating God's Servants in Philippi and in Philippians: The Influence of Paul's Ministry in Philippi upon the Composition of Philippians 2:6–11." *BBR* 20, no. 1 (2010): 85–102.

Hendriksen, William. *Exposition of Philippians*. Grand Rapids: Baker Book House, 1962.

Hengel, Martin. *Crucifixion in the Ancient World and the Folly of the Message of the Cross.* London: SCM Press, 1977.

Henrixk, Hans Hermann. "Paul at the Intersection between Continuity and Discontinuity: On Paul's Place in Early Judaism and Christianity as Well as in Christian-Jewish Dialogue Today." In *Paul and Judaism: Crosscurrents in Pauline Exegesis and the Study of Jewish-Christian Relations*, edited by Reimund Bieringer, and Didier Pollefeyt, 192–207. London: Bloomsbury T&T Clark, 2014.

Henze, Matthias. "The Use of Scripture in the Book of Daniel." In *A Companion to Biblical Interpretation in Early Judaism*, edited by Matthias Henze, 279–307. Grand Rapids: Eerdmans, 2012.

Hess, K. "Serve, Deacon, Worship." In *NIDNTT*, edited by Colin Brown, vol. 3, 544–53. Grand Rapids: Zondervan, 1986.

Höffe, Otfried. *Aristotle.* Edited by Anthony Preus. Translated by Christine Salazar. New York: State University of New York Press, 2003.

Hofius, Otfried. *Der Christushymnus Philipper 2, 6–11: Untersuchungen zu Gestalt und Aussage eines Urchristlichen Psalms.* Tübingen: Mohr, 1976.

Hollander, John. *The Figure of Echo: A Mode of Allusion in Milton and After.* Berkeley: University of California Press, 1981.

Holloway, Paul A. Review of *Philippians: From People to Letter*, by Peter Oakes. *The Journal of Religion* 82 (2002): 434–6.

Holmberg, Bengt. "Understanding the First Hundred Years of Christian Identity." In *Exploring Early Christian Identity*, edited by Bengt Holmberg, 1–32. Tübingen: Mohr Siebeck, 2008.

Hooker, Morna D. "Interchange in Christ and Ethics." *JSNT* 8, no. 25 (1985): 3–17.

Hooker, Morna D. "Philippians 2:6–11." In *Jesus und Paulus: Festschrift für Werner Georg Kümmel zum 70*, edited by E. E. Ellis, and E. Gräßer, 151–64. Göttingen: Vandenhoeck & Ruprecht, 1975.

Hoover, Roy W. "The Harpagmos Enigma: A Philological Solution." *HTR* 64, no. 1 (1971): 95–119.

Horrell, David G. "'Becoming Christian': Solidifying Christian Identity and Content." In *Handbook of Early Christianity: Social Science Approaches*, edited by Anthony J. Blasi et al., 309–35. Walnut Creek: AltaMira Press, 2002.

Horrell, David G. "'"No Longer Jew or Greek": Paul's Corporate Christology and the Construction of Christian Community." In *Christology, Controversy and Community: New Testament Essays in Honour of David R. Catchpole*, edited by David G. Horrell, and Christopher M. Tuckett, 99, 321–44. Leiden: Brill, 2000.

Horrell, David G. "Paul's Narrative or Narrative Substructure? The Significance of 'Paul's Story.'" In *Narrative Dynamics in Paul. A Critical Assessment*, edited by Bruce W. Longenecker, 157–71. Louisville: Westminster John Knox Press, 2002.

Horsley, Richard A. *Paul and the Roman Imperial Order.* New York: Continuum, 2004.

Houlden, Leslie. Review of Paul and the Hermeneutics of Faith, by Francis Watson. *JTS* 56 (2005): 555–8.

Houston, Sam. "Narrative and Ideology: The Promises and Pitfalls of Postliberal Theology." *Religion & Theology* 23 (2016): 161–87.

Howard, George. "Phil 2:6–11 and the Human Christ." *CBQ* 40, no. 3 (1978): 368–87.

Huey, F. B. *Jeremiah, Lamentations: An Exegetical and Theological Exposition of Holy Scripture.* Nashville: Holman Reference, 1993.

Huizenga, Leroy A. *The New Isaac: Tradition and Intertextuality in the Gospel of Matthew.* Leiden: Brill, 2012.

Huizenga, Leroy A. "The Old Testament in the New, Intertextuality and Allegory." *JSNT* 38, no. 1 (2015): 17–35.
Hurst, Lincoln D. "Christ, Adam, and Preexistence Revisited." In *Where Christology Began: Essays on Philippians 2*, edited by Ralph P. Martin, and Brian J. Dodd, 84–95. Louisville: Westminster John Knox Press, 1998.
Hurtado, L. W. *How on Earth Did Jesus Become a God?: Historical Questions About Earliest Devotion to Jesus*. Grand Rapids: Eerdmans, 2005.
Hüsken, Ute. "Ritual Dynamics and Ritual Failure." In *When Rituals Go Wrong: Mistakes, Failure, and the Dynamics of Ritual*, edited by Ute Hüsken, 337–66. Leiden: Brill, 2007.
Huskey, Rebecca K. *Paul Ricoeur on Hope: Expecting the Good*. New York: Peter Lang Publishing Inc., 2009.
Jacobs, Andrew S. "A Jew's Jew: Paul and the Early Christian Problem of Jewish Origins." *The Journal of Religion* 86, no. 2 (2006): 258–86.
Jacobson, Richard. "Satanic Semiotics, Jobian Jurisprudence." In *Semeia 19: The Book of Job And Ricoeur's Hermeneutics*, edited by John Dominic Crossan, 62–71. Chico: SBL, 1981.
Janzen, J. Gerald. "Creation and New Creation in Philippians 1:6." *Horizons in Biblical Theology* 18, no. 1 (1996): 27–54.
Janzen, J. Gerald. "Toward a Hermeneutics of Resonance: A Methodological Interlude between the Testaments." In *When Prayer Takes Place: Forays into a Biblical World*, edited by Brent A. Strawn, 241–99. Eugene: Wipf and Stock Publisher, 2012.
Jeansonne, S. P. *The Old Greek Translation of Daniel 7–12 (Catholic Biblical Quarterly Monograph Series)*. Washington, DC: Catholic Biblical Assn of Amer, 1988.
Jenkins, Richard. *Social Identity*. London: Routledge, 2004.
Jennings, Mark. ""Make My Joy Complete": The Price of Partnership in the Letter of Paul to the Philippians." Ph.D., Marquette University, 2015.
Jenson, Robert. *Systematic Theology, 2 Vols*. New York: Oxford University Press, 1997–99.
Jervis, L. Ann. *At the Heart of the Gospel: Suffering in the Earliest Christian Message*. Grand Rapids: Eerdmans, 2007.
Jewett, Robert. "The Epistolary Thanksgiving and the Integrity of Philippians." *Novum Testamentum* 12, no. 1 (1970): 40–53.
Johnson, Luke Timothy. Review of Paul in Israel's Story: Self and Community at the Cross, by John L. Meech. *JTS* 69 (2008): 433–5.
Kapelrud, Arvid S. "The Main Concern of Second Isaiah." *VT* 32, no. 1 (1982): 50–8.
Käsemann, Ernst. *Exegetische Versuche und Besinnungen II*. Vandenhoeck & Ruprecht, 1970.
Käsemann, Ernst. "Gottesgerechtigkeit bei Paulus." *ZThK* 58 (1961): 367–78.
Käsemann, Ernst. "Kritische Analyse von Phil. 2,5–11." *ZThK* 47, no. 3 (1950): 313–60.
Käsemann, Ernst. "The Righteousness of God in Paul." In *New Testament Questions for Today*, 168–82. London: SCM, 1969.
Kearney, Richard F. *On Paul Ricoeur: The Owl of Minerva*. Transcending Boundaries in Philosophy and Theology. Burlington: Ashgate Pub Limited, 2004.
Keesmaat, Sylvia C. *Paul & His Story: (Re)interpreting the Exodus Tradition*. JSNTSup 181. Sheffield: Sheffield Academic, 1999.
Keppie, Lawrence. *The Making of the Roman Army: From Republic to Empire*. Norman: University of Oklahoma Press, 1998.
Kiley, Mark. Review of *The Story of Christ in the Ethics of Paul: An Analysis of the Function of the Hymnic Material in the Pauline Corpus*, by Stephen E. Fowl. *CBQ* 54 (1992): 151–3.

Kim, Seyoon. *Christ and Caesar: The Gospel and the Roman Empire in the Writings of Paul and Luke.* Grand Rapids: Eerdmans, 2008.

Kleinknecht, K. T. *Der Leidende Gerechtfertigte: Die Alttestamentlich-Jüdische Tradition vom 'Leidenden Gerechten' und ihre Rezeption bei Paulus.* WUNT. 2/13. Tübingen: Mohr Siebeck, 1988.

Klemm, David E. "Philosophy and Kerygma. Ricoeur as Reader of the Bible." In *Reading Ricoeur*, edited by David M. Kaplan, 47–69. New York: SUNY Press, 2008.

Klijn, A. F. J. "Paul's Opponents in Philippians 3." *NovT* 7 (1965): 278–84.

Koester, Helmut. "The Purpose of the Polemic of a Pauline Fragment." *NTS* 8, no. 4 (1962): 317–32.

Kraus, Hans-Joachim. *Theology of the Psalms.* Translated by K. Crim. Minneapolis: Augsburg, 1986.

Kreitzer, Larry J. "Eschatology." In *DPL*, edited by Gerald F. Hawthorne, and Ralph P. Martin, 253–69. Leicester: InterVarsity Press, 1993.

Kreitzer, Larry J. *Jesus and God in Paul's Eschatology.* London: Bloomsbury Academic, 2015.

Krentz, Edgar M. "Military Language and Metaphors in Philippians." In *Origins and Method: Towards A New Understanding of Judaism and Christianity: Essays in Honour of John C. Hurd*, edited by John Coolidge Hurd, and Bradley H. McLean, 105–27. Sheffield: JSOT Press, 1993.

Kruse, C. G. "Afflictions, Trials, Hardships." In *DPL*, edited by Gerald F. Hawthorne, and Ralph P. Martin, 18–20. Leicester: InterVarsity Press, 1993.

Kugler, Chris. "ΠΙΣΤΙΣ ΧΡΙΣΤΟΥ: The Current State of Play and the Key Arguments." *CBR* 14, no. 2 (2016): 244–55.

Kuhn, Thomas S. *The Structure of Scientific Revolutions.* International Encyclopedia of Unified Science. Foundations of the Unity of Science, vol. 2, no. 2. Chicago: University of Chicago Press, 1970.

Kunneman, Harry. "Ethical Complexity." In *Complexity, Difference and Identity: An Ethical Perspective (Issues in Business Ethics)*, edited by Paul Cilliers, and Rika Preiser, 131–64. London: Springer, 2010.

Kwakkel, Gert. "Righteousness." In *DOTWPW*, edited by Longman III, Tremper and Peter Enns, 663–8. Nottingham: InterVarsity Press, 2008.

Lakshmanan, Xavier. "Narrative and Ontology: Paul Ricoeur's Hermeneutic Philosophy as a Guide to Theological Method." Ph.D., Charles Sturt University, 2013.

Leichter, David J. "Collective Identity and Collective Memory in the Philosophy of Paul Ricoeur." *Ricoeur Studies* 3, no. 1 (2012): 114–31.

Leichter, David J.. "The Dual Role of Testimony in Paul Ricoeur's Memory, History, Forgetting." In *Phenomenology 2010, volume 5: Selected Essays from North America. Part 1: Phenomenology within Philosophy*, edited by Lester Embree et al., 373–99. Bucharest: Zeta Books, 2010.

Levick, Barbara. *Roman Colonies in Southern Asia Minor.* Oxford: Oxford University Press, 1967.

Lightfoot, J. B. *Saint Paul's Epistle to the Philippians.* London: Macmillan, 1913.

Lightfoot, J. B. et al. "Recent Editions of St Paul's Epistles." *JCSP* 3, no. 7 (1857): 81–121.

Lim, Kar Yon. *'The Sufferings of Christ Are Abundant in Us': A Narrative Dynamics Investigation of Paul's Sufferings in 2 Corinthians.* LNTS. London: Bloomsbury T&T Clark, 2009.

Lim, Timothy H. *Holy Scripture in the Qumran Commentaries and Pauline Letters.* Oxford: Clarendon Press, 1997.

Lincicum, David. *Paul and the Early Jewish Encounter with Deuteronomy*. Grand Rapids: Baker Academic, 2013.

Lincoln, Andrew T. *Paradise Now and Not Yet: Studies in the Role of the Heavenly Dimension in Paul's Thought with Special Reference to His Eschatology*. Cambridge: Cambridge University Press, 2004.

Linder, Amnon. *The Jews in Roman Imperial Legislation*. Detroit: Wayne State University Press, 1995.

Linebaugh, Jonathan A. "Righteousness Revealed: The Death of Christ as the Definition of the Righteousness of God in Romans 3:21–26." In *Paul and the Apocalyptic Imagination*, edited by Ben C. Blackwell et al., 219–37. Minneapolis: Fortress Press, 2016.

Linington, Silva A. *Covenant (בְּרִית) in Daniel and the Dead Sea Scrolls: An Exposition of Daniel 9–12 and Selected Sections of the Damascus Document (CD), Community Rule (1QS), Hymns Scroll (1QHA) and War Scroll (1QM)*. Pretoria: University of South Africa, 2014.

Loh, I.-Jin, and Eugene A. Nida. *A Translator's Handbook on Paul's Letter to the Philippians (Helps for Translators)*. New York: United Bible Societies, 1977.

Lohmeyer, Ernst. *Die Briefe an die Philipper, an die Kolosser und an Philemon*. Gottingen: Vandenhoeck & Ruprecht, 1964.

Lohmeyer, Ernst. *Kyrios Jesus. Eine Untersuchung zu Phil. 2,5–11*. Heidelberg: Winter, 1928.

Longenecker, Bruce W. *Narrative Dynamics in Paul. A Critical Assessment*. Louisville: Westminster John Knox Press, 2002.

Longenecker, Bruce W. "The Narrative Approach to Paul: An Early Retrospective." *CBR* 1 (2002): 88–111.

Longman, Tremper III. "Disputation." In *DOTWPW*, edited by Longman III, Tremper and Peter Enns, 108–12. Nottingham: InterVarsity Press, 2008.

Loughlin, G. *Telling God's Story: Bible, Church and Narrative Theology*. Cambridge: Cambridge University Press, 1999.

Lukaszewski, Albert L., and Mark Dubis. *The Lexham Syntactic Greek New Testament: Sentence Analysis*. Logos Bible Software, 2009.

Lythgoe, Esteban. "Ricoeur's Concept of Testimony." *Analecta Hermeneutica* 3, no. 1 (2011): 1–16.

Macaskill, Grant. *Union with Christ in the New Testament*. Oxford: Oxford University Press, 2014.

Mallett, Oliver, and Robert Wapshott. "The Challenges of Identity Work: Developing Ricoeurian Narrative Identity in Organisations." *Ephemera* 11, no. 3 (2011): 271–88.

Mallett, Oliver, and Robert Wapshott. "Mediating Ambiguity: Narrative Identity and Knowledge Workers." *SJM* 28, no. 1 (2012): 16–26.

Marchal, Joseph A. "Military Images in Philippians 1–2: A Feminist Analysis of the Rhetorics of Scholarship, Philippians, and Current Contexts." In *Her Master's Tools?: Feminist And Postcolonial Engagements of Historical-Critical Discourse*, edited by Caroline Vander Stichele, and Todd Penner, 265–86. Atlanta: SBL, 2005.

Marshall, I. Howard, and Karl P. Donfried. "The Theology of Philippians: The Shape of the Church." In *The Theology of the Shorter Pauline Letters*, 149–61. Cambridge: Cambridge University, 1993.

Martin, Ralph P. *Carmen Christi: Philippians 2:5–11 in Recent Interpretations and in the Setting of Early Christian Worship*. Grand Rapids: Eerdmans, 1983.

Martin, Ralph P. *Philippians*. NCBC. Grand Rapids: Eerdmans, 1976.

Martin, Ralph P. *Philippians: An Introduction and Commentary*. TNTC 11. Downers Grove: InterVarsity Press, 1987.

Martin, Ralph P. *Philippians: Based on the Revised Standard Version*. London: Marshall, Morgan & Scott, 1976.

Martyn, J. Louis. *Galatians*. New Haven: Yale University Press, 2004.

McAuley, David. *Paul's Covert Use of Scripture: Intertextuality and Rhetorical Situation in Philippians 2:10–16*. Eugene: Pickwick Publications, 2015.

McDonald, L. M. "Philippi." In *DNTB*, edited by Craig A. Evans, and Stanley E. Porter, 787–9. Downers Grove: InterVarsity Press, 2000.

Meadowcroft, T. J. *Aramaic Daniel and Greek Daniel: A Literary Comparison*. Sheffield: Sheffield Academic, 1995.

Mearns, Chris. "The Identity of Paul's Opponents at Philippi." *NTS* 33 (1987): 194–204.

Meech, John L. *Paul in Israel's Story: Self and Community at the Cross*. New York: Oxford University Press, 2006.

Melick, Richard R. *Philippians, Colossians, Philemon. An Exegetical and Theological Exposition of Holy Scripture*. NAC 32. Nashville: Holman Reference, 1991.

Metzger, Bruce M. *A Textual Commentary on the Greek New Testament*. 2nd ed. New York: United Bible Societies, 1994.

Meyer, Ben F. *The Early Christians: Their World Mission & Self-Discovery*. Wilmington: M. Glazier, 1986.

Michael, J. Hugh. "Paul and Job: A Neglected Analogy." *Expository Times* 36, no. 2 (1924): 67–70.

Michaelis, Wilhelm. *Zur Engelchristologie im Urchristentum. Abbau der Konstruktion Martin Werners*. Zürich: Heinrich Majer, 1942.

Michel, O. "Zur Exegese von Phil. 2,5–11." In *Theologie als Glaubenswägnis. Festschrift für K. Heim zum 80. Geburtstag*, 77–95. Hamburg: Furche-Verlag, 1954.

Middleton, Paul. *Martyrdom: A Guide for the Perplexed*. London: T & T Clark International, 2011.

Milbank, John. *Theology and Social Theory: Beyond Secular Reason*. Oxford: Blackwell, 2006.

Miller, Ernest C. "Politeuesthe in Philippians 1:27: Some Philological and Thematic Observations." *JSNT* 15 (1982): 86–96.

Miller, James C. "Communal Identity in Philippians." *ASE* 27, no. 2 (2010): 11–23.

Miller, J. W. "Prophetic Conflict in Second Isaiah." In *Wort - Gebot - Glaube*, edited by Walther Eichrodt, and H. J. Stoebe, Bd.59, 77–85. Zürich: Zwingli Verlag, 1970.

Moessner, David P. "Turning Status 'Upside Down' in Philippi: Christ Jesus' 'Emptying Himself' as Forfeiting Any Acknowledgment of His "Equality with God" (Phil 2:6–11)." *Horizons in Biblical Theology* 31, no. 2 (2009): 123–43.

Motyer, J. A. *Isaiah: An Introduction and Commentary*. Downers Grove: InterVarsity Press, 1999.

Motyer, J. Alec. *The Message of Philippians*. Downers Grove: IVP Academic, 1984.

Moule, C. F. D. "Further Reflexions on Philippians 2:5–11." In *Apostolic History and the Gospel: Biblical and Historical Essays Presented to F. F. Bruce*, edited by W. Ward Gasque, and Ralph P. Martin, 264–76. Exeter: The Paternoster Press, 1970.

Mouzakitis, Angelos. "From Narrative to Action: Paul Ricoeur's Reflections on History." *Rethinking History* 19, no. 3 (2015): 393–408.

Moyise, Steve. Review of *Arguing with Scripture : The Rhetoric of Quotations in the Letters of Paul*. *JSNT* 27 (2005): 85–6.

Muldoon, Mark S. "Ricoeur's Ethics: Another Version of Virtue Ethics? Attestation is Not a Virtue." *Philosophy Today* 42, no. 3 (1998): 301–9.

Nanos, Mark D. "Paul's Reversal of Jews Calling Gentiles "Dogs" (Philippians 3:2): 1600 Years of an Ideological Tale Wagging an Exegetical Dog?" *Biblical Interpretation* 17, no. 4 (2009): 448–82.
Nebreda, Sergio Rosell. *Christ Identity: A Social-Scientific Reading of Philippians 2.5–11*. Göttingen: Vandenhoeck & Ruprecht, 2011.
Neugebauer, Fritz. *In Christus: Eine Untersuchung zum Paulinischen Glaubensverständnis*. Göttingen: Vandenhoeck & Ruprecht, 1961.
Neutel, Karin B. *A Cosmopolitan Ideal: Paul's Declaration 'Neither Jew Nor Greek, Neither Slave Nor Free, Nor Male and Female' in the Context of First-Century Thought*. London: T&T Clark, 2015.
Neutel, Karin B., and Matthew R. Anderson. "The First Cut is the Deepest: Masculinity and Circumcision in the First Century." In *Biblical Masculinities Foregrounded*, edited by Ovidiu Creanga, and Peter-Ben Smit, 228–44. Sheffield: Sheffield Phoenix, 2014.
Nicolet, Valérie. *Constructing the Self: Thinking with Paul and Michel Foucault*. Tübingen: Mohr Siebeck, 2012.
Nixon, Lyn. "New Testament Quotation at the Reader-Author Intersection: Evoking Story for Transformation." Ph.D., Middlesex, 2015.
Noguchi Reese, Naomi. "The Pauline Concept of Suffering in Phil 3.10–11." Th.M., Biola University, 2003.
Nongbri, Brent. "Two Neglected Textual Variants in Philippians 1." *JBL* 128, no. 4 (2009): 803–8.
Oakes, Peter. *Philippians: From People to Letter*. Cambridge: Cambridge University Press, 2001.
Oakes, Peter. "Re-Mapping the Universe: Paul and the Emperor in 1 Thessalonians and Philippians." *JSNT 27* (2005): 301–22.
O'Day, Gail R. "Jeremiah 9:22–23 and 1 Corinthians 1:26–31: A Study in Intertextuality." *JBL* 109, no. 2 (1990): 259–67.
Ogereau, Julien M. *Paul's Koinonia with the Philippians: A Socio-Historical Investigation of a Pauline Economic Partnership*. Tübingen: Mohr Siebeck, 2014.
Onesti, K. L., and M. T. Brauch. "Righteousness, Righteousness of God." In *DPL*, edited by Gerald F. Hawthorne and Ralph P. Martin, 827–37. Leicester: InterVarsity Press, 1993.
Orr, Peter. *Christ Absent and Present: A Study in Pauline Christology*. Durham: Durham University, 2011.
Osborne, G. R. "Hermeneutics/Interpreting Paul." In *DPL*, edited by Gerald F. Hawthorne, and Ralph P. Martin, 388–97. Leicester: InterVarsity Press, 1993.
Oswalt, John N. *The Book of Isaiah, Chapters 40-66*. NICOT. Grand Rapids: Eerdmans, 1998.
Oswalt, John N. "Isaiah." In *NDBT*, edited by T. Desmond Alexander, and Brian S. Rosner, 217–23. Downers Grove: InterVarsity Press, 1993.
Oswalt, John N. *Isaiah*. NIVAC. Grand Rapids: Zondervan, 2003.
Pauw, Amy Plantinga. "The Word is Near You: A Feminist Conversation with Lindbeck." *Theology Today* 50, no. 1 (1993): 45–55.
Pellauer, David. "Narrated Action Grounds Narrative Identity." In *Paul Ricoeur in the Age of Hermeneutical Reason: Poetics, Praxis, and Critique*, edited by Roger W. H. Savage, 69–83. Lanham: Lexington Books, 2015.
Pellauer, David. *Ricoeur: A Guide for the Perplexed*. London: Continuum, 2007.
Peter, Doble. "'Vile Bodies' or Transformed Persons? Philippians 3.21 in Context." *JSNT* 24, no. 4 (2002): 3–27.

Peterlin, Davorin. *Paul's Letter to the Philippians in the Light of Disunity in the Church.* NTSupp 79. Leiden: Brill, 1995.

Petersen, Norman R. *Rediscovering Paul: Philemon and the Sociology of Paul's Narrative World.* Eugene: Wipf & Stock Pub, 2008.

Pfitzner, Victor C. *Paul and the Agon Motif: Traditional Athletic Imagery in the Pauline Literature.* Leiden: Brill, 1967.

Phelan, James, and Peter J. Rabinowitz. "Narrative as Rhetoric." In *Narrative Theory: Core Concepts and Critical Debates*, 3–8. Columbus: Ohio State University Press, 2012.

Phelan, James, and Peter J. Rabinowitz. "Time, Plot, Progression." In *Narrative Theory: Core Concepts and Critical Debates*, 57–83. Columbus: Ohio State University Press, 2012.

Philo. *Philo: On the Embassy to Gaius* (Greek). Translated by F. H. Colson. Vol. X. London: William Heinemann Ltd, 1962.

Pilhofer, Peter. *Philippi. I. Die Erste Christliche Gemeinde Europas.* WUNT 87. Tübingen: Mohr Siebeck, 1995.

Pobee, John S. *Persecution and Martyrdom in the Theology of Paul.* Sheffield: JSOT Press, 1984.

Polhill, John B. "Twin Obstacles in the Christian Path: Philippians 3." *RevExp* 77, no. 3 (1980): 359–72.

Porter, Stanley E. "Tribulation, Messianic Woes." In *DLNTD*, edited by Ralph P. Martin, and Peter H. Davids, 1179–82. Downers Grove: InterVarsity Press, 1997.

Price, Simon R. F. *Rituals and Power: The Roman Imperial Cult in Asia Minor.* Cambridge: Cambridge University Press, 1984.

Punt, Jeremy. "Paul's Jewish Identity in the Roman World. Beyond the Conflict Model." In *Paul the Jew: Rereading the Apostle as a Figure of Second Temple Judaism*, edited by Gabriele Boccaccini, and Carlos A. Segovia, 245–70. Minneapolis: Fortress Press, 2016.

Rainwater, Mara. "Refiguring Ricoeur: Narrative Force and Communicative Ethics." In *Paul Ricoeur: The Hermeneutics of Action*, edited by Richard M. Kearney, 99–110. New Delhi: Sage Publications, 1996.

Rajak, Tessa. "Was There a Roman Charter for the Jews?" *JRS* 74 (1984): 107–23.

Raurell, Frederic. "The Doxa of the Seer in Dan-LXX 12,13." In *The Book of Daniel in the Light of New Findings*, edited by A. S. Van Der Woude, 520–32. Leuven: Peeters Publishers, 1993.

Redditt, Paul L. *Daniel.* NCBC. Sheffield: Sheffield Academic, 1999.

Redditt, Paul L. "Daniel 11 and the Sociohistorical Setting of the Book of Daniel." *CBQ* 60, no. 3 (1998): 463–74.

Reimer, Raymond Hubert. "'Our Citizenship is in Heaven': Philippians 1:27–30 and 3:20–21 as Part of the Apostle Paul's Political Theology." Ph. D., Princeton Theological Seminary, 1997.

Reumann, John. "The (Greek) Old Testament in Philippians 1:19 as Parade Example." In *History and Exegesis: New Testament Essays in Honor of Dr. E. Earle Ellis on His Eightieth Birthday*, edited by Sang-won Son, and S. Aaron Son, 189–200. New York: Bloomsbury T&T Clark, 2006.

Reumann, John. *Philippians.* The Anchor Yale Bible Commentaries. New Haven: Yale University Press, 2008.

Richardson, Brian. *A Poetics of Plot for the Twenty-First Century: Theorizing Unruly Narratives.* Columbus: Ohio State University Press, 2019.

Ricoeur, Paul. "A Response by Paul Ricoeur." In *Hermeneutics and the Human Sciences*, edited by John B. Thompson, 32–40. Cambridge: Cambridge University Press, 1981.

Ricoeur, Paul. "Between Rhetoric and Poetics: Aristotle." In *The Rule of Metaphor*, translated by Robert Czerny, Kathleen McLaughlin, and John Costello, 9–43. Toronto: University of Toronto Press, 1977.

Ricoeur, Paul. *The Course of Recognition*. Translated by David Pellauer. Cambridge, MA: Harvard University Press, 2005.

Ricoeur, Paul. *Freud and Philosophy: An Essay on Interpretation*. Translated by Denis Savage. New Haven: Yale University Press, 1977.

Ricoeur, Paul. *From Text to Action: Essays in Hermeneutics, II*. Evanston: Northwestern University Press, 1991.

Ricoeur, Paul. "The Hermeneutical Function of Distanciation." In *Hermeneutics and the Human Sciences: Essays on Language, Action and Interpretation*, 131–44. Cambridge: Cambridge University Press, 1981.

Ricoeur, Paul. "The Hermeneutics of Testimony." In *Essays on Biblical Interpretation*, edited by L. S. Mudge, 119–54. Philadelphia: Fortress, 1980.

Ricoeur, Paul. "The Human Experience of Time and Narrative." In *A Ricoeur Reader: Reflection and Imagination*, edited by Mario J. Valdes, 99–116. Toronto: University of Toronto Press, 1991.

Ricoeur, Paul. *Interpretation Theory: Discourse and the Surplus of Meaning*. Fort Worth: Texas Christian University Press, 1976.

Ricoeur, Paul. "Life: A Story in Search of a Narrator." In *A Ricoeur Reader: Reflection and Imagination*, edited by Mario J. Valdes, 425–37. Toronto: University of Toronto Press, 1991.

Ricoeur, Paul. "Life in Quest of Narrative." In *On Paul Ricoeur: Narrative and Interpretation*, edited by David Wood, 20–33. London: Routledge, 1992.

Ricoeur, Paul. *Memory, History, Forgetting*. Translated by David Pellauer Kathleen Blamey. Chicago: University of Chicago Press, 2004.

Ricoeur, Paul. "The Narrative Function." In *Hermeneutics and the Human Sciences*, edited by John B. Thompson, 274–96. Cambridge: Cambridge University Press, 1981.

Ricoeur, Paul. "Narrative Time." *Critical Inquiry* 7, no. 1 (1980): 169–90.

Ricoeur, Paul. *Oneself as Another*. Translated by Kathleen Blamey. Chicago: University of Chicago Press, 1992.

Ricoeur, Paul. "Rhetoric – Poetics – Hermeneutics." In *From Metaphysics to Rhetoric*, edited by Michel Meyer, 137–49. Dordrecht: Springer Netherlands, 1989.

Ricoeur, Paul. *The Rule of Metaphor: Multi-Disciplinary Studies of the Creation of Meaning in Language*. University of Toronto Romance Series. Toronto: University of Toronto Press, 1981.

Ricoeur, Paul. "The "Sacred Text" and the Community." In *Figuring the Sacred: Religion, Narrative, and Imagination*, 68–72. Minneapolis: Fortress Press, 1995.

Ricoeur, Paul. "The Text as Dynamic Identity." In *Identity of the Literary Text*, edited by Mario J. Valdés, and Owen J. Miller, 175–86. Toronto: University of Toronto Press, 1985.

Ricoeur, Paul. *Time and Narrative*. Vol. I. Chicago: University of Chicago Press, 1984.

Ricoeur, Paul. *Time and Narrative*. Vol. II. Chicago: University of Chicago Press, 1985.

Ricoeur, Paul. *Time and Narrative*. Vol. III. Chicago: University of Chicago Press, 1988.

Ricoeur, Paul. "Toward a Hermeneutic of the Idea of Revelation." In *Essays on Biblical Interpretation*, edited by L. S. Mudge, 73–118. Philadelphia: Fortress, 1980.

Ritivoi, Andreea Deciu. *Paul Ricoeur: Tradition and Innovation in Rhetorical Theory*. New York: State University of New York Press, 2006.

Rives, James B. "Graeco-Roman Religion in the Roman Empire: Old Assumptions and New Approaches." *CBR* 8 (2010): 240–99.

Robinson, Donald W. B. "Faith of Jesus Christ: A New Testament Debate." *RTR* 29, no. 3 (1970): 71–81.

Romanucci-Ross, L., and G. A. de Vos. "Ethnic Identity: A Psychocultural Perspective." In *Ethnic Identity: Creation, Conflict, and Accommodation*, edited by L. Romanucci-Ross and G. A. De Vos, 349–79. London: AltaMira Press, 1995.

Root, Michael. "The Narrative Structure of Soteriology." In *Why Narrative? Readings in Narrative Theology*, edited by Stanley Hauerwas, 263–78. Eugene: Wipf & Stock Pub, 1997.

Rossow, Justin P. "Preaching the Story Behind the Image. A Narrative Approach to Metaphor for Preaching." Ph. D., Concordia Seminary, 2009.

Ryan, Marie-Laure. "Toward a Definition of Narrative." In *The Cambridge Companion to Narrative*, edited by David Herman, 22–35. Cambridge: Cambridge University Press, 2007.

Saint Augustine, Bishop of Hippo. *The Confessions of St. Augustine*. Translated by E. B. Pusey. Oak Harbor: Logos Research Systems, Inc., 1996.

Sanders, E. P. *Judaism: Practice and Belief, 63 BCE - 66 CE*. Minneapolis: Augsburg Fortress, 2016.

Sanders, E. P.. *Paul and Palestinian Judaism: A Comparison of Patterns of Religion*. Minneapolis: Fortress Press, 1977.

Sandnes, Karl O. *Belly and Body in the Pauline Epistles*. Cambridge: Cambridge University Press, 2002.

Sasson, J. M. "Circumcision in the Ancient Near East." *JBL* 85 (1966): 473–6.

Schoors, A. I. *Am God Your Saviour: A Form-Critical Study of the Main Genres in Is. 40–55*. SuppVT 24. Leiden: Brill Archive, 1973.

Schreiner, Thomas R. *Romans*. BECNT. Grand Rapids: Baker Books, 1998.

Schweitzer, Albert. *The Mysticism of Paul the Apostle*. Translated by W. Montgomery. London: A. & C. Black, 1912.

Schweizer, Eduard. "Discipleship and Belief in Jesus as Lord from Jesus to the Hellenistic Church." *NTS* 2, no. 2 (1955): 87–99.

Selwyn, E. G. *The First Epistle of St Peter, the Greek Text with Introduction, Notes and Essays*. London: Macmillan & Co, 1955.

Seneca, Lucius Annaeus. *Seneca's Letters from a Stoic*. Edited by Richard Mott Gummere. New York: Dover Publications, 2016.

Severy, Beth. *Augustus and the Family at the Birth of the Roman Empire*. New York: Routledge, 2003.

Shaw, David A. "Converted Imaginations? The Reception of Richard Hays's Intertextual Method." *CBR* 11 (2013): 234–45.

Sheppard, Kenneth. "Telling Contested Stories: J. G. A. Pocock and Paul Ricoeur." *History of European Ideas* 39, no. 6 (2013): 879–98.

Silva, Moisés. *Philippians*. 2nd ed. BECNT. Grand Rapids: Baker Academic, 2005.

Silva, Moisés. "Philippians." In *Commentary on the New Testament use of the Old Testament*, edited by G. K. Beale and D. A. Carson, 835–9. Grand Rapids: Baker Academic, 2007.

Silverman, Jason M. "Cyrus II." In *LBD*, edited by John D. Barry et al. Bellingham: Lexham Press, 2016.

Simcox, Carroll E. "The Role of Cyrus in Deutero-Isaiah." *JAOS* 57, no. 2 (1937): 158–71.

Simms, Karl. *Paul Ricoeur*. Routledge Critical Thinkers. New York: Routledge, 2003.

Skarsaune, Oskar. *In the Shadow of the Temple: Jewish Influences on Early Christianity*. Downers Grove: InterVarsity, 2002.

Smit, Peter-Ben. "In Search of Real Circumcision: Ritual Failure and Circumcision in Paul." *JSNT* 40, no. 1 (2017): 73–100.
Somers, Margaret R., and Gloria D. Gibson. "Reclaiming the Epistemological "Other": Narrative and the Social Constitution of Identity." In *Social Theory and the Politics of Identity*, edited by Craig Calhoun, 37–98. Oxford: Wiley-Blackwell, 1994.
Spence, Henry, D. M. Daniel. *The Pulpit Commentary*. London: Funk & Wagnalls, 1909.
Spicq, C. *Theological Lexicon of the New Testament*. 3 vols. Peabody: Hendrickson, 1994. [TLNT]
Stanley, Christopher D. *Arguing with Scripture: The Rhetoric of Quotations in the Letters of Paul*. New York: T&T Clark International, 2004.
Stanley, Christopher D. *Paul and the Language of Scripture: Citation Technique in the Pauline Epistles and Contemporary Literature*. Cambridge: Cambridge University Press, 1992.
Stanton, Graham N. "I Think, When I Read That Sweet Story of Old." In *Narrative Dynamics in Paul. A Critical Assessment*, edited by Bruce W. Longenecker, 125–32. Louisville: Westminster John Knox Press, 2002.
Steiner, Richard C. "Incomplete Circumcision in Egypt and Edom: Jeremiah (9:24–25) in the Light of Josephus and Jonckheere." *JBL* 118, no. 3 (1999): 497–505.
Stendahl, Krister. "The Apostle Paul and the Introspective Conscience of the West." *HTR* 56 (1963): 199–215.
Still, Todd D. "(Im)Perfection: Reading Philippians 3.5–6 in Light of the Number Seven." *NTS* 60, no. 1 (2014): 139–48.
Stiver, Dan R. *The Philosophy of Religious Language: Sign, Symbol and Story*. Cambridge: Blackwell Publishers, 1996.
Stiver, Dan R. *Theology After Ricoeur: New Directions in Hermeneutical Theology*. Louisville: Westminster John Knox, 2001.
Stroup, George W. *The Promise of Narrative Theology*. Atlanta: Wipf & Stock Pub, 1997.
Stuart, Douglas K. *Exodus: An Exegetical and Theological Exposition of Holy Scripture*. NAC 2. Nashville: Holman Reference, 2006.
Stuckenbruck, Loren T. "Posturing 'Apocalyptic' in Pauline Theology: How Much Contrast to Jewish Tradition?" In *The Myth of Rebellious Angels*, 240–56. Grand Rapids: Eerdmans, 2017.
Sumney, Jerry L. *Philippians: A Greek Student's Intermediate Reader*. Grand Rapids: Baker Academic, 2007.
Talbert, Charles H. *Learning Through Suffering: The Educational Value of Suffering in the New Testament and in Its Milieu*. Zacchaeus Studies. New Testament. Collegeville: Liturgical Press, 1991.
Talbert, Charles H. "The Problem of Pre-Existence in Philippians 2:6–11." *JBL* 86, no. 2 (1967): 141–53.
Tannehill, Robert C. *Dying and Rising with Christ: A Study in Pauline Theology*. BZNW 32. Berlin: Topelmann, 1967.
Tappenden, Frederick S. *Resurrection in Paul: Cognition, Metaphor, and Transformation*. Atlanta: SBL, 2016.
Teichert, Dieter. "Narrative, Identity and the Self." *Journal of Consciousness Studies* 11, no. 10–11 (2004): 175–91.
Tellbe, Mikael. *Paul between Synagogue and State: Christians, Jews, and Civic Authorities in 1 Thessalonians, Romans, and Philippians*. Stockholm: Almqvist & Wiksell Intl, 2001.
Tellbe, Mikael. "The Sociological Factors Behind Philippians 3.1–11 and the Conflict at Philippi." *JSNT* 55 (1994): 97–121.

The ESV Study Bible. Wheaton: Crossway Bibles, 2008.
Thiessen, Matthew. *Contesting Conversion: Genealogy, Circumcision, and Identity in Ancient Judaism and Christianity*. Oxford: Oxford University Press, 2011.
Thiselton, Anthony C. "Dialectic in Hermeneutics and Doctrine: Coherence and Polyphony." In *The Hermeneutics of Doctrine*, 119–44. Grand Rapids: Wm. B. Eerdmans, 2007.
Thiselton, Anthony C. *The First Epistle to the Corinthians*. Grand Rapids: Eerdmans, 2000.
Thiselton, Anthony C. "The Hermeneutics of Doctrine as a Hermeneutic of Temporal and Communal Narrative." In *The Hermeneutics of Doctrine*, 62–80. Grand Rapids: Wm. B. Eerdmans, 2007.
Thiselton, Anthony C. "The Hermeneutics of Pastoral Theology. Ten Strategies for Reading Texts in Relation to Varied Reading-Situations." In *Thiselton on Hermeneutics: Collected Works with New Essays*, 349–84. Grand Rapids: William B. Eerdmans Publishing, 2013.
Thiselton, Anthony C. "The Hermeneutics of Paul Ricoeur." In *Hermeneutics: An Introduction*, 228–54. Grand Rapids: Eerdmans, 2009.
Thiselton, Anthony C. *Interpreting God and the Postmodern Self: On Meaning, Manipulation and Promise*. Edinburgh: Wm. B. Eerdmans, 1995.
Thiselton, Anthony C. *New Horizons in Hermeneutics*. Grand Rapids: Zondervan, 1992.
Thiselton, Anthony C. *The Two Horizons: New Testament Hermeneutics and Philosophical Description*. Grand Rapids: Wm. B. Eerdmans, 1980.
Thompson, J. A. *The Book of Jeremiah*. NICOT. Grand Rapids: Eerdmans, 1980.
Thompson, J. A. *Deuteronomy: An Introduction and Commentary*. TOTC 5. Downers Grove: InterVarsity Press, 1974.
Thompson, James W. "Preaching to Philippians." *Interpretation* 61, no. 3 (2007): 298–309.
Thurston, Bonnie B., and Judith Ryan. *Sacra Pagina: Philippians and Philemon*. Collegeville: Michael Glazier, 2009.
Tracy, David. *The Analogical Imagination: Christian Theology and the Culture of Pluralism*. New York: The Crossroad Publishing Company, 1998.
Trench, Richard C. *Synonyms of the New Testament*. London: Macmillan, 1880.
Tucker, J. Brian. *Remain in Your Calling: Paul and the Continuation of Social Identities in 1 Corinthians*. Eugene: Wipf & Stock Pub, 2011.
Vander Hart, Mark D. "The Transition of the Old Testament Day of the Lord into the New Testament." *Mid-America Journal of Theology* 9, no. 1 (1993): 3–25.
Vandevelde, Pol. "The Challenge of the "such as it Was": Ricoeur's Theory of Narratives." In *Reading Ricoeur*, edited by David M. Kaplan, 141–62. New York: SUNY Press, 2008.
Venema, Henry I. *Identifying Selfhood: Imagination, Narrative, and Hermeneutics in the Thought of Paul Ricoeur*. Albany: State University of New York Press, 2000.
Venema, Henry I. "Paul Ricoeur of Refigurative Reading and Narrative Identity." *Symposium* 4, no. 2 (2000): 237–48.
Vincent, M. R. *A Critical and Exegetical Commentary on the Epistles to the Philippians and to Philemon*. ICC. Edinburgh: T. & T. Clark, 1897.
Vlacos, Sophie. *Ricoeur, Literature and Imagination*. New York: Bloomsbury Publishing, 2014.
Vollenweider, Samuel. "Der 'Raub' der Gottgleichheit: Ein Religionsgeschichtlicher Vorschlag zu Phil 2.6(–11)." *NTS* 45, no. 3 (1999): 413–33.
Von Rad, G. "The Origin of the Concept of the Day of the Lord." *JSS* 4, no. 2 (1959): 97–108.
Wagner, J. Ross. *Heralds of the Good News: Isaiah and Paul "in Concert" in the Letter to the Romans*. Boston: BRILL, 2012.

Wagner, J. Ross. Review of *Holy Scripture in the Qumran Commentaries and Pauline Letters*, by Timothy H. Lim. *JBL* 120 (2001): 175–8.
Wallace, Daniel B. *Greek Grammar Beyond the Basics: An Exegetical Syntax of the New Testament with Scripture, Subject, and Greek Word Indexes*. 4th rev. ed. Grand Rapids: Zondervan, 1996.
Wallis, Ian G. *The Faith of Jesus Christ in Early Christian Traditions*. Cambridge: Cambridge University Press, 2005.
Watson, Duane F. "A Rhetorical Analysis of Philippians and Its Implications for the Unity Question." *Novum Testamentum* 30 (1988): 57–88.
Watson, Francis. "Is There a Story in These Texts?" In *Narrative Dynamics in Paul. A Critical Assessment*, edited by Bruce W. Longenecker, 231–9. Louisville: Westminster John Knox Press, 2002.
Watson, Francis. *Paul and the Hermeneutics of Faith*. Edinburgh: T & T Clark, 2004.
Watts, Rikki E. "Consolation or Confrontation: Isaiah 40–55 and the Delay of the New Exodus." *TynBul* 41, no. 1 (1990): 31–59.
Weiss, M. "The Origin of the "Day of the Lord"— Reconsidered." *HUCA* 37 (1966): 29–60.
Weitzman, Steven. "Plotting Antiochus's Persecution." *JBL* 123, no. 2 (2004): 219–34.
Weymouth, Richard J. "The Christ-Story of Philippians 2:6–11: Narrative Shape and Paraenetic Purpose in Paul's Letter to Philippi." Ph.D diss., University of Otago, July 2015.
Whitcomb, Kelly A., and Getachew Kiros. "Circumcision." In *LBD*, edited by John D. Barry et al. Bellingham: Lexham Press, 2016.
White, Eugene E. *The Context of Human Discourse: A Configurational Criticism of Rhetoric*. Columbia: University of South Carolina Press, 1992.
White, Roger M. *The Structure of Metaphor: The Way the Language of Metaphor Works*. Oxford: Wiley-Blackwell, 1996.
Wiles, Nancy V. "From Apostolic Presence to Self-Government in Christ. Paul's Preparing of the Philippian Church for Life in His Absence." Ph.D diss., University of Chicago, 1993.
Wilk, Florian. "The Letters of Paul as Witnesses to and for the Septuagint Text." In *Septuagint Research: Issues and Challenges in the Study of the Greek Jewish Scriptures*, edited by Wolfgang Kraus, and R. Glenn Wooden, 253–71. Atlanta: SBL, 2006.
Williams, Demetrius K. *Enemies of the Cross of Christ: The Terminology of the Cross and Conflict in Philippians*. JSNTSup 223. Sheffield: Sheffield Academic, 2002.
Wilson, Gerald H. *Psalms*. Vol. 1. NIVAC. Grand Rapids: Zondervan, 2002.
Witherington III, Ben. *Paul's Narrative Thought World: The Tapestry of Tragedy and Triumph*. Louisville: Westminster John Knox Press, 1994.
Witherington III, Ben. *The Paul Quest: The Renewed Search for the Jew of Tarsus*. Downers Grove: InterVarsity Press, 1998.
Wright, N. T. "Ἁρπαγμός and the Meaning of Philippians 2:5–11." *JTS* 37, no. 2 (1986): 321–52.
Wright, N. T. *Justification: God's Plan and Paul's Vision*. London: SPCK, 2009.
Wright, N. T. *The New Testament and the People of God*. London: SPCK, 1992.
Wright, N. T. *Paul and the Faithfulness of God*. Philadelphia: Fortress Press, 2013.
Wright, N. T. "Paul's Gospel and Caesar's Empire." In *Paul and Politics: Ekklesia, Israel, Imperium, Interpretation*, edited by Richard A. Horsley, 160–83. Valley Forge: Trinity Press, 2000.

Wright, N. T. *The Resurrection of the Son of God*. London: SPCK, 2003.
Yee, Tet-Lim N. *Jews, Gentiles and Ethnic Reconciliation: Paul's Jewish Identity and Ephesians*. Cambridge: Cambridge University Press, 2005.
Zetterholm, Magnus. *Approaches to Paul: A Student's Guide to Recent Scholarship*. Minneapolis: Fortress Press, 2009.

Index

ἀγῶνα (ἀγών) 103–5
ἀντικειμένων 94
ἀπολογία 127–8
ἁρπαγμός 142–5
ἀσφαλής 170
βεβαιώσει 127–8, 136
δοῦλος 145–6, 149, 154
ἐνάρχομαι 81–2, 129–30, 132–4, 154, 166
ἔνδειξις 5, 97–8
ἐξομολογέω 157–8
ἐπίγνωσις 135
ἐπιτελέω 81–2, 129–30, 133–4, 194
ἐριθεία 113–14, 137–8
ἐριθευόμενοι 113–14
εὐδοκία 111–12
ἡμέρας Χριστοῦ Ἰησοῦ 130–2
θανάτου δὲ σταυροῦ 140–1, 150, 152–3
κάμψει 157–8
κατατέμνω 171
κατατομή 171–2, 173–5, 178
κατελήμφθην 189–90
καυχάομαι 176–7
κενοδοξία 137–8
κύριος 156–7
κύων 171
μορφή 145
μου 126
οἱ πνεύματι θεοῦ λατρεύοντες 176
ὁμοίωμα 148
περιτομή 172, 173–5
πολιτεύ 164
πολιτεύομαι 5, 82–4, 93–5, 103, 172 n.19
  Greco-Roman context 83–7
  Jewish context 87–92
πτυρόμενοι 93, 94
στήκετε 93
συναθλοῦντες (συναθλέω) 93–4
σχῆμα 148
σῶμα 165
σωτηρία 120, 123–5
ταπεινόω 138
τέλειος 192
τελειόω 192
τῇ πίστει τοῦ εὐαγγελίου 95–6
φανερός 108
φρονέω 137, 138
χάρις 126 n.261
ὥστε τοὺς δεσμούς μου φανεροὺς ἐν Χριστῷ γενέσθαι 107–8

actantial model 16, 87 n.32
Alden, Robert 119
aletheia 61 n.111, 75, 125
allegiance 139, 157–8, 204
  contestation between Caesar and Christ 92–5, 102–3, 109–10, 144
  ethnicity and 185
  to newly enthroned Messiah 206–9
  political and military 83–7
allusion 61–3, 90–1, 139, 232
  to Daniel 212–18
  to Isaiah 160–2
  to Israelites 209–11, 218–19
  to Jeremiah 177–9, 232
  to Job 115–25, 231
anti-imperialism 38–9, 102–3
Antiochus IV Epiphanes 88, 93, 213–16, 218
apocalypticism 201–2
apostolic authority 172
Aristotle 45, 52 n.65, 55, 60 n.106, 113–14
Arnold, Bradley 83 n.9, 89–92, 93–4, 103–4
assurance 170
  of being owned by Christ 189–91
  of bodily resurrection 212
  of God's righteousness 181–8
  of the gospel 95–6
  Paul's 115–25, 200
attestation 73 n.189
Augustine, Saint 45, 63
Augustus 84, 164 n.160

Index

Baan, Ariaan W.   71
Barclay, John M. G.   2, 30–3, 172, 184 n.81, 230
Bauckham, Richard   71
Belleville, L. L.   172 n.22
Benveniste, Emile   65
Bertschmann, Dorothea   154 n.96
body
   bodily suffering   162–6, 185 n.90
   transformation of believers' bodies   5, 132–4, 194–8, 200
Boernerianus   126 n.258
Brändl, Martin   93
Brawley, Robert   26–7, 28, 31–2, 204, 230
Brewer, Raymond Rush   86, 92
Brueggemann, Walter   159 n.129
Bryan, Christopher   38–9, 86

Caesar   15, 92–5, 109–10, 144, 164 n.160
Caird, G. B.   192 n.133
Campbell, William S.   2, 27–8, 31–3, 230
character   64–7, 119–22, 222, 228
Chicago school   22 n.91
Christ
   allegiance to   92–5, 102–3, 109–10, 144, 204, 206–9
   being owned by   189–91
   "day of Christ"   5, 130–2, 134, 136, 137, 139, 162, 185, 188–90, 219, 231
   death of   63
   death on the Cross   151–2, 154
   earthly journey of   138–9, 144–9, 151–4, 156–7, 203
   "equality with God"   142–5
   exaltation of   5, 121–4, 144, 156–7
   obedience of   152–4
Christ-Hymn   2, 14, 17–18, 19, 92 n.64
   beginning of   142–7
   contestation of testimonies   140–1
   ending of   155–66
   function of   25–6, 38–9
   influence on Philippians' identity   26–7
   middle of   147–55
   temporal framework of   141–2
Christology   39, 157
circumcision   102, 185 n.90, 188
   avoidance of suffering and   171–3, 183–4, 195–6, 201–2, 222–3, 232
   contestation over definition of   175–81
   redefinition of   194–5
   significance of   173–5
citizenship   83–7
Claromontanus   126 n.258
coherence   13, 51 n.54, 57
Collange, Jean-François   161
collective identity   6, 24, 88–9
   formation of   75–7, 220–1
communal identity   24–5
communal narratives   25
communal self   43
competing narratives   2–3
compositional unity   3, 35
concordance/concordant   47, 49–50, 59–60, 64, 129, 182–5
continuity   27–8, 31–2, 51, 219
cosmological upper limit of time   124, 130–2, 139, 155, 193, 231
counter-imperial narrative   17–18
creative resonance   58–60
criteriology of the divine   70–1, 81, 96, 109, 134–5, 145, 158–9, 173, 175, 194, 210
crucifixion   151–4
Currie, Mark   60 n.106
Cyrus, as God's instrument   157–60, 166, 231

dative of interest   95–6
Davies, W. D.   184 n.83
Day of Christ   5, 130–2, 134, 136, 139, 185, 190, 231
Day of the Lord   130–1
death
   on the Cross   151–2
   "death of Christ"   99, 202–3, 224 n.19, 226
   as earthly upper limit of time   152
   suffering and   98–100, 147–55, 212–18
   testimony and   75
demarcation of time   48 n.40, 59–60, 193–8
de Vos, Craig S.   87 n.37
de Vos, George A.   185
DiMattei, Steven   62
discernment   57 n.91, 125–6, 135–6, 154–5

discontinuity 29–32, 51, 219
discordance/discordant 47, 49–50, 64, 74, 129, 160, 182–5, 222–4
disposition 66–9, 129
divine sovereignty 217–18
Docherty, Susan 90 n.50
Donfried, Karl P. 93
Dowling, William C. 54 n.74
doxa 55, 68, 74
Dunn, James D. G. 1, 3, 12–13, 16, 32 n.155, 33, 50 n.54, 79, 174 n.31, 230

Easter experience 29, 32
Eastman, Susan G. 45 n.12
emplotment 4, 46–51, 160
   of authorities 98–9
   testimony and 70 n.166
endoxa 55, 74
epistemological 70, 72, 128, 135, 139
eschatological era 125–36, 154, 185–6, 198, 199, 202, 231
eschatological lordship 160–2, 165, 166, 178, 200, 211–12, 231–2
ethical disposition 136–9, 222–3, 231
ethical identity 5, 64–9, 124, 138, 222, 231
ethics 51–2, 65–6, 111
ethnic continuity 27–8
ethnic identity 195–6
exaltation 5, 121–4, 144, 156–7
exegesis 79
exemplar 6, 18–20, 79, 102–3, 192–3, 204
external narration 70–1, 135–6, 145, 173, 178, 210

faithfulness, of Christ 156, 164–5, 186
Fanning, Buist M. 189
Fee, Gordon 37 n.15, 38, 97, 108 n.149, 111 n.167, 117 n.204, 118, 130, 153, 170, 176, 180, 190–1, 192 n.133, 213
Fisk, Bruce N. 151 n.74, 152–3
Fitzgerald, John T. 36
Fitzmyer, Joseph A. 140 n.5
five levels of story model 1–2, 3, 4, 12–13, 27, 33, 79, 230
Foster, Paul 187
Fowl, Stephen 18–20, 90, 91, 140 n.3, 210

Frei, Hans 22 n.91
Fried, Lisbeth S. 161
Fuller, J. William 157 n.106
Furnish, Victor P. 170

Gadamer, Hans-Georg 51 n.57
Garland, D. E. 35
Geoffrion, Timothy C. 85, 86, 89 n.45, 94
Gilkey, Langdon 22 n.91
Gnilka, Joachim 121 n.231
God
   absence of 152–3
   active role of 199–200
   approval of Christ's earthly suffering 156–7
   double participation of 112–13
   "equality with God" 142–5
   experience of 57–8, 70
   grace of 126
   involvement in Philippian testimony 129–30
   manifestation of 142–7, 151–4
   manipulation of 173–5, 209–11
   obedience/lack of obedience to 147–55, 209–12, 226
   protection of 175–81, 195–6
   responsive relationship of 130–1
   righteousness of 119, 149, 154–5, 159–60, 173, 176–8, 181–8, 210, 225–6
   story of God 12–13, 32, 132–5
   submission to 157–8
   'sustaining activity' of 134
Gorman, Michael J. 15–16, 36
Gowan, Donald E. 217 n.65
Green, Donald E. 151
Green, Joel B. 63 n.119
Gunther, John J. 37

Hafemann, Scott J. 36
Hansen, G. Walter 86
Harding, Sarah 164
Hauerwas, Stanley 22 n.91
Hawthorn, T. 110
Hawthorne, Gerald F. 116
Hays, Richard 1, 10–11, 16–17, 57 n.91, 58, 230
Heen, Erik M. 38

Index

Heidegger, Martin   46 n.20, 61 n.111, 63, 133 n.306
Hellerman, Joseph H.   38, 161 n.138
Hengel, Martin   151
Henrix, Hans Herman   91 n.59
historiography   76 n.205
history   75–6
Hofius, Otfried   152
Holloway, Paul A.   91 n.60, 104
Holmberg, Bengt   16, 29 n.142
Hooker, Morna D.   140 n.5, 149
Hoover, Roy W.   143
Horrell, David   2 n.11, 22–3, 29 n.42, 31 nn.151–2, 32, 230
Huizenga, Leroy A.   61 n.113
human will   112–13
humiliation   231–2
  of Christ   138–9, 145–6, 150–1
  of crucifixion   151–2, 154
  humiliated bodies   5, 132–4, 163–5, 196–8
  of Paul's imprisonment   146
humility   138–9, 149

iconic augmentation   51 n.56
identity/ies   3, 4–6, 77–8
  as being in Christ   101
  notion of   22–3
  of Paul   27
  of Paul's opponents   3, 37, 171–3
  source of   64
identity formation   2–4, 230, 232–4
  early exemplary formation   181–2, 204–5
  narrative studies on   22–34
  temporality and   56–70, 77–8, 219
idolatry   163
imagination   50, 55, 60 n.107, 65, 68–9, 124, 226
imperial cult/worship   3, 37–9, 86, 92–5, 144, 172, 177, 231
incarnation   150–2, 153
innovation   50–1, 145, 175, 182, 183–4
internal conviction   70–1, 135–6, 145, 178, 210
intersubjective knowledge   77 n.208
intertextuality   61 n.113
Israel, story of   12–13, 90, 185–6, 195–7
Israelites

  grumbling of   209–12
  sufferings of   213–16

Jacobs, Andrew S.   181–2
Janzen, J. Gerald   58 n.95, 59 n.101, 133, 134
Jenson, Robert   43
Jeremias, Joachim   146 n.45
Jervis, L. Ann   36
Jewish Christian leaders
  assurance for   191
  contestation of testimonies between Paul and   100–3, 161–2, 170
  demarcation of time within testimony of   195–6
  disobedience to God   209–12
  grumblings of   211–12
  identity and influence of   171–3
  reappropriation of circumcision   175–6
  salvation and   201–2
  truthfulness and   110–15, 137, 183–4
Jewish identity   171–3
  of Paul   179–81, 204
Jewishness   62 n.118, 88–92
Jewish tradition   83, 87–92
Jews
  exemption for   39
  privileges of   171
  religious identity markers of   179–81
Job
  allusion to   115–17, 231
  confidence of righteousness   119–22
  suffering righteous   117–19
Josephus   102 n.123, 171
Judaism, boundaries between New Christianity and   181–4
Judaizers   110, 172–3
justification   172

Käsemann, Ernst   150 n.68, 187
Kearney, Richard M.   72 n.184
Kleinknecht, K. T.   36, 118–20
Koester, Helmut   171
Kreitzer, Larry J.   131, 161
Krentz, Edgar M.   86
Kuhn, Thomas S.   18–19, 20
Kunneman, Harry   68 n.158

Lightfoot, J. B.   109, 110, 142, 148, 170
Lincoln, Andrew T.   202 n.172

Lindbeck, George 22 n.91
Linebaugh, Jonathan A. 188 n.106
Lohmeyer, Ernst 36, 116, 140, 141, 225 n.19
Longenecker, Bruce W. 11

Macaskill, Grant 199, 202–3
McAuley, David 206 n.1, 207, 208 n.13, 211 n.28, 213, 214, 220
McClendon, James 22 n.91
manifestation 142–7, 151–4
Marshall, I. Howard 134 n.308
Martin, Ralph P. 130, 150
Meech, John L. 43–4
Melick, Richard R. 110, 133 n.304, 165 n.164
memory 75–6, 126–9
metalepsis 58
metaphor, of running 190–1
Meyer, Ben 29–32, 160 n.135, 167, 230
military conflict 85–7
Miller, Ernest 88, 92
Miller, James W. 24–5, 159
Mink, Louis O. 52–3, 54 n.75
Moses 209, 210
Motyer, J. Alec 203 n.178
Moule, C. F. D. 142–3, 146 n.47
Muller, P.-G. 108

Nanos, Mark 27 n.124
narrative(s)
    contestation of 46–7, 54–5, 105–6
    "distinctive religious ethos" between 133, 134
    double contestation of 3, 5, 81–2, 139, 190, 212–18, 230
    as experiments in a laboratory 65 n.128, 215
    temporal demarcations of 193–8
narrative analysis 9–13, 33–4, 230
    general 14–22
    on identity formation 22–33, 230–1
narrative consciousness 54
narrative continuity 13
narrative identity 64–5, 138, 157, 231
    formation of 4–5
    modes of 66–9
    notion of 75
narrative logic 2, 231

narrative necessity 49, 121, 124, 232
narrative spirituality 15–16
narrative substructure 1–3, 10–11, 12–13, 16, 77, 230
narrative theory 3–4, 43, 77–8, 231
narrative unity 74, 137
natural institution 75, 128, 228–9
Nebreda, Sergio 25–6, 64
nesting 4, 6, 57–63, 133, 187, 193, 232
    of stories of Christ and Paul on Isaiah 160–2, 167–8
    of story of Paul upon the story of Christ 146–7, 154–5, 188–9
    of story of Paul upon the story of Jeremiah 177–9, 232
    of story of Paul upon the story of Job 117–25, 187, 231
    of story of Philippians upon the story of Daniel 213–18
    of story of Philippians upon the story of Israelites 209–12
    of story of Philippians upon the story of Ps. 2 207–8
Nongbri, Brent 126

Oakes, Peter 39, 87 n.37, 89, 93, 103–4
obedience 147–55, 226
    lack of 209–12
opponents of Paul, identity and influence of 3, 37, 171–3
Origen 91 n.58

parousia 32, 74–5, 136, 161, 165, 166, 193, 201, 204, 218, 233
past 75–6, 193–8
Paul, St., the Apostle
    commitment to 227–8
    contestation of testimonies between opponents and 100–3
    conviction of 129–33
    demarcation of time within testimony of 196–8
    emplotment of 99–100
    empowerment through suffering 199–200
    imprisonment of 102, 103, 104–7, 108, 110, 146, 154, 183, 222
    Jewish background of 179–81, 204
    and Job compared 115–25

obedience of 154
Philippians' participation in ministry
    of 126–8, 133
Philippians' reconsideration of
    relationship with 221–4
Philippians' role in the narrative world
    of 216–18
present experience of 198–204
relationship with Philippians 125–6
remembrance of 132–5
resonance between Christ and 154–5
retelling of testimony of 226–9
suffering of 36–7, 146–7
theological thinking processes
    of 57–61
truthfulness and 110–15
persecution 36–7, 82, 87–8, 93–8, 228
perseverance 74–5, 225
personal identity 75
Peterlin, Davorin 221 n.8
Pfitzner, Victor C. 95 n.83, 190
Phelan, James 54 n.74
Philippi 84–7
Philo 113–14, 171
Plato 45 n.12
Pobee, John S. 146 n.45
political and military allegiances 83–7,
    206–9
present 198–204
Punt, Jeremy 183 n.79
purposive narrative 54 n.74

Rabinowitz, Peter J. 54 n.74
reading 52–4
    ending of story 122–3
Reddit, Paul L. 214
resonance 117–18, 119
    between Christ and Paul 154–5
resurrection 133, 136, 164
    power of 199–200, 202–3
Reumann, John 89 n.45, 118, 120, 150
rhetoric 54–6
righteousness 5
    confidence of 119–22
    exaltation and 121–4
    of God 149, 154–5, 173, 176–8,
        181–8, 210, 225–6
    God's act in Cyrus as 159–60
Ritivoi, Andreea Deciu 55 n.81

Robinson, Donald W. B. 95
Romanucci-Ross, Lola 185
Rossow, Justin P. 87, 164
Ryan, Judith 92 n.64

sacrifice 75
sameness
    idem 66–9, 228
    of suffering 103–5
Sanders, E. P. 102 n.123
Sandnes, Karl O. 163
Sangermanensis 126 n.258
Schneider, Johannes 164 n.161
Schrenk, Gottlob 111–12
Schweitzer, Albert 36
sedimentation 50–1, 145, 175, 182,
    183–4
self-constancy 67–9, 129, 228
self-engagement 71, 101–2
selfhood (*ipse*) 66–9, 228
self in community 43
Silva, Moisés 32, 90, 97 n.91, 107, 111,
    116, 126, 137, 167
slavery 144–7, 153
social identity 102, 230
    of gentile Christians 172–3
social identity theory 24–5
Spicq, Ceslas 85, 128, 146 n.46
Stanley, Christopher D. 62 n.113
Stanton, Graham N. 16–17
Stendahl, Krister 180 n.62
Stiver, Dan R. 22 n.91, 45
Stuckenbruck, Loren T. 201
substitutionary atonement 152 n.84
suffering 3, 5–6, 45–6, 98–9, 102–3,
    113–14, 132, 134, 170, 175–8
    approval of Christ's suffering 156–7
    avoidance of/unnecessary
        suffering 98–9, 102, 116, 139,
        172–3, 175–6, 178, 183–4, 195–6,
        197, 199, 201–2, 222–3, 232
    bodily suffering 162–6, 185 n.90
    Christ's obedience through 152–4
    empowerment of Paul through 199–
        200
    as essential 135–6
    of Israelites 213–16
    of Job and Paul 115–25
    of Paul 36–7, 146–7

of Paul, alternative testimonies
    of 100–3, 129
of Philippians 54–5, 96–100, 222–3
of Philippians and Paul 103–5
to the point of death 212–18
role of 36–7
suffering slave 146, 153
volitional 138, 149–51
suffering righteous 101, 117–19, 121, 134–5, 136, 167, 197–8, 200–2
    necessity of 216–18
    ultimate vindication of 122–5

Talbert, Charles H. 140–1
Tannehill, Robert C. 36
Tappenden, Frederick S. 200 n.158, 202 n.172
Tellbe, Mikael 37, 38, 171, 172–3, 184 n.81, 198 n.145
telos 155–6, 166
temporality/ies 2, 4–5
    contestation over 193–8
    emplotment and 47–9
    of human experience 44–5
    identity formation and 56–70, 77–8, 219
    of Jewish Christian leaders 201–2
    notion of 46
    of Paul 6
    of Philippians 223
    reading process and 52–4
temporal markers 81–2, 125, 130–2, 133, 136
testimony/ies 56 n.86, 69–77
    contestation of 70–1, 140, 224–6
    contestation of, between "Christ followers" 113–14
    contestation of, between Paul and Jewish Christian leaders 100–3, 161–2, 170, 209–12
    contestation of, between prophet and unbelieving Israelites 159–60
    diverse reception of 106–13
    lack of truthfulness in 137–9
    truthfulness in 71–7
theological appropriation 181–4
Thiselton, Anthony 23, 64 n.126
threefold mimesis 4, 6, 44–5, 66 n.147, 77, 83, 231
    application of 69–70
    mimesis1 45–6, 138–9, 221–4
    mimesis2 46–51, 64, 107, 224–6
    mimesis3 51–6, 76 n.208, 138, 226–9
Thurston, Bonnie B. 92 n.64
time
    as sequence and configuration 47–9
    structure of 31
Tracy, David 19, 22 n.91
transformative reading 51–6
truthful/truthfulness
    contrast between Paul and his opponents 110–15, 137–9
    in nesting 61
    of Paul before Philippians 126–7
    of testimony 71–7, 137–9
Tucker, J. Brian 27
Two Ages 201–2

upper limit of time 63, 99, 124–5, 168
    cosmological 124, 130–2, 139, 155, 193, 231
    earthly 152, 155, 202–3, 204–5

Vandevelde, Pol 56 n.90
Venema, Henry I. 77 n.208
verticality 29, 30–1
vindication 166–7, 231
    of Christ 155–7, 225–6
    of Paul 165
    of Philippian community 164, 188
volitional agent 53–4, 117–18, 226–7
    character and action of 119–22
    Christ as 151–4
Vollenweider, Samuel 144
voluntary 138, 149–51

Wallace, Daniel B. 134 n.307
Watson, Francis 11
Weymouth, Richard J. 2, 17–18, 20–1, 64, 69 n.162
Whitcomb, Kelly A. 174
White, Eugene E. 56
Wiles, Nancy V. 149
Witherington III, Ben 10–11
Wright, N. T. 1–2, 10–11, 14–15, 30 n.44, 153

Yale school 22 n.91

Scripture Index

OLD TESTAMENT

Genesis (Gen)

	130
17	174
17:3-14	179
17:12	193, 195
34	174

Exodus (Ex/Exod)

4:24-26	174
12:43-49	174
15:22–17:7	6, 209, 232
15:22-27	210
15:24	210
16:1-36	210
16:2, 7-12	210
16:20, 28	210
17:1-7	210
17:2, 7	210
17:3	210
17:7	210
51:9	133 n.305
51:10	133 n.305

Numbers (Num)

14–17	6, 209, 232
14:2	210
14:2, 27-29	210
14:11	210
14:22	210
14:27-29	210
16:41	210
17:5, 10	210

Deuteronomy (Deut)

32:4 (LXX)	210, 211
32:5	209, 210, 211

Joshua (Josh)

5	174

Judges (Judg)

7:2	176

1 Kings (1 Kgs)

18:28	174

Job

1:6-12	122
4–27	122
4:7-9	116
6:24-30	118
9–10	119
9:33-35	122
10:1-7	118
11:1ff	117 n.201
12–14	119
12:1ff	117 n.201
13:12-18	117, 119, 121–2, 231
13:13-18	122
13:13-18 (LXX)	117
13:15	119
13:16 (LXX)	115, 117
16:19-21	122
31:35-37	122
33:8-21	116
34:5-20	116
38–42	122–3
42:5	122

Psalms (Ps)

2	207, 209 n.16, 232
2:1-3	207
2:4-6	207
2:10	209 n.16
2:10-11	207
2:11	6
2:11 (LXX)	207, 208
2:11-12	207
2:12	208, 209 n.16
9:3-4	119
22:8	118 n.216
27:1	176
34:3-6	118
48:7	176
52:1	176
68:2-3	119
110	161 n.137

Isaiah (Isa)

40–48	159
40:12-26	159
40:27	158, 159
41:2	159
41:4	158
41:8-10	159
41:25-26	159
42:17-19	163 n.155
42:18-25	159
43:1	133 n.305
43:9-10	159
43:22	159
44:6-8, 24	159
44:9-20	163 n.155
44:23–47:15	158
44:24	159
44:26-28	158
44:28–45:1	157–60
45:1	158, 161
45:1-3	158
45:4	160
45:7, 9, 11-12, 21	159
45:8	159
45:9-10	158
45:9-13	159
45:12, 18	159
45:13	158, 159
45:18-25	156–7, 158
45:19	159
45:23	91, 156, 159, 160, 161
45:23 (LXX)	157–8
45:23b (LXX)	160

45:24 (LXX)	157, 158, 159	12:3 (LXX)	212, 216, 224 n.19	3:22	186		
				3:27	192 n.133		
45:24-25	157–8	12:4	214, 215				
45:25	159, 165	12:10	214 n.43	**Philippians (Phil)**			
46:1-2	159	12:13	215 n.55	1:1b	54		
46:1-5	159			1:3-4	127		
46:2-7	163 n.155	**Hosea (Hos)**		1:3-8	56, 127, 130		
46:5-11	159	7:14	175				
46:8, 12	159			1:3-11	5, 81–2, 139, 231		
46:8-13	158	**Amos (Am)**					
46:11	158	8:11-12	215 n.53	1:3-11, 12-26, 27-30	81		
46:12	158						
48:1	159			1:3-11a	125–36, 139		
48:1-16	159	**NEW TESTAMENT**					
49–55	158	**Acts of the Apostles (Acts)**		1:3-2:4	5, 79, 81, 231		
49:14	158	14:22	202 n.172				
51:9-11	133 n.305	16:11-40	56, 104–5, 221	1:4	127		
51:11	133 n.305			1:4-7	167		
51:17-23	158	16:12	85 n.19	1:4-8	227		
52–3	146 n. 45			1:4-8, 9-11, 27-30	167		
54:11	158	**Romans (Rom)**					
56:10-12	171	1:18	108	1:5	125 n.253, 126, 129, 132		
		1:19	108				
Jeremiah (Jer)		2:18	135 n.315				
9:22-23	176	3:21	186	1:5-7, 27-30	163		
9:23-24	177	3:22, 26	186 n.95	1:6	32 n.155, 125 n.253, 129, 130, 132, 134, 154, 166, 176, 194, 219, 231		
9:23-26	177, 232	3:25	153				
9:25-26	177, 178	3:25-6	98 n.97				
44:15-19	163 n.155	5:8	153				
		6:3	192 n.133				
Ezekiel (Ezek)		8:2-3	148				
8:7-18	163 n.155	8:17	202 n.172				
		9:31	186	1:6, 9	199		
Daniel (Dan)		10:4-5	186	1:6, 10	161, 185		
9:13	218			1:6, 11	190 n.119		
11:21-45	213	**1 Corinthians (1 Cor)**		1:6, 20	122		
11:30	214	1:18	151	1:6bc	144		
11:30–12:4	215 n.51	4:8	202 n.172	1:7	126, 128, 137, 154, 165 n.166, 197 n.143, 200 n.154, 229		
11:32-33	214, 218	15:12	202 n.172				
11:33	214 n.43						
11:35	214	**2 Corinthians (2 Cor)**					
11:45	215	5:18-21	153				
11:45–12:1	218	8:1-5	96, 221				
12 (LXX)	212	11:13	171	1:7a	144, 150 n.68		
12:1	213						
12:1-4	215 n.55	**Galatians (Gal)**		1:7c	148		
12:2	215–16	2:16 (2x), 20	186	1:8	127, 226		
12:3	6, 197 n.143, 213–16, 218, 232	2:21	186	1:8a	150 n.68		
		3:1-4:11	10	1:8abc	148		
		3:21	186	1:8c	150		

1:9	135, 154	1:20	113, 116,	1:29a	126
1:9-11	164		119, 121,	1:29ab	101
1:9-11, 19-20	227		123	1:29a-d	100–3
1:9-26	218, 231	1:20-21	113	1:29b	101
1:10	104, 135, 136, 154, 209	1:20-26 1:21	223 116, 124–5, 203	1:29b-cd 1:29c 1:29d	101 101 101
1:10-11	212	1:22-26	115	1:30	56, 129,
1:11	197, 203	1:27	38–9,		205
1:11a	136		88 n.43,	1:30a	94, 103,
1:11b	137, 227		89, 139,		104
1:12	106, 107, 116 n.200, 124, 154		161 n.141, 187, 219, 227, 231	1:30a-c 1:30abc	82, 96, 103 103–5
1:12-14	48, 103, 161 n.141	1:27-28 1:27-30	129 5, 26,	1:30b 1:30bc	104 104
1:12-18	5, 21, 56, 106, 116, 139, 221–3, 231		32 n.155, 81, 82–106, 108, 114, 139, 162, 178, 231	1:30c 2:1 2:1-4	105 136 5, 81, 82, 129, 136, 138, 139,
1:12-18, 27-29	216	1:27a	83		222, 231
1:12-19	20	1:27a-e	82–92	2:2	137, 227
1:12-26	79, 81, 111	1:27f-28a	82, 92–5,	2:2, 5	209 n.16
1:13	107–8, 109, 161 n.141	1:27ff	103 18–19	2:2, 16 2:3	197 n.143 138
1:13-14	106–7	1:27fg	97	2:5-8	186
1:15	111–12	1:27g	95–6, 99	2:5-11	2, 5, 14, 15,
1:15-17	37, 102, 109, 110–11, 112	1:28	97 nn.91–2, 103, 123, 138, 144, 153,		16, 17, 18, 25–7, 32, 38, 79, 105, 138, 139,
1:15-18	15, 101		162 n.148,		141–2, 144,
1:16	112		178, 190,		169 n.1,
1:17	110, 113, 137, 227	1:28-29	204, 227 37, 208	2:6	206, 231 141, 164
1:18	111, 115, 122, 137	1:28a	94, 95–6, 97	2:6-7 2:6-7b	144–5, 203 142–7
1:18, 25-26	227	1:28b	98 n.104,	2:6-8	138, 150,
1:19	90, 97 n.92, 115, 120, 124, 125, 193, 217, 219	1:28b-29d 1:28bc 1:28c	99 82, 96–7, 103, 104 96–100 101, 108	2:6-11	151, 152–3, 156, 162–3, 226 2, 17, 21, 24
1:19-20	123	1:28c-29a	101	2:6a-7b	142
1:19-26	5, 111, 117, 139, 203 n.178	1:29	6, 161, 166, 178, 197, 199, 205,	2:6b 2:7 2:7-8	142 164 203
1:20-22	163		219	2:7c-8	147–55

2:8	138, 164, 199	2:16b-18	206	3:10	202, 203, 205
2:8b	154	2:18	170	3:10-11	6, 20, 154n.96,169, 189 n.116, 197, 198–204, 216, 217, 219
2:9	156, 163	2:20	102		
2:9-11	5, 155–66, 188, 211, 218, 226, 227	2:25-30	163		
		2:27-28	227		
		2:30	227		
		3	1, 15, 20, 37		
2:9-11, 16	219	3:1	170, 227	3:11	199, 203
2:9-11, 16b-18, 25-30	218	3:1-6	21, 169, 170–81, 188, 193, 194, 204	3:12	188–9, 202 n.172
				3:12-13	25
2:9-13	207, 209 n.16			3:12-14	32 n.155, 167, 188, 191 n.123, 192, 227, 228
			198		
2:9a	156	3:1-9	6, 79, 169–70, 204, 232		
2:9b	156	3:1-21			
2:10-11	90, 157, 161, 162, 193, 217				
		3:2	15, 37, 78, 109, 169, 177, 184	3:12-16	169, 188–93, 204
2:10-11, 12-15	219				
2:11b	156	3:2-3	101–2, 177	3:12-21	198
2:12	112, 206–8, 221, 223			3:13-14	188
		3:2-11	154 n.96	3:14	190
		3:2-16	170	3:15	137, 188, 192, 209 n.16
2:12-13	206–9	3:3	171, 193, 195, 202, 217, 219		
2:12-15	32 n.155, 167, 227			3:15-16	188, 228
2:12-16a	6, 206, 232			3:15ff	192
2:12-18	90	3:4	179	3:17	28, 54, 91, 162–3, 169, 212, 217, 219
2:13	32 n.155, 112, 129, 132 n.302, 134, 166, 199, 200, 208	3:4-6	51, 186		
		3:4-8	27, 204		
		3:4-11	79		
		3:4-11, 20-21	79		
		3:5-6	171	3:17-21	5, 79, 86–7, 105, 139, 155–66, 169–70, 188, 191, 203, 204, 226, 231
		3:5b-6	180		
2:14	209	3:6, 9	186		
2:14-15	209	3:7	180 n.60, 181		
2:14-15b	209–12				
2:15	37, 197 n.143, 209, 212, 216, 217	3:7-8	185		
		3:7-9	169, 181–8, 190, 204	3:18	162
				3:18-19	37
		3:7-14	32 n.155	3:19	162, 165
		3:8	170, 185, 199	3:19-20	97 n.92
2:15-16	197 n.143			3:20	38–9, 85–6, 87, 132, 134, 161 n.141, 162 n.148, 163
2:15c	213, 216				
2:15c-16a	212–18	3:9	14, 185, 186, 187–8, 191, 199–200, 209		
2:16	54, 137, 185, 197				
2:16-18	124–5, 163, 190 n.119, 203				
		3:9-11	51		

3:20-21	5, 32, 54, 123, 132, 157, 160–2, 166–7, 190 n.119, 198, 200, 203, 217–19, 226, 227	4:14	126, 132, 163, 197 n.143	**2 Maccabees**	
				6:1	88 n.39
		4:14-16	96, 129, 221	**4 Maccabees**	
		4:15	85, 132	9:22 (LXX)	164 n.161
		4:18	106	17:11-16	93
		4:22	144, 161 n.141	**Sirach (Sir)**	
				35.3, 16	112–13
		Colossians (Col)		**Wisdom of Solomon (Wis)**	
3:21	163, 164, 202, 203, 208, 218	1:24	202 n.172	2:12-20	118 n.216
		1 Thessalonians (1 Thess)		**JEWISH AUTHORS**	
4:2	227	2:2	105	**Philo**	
4:2, 10	137, 209 n.16	3:3	202 n.172	*On the Embassy to Gaius*	
		4:13–15:11	202 n.172	68	114
4:2-3	222				
4:3	93, 129	**2 Thessalonians (2 Thess)**		**OTHER GREEK AUTHORS**	
4:4-6, 12-13	32 n.155, 167	1:4-8	97 n.91		
4:4, 10	227	**OLD TESTAMENT APOCARYPHA**		**Aristotle**	
4:4-13	228			*Πολιτικά* (Politics)	
4:6	227	**Additions to the Book of Esther (Add Est)**		5.3.1302^{b}4	113–14
4:7, 13, 19	199			1303^{a}14	113–14
4:12-13, 19	227	8:15-16	88 n.38		

www.ingramcontent.com/pod-product-compliance
Lightning Source LLC
Chambersburg PA
CBHW071245230426
43668CB00011B/1589